Lecture Notes in Computer Science   12790

More information about this subseries at http://www.springer.com/series/7409

Xiaowen Fang (Ed.)

HCI in Games

Serious and Immersive Games

Third International Conference, HCI-Games 2021
Held as Part of the 23rd HCI International Conference, HCII 2021
Virtual Event, July 24–29, 2021
Proceedings, Part II

Springer

Editor
Xiaowen Fang
DePaul University
Chicago, IL, USA

ISSN 0302-9743 ISSN 1611-3349 (electronic)
Lecture Notes in Computer Science
ISBN 978-3-030-77413-4 ISBN 978-3-030-77414-1 (eBook)
https://doi.org/10.1007/978-3-030-77414-1

LNCS Sublibrary: SL3 – Information Systems and Applications, incl. Internet/Web, and HCI

This Springer imprint is published by the registered company Springer Nature Switzerland AG
The registered company address is: Gewerbestrasse 11, 6330 Cham, Switzerland

Foreword

Human-Computer Interaction (HCI) is acquiring an ever-increasing scientific and industrial importance, and having more impact on people's everyday life, as an ever-growing number of human activities are progressively moving from the physical to the digital world. This process, which has been ongoing for some time now, has been dramatically accelerated by the COVID-19 pandemic. The HCI International (HCII) conference series, held yearly, aims to respond to the compelling need to advance the exchange of knowledge and research and development efforts on the human aspects of design and use of computing systems.

The 23rd International Conference on Human-Computer Interaction, HCI International 2021 (HCII 2021), was planned to be held at the Washington Hilton Hotel, Washington DC, USA, during July 24–29, 2021. Due to the COVID-19 pandemic and with everyone's health and safety in mind, HCII 2021 was organized and run as a virtual conference. It incorporated the 21 thematic areas and affiliated conferences listed on the following page.

A total of 5222 individuals from academia, research institutes, industry, and governmental agencies from 81 countries submitted contributions, and 1276 papers and 241 posters were included in the proceedings to appear just before the start of the conference. The contributions thoroughly cover the entire field of HCI, addressing major advances in knowledge and effective use of computers in a variety of application areas. These papers provide academics, researchers, engineers, scientists, practitioners, and students with state-of-the-art information on the most recent advances in HCI. The volumes constituting the set of proceedings to appear before the start of the conference are listed in the following pages.

The HCI International (HCII) conference also offers the option of 'Late Breaking Work' which applies both for papers and posters, and the corresponding volume(s) of the proceedings will appear after the conference. Full papers will be included in the 'HCII 2021 - Late Breaking Papers' volumes of the proceedings to be published in the Springer LNCS series, while 'Poster Extended Abstracts' will be included as short research papers in the 'HCII 2021 - Late Breaking Posters' volumes to be published in the Springer CCIS series.

The present volume contains papers submitted and presented in the context of the 3rd International Conference on HCI in Games (HCI-Games 2021) affiliated conference to HCII 2021. I would like to thank the Chair, Xiaowen Fang, for his invaluable contribution in its organization and the preparation of the Proceedings, as well as the members of the program board for their contributions and support. This year, the HCI-Games affiliated conference has focused on topics related to experience design in games, user engagement and game impact, game mechanics, serious games, gamification for learning and Mixed and Virtual Reality games.

I would also like to thank the Program Board Chairs and the members of the Program Boards of all thematic areas and affiliated conferences for their contribution towards the highest scientific quality and overall success of the HCI International 2021 conference.

This conference would not have been possible without the continuous and unwavering support and advice of Gavriel Salvendy, founder, General Chair Emeritus, and Scientific Advisor. For his outstanding efforts, I would like to express my appreciation to Abbas Moallem, Communications Chair and Editor of HCI International News.

July 2021   Constantine Stephanidis

HCI International 2021 Thematic Areas
and Affiliated Conferences

Thematic Areas

- HCI: Human-Computer Interaction
- HIMI: Human Interface and the Management of Information

Affiliated Conferences

- EPCE: 18th International Conference on Engineering Psychology and Cognitive Ergonomics
- UAHCI: 15th International Conference on Universal Access in Human-Computer Interaction
- VAMR: 13th International Conference on Virtual, Augmented and Mixed Reality
- CCD: 13th International Conference on Cross-Cultural Design
- SCSM: 13th International Conference on Social Computing and Social Media
- AC: 15th International Conference on Augmented Cognition
- DHM: 12th International Conference on Digital Human Modeling and Applications in Health, Safety, Ergonomics and Risk Management
- DUXU: 10th International Conference on Design, User Experience, and Usability
- DAPI: 9th International Conference on Distributed, Ambient and Pervasive Interactions
- HCIBGO: 8th International Conference on HCI in Business, Government and Organizations
- LCT: 8th International Conference on Learning and Collaboration Technologies
- ITAP: 7th International Conference on Human Aspects of IT for the Aged Population
- HCI-CPT: 3rd International Conference on HCI for Cybersecurity, Privacy and Trust
- HCI-Games: 3rd International Conference on HCI in Games
- MobiTAS: 3rd International Conference on HCI in Mobility, Transport and Automotive Systems
- AIS: 3rd International Conference on Adaptive Instructional Systems
- C&C: 9th International Conference on Culture and Computing
- MOBILE: 2nd International Conference on Design, Operation and Evaluation of Mobile Communications
- AI-HCI: 2nd International Conference on Artificial Intelligence in HCI

List of Conference Proceedings Volumes Appearing Before the Conference

38. CCIS 1420, HCI International 2021 Posters - Part II, edited by Constantine Stephanidis, Margherita Antona, and Stavroula Ntoa
39. CCIS 1421, HCI International 2021 Posters - Part III, edited by Constantine Stephanidis, Margherita Antona, and Stavroula Ntoa

http://2021.hci.international/proceedings

3rd International Conference on HCI in Games
(HCI-Games 2021)

Program Board Chairs: **Xiaowen Fang,** *DePaul University, USA*

- Amir Zaib Abbasi, Pakistan
- Abdullah Azhari, Saudi Arabia
- Barbara Caci, Italy
- Darryl Charles, UK
- Benjamin Ultan Cowley, Finland
- Khaldoon Dhou, USA
- Kevin Keeker, USA
- Xiaocen Liu, China
- Haipeng Mi, China
- Keith Nesbitt, Australia
- Daniel Riha, Czech Republic
- Owen Schaffer, USA
- Fan Zhao, USA
- Miaoqi Zhu, USA

The full list with the Program Board Chairs and the members of the Program Boards of all thematic areas and affiliated conferences is available online at:

http://www.hci.international/board-members-2021.php

HCI International 2022

The 24th International Conference on Human-Computer Interaction, HCI International 2022, will be held jointly with the affiliated conferences at the Gothia Towers Hotel and Swedish Exhibition & Congress Centre, Gothenburg, Sweden, June 26 – July 1, 2022. It will cover a broad spectrum of themes related to Human-Computer Interaction, including theoretical issues, methods, tools, processes, and case studies in HCI design, as well as novel interaction techniques, interfaces, and applications. The proceedings will be published by Springer. More information will be available on the conference website: http://2022.hci.international/:

General Chair
Prof. Constantine Stephanidis
University of Crete and ICS-FORTH
Heraklion, Crete, Greece
Email: general_chair@hcii2022.org

http://2022.hci.international/

Contents – Part II

Gamification and Learning

Mixed and Virtual Reality Games

Contents – Part I

User Engagement and Game Impact

Game Mechanics

Serious Games

Mindful Gaming: User Experiences with *Headspace* and *Walden, a Game*

Matthew Hamilton[1(✉)], Betsy DiSalvo[2], and Tracy Fullerton[1]

[1] University of Southern California, Los Angeles, CA 90008, USA
criticalgameliteracy@gmail.com, tfullerton@cinema.usc.edu
[2] Georgia Institute of Technology, Atlanta, GA 30332, USA
bdisalvo@cc.gatech.edu

Abstract. *Headspace* is a gamified app designed to teach mindfulness, and *Walden* is an experimental game that moves beyond traditional game mechanics in order to encourage mindful play. Through semi-structured interviews and contextual inquiry think-aloud sessions, this phenomenological case study compares user experiences with these two pieces of software. Findings include descriptions of how participants experienced mindfulness as contemplative self-reflection, as a long-term process, as a byproduct of play, and as a tension between exploration and completing objectives. These findings are analyzed in relation to extant theories of game design and mindfulness, especially Brian Upton's theory of ludic semiotics [1]. The resulting insights have informed the first and third authors' development of two new pieces of software: a mindfulness practice module that is a component of a new version of *Walden* designed for use in schools, and a study aid called *Lofi Hip Hop Worlds to Study In*. This outcome highlights the relevance of qualitative user experience research for the iterative, playcentric design [2] of educational technologies.

Keywords: Mindfulness · Games · Learning

1 Introduction and Related Literature

Mindfulness has been defined as the "regulation of attention" [3], the ability to consciously reflect upon one's experiences [4], and being emotionally and cognitively [5] present in the moment [6] with non-judgmental acceptance of one's experiences [7]. There is a growing interest in teaching and learning mindfulness practices, fueled by research on their benefits for improving self-regulation [3]. Proponents (e.g. [8]) and critics (e.g. [9]) of this trend both focus on mindfulness's role in maintaining attention in an era of ubiquitous digital media. *Headspace* (https://www.headspace.com/) and *Walden* (www.waldengame.com) both attempt to promote mindfulness using digital media itself, but in very different ways.

© Springer Nature Switzerland AG 2021
X. Fang (Ed.): HCII 2021, LNCS 12790, pp. 3–19, 2021.
https://doi.org/10.1007/978-3-030-77414-1_1

1.1 *Headspace* and the Gamification of Mindfulness

Headspace is a mobile app that provides reminders and verbal assistance with self-regulating the practice of meditation [10]. Studies have found that using *Headspace* has multiple benefits, such as reducing stress (e.g. [11]) and the severity of depression symptoms [10].

The design of mindfulness apps like *Headspace* is part of a larger trend among Human-Computer Interaction (HCI) researchers to design technologies aimed at changing users' behaviors [12]. Building on the Octalysis framework of gamification [13], *Headspace* uses game-like elements to promote mindfulness; Yu-kai Chou [13], the creator of the Octalysis framework, defines gamification as "the craft of deriving fun and engaging elements found typically in games and thoughtfully applying them to real-world or productive activities". For example, *Headspace* provides rewards for meditation streaks and allows users to share their meditation progress with their peers [10].

1.2 *Walden* and Traditions of Mindful Play

Synonymous with contemplation [3], mindfulness practices are rooted in multiple Asian cultural, spiritual, and philosophical traditions, especially Buddhism [5]. Contemporary practitioners have modified and merged these with various Christian and secular contemplative practices. One prominent example is the 19th century American philosopher Henry David Thoreau's attempt to "live deliberately" [14].

Tracy Fullerton, the third author of this paper, has created games that explore the ways these contemplative traditions are themselves already full of game-like elements [15]. Her game *The Night Journey* poses the question, "What is the game mechanic of enlightenment?" Her more recent *Walden, a Game* (see Fig. 1), asks, "What is the game mechanic of Thoreau's experiment at Walden Pond?".

Fig. 1. Screenshot from *Walden, a Game*

Walden is an open-world walking simulator game where players take on Thoreau's perspective, exploring the woods around Walden Pond, attending to basic needs; engaging in correspondence with friends and family; interacting with plants and animals;

and participating in abolitionist activities. As an experimental game, *Walden* eschews traditional game mechanics like points or a win state, instead opting for feedback that prompts the player to reflect on how she wants to spend her time and energy as she explores the world. For example, if the player does not complete tasks in the game to meet Thoreau's basic needs, she becomes fatigued and moves slowly. On the other hand, if the player works too hard at these tasks, the graphics and music become duller, and their vibrancy can be restored through meditation, reading, and listening to birdsongs. This mechanic and others prompt the player to act like Thoreau himself did, playfully deciding how to direct his attention in the world around him. In this sense, *Walden* is part of a mindful gaming practice that is older and broader than the gamification of mindfulness; it is a digital re-creation of a historical influence on how mindfulness itself has been understood, especially in the United States.

1.3 Qualitative Studies on User Experiences and Why They Matter for Studying Mindfulness

In their critical review of HCI literature, Rapp, Tirassa, and Tirabeni [16] argue that HCI researchers designing technologies supporting personal change generally assume change happens at the behavioral level, and that it is "externalistic, monistic, mechanistic, fragmented, and episodic"; the findings of their phenomenological interviews on how people experience change suggest that change also happens in ways that are "internalistic, multiple, intentional, holistic, and continuous". To study and design for such change, quantitative HCI research can be supplemented with qualitative studies of how players make sense of their experiences with changes such as learning or becoming more mindful. Consistent with the Third Wave of HCI, this approach might help us design software that can prompt people to reflect upon their own efforts to change and grow [16].

Such an approach is particularly relevant for studying mindfulness software, since mindfulness is not simply a set of practices and behaviors that can be tracked through external measures the way a Fitbit might track someone exercising. It also involves *how* behaviors such as meditation or gaming are conducted, e.g. with an attitude of non-judgmental acceptance of experiences [7]. For this reason, research participants' self-reported experiences of mindfulness have been included in quantitative scales that psychologists use to measure mindfulness (e.g. [7, 17]); for example, the Philadelphia Mindfulness scale measures participants' self-reported attention and acceptance [7]. Qualitative methods such as contextual inquiry think-alouds [18] can prompt users to reflect on how they make sense of the construct of mindfulness as a process over a period of time as they interact with software that is designed to facilitate mindfulness, allowing researchers to analyze how users describe this process in their own words.

Park and colleagues' 2013 systematic review of the quantitative measures of mindfulness used by psychologists found that "There is a great need to establish the content validity of the extant measures of mindfulness using qualitative methods, such as semi-structured interviews and focus groups" [17]. While the current study does not aim to improve the content validity of a particular quantitative scale, it does aim to better describe the construct of mindfulness by asking how participants experience it in a game and a gamified app; this could inform future mixed methods studies that could measure mindfulness in gaming contexts while supplementing the measures with interviews and contextual inquiries regarding players' experiences.

Rapp and colleagues' call to center users' lived experiences in the design of software [16] echoes substantial and growing conversations among educators, game designers, and game studies researchers about the agency of players to shape how they play and what they learn through play. For example, discourses of playcentric game design [2], critical play [19], metagaming [20], and connected gaming [21] all focus on player experience. So far, however, these perspectives have not been applied empirically to study player experiences with mindfulness software that involves playing games or engaging in game-like activity.

1.4 Research Questions and Scope of This Study

To fill these gaps, this study took an inductive, comparative case study approach [22] to generate theory and design ideas to be tested in further design practice and research. It extended Rapp and colleagues' [16] phenomenological approach to human-computer interaction to pose the following research questions: How, if at all, do players experience mindfulness while learning to use software designed to facilitate mindfulness? In particular, how, if at all, do they experience it while playing *Walden*? And how, if at all, do they experience it while using *Headspace*?

Mindful gaming is a potentially vast subject, and a wide range of games could be played more or less mindfully. This inquiry was bounded and scoped as a comparative case study of experiences with these two games in particular because they each represent a unique entry point into opposite ends of the conversation about gamification, and a comparison between them can help move that conversation forward. *Headspace* intentionally gamifies mindfulness, applying popular video game mechanics like streaks and rewards to motivate users to practice meditation. In contrast, *Walden's* non-leveled and non-competitive mechanics diverge from game elements usually included in gamification designs. Instead, *Walden* digitizes the subtler game-like elements of Thoreau's historic experiment in living mindfully, encouraging users to interact mindfully with the world of the game and the world around them. By asking how players experience this experimental game that jettisons traditional game mechanics in order to facilitate mindfulness, in comparison to a non-game app that adopts these same mechanics for the same purpose, this study generated theoretical analyses of player experiences that have been informing our designs of new mindfulness software.

2 Theoretical Framework

This research adapts and extends game designer Brian Upton's theory of ludic semiotics [1]; this theory of meaning-making in games examines how "meaning is not transmitted but constructed, and constructed in such a way that it takes into account both player agency and motivation". Knowledge is a not a collection of facts, it is a collection of ways to interact with situations and worlds, what Upton calls constraints and what game literacy researcher James Paul Gee calls surmising possibilities [23]. As Upton puts it, knowing about something means having internal constraints that orient one toward particular courses of action and away from others. Upton calls the process of developing such knowledge the "epistemological cycle": players explore their constraints to predict the future, check to see if their predictions come true, and then adjust their constraints in response to the outcome [1]. This framework is consistent with phenomenology, which emphasizes that every act involves consciousness of something [4]. It allows us to conceptualize players' awareness of their own internal constraints as a possible component of mindful play.

3 Method: Phenomenological Case Study

Data was collected using both contextual inquiry think-alouds [18] and semi-structured interview methods with 15 participants. Researchers were well-trained graduate students currently enrolled in a graduate level course in qualitative methods for both masters and PhD students in human computer interaction (HCI) and related majors at a large public U.S. institution. For masters students, this was their second course in HCI methods and many had industry experience with qualitative data collection previously. Ph.D. students typically had previous experience in conducting interviews and took this course to improve their qualitative research skills. These interviews were conducted as part of the final project, after students had practiced interviews and think-aloud protocols multiple times in class and for previous assignments.

Researchers recruited participants from word of mouth and social networks using a snowball approach to recruitment. They only recruited participants who were fluent in English. Students worked in teams of 3–4, with two students present for each contextual inquiry/interview to ensure all questions were asked. Research was approved by researchers' Institutional Review Board and all participants signed consent forms. Because the third author of this paper has intellectual property in *Walden*, she was not involved in data collection or analysis and did not have access to the data.

The interviews began with a think-aloud protocol while participants used *Headspace* and *Walden* for a short time (~15 min). The order the interfaces were presented was random. Participants were asked to talk aloud about what they were doing while using the software and why they were making their choices with the software. Researchers prompted the participants when they did not vocalize their actions. Researchers then conducted semi-structured interviews with the participants asking to reflect on the software they just used as well as their experiences with mindfulness, relaxation, meditation, behavioral changes, motivation, and other digital and analog technologies and games they use to support these practices. This portion of the interview took about 30 min.

There were 15 participants total. Ten self-identified as "male" and five self-identified as "female". Ten were born in the U.S, three in India, one in Hong Kong, and one in Indonesia. Thirteen were students, one self-employed, and one a part-time worker. Twelve were 18–25 years old and three were 26–30. Race, ethnicity, and class demographics were not collected. All participant names were replaced with numerical codes to protect their anonymity.

The first author analyzed the data using an inductive approach informed by phenomenological methods in social and educational psychology [24]. The goal of phenomenological analysis is to attempt to understand a phenomenon (in this case mindfulness) from the perspective of the research participants themselves, rather than assessing the participants' behaviors or the software they are using based on an a priori set of criteria [24]. To do this, the first author set aside assumptions about mindfulness and games as much as possible. They conducted open readings of interview and think-aloud transcripts with a curious and non-judgmental attitude, noting aspects of the phenomena that participants demonstrated as they used the software and reflected on as they answered the interview questions. They recorded these in memos, including holistic profiles of participants. Then, they began differentiating the transcripts into meaning units [24], generating inductive codes to name patterns that began to emerge across the data set. Saturation was reached when inductive readings of additional transcripts no longer generated codes, and existing codes were consolidated into a table with examples and criteria for how they should be applied across the data set. These codes were used to code the rest of the data.

The first author then analyzed similarities and tensions across the coded excerpts, asking what each excerpt might demonstrate regarding users' experiences of mindfulness while engaging with the software. They compared and contrasted users' experiences to each other and engaged in eidetic analysis [24], imagining different possible variations on these experiences of mindfulness and gaming, noting emergent theoretical insights. Through writing memos about this, they generated axial codes linking the inductive codes to the study's research questions, and compared and contrasted these coded excerpts with conceptualizations of mindfulness and gaming from extant literature. This process consolidated the axial codes into the four main thematic findings reported here. To maintain the scope of this study as a comparative case study analysis, the findings reported reflect only the axial codes for experiences of mindfulness that participants articulated in their interviews *and also* demonstrated in interactions with *Walden* and/or *Headspace* in the contextual inquiries.

4 Findings

Participants reported experiencing mindfulness in the following four ways as they engaged with *Walden and Headspace*: mindfulness as contemplative self-reflection, as a long-term process, as a byproduct of play, and as a tension between exploration and completing objectives. Because the final theme most directly informed the first and third authors' ongoing iterative design processes, it is emphasized here in greater detail than the first two.

4.1 Mindfulness as Contemplative Self-reflection

Participant T11P4 stated that "being mindful is, I think it's more spiritual in the sense that you're just becoming more mindful of your own emotions, of your own thoughts, stuff like that". Similarly, T7P2 stated that "the point of meditation is to go inwards, like, look at yourself." These concepts reflect literature that defines mindfulness as reflective self-consciousness [4] and contemplation [3].

This concept of mindfulness was present in T11P4's description of his experience playing *Walden*; he noted that "it was so philosophical and stuff, which is pretty good. I don't think many games make you think about life... I found it really interesting, pretty novel". It was also present in T7P2's reaction to the profile page in the *Headspace* app; after looking at it, he said "I hate the networking aspect of most of these apps…What am I going to do with that? Like, your friend spent 3 min like, breathing today, like ok cool". Reflecting his understanding that mindfulness should be an inward process, he argued that "It's not genuine if it's not only about yourself, cause then it's like, you're being influenced by other people's opinions and you can't really say whether or not that's like, what you wanted to do…Or it's like you might like try and curate something like show people like oh you know 'let me do um physical health meditation to show people how healthy I am'". This participant preferred *Walden's* single-player design over the gamified social networking aspects of *Headspace* because it corresponded more with his concept of mindfulness as inward-facing and autonomous. This concept of mindfulness may be popular in individualistic cultures such as the dominant culture of the United States, and is reflected in Thoreau's own writings. Alternatively, it could be an attempt to avoid a different but related kind of individualism, namely the pressure to curate an individual online identity that projects an image of mindfulness as defined by wellness industries.

4.2 Mindfulness as a Long-Term Process

T5P2 described mindfulness as a process of "becoming mindful", saying "I wouldn't put any single activity in there. I would put like maybe years of growth in there". This distinction between mindfulness and particular activities associated with it came up among several participants, but T5P2 demarcated it most clearly, making a distinction between mindfulness as a long term process vs. meditation as an episodic practice. Speaking of meditation, she stated "that's what Headspace is designed for… it's entirely meant to be a whole thing in of itself". This and the rest of her transcript suggest she experienced *Headspace* as effective, but effective in an episodic and modular way, rather than as holistic and continuous. This reflects Rapp and colleagues' analyses of HCI behavioral change interventions more broadly [16]. While T5P2 felt that self-contained meditation sessions might help build mindfulness, she also suggested that more than an app might be necessary to sustain the behavioral changes involved in mindfulness: "it's a process of change. Potentially taking on meditation, potentially learning more about how you think, that feels like a lot more like a job for a psychologist plus an app." She did suggest that *Headspace's* Journey function might help with this long-term commitment, saying that if the app were to report that she had engaged in a streak of meditation she would feel like "I'm doing this good thing habitually every day." This reflects a tension in the design of *Headspace*, where its modular design allows for a low barrier of entry, encouraging people to use it casually for short periods of time, but at the same time the app also attempts to support people in sustained long-term practice.

4.3 Mindfulness as a Byproduct of Play, and a Third-Order Design Problem

Several participants described mindfulness as a byproduct of play, not something that can be directly pursued. T11P4 said that "something that I can play would motivate me to use it more. If it's just a regular meditation app, then I won't use it that often. Cause like it's an app which is basically lecturing you to do this, do that. The game is allowing you to play and interact and engage more with it, which is fun". T7P2 described *Walden* as "actually relaxing for me as opposed to this [*Headspace*]. Cause that [*Walden*] just comes naturally, right?" These participants are contrasting *Walden's* open world design with *Headspace's* gamified, leveled instructional design, seeing the later as too didactic.

T7P2's preference for *Walden* might also stem from the fact that it is recognizable as a video game. T7P2 closely associates mindfulness with relaxation, and describes relaxation as a "byproduct" of playing games, saying that "playing games is like, you know you just wanna have fun, you wanna chill out. So that's already there, whereas this [*Headspace*]...it's almost like you're going out of your way to do it". In contrast, "That [*Walden*] is just an existing outlet to I guess spend time". This might reflect a limit to gamification, that some of the motivations people experience while playing games may not automatically transfer over to other pieces of software just because they incorporate select game mechanics. Conversely, T6P3 associates video games with a "waste of time" so he felt that *Walden* could not make a "deep" impact on his life even though he liked its philosophical narrative. As someone who meditates regularly, he felt that using *Headspace* to meditate could be as effective as "actually going to some far off place in the woods like Walden Pond".

While T7P2's preference for recognizable games stems from associating mindfulness with relaxation, it also reflects literature that associates mindfulness with an attitude of non-striving [25], drawing from its roots in Buddhist philosophy about striving leading to suffering. T7P2 describes using *Headspace* as "almost like forcing it, like I'm gonna chill out, I'm gonna relax or something" whereas with *Walden* there is no "anterior [sic] motive". This suggest a paradoxical implication for designing mindfulness games: they need to encourage players to exert effort to become more mindful, without striving toward this goal in a way that leads to anxiety and suffering [25]. Game designers Katie Salen Tekinbaş and Erik Zimmerman describe play as a second-order design problem, an emergent experience that arises indirectly from the rules the designers create [26]. Perhaps mindfulness is a third-order design problem, a phenomenon that emerges indirectly from playful experiences of non-striving that emerge indirectly from certain types of games.

4.4 Mindfulness as a Tension Between Exploring vs. Completing Objectives

Several participants described their experiences with the software as open, mindful exploration. For example, T7P2 said that gameplay "serves as an extension of your thought process or your growth as a person...You look at that and see how far you've come and say like, 'Oh, this is how I'm living... And that makes you more mindful or in tune with yourself'". While engaging with the crafting mechanics in *Walden*, he argued that they might motivate people to "just like get in there and start messing around", similar to his experiences with *Minecraft* where "you're putting your fingerprints onto that landscape". He argued this experience is possible because of the game's open-world design: "if you go into it knowing that there's no like ultimate goal then there's almost no pressure to get to start working towards that. So, it leaves it open for you to just explore" instead of worrying about preparing for "a boss battle at the end". This experience suggests that open-world game design might support mindfulness as being-in-the-moment [5, 6]. Similarly, while playing *Walden*, T11P4 zoomed in on an object in the world and said "as soon as I zoom in, I learn about this thing. That motivated me to try and zoom in on every object and just learn more about it. I was curious". This experience offers insight into the specific ways the game's mechanics encourage the kind of open exploration T7P2 talked about.

However, *Walden* does have objectives and quests that constrain and shape this process of exploration, and players responded to these in different ways. T1P3 said, "All of the game is supposed to be me meditating and calming and stuff and the food running out is making me anxious to look for food and stuff instead of just exploring". While she shared T7P2 and T11P4's association between open exploration and mindfulness, the internal constraints that *Walden's* objectives generated ended up limiting, rather than encouraging, her exploration, and hence her experience of mindful play. T8P1 also said he experienced stress from these game mechanics, but he associated this experience with survival games he likes to play, calling it a "good stress" that motivates him by challenging him to get better at the game. He felt *Walden* did not have enough of this kind of stress at the beginning of the game, but anticipated that it might later on as winter sets in. After reading a quote from Thoreau embedded in the game, he drew the conclusion that "it'd be very easy to survive, like just eat with the animals, eat and you'll be fine". He thought this was an intentional choice on the part of the designers, that the game "is meant to be like relaxing and not stressful", with the survival mechanics "pushing you to explore things" rather than threatening the main character with death if the player does not complete certain tasks. For T8P1, *Walden* creates dramatic tension by presenting the challenge of acquiring essential needs in the woods, but it intentionally modulates this tension in order to prompt the player to reflect on what really is essential after all. This mirrors feedback the third author has received from teachers and students who have used *Walden* during the COVID19 pandemic to prompt reflection on the question: "what is essential?".

Multiple participants named a related tension in their broader experiences: that objectives can encourage *and* limit open exploration, so game designs that overemphasize or underemphasize them can fail to encourage mindful behavior. For example, T11P4 analyzed one mindfulness app he had used that was too open-ended, contrasting it to another that had too many objectives. The first was a doodling/ art therapy app that he could imagine working for someone who "doesn't care and just wants to enjoy the experience of drawing patterns" but it didn't work for him because it brought out his "inner perfectionist" as he stressed himself out trying to improve his drawings. T3P4 described something similar happening when she tries meditate; she thinks "I'm relaxing and there's stuff I could be doing" and her mind starts to wander. To solve this problem, she plays games with puzzles to focus her attention, and she enjoyed the small daily tasks in *Walden* because they reminded her of these puzzles. The anxiety that these participants express could be a kind of terror of the blank page; as Upton [1] put it, playfulness is only possible with constraints, when the player can choose among a series of interesting moves. If there are too many possible moves that could be made, the player might become confused or anxious about deciding where to focus. In contrast, when every move is easily mapped out, the player becomes bored or feels patronized. For example, T11P4 described a behavioral change app that he felt "was trying to control your day":

"every one hour it'll send you a small pop up saying, Hey, have a glass of water". This also did not work for him.

Extending his analysis of this tension to the apps in this study, T11P4 said that he liked using *Walden* to de-stress by "exploring a new world and how serenely and slowly the game goes on maintaining a story". T9P1 echoed this, noting that Walden's character motion controls seem intentionally slow so that when the player walks to a place to complete one task there is more of a chance that they might notice other things on the way; tasks like meeting basic needs become a prompt to open up exploration.

However, in contrast to T1P3's experience, T11P4 wished the game's basic needs system were more like a traditional game health meter, suggesting the game "tell me that I need to collect four jars by tonight, otherwise I'll die of hunger or something". While T3P4 felt "bothered" by the time pressure to accumulate resources, she shared this desire for a clearer metric of basic needs, expressing frustration that "there's no indication on your own food jar...how much is full?" Similarly, T11P4 said he wished *Headspace* would state more directly that "if you do this meditation exercise on a regular basis this is going to benefit you like this". While some participants agreed that *Headspace* did not offer clear enough objectives, others felt it was too prescriptive or didactic. These findings show that designing game-based mindfulness apps requires fine-tuning the balance between objectives and open exploration, recognizing that different players experience this balance in different ways.

Other players' experiences emphasize the difficulty in fine-tuning such a balance in an era of ubiquitous media. When T5P1 encountered the possibility of seeking hidden badges in *Headspace* as an incentive for meditating, he said "I would first of all Google every single badge...to see if I could get them instead... I tend to be more of a completionist in games and that's how I'd probably approach something like this as well". In an era of metagaming [20] where users frequently share information online, game designers cannot rely on hiding information from players in order to create an experience of mindfully exploring a mysterious or unknown world. Other mechanics are needed to encourage players to stay in the moment rather than leaving the game to search the internet for clues.

However, T5P1's desire for the satisfaction of completion also cannot be met by casual-game-like mechanics in mindfulness apps such as quick feedback from the user interface or non-player characters. Critiquing an animation in *Headspace*, he said "I feel like it's the same problem with, like a smartphone being like "Good job! You've completed your task" or whatever. I don't really feel any derived reward from that. I feel like somebody just wrote a line of code, and it showed up because I did something. I'd rather just be satisfied that I did the task in of itself". This sentiment was echoed by other participants; more passages in the data were coded for intrinsic than extrinsic motivation and more were coded for mastery than performance-oriented motivation (these codes used definitions for these constructs drawn from Plass and colleagues' 2015 review of game-based learning research [27]). This shows the importance of intrinsic motivation in the experience of mindfulness practice, challenging reward-oriented aspects of gamification.

This tension that participants named between open exploration and objectives is similar to a tension that Upton [1] names between coherence/closure gameplay and expansion gameplay. Coherence is the player's sense they are "getting it right", that the game is going the way it should, and the moves they make to sustain that fantasy. Closure, like T11P4's "completionism", means making moves to close off ambiguities and tie up loose ends. Expansion means making moves to open up the play space, to increase the number of future moves available, to risk the chance of failure in order to avoid habitually repeated situations that have been played out. Upton says that to achieve expansion, a game must help a player know they are moving into the unknown. "We generally don't seek out situations that increase our uncertainty and that pose more questions than they answer. However, since play itself is pleasurable, we're willing to avoid closure in order to sustain it". Mindfulness might involve making moves that challenge some of the internal constraints we have inherited from our lived experiences, embracing the unknown, critically questioning, and opening up a wider range of moves we can make in our lives. Practicing how to do that requires games that encourage us to explore while also making us feel safe and supported enough to do.

Participants' Suggestions for How to Resolve This Tension in Future Designs

In the interview protocols, participants were invited to imagine ways to improve mindfulness software, and they generated a range of promising design ideas that could address the tension they named between exploring and completing objectives. For example, T1P3 suggests modifying *Walden*: "I would have different tracks kind of thing. Like one is probably goal-oriented, you're collecting food or arrows or whatever, and one... there's no time limit. You're just exploring. So those two tracks can help different people". This idea offers players the chance to choose their own balance between open mindful exploration and the pursuit of objectives set by the game. T9P1 regularly plays console games "casually" by just exploring their worlds in order to get away from his work computer; to enhance that kind of activity, he imagined a virtual reality version of *Walden* with "an infinite treadmill that you could just walk anywhere and explore the woods that would be way more relaxing because you're physically involved in it and just physical motion and using your body is going to be more stress relief than sitting idly".

Expanding these ideas, T11P4 imagined a mindfulness app that's similar to *Walden*, but customizable like *Headspace*: "*Walden* gave me this thing that I'm in a forest and stuff. What if I wanted to explore, like a mountain and stuff? So that's what *Headspace* does. One of the relaxation techniques asks you to explore, to like choose your most favorite place and then explore the details of that place... So if *Walden* could allow me to like customize aspects of it and then explore, I think that would be more engaging". He recognized that this level of customization would transform world exploration into "building your own world". Drawing from *Headspace's* timed meditations, T1P3 suggests that such an app could be part of a Pomodoro-style productivity aid, with a 10-min timer to "explore...with no purpose" as a break from her schoolwork without getting lost and distracted. This suggestion is consistent with the ways that several participants described using games to relax during breaks in schoolwork. It builds on the affordances of desktop and laptop computers by integrating mindful play into the same equipment and setting where work happens, analogous to how *Headspace* builds on the affordances of mobile devices that can play audio while they are set to the side during meditation or preparation for sleep.

T1P3 also recommends creating a feature where players can write and reflect in the journal that pops up in *Walden*, which echoes Rapp and colleagues' [16] suggestion that "behavior change technologies could help people reflect on the quality of their motivations to change". This would allow players to act like Thoreau by engaging in mindful journaling, essentially creating their own version of *Walden* the book by setting their own reflective, playful goals.

5   Practical Applications of this Research for Iterative, Playcentric Design of Mindfulness Software

Based on these findings, the third and first authors are currently developing two new mindfulness apps based on expansion gameplay. The impact of this study on the design of these projects illustrates the relevance of qualitative player experience research for the playcentric development [2] of mindfulness and educational software. A playcentric design process involves setting user experience goals and iterating towards them through successive rounds of playtesting. It can be extended after a game is published through research on user experiences with the game that can inform new versions of the game or related works that build on its design. In this sense, this study connects playcentric design with a longer process of design-based research [28].

The third and first author (Tracy Fullerton and Matthew Hamilton), their team at the Game Innovation Lab, and education researcher Matthew Farber are working on a mindfulness learning module that is part of a new web-based educational version of *Walden*. The overall project consists of a series of web-based modules optimized to run on Chromebooks in high school classrooms, or incorporated into online learning environments, with accompanying lessons and activities. This will help support the growing interest in using *Walden* for remote learning during the COVID19 pandemic. Following T1P3's suggestion, some of these modules focus on meeting goals that are more clearly defined than in the original game, whereas in the mindfulness module called *What I Lived For*, players can explore the pond at their own pace, without the pressure of a basic needs meter.

The tension between objectives and exploration that study participants experienced with *Walden* might partially be a result of the short play sessions during the study. The original version of *Walden* attempts to address this tension through the inspiration meter that grays the graphics if players work too hard, but most players in this study did not play long enough to notice it and adjust their play style in response to it. This finding is useful because the length of the contextual inquiries (~15 min) is similar to the length of time students will likely play with the app if it is used in schools for various learning purposes, including social emotional learning around mindfulness (surveys with teachers interested in *Walden* suggest 15–30 min as an optimal time frame). For that reason, the authors broke the game up into shorter modules. Some have objectives more defined than the original game, while the mindfulness module has no objectives.

This new module, called *What I Lived For* (see Fig. 2), explores Thoreau's own attempts to live in the moment through connection with nature. It will model a contemplative walk around the pond with special spots marked with stone cairns that prompt the user to stop and reflect. The inspiration meter is de-emphasized and replaced with

Fig. 2. Screenshot from *What I Lived For*, the new *Walden* mindfulness module, with a cairn in the foreground

mechanics that aim to prompt mindfulness more quickly. For example, the game models a breathing exercise at each of the locations; in a current draft, an interface alert pops up saying: "Take some time to breathe along with Thoreau at each of the cairns and enjoy the moment. Thoreau will begin to hum when it's time to move along". The most important instruction is the way the game models how to do this meditation through timed sound effects of Thoreau breathing in and out, which hopefully will invite the player to breath in sync. While the game will record how long the player stops at each cairn and will reflect this back to the player, this variable is not tied to an objective or win state. Consistent with the findings of this study about non-striving and expansion play, the game does not insist that players participate in the meditation, and gives them the option to just explore if they wish.

The second piece of software is called *LoFi Hip Hop Worlds to Study In*, developed by the first author (Matthew Hamilton) and their colleague Israel Jones (see Fig. 3). Recently released on Itch.io (https://lofiworlds.itch.io/study), it is a collection of 3D worlds full of study spots with instrumental music and ambient sounds. Users can explore these worlds to relax while they take breaks from studying, as participant T1P3 suggested, and they can set a timer so they do not explore for too long. When they are ready to study again, they can set another timer and put the software in the background, using it as part of a Pomodoro method to sustain a rhythm of focused work punctuated by breaks. To help users focus, the software continues to provide relaxing sounds and beats with no ads during study sessions.

LoFi Hip Hop Worlds To Study In is a walking simulator based on the design of open world video games like *Walden*. Unlike the original version of *Walden*, it does not have quests or game objectives beyond the study goals players set for themselves; this design choice was based on the findings of this study regarding expansion play and non-striving. Like *Headspace*, it allows players to customize their experience, choosing which worlds

Fig. 3. Screenshot from *LoFi Hip Hop Worlds To Study In*

they want to explore, as participant T11P4 suggested. It also allows users to customize their study soundscape by moving closer or farther away from radios that emit music as well as other diegetic sound sources such as waves, fireplaces, and non-player characters doing breathing meditations. The intention is to give users more control over their sonic environment, to help meet the needs of students who are engaged in remote learning during the pandemic in environments where they may not otherwise have much choice in what they hear (a recent survey of Los Angeles Unified School District students found that just one in three families report that their children always have a spot free of distraction where they can engage in remote learning [29]).

Further research is needed to see how, if at all, players experience mindfulness while using these new pieces of software. Education researchers and teachers might also be interested in whether use of the software contributes to motivation, self-regulation, and learning outcomes.

6 Limitations and Suggestions for Future Research

This current study is limited by its small and non-representative sample, and future research is needed to see if the findings reported here also apply among players with different backgrounds, genders, cultures, and social contexts. Aspects of the qualitative methodology used here could be coupled with quantitative measures of mindfulness used in studies of larger, randomized, representative samples to see how participants themselves experience the constructs being measured, increasing the content validity of the quantitative measures [17].

On the other hand, purposeful sampling could be conducted to see if specific groups of potential users might be particularly responsive to the various design features of apps like *Walden* and *Headspace*. For example, *Walden's* status as an experimental game might attract specific kinds of gamers, and results might be different among people who intentionally seek out this kind of game; similarly, they may differ among clients of therapists or students of teachers who refer people to it. Because analyses of player types were not conducted in this study, we cannot report whether patterns in players' experiences relate to differences on measures such as the Hexad scale [30]. Future research that includes such analyses could support future design efforts, especially around tuning the balance between objectives and exploration to meet the needs of different users.

Interview responses and think-aloud transcripts did not suggest that the order the software was presented affected findings for this phenomenological study. However, in a larger sample study involving mixed methods and statistical analyses, the order of presentation should be tracked as a variable to see if it might explain variation in the outcomes.

Finally, it is possible that the think-aloud protocol primed participants to be more self-aware and attentive because they were engaging in metacognition about their play experiences. For some, this it might have resulted in a greater degree of mindfulness than they may have experienced using the software in everyday life settings. Research on how the apps are used in such settings could supplement these findings. For example, observations and interviews could be conducted on how *Walden* and *Headspace* are used in social-emotional learning activities in schools or online classes. Conversely, metacognitive reflection about playing a game might itself be a desired outcome of a design process aimed at producing educational software [23], and aspects of a think-aloud protocol could be incorporated into the design of games and their accompanying curricular materials, especially if the learning objectives include both mindfulness and game literacy. The new *Walden* educational modules begin to do this through prompts for class discussions before and after gameplay sessions; they also provide students with an editable journal feature that prompts them to reflect on their play as participant T1P3 suggested.

More broadly, the purpose of the current study was not to evaluate these two pieces of software to assess their effectiveness in producing mindfulness or related outcomes. Evaluation studies of *Walden* are needed, especially as it is used more frequently in schools.

7 Conclusions and Suggestions for How to Develop Mindfulness Software

This study asked participants how they experience mindfulness while interacting with *Walden* and *Headspace*. Many of them reported experiencing a tension between mindfulness as open exploration, and mindfulness as a scaffolded set of objectives to meet, reflecting and extending Upton's [1] concepts of expansion and coherence/closure. Participants' design suggestions focused on ways to resolve this tension by customizing and differentiating the experience in mindfulness apps, combining aspects of *Headspace's* gamification with aspects of *Walden's* open-world design. Mindfulness might be a game that people create for themselves, like Thoreau did by giving himself the challenge of living within the constraints of Walden Pond. Software, including video games, might be the equipment that designers provide to help build such a game [20].

To support the design of such equipment, software developers should engage in a play-centric [2] design process, carefully noting how users experience their software, attempting to facilitate experiences closer to their goals in the next iteration of the software. In this process, qualitative research methods can be helpful in generating descriptions of player experiences, especially considering this study's finding that mindfulness may be a third order design challenge, a byproduct of play which is itself a byproduct of design. Such a meta-gaming [20] experience requires research tools that prompt metacognition.

Echoing Upton [1], and Rapp and colleagues [16], developers of mindfulness apps should not just design ways to encourage specific behaviors like meditation, they should design situations where players can actively reflect on these behaviors. As the think-aloud contextual inquiries in this study show, players are making what Upton calls interpretative moves, reflecting on their experiences, even when they are not immediately making an external move such as manipulating a game's controls or doing a particular meditation technique. The spaces between techniques and game-like achievements are just as important for mindfulness as the techniques and achievements themselves. For this reason, designers should draw from the full range of game design theory and practice, including Upton's situational game design, which provide frameworks to design for these contemplative moments. This might help the design of mindfulness apps move beyond what has been achieved so far under the framework of gamification, cultivating a more holistic practice of mindful gaming.

References

1. Upton, B.: Situational Game Design. CRC Press, Boca Raton (2017)
2. Fullerton, T.: Game Design Workshop: A Playcentric Approach to Creating Innovative Games, 4th edn. CRC Press, Boca Raton (2019)
3. Shapiro, S., Lyons, K., Miller, R., Butler, B., Vieten, C., Zelazo, P.: Contemplation in the classroom: a new direction for improving childhood education. Educ. Psychol. Rev. 27(1), 1–30 (2015)
4. Micallef, J.: Play, effect, reflect: a phenomenological study of reflective self-consciousness in players' experiences of digital games. In: Proceedings of the 2016 Philosophy of Computer Games Conference (2016)
5. Batacharya, S., Wong, Y. (eds.): Sharing Breath: Embodied Learning and Decolonization. Athabasca University Press, Edmonton (2018)
6. Kosa, M., Uysal, A.: Trait mindfulness and player experience. In: Extended Abstracts Publication of the Annual Symposium on Computer-Human Interaction in Play (CHI PLAY 2017 Extended Abstracts), pp. 463–470. Association for Computing Machinery, New York (2018). https://doi.org/10.1145/3130859.3131301
7. Cardaciotto, L., Herbert, J.D., Forman, E.M., Moitra, E., Farrow, V.: The assessment of present-moment awareness and acceptance: the Philadelphia mindfulness scale. Assessment 15, 204–223 (2008)
8. Kabat-Zinn, J.: Coming to Our Senses: Healing Ourselves and the World Through Mindfulness. Hyperion, New York (2005)
9. Reveley, J.: School-based mindfulness training and the economisation of attention: a Stieglerian view. Educ. Philos. Theory 47(8), 804–821 (2015)

10. Fish, M., Saul, A.: The gamification of meditation: a randomized-controlled study of a prescribed mobile mindfulness meditation application in reducing college students' depression. Simul. Gaming **50**(4), 419–435 (2019). https://doi.org/10.1177/1046878119851821

11. Economides, M., Martman, J., Bell, M.J., Sanderson, B.: Improvements in stress, affect, and irritability following brief use of a mindfulness-based smartphone app: a randomized controlled trial. Mindfulness **9**(5), 1584–1593 (2018). https://doi.org/10.1007/s12671-018-0905-4

12. Hekler, E., Klasnja, P., Froehlich, J., Buman, M.: Mind the theoretical gap: interpreting, using, and developing behavioral theory in HCI research. In: Proceedings of the SIGCHI Conference on Human Factors in Computing Systems (CHI 2013), pp. 3307–3316. Association for Computing Machinery, New York (2013). https://doi.org/10.1145/2470654.2466452

13. Chou, Y.-K.: Actionable Gamification: Beyond Points, Badges, and Leaderboards. Octalysis Media, Fremont (2015)

14. Thoreau, H.D.: Walden and Other Writings. Barnes and Noble, New York (1993)

15. Plate, B.: Religion is playing games: playing video gods, playing to play. Relig. Stud. Theol. **29**(2), 215–230 (2011). https://doi.org/10.1558/rsth.v29i2.215

16. Rapp, A., Tirassa, M., Tirabeni, L.: Rethinking technologies for behavior change: a view from the inside of human change. ACM Trans. Comput.-Hum. Interact. **26**(4), Article 22 (2019). https://doi.org/10.1145/3318142

17. Park, T., Reilly-Spong, M., Gross, C.R.: Mindfulness: a systematic review of instruments to measure an emergent patient-reported outcome (PRO). Qual. Life Res. **22**(10), 2639–2659 (2013). https://doi.org/10.1007/s11136-013-0395-8

18. Holtzblatt, K., Wendell, J.B., Wood, S.: Rapid Contextual Design: A How-to Guide to Key Techniques for User-Centered Design. Elsevier, San Francisco (2005)

19. Flanagan, M.: Critical Play: Radical Game Design. MIT Press, Cambridge (2009)

20. Boluk, S., LeMieux, P.: Metagaming: Playing, Competing, Spectating, Cheating, Trading, Making, and Breaking Videogames. University of Minnesota Press, Minneapolis (2017)

21. Kafai, Y., Burke, Q.: Connected Gaming: What Making Video Games Can Teach us About Learning and Literacy. The MIT Press, Cambridge (2016)

22. Eisenhardt, K., Graebner, M.: Theory building from cases: opportunities and challenges. Acad. Manag. J. **50**(1), 25–32 (2007)

23. Gee, J.P.: Good Video Games+ Good Learning: Collected Essays on Video Games, Learning, and Literacy, 2nd edn. Peter Lang, New York (2013)

24. Wertz, F., Charmaz, K., McMullen, L., Josselson, R., Anderson, R., McSpadden, E.: Five Ways of Doing Qualitative Analysis: Phenomenological Psychology, Grounded Theory, Discourse Analysis, Narrative Research, and Intuitive Inquiry. Guilford Press, New York (2011)

25. Shapiro, S., Siegel, R., Neff, K.D.: Paradoxes of mindfulness. Mindfulness **9**(6), 1693–1701 (2018). https://doi.org/10.1007/s12671-018-0957-5

26. Salen-Tekinbaş, K., Zimmerman, E.: Rules of Play: Game Design Fundamentals. MIT press, Cambridge (2004)

27. Plass, J., Homer, B., Kinzer, C.: Foundations of game-based learning. Educ. Psychol. **50**(4), 258–283 (2015). https://doi.org/10.1080/00461520.2015.1122533

28. Barab, S., Squire, K.: Design-based research: putting a stake in the ground. J. Learn. Sci. **13**(1), 1–14 (2004)

29. Aguilar, S., Galperin, H., Baek, C., Gonzalez, E.: When school comes home: how low-income families are adapting to distance learning (2020). Edarxiv.org/su8wk. Accessed 11 Feb 2020

30. Tondello, G.F., Mora, A., Marczewski, A., Nacke, L.E.: Empirical validation of the gamification user types hexad scale in English and Spanish. Int. J. Hum. Comput. Stud. **127**, 95–111 (2019)

Gamification of ERP Training in Local Governments

Volha Knysh, Kaitlyn Patrick(✉), and Fan Zhao

Florida Gulf Coast University, Fort Myers, FL 33965, USA
{vmknysh,kapatrick6268}@eagle.fgcu.edu, fzhao@fgcu.edu

Abstract. Local government organizations are actively adopting and utilizing ERP technology in their operations but often face challenges in facilitating effective use of the system. The application of gamification in employee training and education has grown in popularity in recent years and displayed its effectiveness. The case study focuses on the possibilities of improving ERP training by adapting the educational gamification concepts in the training process. Two case studies of the ERP training approaches were conducted with two local governments in Florida. Common issues such as lack of formal training and the absence of incentives or motivation for continued education with the ERP system. This case study outlines the model that can be used to design the ERP training with gamification elements. The proposed model incorporates the following gamification mechanics and dynamics elements: immediate feedback, points and leaderboards, narratives, missions, quests, competition, and compensation. The gamification elements can be included without significant investments in technology and within the local legislation's boundaries concerning the governmental employees' incentivization.

Keywords: Gamification · ERP · Training

1 Introduction

Local government plays a vital role in the development of the region or municipality. As an active and important participant in the area's economic growth, local governments naturally cannot be immune to the need to manage large quantities of data and the effects of technological advancement. There is also the question of the effectiveness and efficiency of such an organization. Any governmental organization is inherently viewed as bureaucratic, not very efficient and often lags in adopting or entirely using technology. In most cases, the local governmental entity does not measure its performance through profits and revenue, making it more challenging to measure the benefits of the adaptation and effective utilization of technology like ERP (Enterprise Resource Planning).

ERP software is a large software package designed to provide a single comprehensive database for business activities and integrate business processes across business functions into a single computer system. Through data standardization and process integration, ERP systems have the potential to facilitate communications and coordination, enable the centralization of administrative activities, reduce IS maintenance costs, and increase the

X. Fang (Ed.): HCII 2021, LNCS 12790, pp. 20–32, 2021.
https://doi.org/10.1007/978-3-030-77414-1_2

ability to deploy new IS functionality [1]. When they are well implemented, ERP systems are able to bring operational, managerial, strategic, IT infrastructure, and operational benefits to their customers [2]. However, in order to reap the benefits of an ERP system, ERP users are critical. They have to understand how to use the ERP systems skillfully. Hundreds of previous studies mentioned system education and training as one of the key success factors in Information Systems implementations and operations. Alcivar and Abadclaim demonstrate that issues with ERP systems are due to poor user training and underestimating the importance of training [3]. ERP systems have a long history of training issues that led to failure. Companies are usually surprised by the knowledge gap between the training provided by the ERP system's vendor and the knowledge required by staff for them to work effectively with a new ERP system. This can be due to training being provided too early, insufficiently or even incorrectly [4]. Users must have a firm understanding of how to use a system, or they will make critical errors when attempting to perform basic business functions, which results in money and man-hours spent fixing the issue when they should have been spent on training. Getting users trained and up to speed as the implementation is performed will help achieve the benefits of the ERP system [5]. However, in most cases, governmental employees do not have an incentive for actively seeking training, improvement, and technology adaptation. "The use of technology in doing tasks is involuntary" [6].

Gamification is the application of game design elements in non-game contexts [7]. The application of gamification in employee training and education has grown in popularity in recent years, and positive results have been observed. For example, a 2020 study detailed a gamification approach to statistics education and its impacts on student learning outcomes. The study found those game design elements such as points, levels, challenges, and leaderboards improved student performance by 34.75% compared to traditional teaching methods [8]. Positive results like this have increased the prevalence of gamification in the education field. The education field can offer tested gamification models, but how does this approach impact intrinsic motivation for learning in the professional environment? How do local governments adopt this new training technology to improve their employees' productivity?

2 Literature Review

2.1 Gamification Features

Gamification features include badges, quests, points and levels, avatars. Alsawaier [9] describes the connection between behavioral science, psychology, and gamification. The author also provides an overview of the existing studies and findings. One of the crucial insights is that many studies suggest a significant increase in students' engagement levels following game elements' introduction [9]. The author also points out that many studies focused on gamification in the educational kids' and young adults' environment; however, many of the conclusions were based on quantitative data and insufficient observations and qualitative data.

A common criticism of gamification is that it inspires participants to learn the topic on a very superficial level. Current literature addresses the concerns with extrinsic, intrinsic motivation, and retention of the information in education.

2.2 Extrinsic Motivation

Generally speaking, the incorporation of game design elements in training programs and education positively impacts extrinsic motivation for users. This may appear obvious because gamification makes the process of completing training programs and education more enjoyable. In fact, a common criticism is that gamification encourages extrinsic motivation and, as a result, diminishes the role of intrinsic motivation. Markopoulos et al. [10] evaluated gamification literature and concluded that gamification could make difficult subjects like engineering more manageable, easier to understand, increase collaboration, interest, and reduce or manage workload.

2.3 Intrinsic Motivation

Gamification tools have a clear, positive impact on users' extrinsic motivation. However, do these tools have the same impact on intrinsic motivation? In 2014, Michael Armstrong and Richard Landers used an online leaderboard to improve college student engagement with course material and student learning. They found that points and leaderboards increased students' perception of a future training program [11]. Their findings were consistent with an online experiment detailed in Mekler et al.'s experiment [12] that examined gamification elements and other factors through an image-tagging task. Mekler et al. [12] found that gamification elements positively impacted extrinsic motivation, but intrinsic motivation was not affected. A systematic review of 46 empirical research papers published in the Web of Science database between 2016 and 2019 conducted in 2020 revealed that game-based elements promote students' extrinsic motivation and increase their intrinsic value for learning [13]. Additionally, a study from Pereira et al. [14] concluded that gamification has the potential to promote employee involvement within the organization, provides managers with better tools to make practical sense to employees and that employees are led to a search for learning.

2.4 Retention of Information

It is important to consider how gamification impacts the retention of information. The positive effects on extrinsic and intrinsic motivation are rendered useless if users cannot retain the information. Fouche and Mangle [15] proposed a solution to address barriers to entry in the cybersecurity field. Their solution involved leveraging Code Hunt, an existing training platform to address expensive training, exclusionary culture, and the need for costly infrastructure. They specifically suggest using incremental exercises to improve the retention of information. A longitudinal gamification study [16] found that an augmented-reality game resulted in students' highest knowledge retention. This study utilized Logistify, an augmented-reality game that incorporates time constraints, avatars, points, clear goals, immediate feedback, and storytelling.

2.5 The Effectiveness of Traditional ERP Training

Sreehari et al. [17] assessed the effectiveness of the traditional ERP university course by conducting questionnaires with 120 students. The study was focused on evaluating the effectiveness of the training, the effectiveness of the resource people, and the usefulness of such courses in a professional environment. However, the desired transfer of knowledge from the classroom to the workplace is not evident. On the other hand, Zadeh et al. [18] demonstrate that focusing on the technical aspects of the ERP can be a more effective way of teaching the subject than only concentrating on the functional aspects of the ERP. The study used a modified version of the existing ERP course to learn more technical aspects of the Microsoft Dynamics ERP in a major Midwestern University as a learning experiment. Using surveys and analysis of the students learning outcomes, authors found evidence that involving students in the technical aspects of ERP and going beyond the ERP's data analytic functionality allowed students to unlock a wealth of additional information. The students had a better understanding of how things are all intertwined in a complex system like an ERP. These findings emphasize the idea that hands-on engagement and deeper learning has more potential in improving training outcomes.

2.6   Experience of Local Governments in Training for New Technology

Batara et al. [6] examine the adaptation of the e-government technology, using quantitative methods, by the employees of Indonesia and the Philippines. The study concluded that attitude was a pivotal predictor, and performance expectancy, social influence, and facilitating conditions were critical positive factors in the ability to influence acceptance and organizational change in the adaptation process. The study also admits the importance of the length of employment as a moderating variable. The limitation of this study's applicability to this research is its potential cultural differences and the fact the authors used purposive sampling in the model. E-government has more exposure outside of the organization. However, the findings still can be useful to the understanding of the problems with adaptation and training of ERP technology. This study clearly shows that emotional and social components are valid factors, so the potential of gamification as a tool is evident.

2.7   Gamification Application in the Enterprise Environment

Deliberate design choices are crucial to the successful gamification concept application [19]. Gamification must be approached structurally and cannot be oversimplified to the existing info systems' fun video game layer. Ruhi [19] presents the MDA (Mechanics, Dynamics, Aesthetics) framework that aims to facilitate interactive gameplay within the business process and drive positive behavioral and business outcomes. The author describes the elements of the framework as the following: mechanics includes components and controls; dynamics consists of all user interaction elements, and aesthetics includes all emotional response elements. The model is generic and logical and is intended to be applied in for-profit enterprise and within the governmental entity.

Leaderboards and social groups are team-based gamification elements that are essential for human information processing in a gaming team environment. Performance is important to facilitate team cohesion [20]. This leads to the conclusion that team engagement in the gamification process must be an essential element in designing ERP training for governmental employees.

Additionally, Kocadere et al. [21] bring the importance of considering different player types during gamification design. The study identifies four player types: killer, achiever, explorer, and socializer, and what game mechanics such as reward positively or negatively affect the player. It concludes that design features in the gamified learning environment can affect players' characteristics, and different player types get a different effect from the same mechanics.

There is a significant body of information on the potential of gamification as a tool of technology adaptation and effective technology utilization. Observation of a gamification tool in the education field or in a training session may lead one to believe that gamification directly impacts users' extrinsic motivation. However, gamification can make difficult subjects like engineering more manageable, easier to understand, increase collaboration, interest, and reduce or manage workload [10].

2.8 Gamification Models in Education

Analysis of Gamification Models in Education Using MDA Framework Using MDA Framework
Kusuma et al. [22] developed the Mechanics, Dynamics, and Aesthetics (MDA) framework to analyze various gamification models in the education field. The MDA framework analyzes three components of game design: mechanics, dynamics, and aesthetics. Mechanics are the core components of the game, and dynamics are the way the mechanics affect gameplay and interact with input from the player. Aesthetics refer to the emotional response from the player.

Game mechanics identified in various previous studies include points, leaderboard, levels, mission, role-playing, feedback, background story, items, etc. Kusuma et al. [22] state that the easiest mechanics to implement are points and are generally used to reward a player based on their actions. They further identify eight types of aesthetics in their paper: sensation, challenge, discovery, fellowship, expression, fantasy, submission, and narrative. Game mechanics should be chosen to create dynamics that will result in different aesthetics.

Gamification in engineering education and professional training
Markopoulos et al. [10] discuss the benefits and criticism of gamification, game mechanics, and gamification in education. The authors identified several game mechanics they found to have positive impacts on students. These mechanics include achievements, levels, progression, quests/challenges, status, community collaboration, loss aversion, and leaderboards. Implementing these mechanics to gamify learning for students can have positive effects. Markopoulos et al. stated these benefits might result in students taking responsibility for and controlling their learning. Students may become more comfortable trying new things and making mistakes. Students are more likely to enjoy learning.

However, critics of gamification state that students do not develop or increase intrinsic motivation for learning, gamification is perceived as easy and should only be used with young students, and teachers have difficulty implementing gamification in the classroom. Markopoulos et al. examine different gamification elements and platforms and emphasize the importance of immediate feedback. Immediate feedback gives the player the ability to understand the effects of their actions. The authors ultimately conclude that gamification has a positive effect on learning by making content easier to understand, increasing intrinsic motivation, and reducing students' workload.

Gamification of employee training and development
Both Kusuma et al. [22] and Armstrong and Landers [11] found the implementation of points to be effective and simple. The trainees or players are motivated to do well in order to receive points. This motivation can also be increased by implementing a badge system or displaying players' scores on a leaderboard. Armstrong and Landers [11] point out that while these game elements are easy to implement, critics state that these elements only increase extrinsic motivation within the player. These elements manipulate the player into completing the lesson or training.

How a company's gamification strategy influences corporate learning: A study based on gamified MSLP (Mobile social learning platform)

Kim [23] analyzed the effects of various gamification strategies in the context of a mobile social learning platform. A competition strategy aims to increase a person's participation by having users compete against each other. Research has shown that a competition strategy has a positive effect on both intrinsic motivation and performance. Game mechanics such as points, leaderboards, and levels can be implemented when using a competition strategy. A challenge strategy determines a person's skills by the completion of certain tasks and has been shown to help keep users interested. Kim states this strategy is often associated with the compensation strategy. For example, a user is compensated or rewarded for the completion of a task with a badge, trophy, etc. A relationship strategy is an approach to gamification that encourages users to interact with each other. Applying the relationship strategy can motivate users to continue the training or lesson. The last strategy discussed in Kim's paper is the usability strategy. This strategy provides support for using the system. If there is perceived ease of use amongst users, then continuous usage is more likely.

Kim's study [23] tested the relationships between these strategies and Flow and Continuous usage intention. In the gamification context, flow is a desirable state where users are absorbed and wholly involved in their actions. Continuous usage refers to whether the person will use the system again. The results found that the competition strategy did not affect Flow and Continuous usage intention, but this strategy should not be discounted because it has positive learning effects. Kim's study found that the challenge strategy had a positive effect on flow but no effect on Continuous usage intention. The compensation strategy did not affect Flow and Continuous usage intention, but like the challenge strategy, it should not be discounted because it can have a positive effect on motivation. The relationship strategy had a positive impact on Flow but did not affect Continuous usage intention. Finally, the usability strategy had a positive effect on both Flow and Continuous usage intention.

However, there is limited data on applying the gamification concept and improving motivation overall in not-for-profit, governmental organizations. The literature findings suggest that existing gamification has the potential to enhance ERP training and overall better adaptation of the technology in a governmental organization. How can gamification be applied in the environment of the local government for ERP training?

3 Case Study

This research adopted a case study method to study our research questions. Two case studies of the ERP training approach were conducted using information for the interview with the local government employees of two counties in Florida. The interview reveals some common issues with the current ERP training and utilization overall. Government Entity #1 was founded in 1887. It is the legislative and governing body of the local territory. The entity has over 2500 employees, not including special districts, and is the fourth largest employer in the county. The county-wide information systems are used by most of the special districts and departments within the organization. The innovation and technology department supports county operations and multiple special districts and departments. Government Entity #1 uses the well established JD Edward cloud-based ERP. The system is mature and was implemented in 2000. The system does not satisfy all organizational needs. Local governments usually manage a variety of functionally different units. The needs of the port authority will be different from the needs of the utility unit or library. Only one division uses the Account Receivable module from ERP. The remaining units of the county use third-party software.

In most cases, the third-party software is not integrated into the ERP and requires employees to duplicate accounting entries from one system to another. This forces employees to invest significant time in the multiple systems reconciliations. The entity uses the Fixed Assets module, Accounts Payable, and Procurement. According to the interview, Accounts Payables functionality is not fully used. The vendor self-services module is purchased but not utilized due to the lack of training and user understanding.

Government Entity #1 attempted to utilize it, but the outcome was not satisfying. There is no centralized training program, and when a new ERP feature is deployed, users must find that information by themselves. Every department of Government Entity #1 provides individual training to the newly onboarded employees through the shadowing process. Currently, there are no established training requirements to access ERP. Departments can make subjective decisions on the level of access for each employee. The organization does not encourage or gives open access to the Oracle provided training to employees to upgrades of the system first performed on the "Test" environment, which is supposed to give users the appropriate time to adjust and test. However, there is no incentive or any controls in place to ensure that testing is happening. During system upgrades, some departments assemble a testing team that follows testing scripts and communicates with the manager on the potential issues and challenges prior to switching to production. However, this practice is not mandatory and not utilized by every department or special district. The innovation and Technology Department provides the support of the ERP but is not involved in the facilitation of any training activities.

Government Entity #2 employs about 1,800 people in total, and the Information Technology Services (ITS) department employs around 75 people. The ITS department is responsible for satisfying IT requirements for each of the various departments within the county. Government Entity #2 utilizes CentralSquare's Finance Enterprise as its ERP. Overall, the ITS department is satisfied with the system's performance, and organizational needs are met. However, automatic depreciation calculations for assets are sometimes incorrect and require manual intervention. Another recurring issue is that certain reconciliation jobs get stuck in the system and also require manual intervention.

The ITS department hopes these issues will be resolved after upgrading to the newest version of Finance Enterprise. ERP training occurs every few years after an upgrade. Government Entity #2 is in the process of implementing an upgrade; however, they are experiencing delays. The ITS department plans to use a "train the trainer" approach to train subject matter experts and employees of the Board of County Commissioners. New employees that are hired after training is no longer offered will likely be trained by a subject matter expert in their department. Initial training for subject matter experts will consist of virtual, two-hour courses. The organization has used the ERP system for decades, but training knowledge is not formalized in an ERP training manual.

In both cases, there were similarities in the lack of a formal training process in place for new employees and no incentives to motivate the existing employees to better understand and use the system. As a result, there is a lost opportunity to utilize the system to its full ability.

4 Proposed Research Model

According to the case studies, we propose an approach that local governments can use to gamify ERP training based on current research and gamification models. First, local governments should create a project team that will gamify ERP training (or ERP vendors should come up with a more attractive gamified training package). This project team will utilize Armstrong and Landers' [11] recommendation to assess areas of improvement. After the areas of improvement have been identified, appropriate gamification mechanics should be selected based on resource and time constraints. However, these gamification mechanics should aim to create game dynamics [22]. The five strategies discussed in Kim's study [23] can be used in conjunction with or as an alternative to creating game dynamics that result in the desired aesthetics. Finally, Armstrong and Landers' [11] recommendation to analyze data related to the effectiveness of the gamified training should be utilized. Analyzing the data will give the project team an understanding of whether the gamified training is effective and what areas, if anything, needs to be improved.

Therefore, we propose the following Application of the Gamification training guideline:

- The first step of implementing the gamification approach to the organization will be the assessment of the existing training attitude among the personnel. As a branch of the local government that uses the system for many years, there can be multiple reasons why the training is an opportunity for an organization. What kind of needs must be addressed behavioral, attitudinal, or motivation?
- Points are a very effective element [10, 11, 22]. The local government can create a system of assigning points for completing the ERP training activity. The number of points can be proportionate to the difficulty of training.
- The next step is to apply a competition strategy. This can include the incorporation of the ERP leaderboard and assigning levels to the learners who achieved a specific number of points—making the board visible using Sharepoint or another organizational intranet technology. Including the top 10 learners in the electronic organizational publication can also be a solution.

- The next step is to create realistic narratives that give background and the example of "why" behind a particular training module. For example, the narrative for completing posting revenue journal entries: "Fixed Assets that no longer have any use for the organization are getting sold on the GoveDeals.com. Revenue from the sales is recorded to the revenue account string #11111 and cash account string #2222. On 10/01/2020, payment was received from GoveDeals.com in the form of an ACH. Your supervisor has asked you to prepare the entry and post it to ERP".
- Creating quests. Narratives created for the individual task can be united into one story quest for the complete training for the particular module.
- The existing testing system usually does not have built-in immediate feedback for training purposes. However, this game element can be incorporated on some level by providing a visual of the expected outcome on the screen and requiring trainees to compare them to their outcome. After completing the critical portion of the training module, the trainee can be required to seek feedback from the trainer or direct supervisor as well.
- Addressing compensation. It is more challenging to incorporate compensation into the gamification process for the local governments. Local municipalities and counties are subject to strict state and local statutes and ordinaries. However, the organization can use time-off or parking privileges or other available perks as a form of compensation (Table 1).

Table 1. Game mechanics and dynamics incorporated into our model

The game mechanic and dynamics	Description
Immediate Feedback	Game mechanic where a user receives an immediate response after making
Points, leaderboards, etc.	Game mechanic that assigns points to users based on their actions. The leaderboard displays the number of points each user has
Narrative	Game mechanic that adds a background story, context, or overarching story to gamify the content of training
Missions, quests, etc.	Game mechanic that requires users to complete tasks in order to progress through training
Competition	Game dynamic that pits trainees against each other. This strategy motivates users to successfully complete training
Compensation	Game dynamic that rewards users for making correct choices/actions

We designed an example of the adaptation of the gamification approach to the training assignments in one the local government (see Appendix).

5 Conclusion

Gamification can influence employee engagement, retention, and organizational commitments, and there are possible positive effects on the employee's mental health, stress reduction, and healthier life from the game elements in the work environment [24]. In this paper, we conducted a literature review to determine how gamification impacts intrinsic motivation and information retention in the professional environment, the effects of current ERP training models, and how local governments adopt new technology. Research indicates that gamification has a positive effect on both intrinsic motivation and retention of information. Current ERP training models conclude that design features impact the individual experiences of each user and utilizing team engagement has positive results. Emotional and social factors are valid factors in government employees adopting new technology, so it is possible gamification can have positive effects. The important factor is that including gamification mechanisms will not require significant investments in the training programs but rather formalizing the training process.

We reviewed current gamification models in education and used these models to create a gamification model that can be applied to ERP training in local government. We recommend that the local government creates a system to assign points for completing the ERP training activity. A competition strategy should then be applied to the ERP training program through the points, achievements levels, and leader dashboard. It is also important to incorporate creating narratives or background stories for each training module and combining the stories from individual models into one quest from the trainee. Immediate feedback is extremely beneficial to users and can be incorporated in different ways. Finally, compensation should be incorporated into the ERP training program.

Local governments have definite limitations in using compensation for the training; however, there are other instruments that can be used for that purpose. In this paper, we show the potential of the education gamification models by providing an example of applying the proposed gamification approach to an ERP training program in a local government. However, we understand that gamification application to the ERP training is theoretical only, and implementation and results analysis necessary to be confident that it is a valid and valuable approach.

Appendix: Proposed Sample of the Gamification Training in One Local Government

Centralsquare is utilized by the Governmental Entity #2. Governmental organizations commonly use this software. The Enterprise Asset Management module can be used as a part of the Public Administration Suite of the Centralsquare and used as a stand along with the solution. The EAM module can offer work and asset management functionality with GIS integration. The proposed approach incorporates such game elements as narrative, immediate feedback, and compensation to engage better users into knowing and understanding the technology. Currently, Government Entity #2 does not utilize Fleet management at the moment.

- Review ERP training leadership board. Log in to the Centralsquare EAM

  Instruction: Use Log in the information provided by your supervisor.

Adding Game Element - Competition Strategy and Leader Dashboard, Compensation: Log in to the Organization's Intranet and identify the top three employees with most of the points on the ERP training leadership board. Document in the email to your supervisor what are the levels of achievement that can be achieved through that training? What are the perks and benefits top learners enjoy from the organization?

- Asset information Lookup using multiple search criteria:

a. Asset tag number
b. Year/Make/Model of the Vehicle
c. VIN Number

Adding Game Element - Narrative: Maintenance department reached out to you with the questions about three vehicles. Department has no use for the referred vehicles and planning to sell them using GovDeals. Department was able to provide the following information:

- Vehicle #1 - VIN Number # FG12h234k,
- Vehicle #2 Model/Maker - Ford focus/2005
- Vehicle #3 - general description information.

  Research the assets and document the following information:
  Fleet record for Vehicle #1
  Summary for #Vehicle #2
  Fleet Inspection due date for Vehicle #3

Adding Game Element - Points: Completing each step of the assignment worth 1 point.

  Instructions:

- Home->Fleet/Wherehouse->Fleet Information -> Fleet Record lookup.

Adding Game Element - Immediate Feedback. Select Fleet Record. Compare Screenshot below with the Fleet Record information for Vehicle #1:

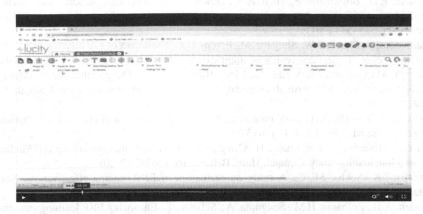

After the employee completes the assignment, his/her dashboard standing needs to be updated in a timely matter. The next step will be providing the employee with the perks and compensation in accordance with the achieved training level.

References

1. Gattiker, T., Goodhue, D.: Understanding the plant level costs and benefits of ERP: will the ugly duckling always turn into a swan. In: Proceedings of the 33rd Hawaii International Conference on System Science, Hawaii (2000)
2. Shang, S., Seddon, P.B.: A comprehensive framework for classifying the benefits of ERP systems. In: Proceedings of the Americas Conference on Information Systems, Long Beach, CA (2000)
3. Alcivar, I., Abad, A.G.: Design and evaluation of a gamified system for ERP training. Comput. Hum. Behav. **58**, 109–118 (2016)
4. Chang, H., Chou, H.: Drivers and effects of enterprise resource planning post-implementation learning. Behav. Inf. Technol. **30**(2), 251–259 (2011)
5. Dorobat, I., Nastase, F.: Training issues in ERP implementations. Acc. Manag. Inf. Syst. **11**(4), 621–636 (2012)
6. Batara, E., Nurmandi, A., Warsito, T., Pribadi, U.: Are government employees adopting local e-government transformation?: The need for having the right attitude, facilitating conditions and performance expectations. Transf. Govern.: People Process Policy **11**(4), 612–638 (2017)
7. Deterding, S., Dixon, D., Khaled, R., Nacke, L.: From game design elements to gracefulness: defining "gamification". In: Proceedings of the 15th International Academic MindTrek Conference: Envisioning Future Media Environments, pp. 9–15 (2011)
8. Legaki, N.Z., Xi, N., Hamari, J., Karpouzis, K., Assimakopoulos, V.: The effect of challenge-based gamification on learning: an experiment in the context of statistics education. Int. J. Hum.-Comput. Stud. **144**, 102496 (2020)
9. Alsawaier, R.S.: The effect of gamification on motivation and engagement. Int. J. Inf. Learn. Technol. **35**(1), 56–79 (2018)
10. Markopoulos, A.P., Fragkou, A., Kasidiaris, P.D., Davim, J.P.: Gamification in engineering education and professional training. Int. J. Mech. Eng. Educ. **43**(2), 118–131 (2015)

11. Armstrong, M.B., Landers, R.N.: Gamification of employee training and development. Int. J. Train. Dev. **22**(2), 162–169 (2018)
12. Mekler, E.D., Brühlmann, F., Tuch, A.N., Opwis, K.: Towards understanding the effects of individual gamification elements on intrinsic motivation and performance. Comput. Hum. Behav. **71**, 525–534 (2017)
13. Zainuddin, Z., Chu, S.K.W., Shujahat, M., Perera, C.J.: The impact of gamification on learning and instruction: a systematic review of empirical evidence. Educ. Res. Rev. **30**, 100326 (2020)
14. Pereira, M., Oliveira, M., Vieira, A., Lima, R.M., Paes, L.: The gamification as a tool to increase employee skills through interactives work instructions training. Proc. Comput. Sci. **138**, 630–637 (2018)
15. Fouché, S., Mangle, A.H.: Code hunt as platform for gamification of cybersecurity training. Paper Presented at the, pp. 9–11 (2015)
16. Putz, L., Hofbauer, F., Treiblmaier, H.: Can gamification help to improve education? Findings from a longitudinal study. Comput. Hum. Behav. **110**, 106392 (2020)
17. Sreehari, K., Sekhar SF, C.: A study on evaluation of ERP training effectiveness. Srusti Manage. Rev. **7**(2), 30–33 (2014)
18. Zadeh, A.H., Zolbanin, H.M., Sengupta, A., Schultz, T.: Enhancing ERP learning outcomes through microsoft dynamics. J. Inf. Syst. Educ. **31**, 83–95 (2020)
19. Ruhi, U.: Level up your strategy: towards a descriptive framework for meaningful enterprise gamification. Technol. Innov. Manage. Rev. **5**(8), 5–16 (2015)
20. Kwak, D., Ma, X., Polites, G., Srite, M., Hightower, R., Haseman, W.D.: Cross-level moderation of team cohesion in individuals' utilitarian and hedonic information processing: evidence in the context of team-based gamified training. J. Assoc. Inf. Syst. **20**(2), 161–185 (2019)
21. Kocadere, S.A., Caglar, S.: Gamification from player type perspective: a case study. Educ. Technol. Soc. **21**, 12–22 (2018)
22. Kusuma, G.P., Wigati, E.K., Utomo, Y., Putera Suryapranata, L.K.: Analysis of gamification models in education using MDA framework. Proc. Comput. Sci. **135**, 385–392 (2018)
23. Kim, S.: How a company's gamification strategy influences corporate learning: a study based on gamified MSLP (mobile social learning platform). Telemat. Inf. **57**, 101505 (2020)
24. Hussain, S., Qazi, S., Ahmed, R.R., Streimikiene, D., Vveinhardt, J.: Employees management: evidence from gamification techniques. Montenegrin J. Econ. **14**(4), 97–107 (2018)

Orpheus: A Voice-Controlled Game to Train Pitch Matching

Jiahui Li and Zhenyu Gu[✉]

Shanghai Jiao Tong University, Shanghai, People's Republic of China
zygu@sjtu.edu.cn

Abstract. Pitch matching is one of the most basic musical skills, but is hard to stick to because of its monotony. To solve this problem, *Orpheus*, a serious game based on Greek mythology for training pitch matching is proposed. The player needs to act as Orpheus, the main character of the story who is known as "the father of songs", to use his great power of music to experience the famous love story with Eurydice. The player needs to control Orpheus by singing specific pitches to change his position and action so that Orpheus can complete the tasks and drive the plots. A game prototype was developed with Unity, and a pilot case study was conducted to measure the game experience and assess the game effectiveness. Results showed that players considered *Orpheus* as challenging but engaging, and they thought *Orpheus* was better in training pitch matching than the traditional method. In conclusion, *Orpheus* provides a new training method for pitch matching that is both engaging and effective.

Keywords: Pitch matching · Serious games · Orpheus · Greek mythology · Voice control · Music education

1 Introduction

Good intonation is a basic but challenging skill for singers and instrumentalists. One of the most widely used training techniques for improving intonation is pitch matching, in which the student is required to vocally reproduce the pitches played on an instrument and the teacher will analyze the accuracy and help fix the out-of-tune notes. Although this traditional master-apprentice model works well in music education, it still has disadvantages and some are obvious:

First, it is monotonous, just like any other kind of learning that needs repetition.

Second, the feedback is ambiguous because teachers often use imagery to instruct the students such as "sing as if through the top of your head" [9].

To date, a lot of electronic tools that can synthesize musical notes and assess intonation performance with real-time visualization of users' pitches have been developed such as SINGAD [10] and SING & SEE [2]. These apps can provide more precise and explicit feedback for users but have not improved much in enhancing the fun of pitch matching. On the other hand, serious games are growing rapidly both in the gaming

© Springer Nature Switzerland AG 2021
X. Fang (Ed.): HCII 2021, LNCS 12790, pp. 33–41, 2021.
https://doi.org/10.1007/978-3-030-77414-1_3

industry and in the academic research field. The addictive nature of game play can facilitate the learning process [7], so creating a serious game for pitch matching seems to be
a possible solution to help overcome boredom and motivate the learners to stick to it.

Therefore, we decided to design and develop a serious game that can help players
train pitch matching. An ideal learning-assisted game should integrate the advantages
of traditional learning and traditional gaming:

First, the game should make the player feel engaged.

Second, the game should drive the player to learn effectively.

To create a game that met the criteria, we conducted a competitive analysis first to
prepare for the game design, and after the game development, a pilot case study was
carried out to check whether the game met the expectations.

2 Related Works

Since the music terms related to pitch matching are literally similar, it is necessary to
clarify their definitions and relationships at the very beginning. After that, a competitive
analysis on serious games designed for pitch matching is presented.

2.1 Basic Concepts in Pitch Matching

Pitch Matching: Pitch matching is the ability to reproduce exactly a given pitch or a
given sequence of pitches [15].

Pitch Discrimination: Pitch discrimination is the ability to distinguish between two
successive pitches or two dissimilar examples of a single pitch [15].

Pitch Production: Pitch production is the ability to produce an intended pitch or an
intended sequence of pitches.

Pitch Recognition: Pitch recognition is the ability to accurately state the tone or tones
being performed [14].

Pitch matching can be broken down into finer steps. First, the learner needs to perceive
the pitch accurately. Second, the learner needs to store the pitch in his memory. Third,
the learner needs to vocally reproduce the pitch. Finally, the learner needs to compare
his pitch with the one played on the instrument or the one stored in his memory and keep
them similar. It is obvious that pitch matching is closely related to pitch discrimination
and pitch production, while pitch recognition is less used in pitch matching.

2.2 Serious Games for Pitch Matching

Only a small number of researchers have tried to design serious games for pitch matching.
SingingCoach can score the accuracy of the user's singing of a song. It displays the
contour of the song and the contour of the singing at the same time to give the user intuitive
visual feedback [1]. *SingingCoach* is very similar to the electronic tools mentioned above
both in appearance and functionality, thus leading to its shortage in playfulness as a game.

Chung [4], Yang and Cheng [18] did better in applying gamification strategies. Chung constructed an impressive scene for pitch matching in his game, where a rainbow ladder with seven steps visually stands out. The player needs to touch the corresponding steps after listening to the tone samples and will be told whether his matching is correct. Yang and Cheng combined the elements of shooting game in VR environment with the pitch recognition training game. The player needs to use the VR controller as a gun to select the targeted note as a bullet and shoot the monster that produces the pitch. Though this game is not designed for pitch matching, the authors' pratice of naturally combining different elements to enrich the gameplay can be learned from.

We can find that these games didn't pay much attention to narrative, the tenichque appreciated and advocated by many researchers. Narrative, namely storytelling, is considered to be central to serious games because it can add layers of meaning to games [16] and foster greater immersion, engagement, motivation and learning [12]. Therefore, it should be adopted to further optimize the game experience.

3   Design and Implementation

3.1   Game Design

Game Objective: *Orpheus* aims to enhance the fun of intonation training by combining the content of pitch matching with the form of serious games. *Orpheus* is designed for users of all ages who want to improve their pitch matching abilities in an engaging and effective way.

Story Selection: An ancient Greek story about Orpheus is selected to construct the virtual world in the game, because it is rich in plot and closely related to music. Orpheus is a talented musician who can charm animals and make trees dance by playing Lyre. He won the heart of Eurydice and married her under the blessings of the gods. Unfortunately, Eurydice soon died from a snakebite and was trapped in the Underworld ruled by Hades. To save Eurydice, Orpheus went to the Underworld and softened Hades' heart with the great power of music. He was allowed to bring Eurydice back to the ground at the only expense of not looking back before reaching the surface. However, Orpheus finally failed because he broke his promise with Hades [13].

Chapter Design: The game is designed based on a modified version of the mythology mentioned above and contains four chapters where the player needs to control Orpheus to complete specific tasks and drive the plots using their voices. If the player fails to complete the task, the current chapter will be restarted and the next chapter cannot be unlocked.

In the first chapter, Orpheus is set to be wandering in the forest and be blocked by various animals that require him to sing the pitches they demonstrate. If the player reproduces the pitches correctly, the animals will be charmed and give way to Orpheus proactively. At the end of the road, Eurydice is waiting for her beautiful encounter with Orpheus.

Orpheus and Eurydice will get married in chapter two, where the player must act as the groom and follow the priest to sing given melodies to promote the wedding ceremony. Eurydice will get bitten by a snake at the end of the wedding.

Orpheus needs to traverse an underground cave to get to Hades' kingdom in chapter three. The player must sing reasonable pitches, the frequency of which corresponds to Orpheus' flying altitude, to avoid obstacles in the cave.

In the last chapter, Orpheus and Eurydice intend to escape from Hades and the player needs to frequently change their position as in chapter three. Eurydice will be grabbed back to the Underworld if they hit the monsters ambushing on their way back to the ground. The original bad ending can be rewritten if the player finally develops good intonation and successfully dodges all the monsters.

Challenge Design: Task difficulty increases as the plot thickens. The first two chapters are designed to train the player's ability to perceive the pitches correctly and imitate the pitches accurately by letting the animals or the priest to demonstrate the target pitches first. The last two chapters, however, require more skills. The target pitches will no longer be presented directly, but a background pitch at a constant frequency will be provided instead. The player has to take the background pitch as a baseline, estimate their intended pitches and adjust the pitches according to the feedback. The variability of pitch stimuli for learning also differs among the chapters. The game trains on single pitches in odd-numbered chapters, and sequences of pitches in even-numbered chapters.

Visualization Design: Visual feedback is proved to be effective in developing conscious pitch control [17]. *Orpheus* also adopts this strategy to give players a more intuitive understanding of the intervals between their pitches and the target ones. For example, in chapter three, the player can quickly find out whether he hums the pitch in tune by comparing the position of Orpheus with that of the cave wall, and he can also learn the pitch name by checking the 'note scale' on the left side of the interface (see Fig. 1 and Fig. 2).

Personalized Design: Everyone has his own vocal range, and everyone can expand his vocal range by training. Therefore, it is necessary to customize the training content for each player and each use. Every time a player launches *Orpheus*, he will be asked to sing the lowest pitch and the highest pitch first as best as he can, and then the program will select the training notes from the interval for him (see Fig. 3).

3.2 Prototype Implementation

The prototype was developed with Unity Game Engine in 2D and built for Windows x86-64 platform. The game required the use of the device microphone to sample human vocals and adopted the Robust Algorithm for Pitch Tracking (RAPT) to analyze the corresponding notes [5]. Art assets were made with Adobe Illustrator and Adobe After Effects.

Fig. 1. The player sings C#4 and passes through the cave when C#4 is required.

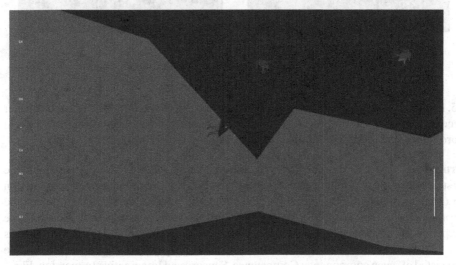

Fig. 2. The player sings C#4 and hits the cave wall when A#3 is required.

4 Pilot Case Study

A pilot case study was conducted in order to measure the game experience of Orpheus and assess the game effectiveness in pitch matching training.

Participants: We recruited 12 non-music college students (6 males and 6 females) to participate in the study. Two male participants were not included in the final sample: One found his microphone not working properly, and one spent far less time playing the prototype than the study stipulated. The average age of the remaining samples was

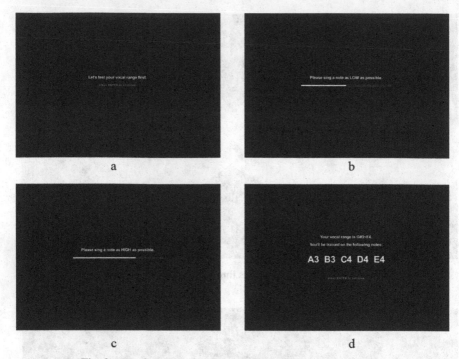

Fig. 3. Interfaces that test vocal range and select training notes

25.1 years old ($SD = 2.98$). Three of them had tried pitch matching before but had never received professional training. The participants reported no auditory disability or vocal cord injury, and they were familiar with the Windows x86-64 platform.

Procedure: The entire procedure took approximately 40 min. The participants were first asked to fill in a demographic questionnaire. They then read a brief introduction to *Orpheus*, watched a tutorial video illustrating the basic game rules, and played the prototype for at least 15 min. After that, participants were required to complete a Game Experience Questionnaire (GEQ) [11], a widely acclaimed 5-point Likert scale (0 stands for "not at all" and 4 stands for "extremely") assessing player experience. The scale consisted of seven components: Competence, Sensory and Imaginative Immersion, Flow, Tenson/Annoyance, Challenge, Negative Affect and Positive Affect, which were related to learning [3, 7, 8]. Finally, we collected game data from the participants, and asked them about their attitude toward *Orpheus* and their suggestions on *Orpheus*.

Results: GEQ results (Fig. 4) showed that participants had a moderate positive affect ($M = 2.06$, $SD = 1.08$) and a slight negative affect ($M = 0.88$, $SD = 1.08$). They felt slightly to moderately successful and competent ($M = 1.6$, $SD = 1.44$), moderately challenged ($M = 1.98$, $SD = 1.42$) and slightly tensed or annoyed ($M = 0.73$, $SD = 0.89$) when playing the game. They thought the game was fairly immersive ($M = 2.72$, $SD = 1.02$) and they were moderately to fairly concentrated in the game ($M = 2.40$, $SD = 1.06$). To sum up, the participants considered Orpheus as challenging but engaging.

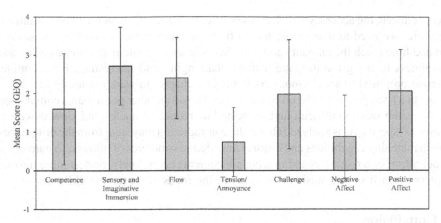

Fig. 4. Results of the GEQ

Each participant was required to play the prototype several times and record their game performance. The data showed that the average passing rate of a chapter was 22.3%, which was consistent with the participants' subjective evaluations that the game was challenging. We invited some participants that achieved fairly high scores (50% passing rate) and fairly low scores (0% passing rate) to participate in a more in-depth interview. Results showed that those who performed well in the game had learned music theory more or less before while those who played poorly had not. Those who performed well could easily read the "note scale", quickly adapted to the game and even developed their own game strategies, while those who played poorly could not understand the difference between C4 and C#4 and lost their control of the character frequently. Those who performed well got a sense of confidence at the beginning of the game and successfully built a positive cycle of "succeed-motivated-succeed", while those who played poorly lost their confidence initially and were trapped in a negative cycle of "fail-anxious-fail". All these mean that *Orpheus* may be more suitable for the players with musical knowledge, and it may be necessary to add some tutorial chapters that dedicate to popularizing the most basic musical concepts before the pitch matching training.

In terms of game effect and game appeal, *Orpheus* did quite well. Although the participants played the game only for 15 min, five of them reported feeling an improvement in pitch discrimination and production: five strengthened their ability to determine whether one pitch is higher or lower than another pitch, and three developed an ability to estimate the intended pitches based on the background pitch. Nine participants thought *Orpheus* was better than the existing method of pitch matching, and the remaining one thought the effects were the same. Eight participants believed that their intonation would be improved if they used *Orpheus* for a longer time and they all showed the willingness to train their intonation with *Orpheus* in their daily life.

Suggestions were also collected from the participants and summed up into two main points. First, many participants reported that there was an obvious time delay between the player's producing pitches with the character's taking corresponding action. The delay exists because the system has to take a period of time to sample enough audio signals, so that it can accurately analyze which pitch the player is singing. If the sample time is reduced, the accuracy will decrease while the game experience will be optimized. Therefore, we need to make more trade-offs to decide whether to shorten the sample time and how much the amount should be. Second, some participants suggested us add randomness to the game to make it more challenging and interesting. For example, someone proposed to set the monsters in the last chapter to walk randomly instead of waiting at a fixed position to be hit by the player. However, other participants complained that the game was too difficult and suggested us reduce obstacles and slow down the characters' speeds. As is analyzed above, the contradiction may stem from the differences in pitch matching capabilities and musical knowledge structures of players, so narrowing the definition of target users and making adjustments accordingly, or designing tutorial chapters to teach simple music theory, may be the focus of the next working phase.

5 Conclusion

The goal of our work is to design, develop and evaluate a voice-controlled serious game that can help the players train their pitch matching abilities in an engaging and effective way. We adopted the technique of narrative to add layers of meaning to the game and selected the Greek mythology about Orpheus to construct the virtual world in the game. Orpheus' attributes such as position and action can be modified by singing specific pitches, so that the player can vocally control Orpheus to complete the tasks and drive the plots.

A prototype of *Orpheus* was developed with Unity and was later tested in the pilot case study. GEQ was used to measure the players' game experience and results showed that *Orpheus* was evaluated as challenging but engaging. Players also indicated that *Orpheus* was more effective in intonation training than the traditional method of pitch matching, and they had a positive willingness to play *Orpheus* for a longer time. So far, the study has provided evidence to prove that *Orpheus* is both engaging and effective, which is in line with the design standards proposed at the beginning.

In conclusion, *Orpheus* provides a new training method for pitch matching and it is expected that the players can get an impressive game experience and make continuous progress in pitch matching after using *Orpheus*.

References

1. Andrew, S.P., Ann, C.K.: Developing singing in third-grade music classrooms: the effect of a concurrent-feedback computer game on pitch-matching skills. Update: Appl. Res. Music Educ. **34**(1), 42–49 (2015). https://doi.org/10.1177/8755123314548047
2. Callaghan, J., Thorpe W., van Doorn, J.: The science of singing and seeing. In: Parncutt, R., Kessler, A., Zimmer, F. (eds.) Proceedings of the Conference on Interdisciplinary Musicology (CIM04), Graz, Austria, pp. 15–18 (2004)
3. Cheng, M., She, H., Annetta, L.: Game immersion experience: its hierarchical structure and impact on game-based science learning. J. Comput. Assist. Learn. **31**, 232–253 (2015). https://doi.org/10.1111/jcal.12066
4. Chung, S.-M.: Serious music game design and testing. In: Ma, M., Oliveira, M.F., Baalsrud Hauge, J. (eds.) SGDA 2014. LNCS, vol. 8778, pp. 119–133. Springer, Cham (2014). https://doi.org/10.1007/978-3-319-11623-5_11

5. David, T.: A robust algorithm for pitch tracking (RAPT). In: Klejin, W.B., Palatal, K.K. (eds.) Speech Coding and Synthesis, pp. 497–518. Elsevier Science (1995). https://www.ee. columbia.edu/~dpwe/papers/Talkin95-rapt.pdf
6. Fedwa, L., Mohamad, E., Abdulmotaleb, E.S.: An overview of serious games. Int. J. Comput. Games Technol. **2014**, 15 (2014). https://doi.org/10.1155/2014/358152
7. Fullagar, C.J., Knight, P.A., Sovern, H.S.: Challenge/skill balance, flow, and performance anxiety. Appl. Psychol.: Int. Rev. **62**, 236–259 (2013). https://doi.org/10.1111/j.1464-0597. 2012.00494.x
8. Harmari, J., Shernoff, D.J., Rowe, E., Coller, B., Asbell-Clarke, J., Edwards, T.: Challenging games help students learn: an empirical study on engagement, flow and immersion in game-based learning. Comput. Hum. Behav. **54**(C), 170–179 (2016). https://doi.org/10.1016/j.chb. 2015.07.045
9. Hoppe, D., Sadakata, M., Desain, P.: Development of real-time visual feedback assistance in singing training: a review. J. Comput. Assist. Learn. **22**(4), 308–316 (2006). https://doi.org/ 10.1111/j.1365-2729.2006.00178.x
10. Howard, D.M., Welch, G.F.: Microcomputer-based singing ability assessment and development. Appl. Acoust. **27**(2), 89–102 (1989). https://doi.org/10.1016/0003-682X(89)900 02-9
11. IJsselstejin, W.A., de Kort, Y.A.W., Poels, K.: The game experience questionnaire. Technische Universiteit Eindhoven (2013). https://pure.tue.nl/ws/files/21666907/Game_Experie nce_Questionnaire_English.pdf
12. Naul, E.A.: Why story matters: a review of narrative in serious games. https://repositories.lib. utexas.edu/bitstream/handle/2152/68898/NAUL-MASTERSREPORT-2018.pdf?sequence= 1&isAllowed=y. Accessed 12 Feb 2021
13. Greek Mythology. https://www.greekmythology.com/Myths/Mortals/Orpheus/orpheus.html. Accessed 10 Feb 2021
14. Salim, P., Pontifica, U.J.: Pitch recognition through template matching. https://members.loria. fr/sperchy/assets/pdf/pitch_recog.pdf
15. Steven, J.M., Janina, F.: Intonation. In: Richard, P., Gary, M. (eds.) The Science & Psychology of Music Performance: Creative Strategies for Teaching and Learning. Oxford Scholarship Online (2011) https://doi.org/10.1093/acprof:oso/9780195138108.003.0012
16. Lim, T., et al.: Narrative serious game mechanics (NSGM) – insights into the narrative-pedagogical mechanism. In: Göbel, S., Wiemeyer, J. (eds.) GameDays 2014. LNCS, vol. 8395, pp. 23–34. Springer, Cham (2014). https://doi.org/10.1007/978-3-319-05972-3_4
17. Welch, G.F.: Variability of practice and knowledge of results as factors in learning to sing in-tune. Bull. Council Res. Music Educ. **85**, 238–247 (1985)
18. Yang, J.S., Cheng, C.W.: A pitch perception training game in VR environment for enhancing music learning motivation. In: 2020 IEEE International Conference on Consumer Electronics – Taiwan (2020)

Influence of a Video Game on Children's Attention to Food: Should Games Be Served with a Character During Mealtime?

Weiwei Ma, Bo Liu[✉], and Zhao Liu

School of Design, Shanghai Jiao Tong University, Shanghai, China
bibobox@sjtu.edu.cn

Abstract. Young children always have picky eating behavior or easily distracted during mealtime. Different game-based approaches have increasingly been used in dietary interventions for children. Characters are often used in gamification applications that aim to motivate proper eating behavior. This study aims to examine whether playing a video game with characters affects fruit intake among young children. An electronic game was developed to encourage children to eat daily necessary fruit positively. The child will receive a medal of victory. Children used an iPad Pro to play the game with a display screen of 9.7 in. Two-and six-year-old children (N = 10) were recruited. Within sex, children were randomly assigned to two conditions: a character in the app, or a non-character control group. Children were told that they could eat fruits freely during playing the game and stop anytime. After app-play, the researchers measured intake and counted the total time the children spent eating and the time they focused on eating fruits. Furthermore, the researchers examined the children's attitude to the eating-game with Smiley-ometer. The results show that the treatment group of children who played the video game with the character has consumed more fruits than the control group, but there were no significant differences (p = 802). As for the the eating time spent on fruit, there was also no difference between the two groups (p = 0.933). Additionally, the mean ratings for the game's fun were 2.06 for the character group and 3.13 for the non-character group.

Keywords: Children · Eating behavior · Gamification

1 Introduction

Healthy eating habits are essential for the normal growth and development of pre-school children. However, the incidence of dietary behavior problems of Chinese young children has been increasing in recent years. The most common eating behaviors include picky eating behavior and easily distracted during mealtime, about 40% of children usually eat more than 25 min. A survey by Jin found that the incidence of picky eating problems increased rapidly from 1–3 years old, from 12.2% to 46.1%, and still showed an increasing trend at 3–6 years old, from 46.1% to 49.2% [1]. Faced with children's unhealthy eating behaviors, parents of young children feel anxious about their children's

© Springer Nature Switzerland AG 2021
X. Fang (Ed.): HCII 2021, LNCS 12790, pp. 42–50, 2021.
https://doi.org/10.1007/978-3-030-77414-1_4

improper eating behaviors and are worried and fearful of insufficient growth and development [2]. Most parents are not experts in improving their children's bad eating habits. They choose to use inducement measures to improve the situation, such as telling stories during meals, watching TV, playing with toys, which will even aggravate children's bad behaviors.

2 Background

2.1 Related Work

In the field of design, in order to improve children's unhealthy eating behaviors, colorful plates, and cute spoons have become early solutions to achieve this goal. With the development of mobile devices such as mobile phones and tablets, over recent decades, various game-based interventions have been developed to promote health or education-related results. Gamification and serious games have been increasing for children's diet intervention [3].

Behavior Improvement Using Gamification. More video games based on tablets and mobile phones are used. Baranowski et al. experimented with a video game named 'Squire's Quest!' [4]. Children need to eat more fruits and vegetables in the game to save the kingdom. As a result, children who played Squire's Quest! significantly increased their FV and juice consumption by 1.0 serving compared to the control condition. Bell et al. examined the effect of the interactive mobile gardening game 'Virtual Sprouts' on children's food intake and psychological determinants of eating behavior [5]. In this game, players must choose a recipe that meets Dotty's nutritional needs and preferences, and grow certain ingredients required for that recipe. Researchers found that children in the intervention group had significantly improved self-efficacy to eat and cook FV compared with the control group. No differences in food intake were found between the two groups.

Augmented Daily Items Using Technology. There have been other projects that use embedded sensors and mobile devices during mealtime. Kadomura et al. developed a sensing fork-type device that provided simple audio feedback when a user was consuming food [6]. It was found that users could eat their disliked foods more easily than usual while enjoying a playful environment. The team subsequently added an application "Hungry Panda" to address children's eating issues, including picky and distracted eating, using different game elements such as roles, challenges, feedback, and persuasive technology [7]. The conclusion proves that it is more easily accepted by children when sensor technology is embedded in daily use. Joi et al. present an interactive and connected tableware system that comprises a food tray, a spoon, and a smartphone cradle [8]. It aims to promote children to eat more vegetables. The conclusion showed that children changed their attitudes to the disliked vegetables and they also showed good knowledge on the benefits of the vegetable.

2.2 Literature Review

Different game-based approaches have increasingly been used in dietary interventions for children. Game elements such as characters, narrative, challenge, and progress have been proved to be effective in encouraging and promoting children to build healthy eating behavior [3]. However, some learners become annoyed with gamification elements and others are distracted by them [9]. Especially for young children whose attention is easy to be distracted, so we need to explore the proper gamification elements for them.

Among them, characters are often used in gamification applications that aim to motivate proper eating behavior. Children's repeated exposure increase their liking of the character and consume more healthy or unhealthy food, compared with non-character games [10].

However, the positive effect of most game-based approaches using characters to promote children's intake and preference of food are post-intervention. We aim to attract children's attention to the food they need to eat or increase healthy food intake with a video game during mealtime, which replied immediately and meaningfully to children's actions. It is unknown whether the use of video games and adding characters during eating will distract children from the food they eat.

In psychology, attention can be divided into four dimensions[11, 12]: 1) the breadth of attention. It refers to the number of objects that an individual can perceive at the same time; 2) the stability of attention. It refers to keeping attention in a certain activity for a long time; 3) Attention distribution. It refers to the ability of an individual to direct attention to different objects when engaged in two or more activities; 4) Attention shift. It refers to Individuals take the initiative to turn their attention from one activity to another according to a certain purpose.

In terms of children's attention to food, we emphasize the stability of children's attention to food, that is, the ability to keep their attention on eating food for a certain period of time.

3 Design Concepts

In this section, we describe the design concepts employed to achieve the goals of improving young children's eating behaviors.

3.1 Theoretical Basis

Game-based interventions have been proven to be potential for increasing fruit and vegetable intake and educating children about healthy eating, but it also has shortcomings. One type is video games that are separated from eating behaviors teach nutrition knowledge through playing games, and then improve children's unhealthy eating habits such as picky from the inherent motivation. They have the disadvantages of excessive entertainment and long-term intervention and are more suitable for older children who are able to play complex games. The other type is a product that uses a combination of hardware and software to intervene during the meal, but its overly rich stories and vivid characters can easily distract children and make them unable to focus on the food they eat.

We have proposed a video game that meets the needs of children aged 2–5 and the needs of parents and encourages children to actively consume daily essential fruits.

3.2 Feedback Design

In order to encourage children to eat gamification for persuasion, we decided to generate feedback when children use forks. The feedback that the Pad can provide now includes visual (such as pictures/animation), hearing (such as sound/music), and tactile (such as vibration). Among them, vibration feedback is suitable for use in a handheld state, but not suitable for the scene of intervention in eating. Visual feedback is very expressive, but it is worth noting that overly complex and concrete pictures may reduce the child's attention to food and make them think of other things and become more distracted. So we chose to design a kind of abstract and dynamic image feed-back that is out of the narrative to encourage children to eat continuously. At the same time, the sound is played when the click is felt. In this way, it is encouraged to continue the cycle of forking food-eating food-forking food, to achieve the purpose of encouraging children to eat continuously.

In this process, the rhythm of the dynamic changes of the image is also very important. Rhythm plays an important role in various forms of human expression. It communicates with us, attracts our attention, and has an impact on our emotions.

Rhythm perception is a unique cognitive phenomenon for humans. A study showed that when the amplitude of visual cues with motor attributes increases, the amplitude of finger tapping in the synchronous task will also increase, which indicates that visual motion information can enhance the synchronicity of rhythm and body movement [13]. When this conclusion is applied to dietary intervention, it can increase the rate at which children click on food by accelerating the speed of image changes around food.

When the child eats, the iPad will display a colorful beating energy ring, which surrounds the food plate. The frequency of the energy ring beating changes with the child's action of clicking on the food. After each click, the energy ring disappears and releases energy particles. Then it reappears, and the frequency of beating gradually increases, waiting for the next click (see Fig. 3).

3.3 Character Design

The goal of this game is to help Panda Panpan (we use pandas as cartoon characters because most children in Asian countries are familiar with pandas) to accumulate energy to get his favorite medal. Every time the child forks a fruit, the energy ball will be released and passed to Panpan. And if he gets the energy, he will show a happy smile and move towards the terminal. When the child has eaten all the food, Panpan will get the medal as a reward.

4   Materials and Methods

We recruited 10 pairs of parents and children as subjects. The children's age ranged from 2 to 6 years old. Every mother had her own complaints about the children's eating habits. Both parents and children verbally agreed to participate in this study.

4.1 Materials

The picture shows the fruit-eating intervention product we designed. The fruit is placed on the top of the iPad, and the child uses a fork to interact with the application in the iPad below. The application is developed with Unity, and two modes are de-signed with a role (see Fig. 1) and no role (see Fig. 2).

Fig. 1. Game with a role.

Fig. 2. Game with no role.

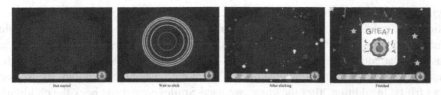

Fig. 3. Pattern changes in the game during fruit eating.

4.2 Pre-survey

We asked these mothers the following questions:

(1) In the past 7 days, how many days did your child eat fresh fruits (such as apples, bananas, oranges, strawberries, etc.)?
(2) What is your child's least favorite fruit?
(3) How do you evaluate your child's fruit intake

Table 1 lists the mothers' answers to questions (1) and (2).

Table 1. Each child's fruit eating frequency and preference.

Child	Days to eat food	Dislike fruit
1	5/7	Banana
2	2/7	Orange
3	2/7	Pear
4	7/7	Pear
5	6/7	Banana
6	6/7	Grapes
7	6/7	Banana
8	5/7	Pear
9	3/7	Apple
10	7/7	Banana

All children have their disliked fruit and half mothers stated, "my child sometimes refuse to eat certain fruits, I am a little worried". The other said, "I am not worried about my child eating fruit.

4.3 Procedure

Within sex, children were randomly assigned to two conditions: a character in the app, or a non-character control group. Children were told that they could eat fruits freely during playing the game and stop anytime. Each child played the app during a videotaped session in a quiet room. After app-play, to measure intake, we calculated the weight difference before and after in grams as the intake. We use behavioral observation, a measure of attention, to evaluate children's dietary attention. We looked back at the video and counted the total time the children spent eating and the time they focused on eating fruits. In addition, after the game, we used Smileyometer to check the children's scores on the fun of eating games [14]. Smileyometer (see Fig. 4). is an adaptation based on the 5-level Likert scale. It is presented in the form of a smiley face, supplemented by words and descriptions below, and requires children to tick their faces.

Children used an iPad Pro to play the game with a display screen of 9.7 in.

Awful   Not very good   Good   Really good   Brilliant

Fig. 4. The Smileyometer.

5   Results

We compared fruit intake and the eating time spent on fruit for Group A ("Character") and Group B ("non-character"). As for the number of fruit intake, there were no significant differences (p = 0.802) between "Character" and "non-character" (see Fig. 5). As for the eating time spent on fruit, there was also no difference between the two groups (p = 0.933) (Fig. 6).

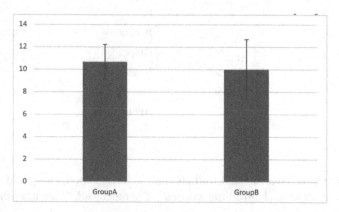

Fig. 5. Comparison of the fruit intake. (Gramme) - Mean: 10.67, 10.00 - SD: 1.53, 2.65

Each of the 10 children in two groups completed the Smileyometer after they had played the game, and the results are summarized in Fig. 7. The mean ratings for the game's fun were 4.67 for the character group and 4.33 for the non-character group.

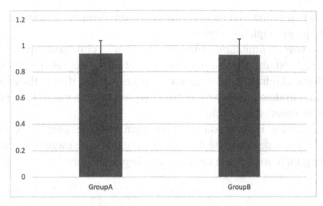

Fig. 6. Comparison of the eating time spent on fruit. (%) - Mean: 0.942, 0.932 - SD: 0.10, 0.12

To determine whether there was a difference in the fun between the two groups, a t-test was performed on the results from the Smileyometer after gameplay (see Fig. 7); this showed no significant difference between the two (p = 0.667).

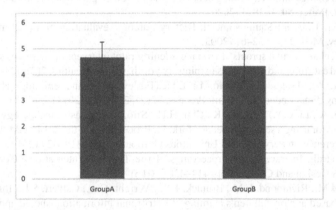

Fig. 7. Results of Smileyometer. - Mean: 4.67, 4.33 - SD: 0.58 0.58

6 Conclusion and Discussion

This video game is about food and how we eat it. Its goal is to address children's eating issues, including distracted eating and picky through simple media technology, by turning food into a medium for children's sensory explorations. It creates a synesthetic and original experience during mealtime and automatically influenced children's eating behavior.

It can be found that the presence or absence of a character in the game has no obvious effect on the amount of food the child eats, and the character does not make the child more distracted when eating. But games with a cartoon character will make children find it more interesting, although not obvious.

Our study has several limitations. First, the number of child participants in this study is limited to a few. Next, the game should be more closely integrated with the food need to eat, and teach the children about food nutrition knowledge during the eating process. Finally, given that children are easy to be bored with the same visual feed-back, various ways of playing are needed to develop.

Our future direction is to conduct a long-term real-life user study that involves mother-child subjects to demonstrate that our video game with more different interactive ways at the dining table to improve children's eating behavior.

References

1. Jin, X., Shi, R., Shi, Z.: Epidemiological investigation on eating behavior problems of children aged 1 to 6 years in Shanghai. Chin. J. Child Health 17(04), 387–389+392 (2009)
2. Kim, H.J., Chung, K.M., Park, M.J., Choe, Y.H.: Parental survey for children with feeding problems. Korean J Pediatr. Gastroenterol. Nutr. 11(2), 179 (2008)
3. Chow, C.Y., Riantiningtyas, R.R., Kanstrup, M.B., Papavasileiou, M., Liem, G.D., Olsen, A.: Can games change children's eating behaviour? A review of gamification and serious games. Food Qual. Prefer. 80, 103823 (2020)
4. Baranowski, T., et al.: Squire's quest!: Dietary outcome evaluation of a multimedia game. Am. J. Prev. Med. 24(1), 52–61 (2003)
5. Bell, B.M., et al.: Virtual sprouts: a virtual gardening pilot intervention increases self-efficacy to cook and eat fruits and vegetables in minority youth. Games Health J. 7(2), 127–135 (2018)
6. Kadomura, A., Tsukada, K., Siio, I.: EducaTableware: sound emitting tableware for encouraging dietary education. J. Inf. Process. 22(2), 325–333 (2014)
7. Kadomura, A., Li, C.Y., Tsukada, K., Chu, H.H., Siio, I.: Persuasive technology to improve eating behavior using a sensor-embedded fork. In: Proceedings of the 2014 ACM International Joint Conference on Pervasive and Ubiquitous Computing, pp. 319–329 (2014)
8. Joi, Y.R., et al.: Interaction. In: Proceedings of the The 15th International Conference on Interaction Design and Children, pp. 414–420 (2016)
9. Putnam, M.M., Richmond, E.M., Brunick, K.L., Wright, C.A., Calvert, S.L.: Influence of a character-based app on children's learning of nutritional information: should apps be served with a side of media characters? Games Health J. 7(2), 121–126 (2018)
10. Putnam, M.M., Cotto, C.E., Calvert, S.L.: Character apps for children's snacks: effects of character awareness on snack selection and consumption patterns. Games Health J. 7(2), 116–120 (2018)
11. Zhou, T., Qiu, S., Song, H.: Multi-dimensional Attention Test Instruction Manual. Psychological Press, Taiwan (1992)
12. Ye, Y., Zhu, B.: Psychology. East China Normal University Press (1988)
13. Hove, M.J., Keller, P.E.: Spatiotemporal relations and movement trajectories in visuomotor synchronization. Music Percept. 28(1), 15–26 (2010)
14. Read, J.C.: Validating the fun toolkit: an instrument for measuring children's opinions of technology. Cogn. Technol. Work 10(2), 119–128 (2017)

Ludus Magnus - A Serious Game
for Learning the Latin Language

David A. Plecher$^{(\boxtimes)}$ⓘ, Christian Eichhornⓘ, Moritz Naser,
and Gudrun Klinkerⓘ

Chair for Computer Aided Medical Procedures and Augmented Reality,
The Technical University of Munich, Munich, Germany
{christian.eichhorn,moritz.naser}@tum.de, {plecher,klinker}@in.tum.de

Abstract. In this paper we want to introduce an open world Serious
Game for learning the Latin language. We are using mechanics that are
well known from games like *Assassin's Creed* or *Witcher 3* and combining
them with a tense story and the learning content based on chapters of
a textbook that is used in conventional school lessons. In specific, this
learning content will be an important part of the game and is webbed
into the story and game mechanics fluidly. Therefore, the students will
play as a young Marcomanne, that is enslaved by the Romans and has
only one chance to free himself by becoming the best gladiator in the
town.

Keywords: Serious games · Latin · Open world · Photorealistic
graphics · Historical

1 Introduction

The Latin language is commonly called a "dead language" [5], which is technically correct because there are no native speakers anymore. But it is also known
for to be the "mother of all languages" [1]. Latin is still used in medicine or law
terms and all Romance languages are related to Latin, for example Italian has
only a difference rate of twelve percent [6]. By studying ancient Roman authors
such as Cicero, Livy, or Tacitus, the reader gains insight into Roman history, politics, philosophy, and much more. Furthermore scientists believe learning Latin
trains the logical thinking [23]. Consequently, Latin continues to be taught in
schools. But the language is not easy to learn because of its complexity. Nevertheless, it is definitely worth the effort or as the Romans would have said: *"per
aspera ad astra"* (through hardships to the stars).

With our Serious Game "Ludus Magnus" we would like to interweave the
game world with the learning content and thus support pupils and students in
learning the Latin language. Wong et al. describes how learning and games can
be combined:

© Springer Nature Switzerland AG 2021
X. Fang (Ed.): HCII 2021, LNCS 12790, pp. 51–61, 2021.
https://doi.org/10.1007/978-3-030-77414-1_5

"The optimal state of this relationship requires a *sweet spot*, in which the entertainment elements function sufficiently enough to serve as a motivator for information processing without distracting people from valuable knowledge content" [28]

Playing a game with reasonable flow can lead to an intrinsic motivation which is a good precondition for learning purposes. In contrast to school-based learning, which is mainly extrinsically motivated [4] and hence does not last long. To create this flow in Serious Games, it is necessary to find again the *sweet spot* between overwhelming and boring the player. The solution is to confront the player with solvable challenges in the playing and also in the learning part [8].

Therefore both parts should match and not disturb each other, for example a vocabulary trainer should not interrupt the gameplay flow by being placed completely offside the current story or context. Taking this into account, we generated an open world map based on the area around the Roman city of Carnuntum and combined the story of the career of a barbarian gladiator with the learning of game controls such as fighting techniques but also with Latin vocabulary and grammar exercises based on chapters and exercises of a classical textbook.

2   Related Work

It is not an easy task to create a Serious Game that fulfills the requirements of a game in terms of entertainment, graphics or story and additionally conveys knowledge to the player. In terms of graphics, Serious Games usually cannot compete with the AAA titles of the gaming industry, because they are developed with a low budget. But even when developers overcome this barrier, they still often fail due to reluctant or disconnected mechanics besides the modern graphics.

A good example for gameplay that makes boring bureaucratic work fun and let's the player think about the consequences of his or her decisions, is *Papers, Please*. Even if the graphics of the game are not photo-realistic and detailed as in games with a greater budget, the developers were able to create a reasonable atmosphere where the player has to make difficult decisions about whether a human is able to cross the border or not. With the serious context in the background, the game still provides a fun experience, because all the serious actions of the game the player has to make, are interwoven with the gameplay very well.

However, history is more than ancient buildings and names because cultural heritage is very diverse. Beside the "physical" world, there is also the natural environment side, which includes flora and fauna, landscape and geological elements [14]. According to Mortara et al. [14] there a three ways of presenting cultural heritage in a Serious Game: cultural awareness, historical reconstruction and heritage awareness which can be split into artistic/archaeological heritage and architectural/natural heritage.

One famous video game that deals with different historic contexts is *Assassins Creed*. The latest title takes place in ancient Greece and the player takes part either on the Greek's or the Spartan's side during the Peloponnesian War [24]. However, even if they mainly try to keep the heritage awareness, especially the archaeological heritage, with a detailed reconstruction of the ancient buildings, the story of the game cannot be used for teaching Greek history. The addition of the so-called Discovery Tour of an *Assassins Creed* title takes the player on a virtual tour of famous ancient Greek sites. This is informative and can be used as a learning tool as it offers reconstructions of ancient buildings combined with explanations and additional information. However, in this mode all game mechanics are disabled. Therefore, the goal should be to provide learning content and playful entertainment at the same time.

An example of a Serious Game for intangible and tangible cultural heritage is *Oppidum* [16]. It is a Serious AR Game that uses Augmented Reality (AR) to transfer knowledge about the Celtic life and history to the player. All buildings shown in the game were modelled historically accurate in 3D and can be inspected virtually. AR is also part of *DragonTale* [15], which is a story driven Serious Game for learning Japanese Kanji. Another example of a Serious Game for learning languages and corresponding characters is HieroQuest [17], which is a puzzle/escape room game for learning Egyptian hieroglyphs. These games are examples for Serious Games that combine the gaming and the learning content. In the "Tactical Language Training System (TLTS)" [13,20] which is a Serious Game for learning foreign language and culture, the player explores also a world by speaking with citizens and solving quests and has also a collection of minigames to choose from to improve language skills. Minigames are often the main ingredient of so called educational games which is a subgroup of Serious Games.

3   Concept of Ludus Magnus

As we already mentioned in the introduction, our game is an open world game, that is combined with learning content and quests supported by game mechanics inspired from usual open world games to improve the gameplay flow and provide a fun experience. It is necessary to naturally web the learning content into reasonable actions of the player to not disturb the flow. Therefore, we carefully exposed the background story of the main character.

4   Story of Ludus Magnus

The story of our game takes place right after the Marcomannic wars. Our protagonist, a young Marcomanne, fought for his ruler Ballomar against the legions of Emperor Mark Aurel. In one of the battles near Carnuntum, he got enslaved by the Romans and started to attend a school for Gladiators (lat. ludus magnus) as he fought well in the battles before. The "lanista" (manager of gladiators) promised him that, if he becomes the best gladiator of the city he can become a free man again and get a wooden sword (lat. rudis) as a sign for his freedom [11]. But he also needs to learn the Latin language as a requirement, since he only speaks anglo-frisian as his tribe does. Encouraged by this unique possibility the protagonist tries to take the chance to become the best gladiator of the town, as well as learning the Latin language.

Fig. 1. Interactive learning objects in the game world

5   Important Gameplay Mechanics

In the following we want to discuss the most important gameplay mechanics of Ludus Magnus and how they are contributing to the story.

5.1   Game Engine

Before we talk about the gameplay mechanics in specific and talk about the foundation of every game, its Game Engine. Over the past couple of years, more and more engines were released - each with its own pros and cons. The most famous engines for independent developers (INDIE developers) are probably the *Unreal Engine 4*, *Unity 5*, and *Cry-Engine 3* [18]. We went for the Unreal Engine. In recent development steps EPIC has added major improvements for implementing realistic open worlds with its own world composition tool[3] as well as with free 3d models to achieve a photo-realistic environment such as the Quixel megascans library [2].

5.2   Quest System

A quest system is a key factor in every open world game. Every quest can have multiple goals which need to be accomplished. For solving a quest, the player gains experience and other rewards. Especially in open world games quests can be used to guide the player through the story. In our game the player has several options to follow quests. Firstly, at the top a compass displays the directions as well as way-points for landmarks, unknown places or enemies. Secondly, the player can open a map with the same way-points as well as a marker of the player itself to indicate his current position. Thirdly, by clicking the "Q" key the player can open the quest menu, that displays all the currently accepted quests with all goals and rewards. By talking to NPC's and discovering the world the player can accept new quests. Also the lanista gives the player weekly and daily quests that are basic tasks to improve the overall players skills which should make him over time the best gladiator in the town.

5.3 Interactive Objects

In such a game, it is important to make the game world interesting so that the player wants to explore it. We have integrated the learning content into this world through various objects. The player can search or "scan" certain locations to discover them. When an object is found, it is highlighted and either the Latin name or the corresponding translation is displayed (see Fig. 1). The player can collect these objects in an inventory (see Fig. 2). The corresponding vocabulary will be later part of a memory game where the player can test his learned knowledge and improve it.

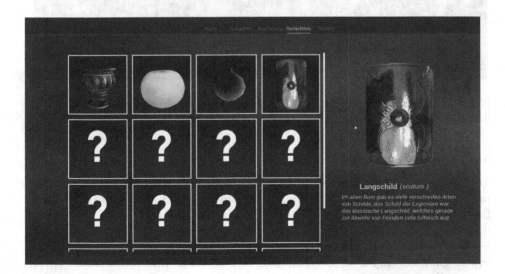

Fig. 2. The inventory with collected objects and translations

5.4 Equipment System

The player is able to equip himself with different weapons, armors and helmets to play different gladiator types (see Fig. 3). Each gladiator type, from Trax to Murmillo [12], has his own attributes and benefits. Each item is assigned to one gladiator type and for each item the specific gladiator type gets a bonus. Being equipped with only items of one gladiator type the player gets extra bonuses, which should enforce him to commit to one historically correct gladiator armory. With earned rewards from quests the player can buy new items in a shop and customize his gladiator to his own favor and learn more about gladiators and their different fighting skills.

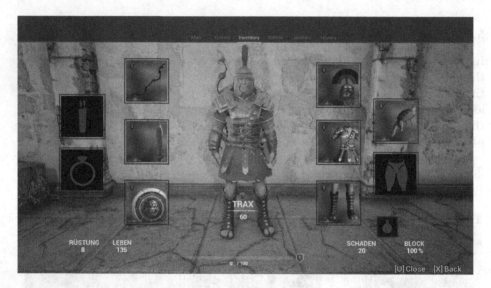

Fig. 3. The equipment system, with armor and weapons already equipped and Trax bonus set to 60.

5.5 Combat System

To become the best gladiator in town and more importantly to become a free man, the protagonist has to train gladiator skills. To make this part of the game fun and challenging, we implemented a combat system that is not only determined by the equipment, which can be improved mainly by quests about the learning content, but also by the player's playing and tactical skills. In many towns gladiator fights were celebrated, one of them was *Carnuntum* [7], an ancient Roman town in today's Austria, that is our historic basis of the game. The player is able to fight in an arena against other gladiators and improve his fighting skills. The system provides a strong learning curve and the player will immediately feel the impact of better equipment and improved skills. We plan to add more attack variants in the future and provide for each gladiator type specific skills (Fig. 4).

Fig. 4. A screenshot from a combat between the player and another gladiator.

5.6 Vocabulary Trainer

One possibility to add suitable weakly/daily quests to the game is our vocabulary trainer that is focusing on words of the latest chapter of the learning material. The player has to choose the right translation out of four options for the Latin vocabulary. For every correct choice the multiplier increments and the score rises. When the wrong answer is chosen, the multiplier resets. This should motivate the students to carefully think about the right answer. Reaching a certain score the player earns a reward which can be spend for new character customizations.

5.7 Grammar Exercises

Apart from the vocabulary trainer, the player has to solve some quests with grammar exercises. The lanista reminds the player after each gladiator training that he has also to master the Latin language. For example, after the gladiator training the player gets a text about roman history from the lanista which he has to translate until the next training session, otherwise he is not allowed to take part in the training. In another quest, the player must deliver a message. Unfortunately, during the process it starts to rain and some words are made illegible. The player must then use his knowledge of Latin vocabulary and grammar to restore the message. Each exercise will be part of a quest and has a credible reason to be solved by the player according to the story. The grammar exercises (see Fig. 5) could also be part of the weekly quests and are taken out of the textbook [26].

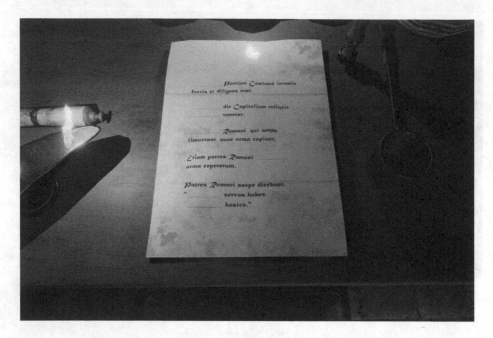

Fig. 5. A grammar exercise which the player has to solve by adding the correct form of *idem* (engl. the same) in the gaps.

5.8 Level Design

A good level design can improve the player's flow. Our world is as already mentioned based on the Roman town *Carnuntum*. It is a gladiator city in today's Austria founded 100 AD and was a very important town for protecting the Limes. We used material provided by the archaeological team in *Carnuntum* as a model. Figure 6 gives a first impression of how the ancient city is brought to new life in the game and thus serves as the historical background of the game.

6 Future Work

In this section we would like to present the future improvements and extensions of the project as well as the planned evaluation in a school.

6.1 Future Game Content

First of all, we will add more quests based on the chapters of the textbook. Each chapter should have its own sequence of quests the player can follow. Each sequence of quests will include grammatical and vocabulary exercises, explorations of the map and training of fighting techniques. Also, we plan to increase the scale of the city over time. One main goal is also to fill the streets with NPC's the player can talk to. Each NPC should have an own life cycle and role inside

(a)   (b)

Fig. 6. Screenshots of the game: streets and buildings (a) and the marketplace (b) of *Carnuntum*.

the story. A main future plan is to include a multiplayer option in the game. This could help social player types to interact with other players and provide them with a more fun and also competitive experience [19].

6.2   Future Evaluation

Due to the Covid-19 pandemic, we had to postpone the evaluation. But our plans are to have two groups of students playing the game. One group with the interactive objects activated and one without them. This way we can compare afterwards the impact on the knowledge transfer. One major problem we face is the feasibility of testing a game with a photorealistic graphic style at school. The PC's in schools are mostly out-dated and by far not powerful enough to run the game. Therefore we are looking forward to the new technology of streaming games via the internet. The most famous platform for this is *Google Stadia* [10], which streams a variety of games over the internet and might be the perfect solution to play a high quality game at school.

7   Conclusion

To conclude, our game is still work in progress. However, we think that the game has good potential. Ludus Magnus supports students to learn Latin vocabulary or grammar and offers an interesting story of a man who tries to free himself. The learning content is meaningfully and comprehensibly integrated into the graphically appealing game world. This offers the players a serious learning environment and a motivating gaming experience at the same time.

Acknowledgments. We would like to thank all the developers that supported us with providing assets and feedback. Especially, thanks to Grzegprz Szewczyk providing the basic combat and equipment system [21] and Thomas Vogel for providing all the clothes and weapons for the gladiators [27]. Also, thanks to Tala Esenlikler for great support on his quest system that was a great starting point [9], the same goes for Peter Sekula with his great support for all the Roman buildings [22] and to MAWI United that gave us great feedback on the environment [25]. We would also like to express our special thanks to the archaeological team of Carnuntum for their support.

References

1. Latin, the mother of many languages—benefits of learning latin. https://www.thelatinroad.com/articles/latin-mother-many-languages/. Accessed 24 Jan 2021
2. Quixel megascans. https://quixel.com/megascans/home. Accessed 24 Jan 2021
3. World composition user guide. https://docs.unrealengine.com/en-US/BuildingWorlds/LevelStreaming/WorldBrowser/index.html. Accessed 24 Jan 2021
4. Ainsworth, S.: Running head: evaluating intrinsic integration in educational games (2011)
5. Babbel.com, Lesson Nine GmbH: Fact vs. fiction: Is latin a dead language? https://www.babbel.com/en/magazine/fact-vs-fiction-is-latin-a-dead-language. Accessed 24 Jan 2021
6. Bily, J.: Latein - die Mutter aller Sprachen? Accessed 24 Jan 2021
7. Carnuntum: Römerstadt carnuntum. https://www.carnuntum.at/de/roemerstadt-carnuntum. Accessed 24 Jan 2021
8. Csikszentmihalyi, M.: Flow and the Foundations of Positive Psychology. Springer, Netherlands (2014). https://doi.org/10.1007/978-94-017-9088-8
9. Esenlikler, T.: Mission component by tala esenlikler in blueprints - UE4 marketplace. https://www.unrealengine.com/marketplace/en-US/product/advanced-mission-and-notification-system. Accessed 24 Jan 2021
10. Google: Stadia premiere edition: games ohne konsole und downloads - google store (2020). https://store.google.com/de/product/stadia. Accessed 24 Jan 2021
11. Hellenicaworld: Gladiator. http://www.hellenicaworld.com/Italy/RomanEmpire/LX/de/Gladiator.html. Accessed 24 Jan 2021
12. Hellmayr, L.: Gladiatoren: 100 Seiten. Reclam 100 Seiten, Reclam, Ditzingen (2018)
13. Johnson, W.L., Vilhjálmsson, H.H., Marsella, S.: Serious games for language learning: how much game, how much AI? In: AIED, vol. 125, pp. 306–313 (2005)
14. Mortara, M., Catalano, C.E., Bellotti, F., Fiucci, G., Houry-Panchetti, M., Petridis, P.: Learning cultural heritage by serious games. J. Cult. Herit. **15**(3), 318–325 (2014)
15. Plecher, D.A., Eichhorn, C., Kindl, J., Kreisig, S., Wintergerst, M., Klinker, G.: Dragon tale-a serious game for learning Japanese Kanji. In: Proceedings of the 2018 Annual Symposium on Computer-Human Interaction in Play Companion Extended Abstracts, pp. 577–583 (2018)
16. Plecher, D.A., Eichhorn, C., Köhler, A., Klinker, G.: Oppidum - a serious-AR-Game about celtic life and history. In: Liapis, A., Yannakakis, G.N., Gentile, M., Ninaus, M. (eds.) GALA 2019. LNCS, vol. 11899, pp. 550–559. Springer, Cham (2019). https://doi.org/10.1007/978-3-030-34350-7_53
17. Plecher, D.A., Herber, F., Eichhorn, C., Pongratz, A., Tanson, G., Klinker, G.: HieroQuest - a serious game for learning Egyptian hieroglyphs. J. Comput. Cult. Heritage (JOCCH) **13**(4), 1–20 (2020)
18. Dörner, R.: Entertainment computing and serious games. Lecture notes in computer science. Springer, Heidelberg (2016). https://doi.org/10.1007/978-3-319-46152-6

19. Reichart, B.: Serious game patterns. Ph.D. thesis, Technische Universität München (2018)
20. Sørensen, B.H., Meyer, B.: Serious games in language learning and teaching-a theoretical perspective. In: DiGRA Conference (2007)
21. Szewczyk, G.: Dynamic combat system - bundle by grzegorz szewczyk in blueprints - UE4 marketplace. https://www.unrealengine.com/marketplace/en-US/product/dynamic-combat-system-bundle. Accessed 24 Jan 2021
22. Theory, Q.: Rome fantasy pack i by quantum theory in environments - UE4 marketplace. https://www.unrealengine.com/marketplace/en-US/product/rome-fantasy-pack-i. Accessed 24 Jan 2021
23. Thomas Ribi: Latein ist mehr als eine Sprache. https://www.nzz.ch/meinung/llatein-ist-mehr-als-eine-sprache-frischluft-fuer-den-geist-ld.1471669. Accessed 24 Jan 2021
24. Ubisoft: Assassin's creed odyssey available now on ps4, xbox one, pc—ubisoft (us) https://assassinscreed.ubisoft.com/game/en-us/home. Accessed 24 Jan 2021
25. United, M.: Broadleaf forest biome by mawi united GMBH in environments - UE4 marketplace. https://www.unrealengine.com/marketplace/en-US/product/broadleaf-forest-collection. Accessed 24 Jan 2021
26. Utz, C., et al.: Campus C2. C. C. Buchner Verlag, Bamberg (2019)
27. Vogel, H.: Modular Rome equipment by polyphoria in characters - UE4 marketplace. https://www.unrealengine.com/marketplace/en-US/product/modular-rome-equipment. Accessed 24 Jan 2021
28. Wong, W.L., et al.: Serious video game effectiveness. In: Proceedings of the International Conference on Advances in Computer Entertainment Technology, pp. 49–55 (2007)

PLAY for LEARNING: Serious Games to Assist Learning of Basic Didactic Concepts: A Pilot Study

Tânia Rocha$^{(\boxtimes)}$ ⓘ and João Barroso ⓘ

INESC TEC and University of Trás-os-Montes e Alto Douro, Vila Real, Portugal
{trocha,jbarroso}@utad.pt

Abstract. In this paper, the study of the design and implementation of a game-based application for learning new basic concepts and/or re-learning these concepts within a cognitive rehabilitation perspective, is presented. Specifically, in this first version, the topics considered were: colours, animals, objects, and vehicles.

The solution was developed to be usable and accessible to two user groups, children with special education needs and seniors in need of cognitive training and/or rehabilitation.

The two main goals are: (1) to develop a game-based interface for the two specific user groups – children with special educational needs and seniors; (2) and, assess user engagement and acceptance. To achieve the first goal a universal design methodology was followed. For the later, we performed a preliminary usability assessment. Specifically, a Cognitive Walkthrough reinforced with a post- test semi-structured interviews was conducted.

Overall results showed a good user engagement and acceptance. The game-based solution seemed to facilitated children' apprenticeship of basic contents and the helped in the cognitive rehabilitation by the seniors. The preliminary results indicated the solution could be used as an assistive tool, in a special education or in rehabilitation contexts, with tutors, teachers or clinicians; but also, in a more without obstruction and autonomous interaction, at home.

Keywords: Serious games · Inclusive design · Children with special educational needs · Seniors · Technologies for education · Cognitive stimuli · Mobile app · Accessibility · Usability

1 Introduction

Learning environments can be boosted through technology [1–4]. Particularly, game-based interfaces for learning (serious games) can be powerful tools to develop and train the acquisition of new or "old" knowledge [5, 6].

In this context, studies on interface design and implementation are mandatory as provides information to analyze user engagement and acceptation of the technology per specific publics.

© Springer Nature Switzerland AG 2021
X. Fang (Ed.): HCII 2021, LNCS 12790, pp. 62–71, 2021.
https://doi.org/10.1007/978-3-030-77414-1_6

In this research we intend to analyze two game-based interfaces, in an educational and rehabilitation context, for two specific user groups, children with special needs and seniors. We wanted to test how the solution provided can be developed as a truly accessible solution for these two groups.

The idea was based in an accessibility perspective where universal design is mandatory for establishing cognitive boost, in training or therapy, that we think is needed for these specify users - one with special education and the other with rehabilitation needs.

Therefore, the research problem was on the development of an accessible game-based interface for different users' profile, focusing on two interaction contexts: education and rehabilitation, to ultimately achieve a universal design.

Our motivation was to develop a solution that could assist children in achieving new knowledge and to stimulate seniors on the re-training of old concepts, within a cognitive rehabilitation perspective. In due course, enhancing their learning skills or cognitive rehabilitation through technology.

For that, two specific goals were defined: (1) to design, implement and assess a game-based interface for two specific user groups – children with special educational needs and seniors; (2) and, to point out user engagement and acceptance.

Furthermore, the research question is: can a serious games-based solution support cognitive training or rehabilitation for different user groups?

Regarding methodology, a universal design was followed. Furthermore, for a preliminary usability assessment a Cognitive Walkthrough was conducted. This task-specific approach to assess usability was reinforced with post- test semi-structured interviews.

This paper is structured as follows: in the background, a brief presentation of the thematic is made; then, it is described the research methodology followed; and, the solution development process - the interaction design description, implementation, and the preliminary usability assessment. In the latter, a description of the participants involved, the experimental design, procedures and apparatus. Also, results and discussion are presented. Finally, we present our conclusions and future work.

2 Background

With an exponential growth, digital and mobile devices, are used in many everyday activity, particularly by children [1]. Their daily habits are undoubtedly influenced by different and varied technologies and the applications used can influence socialization, apprenticeship [2] but also support in a rehabilitation context [38–40].

In literature it is long-established, technologies can create entirely new learning environments by significantly increasing effectiveness, efficiency and sophistication of apprenticeship, giving the opportunity to experience new knowledge [3, 4]. Particularly, games are one of the most successful applications on the market [3].

Serious games can be powerful tools to develop and train acquisition of new knowledge. That is why it can be found several games apps to enhance learning designed for specific public [5, 6].

Teachers are aware of the enormous potential of using games in the classrooms [7–10, 30, 31] confirming students were more motivated, many times, without realizing that were essentially learning. Indeed, serious games have a positive effect, in terms of increasing study motivation, proving to be a valuable tool to support teaching [11, 32].

In literature, many studies presenting the importance of serious games, mobile learning apps, and supporting a game developing approach for education [30–34, 36, 37].

Moreover, play contexts can be resourceful frameworks to help children in cognitive and social developments [12–14]. When interacting with games, children can develop basic skills and competences [15] as they interact with the interface, for example: language skills, when giving instructions, discussing, sharing opinions and answering questions; mathematics, when have to interacting with scores; reading, when appears a game dialogue; and, socially, if children can play in groups and/or or talk about the game. In addition to resources for educational context, games are also used to address problems, of communication [16], spatial skills [17], problem solving exercises [18] and specific mathematical problems [19].

Regarding users with (dis) abilities, a large number of users are still unable to play [23–25]. A game should be accessible to as many people as possible, regardless of their abilities and/or skills. Despite the interest on developing accessible games, interfaces were not accessible when compared to other technologies [20–22]. While in serious games, accessibility is a condition, in entertainment games it seems there is still no concern, in accessible development for most game designers [27]. The accessibility concern, on the game development process, is central. However, is seen as a problem because it can be necessary to integrate or develop new technologies (e.g.: text-to-speech or speech-to-text, speech processing models) or even to produce hardware, or to adapt devices and/or controllers [26]. These factors are considered demotivating to game developers.

It is believed, when developing a game, it is necessary to present an accessible and aesthetically appealing design for various user profiles. Thus, we have to consider both game rules and graphic elements that captivate various player profiles aiming at greater adherence [28].

3   Research Methodology

Regarding methodology, a universal design philosophy was followed towards creating an interface that allowed training and acquiring of new knowledge for different user groups. The universal design philosophy for different user groups was to be achieved by customization of the game topics and levels of difficulty.

Furthermore, the direct observation of the user interaction was important for a preliminary interface assessment hence user testing was conducted using cognitive walkthrough method. This task-specific approach to assess usability was reinforced with post- test semi-structured interviews [29].

In this context, we invited two groups of participants: children with special educational needs and seniors in cognitive rehabilitation aiming to encounter interaction problems, and assess user engagement and acceptance of the interface.

In the user tests, we registered effectiveness, efficiency and satisfaction criteria. In detail, for effectiveness, we registered how many participants performed the tasks with success and without giving up. In efficiency, we registered resources spent to achieve effectiveness, such as: time to perform the task and difficulties observed. In satisfaction, we observed if the participants showed comfort when performing tasks and if they want to repeat the tasks.

The topics for assessment was chosen with conformance with the special needs education teachers and approved by seniors' speech therapists and psychologist. they were: colors, animals, objects, vehicles.

End-users were observed in two interaction phases: one, structured with specific tasks to interact, and consequently assessed; and other, free and autonomous interaction, where they could choose any game thematic.

4 Solution Design Proposal

4.1 Interfaces and Interaction Design

The first version of the solution was designed with a simple interactive interface, aiming to assist new learning (or to reinforce previous learning) of basic concepts, for example: colours, animals, objects, and vehicles.

Though we tested the interface for basic (re)learning concepts, the solution presented is adaptable to different learning profiles. Users (teachers, tutors or parents, …) have options to change the learning contents, i.e., it is possible to add, eliminate or change learning themes (by adding text, images and audio contents) and add or remove levels of difficulty (number of questions).

The solution presented a clear-cut design and usable layout. The simplicity of its design, language used and addition of both visual and audio cues were key features for the user interface design.

Specifically, for interaction, users needed to: (1) register or login (after that the interface displayed specific content for a specific user). Then, (2) they can access the 'Main' menu and (3) play one of the four thematic games available by clicking in the respective 'New Game' button.

At the 'New Game' menu users can choose audio options - on or mute -, by clicking on the sound icon located in the upper right corner of the interface. Additionally, users must choose one of three difficulty levels: level 1, the interface presents two answer choices (one right-one wrong); level 2, three choices (one right-two wrong); and, level 3, four (one right-four wrong). After that, can 'start' the game by clicking in the specific button.

At the end of the game, users can advance to the next level through the 'Next' button and access a 'Score' Menu, with the results obtained on each game/level played.

In the 'Main' menu, users (teachers/tutors or physicians) can select an 'Add Levels' option. This option allows to adapt exercises, including adding new images, sounds and thematic to exercises options, for a specific user profile. Explicitly, to access this menu, they have to click in the option and will be redirected to a new level data entry screen and fill in all fields: thematic or learning topic, correct answers (text content), wrong answer(s) (text content), pictures (images or videos) and sound files. Then, have to click the 'Save' button, this will save the new input within the database.

An audio and a text manual is also available for explaining the game rules and features, and information about user interaction.

4.2 Design Implementation

The application was developed on the Visual Studio platform, using the C# language and Windows Forms. GitLab (Team Explorer) tools were also used. There were defined and developed five key components: Main Menu; Game Menu; Score Menu; Review Menu and Add New Level Menu.

4.3 Preliminary Assessment

Participants

Thirty-eight persons participate in this preliminary assessment. Specifically, twenty children with special educational needs (eleven boys and nine girls - age from 6 to 13 years old); ten elderly people attending a rehabilitation center (three men and seven women - age from 76 to 80 years old); two teachers; and, six parents (age range 29 to 33).

The children participants were nominated by a special education teacher and a psychologist, according to the average rate of literacy and primary education: ten participants in the 2th grade; eight, in the 3th grade; and, two, in the 4th grade.

The seniors were selected by a speech therapists and psychologist working in the rehabilitation center.

All participants were volunteers and had permission of their parents or tutors to participate in the assessment stage.

Furthermore, teachers and parents were invited to observe but also to give their input to improve the application.

Experimental Design

All participants used the application in two assessment phases: one, a task-specific approach to assess usability, (recording effectiveness, efficiency and satisfaction criteria; and a second where users could play freely and autonomously without specific tasks to test. This latter aimed at observing user engagement and interface acceptance.

We observed and registered: quantitate data, such as: the number of successfully conclude tasks, time to conclude tasks; but also qualitative data, comments regarding difficulties and interaction.

Audio recording and writing notes were used.

Participants were divided in four groups: two, with seniors; and, two children special educational needs.

The specific tasks defined were:

- (T1) choose and play the Colors thematic game (level 1);
- (T2) choose and play Animals thematic game (level 2);
- (T3) choose and play Objects thematic game (level 3);
- (T4) choose and play Vehicles thematic game (level 3);
- (T5) choose Score Menu in order to see the final score.

The first four game topic tasks were performed randomly. The level of difficulty remained in the same sequence, users must always to start in level 1 (two-answer choices) to level 3 (four-answer choices).

After this first phase of assessment, with mandatory tasks, we invite the participants to play at will. They could choose the game topics and levels of difficulties.

Note: efficiency criteria is defined as task conclusion with success. The total score obtained in each game was registered but not used to assess efficiency.

Procedures
Participants were seated correctly in front of the screen in a controlled environment. After we explained user interaction and game features they started the assessment activities. Experiments were made one participant at a time with at less two observers.

Apparatus
The resources used to perform the user tests were: an Asus Intel Core i7-4500U 64-bit Operating System Laptop, Windows 8.1 and an Asus Intel Core i7-3610 64-bit Operating System laptop computer, Windows 10. The touch screen of the described laptop was used during the assessment phase to facilitate the user interaction.

4.4 Results and Discussion

Overall, in the preliminary assessment, it was observed a good user interaction. Specifically, the solution seemed to facilitated children apprenticeship of basic topics. Regarding seniors, it seemed to allowed a cognitive stimulus.

Furthermore, within the two groups, it was observed, throughout the experiment, an increase of motivation when interacting with the solution. This was noticed with the results obtain in the effectiveness criteria. Specifically, all participants, seniors and children with special educational needs concluded all tasks with success and no one dropped out. Also, in the autonomous testing phase, all repeated interaction and played with the interface, freely.

Regarding efficiency, specifically time to conclude the tasks:

– children took approximately 3 min to conclude Task 1 and Task 2, and about 6 min to complete the Task 3 and 4;
– seniors, took about 3 min in Task 1 and Task 2, and, 7 min in Task 3 and 4. Notice that the time increased in higher difficulty levels.

No participant comments one difficulties in the score consultation option (Task 5).

No errors or major difficulties were described by the participants or observed in user interaction. Though, in content assessment, i.e., game scores, users obtained different scores, showing more difficulties in a high difficulty level 3 (four-answer choices).

In the autonomous assessment, users tried different difficulty levels, in different game topics. They seemed engaged and positively accepted to use the interface, repeating several times (up to 10 times) the interaction.

Other observation and notes were register: for instance, the visual and audio cues were indicated as important for assistance in word writing. Furthermore, adding of an animated figure with voice was considered to be helpful to assist user interaction. This animation explained the games topics/ aims and reproduced the audio help (if needed). Additionally, the audio and visual wrong and right feedback screens were much appreciating by seniors' participants. These features help them to understand the next step (if they could "continue" or "try again").

Another appreciated feature was the background choice option, must appreciated by the children. They were observed to try several options for the background, in the autonomous assessment. When questioned, they said they liked to customized the background and requested for the possibility of uploading an image of their choice. This option was not considered in the version presented but will be implemented in future work.

The exit option was ignored. No one uses this button. When asked why, several participants said they did not see it.

Overall, in concern of the design features (buttons, illustrations, audio option) participants confirmed were easy to find and use.

Regarding satisfaction, participants seemed to be enrolled in the game activities and several said they would use the application in other contexts. Specifically, children said they liked using it, with their parents, at home; and, the seniors affirmed they could use it in rehabilitation context as an assistive tool.

Moreover, teacher and parents gave their feedback regarding the observations made. Specifically, teachers stated the solution facilitated the children's apprenticeship of basic didactic contents; and, parents would like to try the topic customization option ('Add' level option) at home.

5 Conclusion and Future Work

Overall conclusion, the solution provided a simple and user-friendly interface to effectively assist users with special education needs or seniors in need of cognitive rehabilitation.

The two participant groups of the preliminary assessment and teachers and parents involved seemed very satisfied and expressed positive feedback regarding the solution presented.

All participants – children with special educational needs and seniors - performed the two assessment moments and no one give up.

Several children asked to repeat the experiment, preferring the autonomous interaction, without structured tasks to perform. On the other hand, seniors enjoyed the controlled experience with direct assistance, sustaining the will of having "someone to indicates which task to performed".

Therefore, it seems that effectiveness, satisfaction and user engagement results were promising.

Teachers' feedback was the app facilitated children apprenticeship of basic topics and could use it in different class learning contexts.

Parents affirmed that they could use the solution at home also to assist training. Children were happy and satisfied after tests and said they did not mind to use it in school or at home.

Despite the results were very prominent, we registered some improvements to implement as future work, for example: add more game topics (with visual and audio cues); add background images, allowing users to upload an image of their choice.

Additionally, we intend to follow this research field by further studying universal design of different types of content (audio, image, animation, text) to enhance cognitive stimuli (e.g. audio, visual, and tactile), in education and rehabilitation contexts. We believe it is needed further and deep analysis to provide accessibility in game design interface.

Also, it is intended to enhance the number of participants to performed a second usability assessment.

Acknowledgements. This work is a result of the project INOV@UTAD, NORTE-01-0246-FEDER-000039, supported by Norte Portugal Regional Operational Programme (NORTE 2020), under the PORTUGAL 2020 Partnership Agreement, through the European Regional Development Fund (ERDF). Furthermore, the authors would like to thank all participants that help in different phases of the iterative inclusive development of the solution presented, in particular to our students.

References

1. Palazzi, C.E., Maggiorini, D.: From playgrounds to smartphones: mobile evolution of a kids game. In: IEEE Consumer Communications and Networking Conference (CCNC), pp. 182–186. IEEE (2011)
2. Hromek, R., Roffey, S.: Promoting social and emotional learning with games: "it's fun and we learn things". Simul. Gaming (2009). https://doi.org/10.1177/1046878109333793
3. Rocha, T., Nunes, R.R., Bessa, M., Paredes, H., Barroso, J., Martins, P.: Multimedia technologies as strategy for enhancing learning for students with intellectual disabilities. In: 12th Annual International Conference of Education, Research and Innovation – ICERI 2019 (2019)
4. Hoogerwerf, E.J., et al.: Digital inclusion. A white paper (2016). https://www.entelis.net/sites/all/files/digital_inclusion-a_white_paper_final_0.pdf
5. Rocha, T., Nunes, R.R., Martins, P., Barroso, J.: Learning how to use a QWERTY keyboard with a game interface for children: a usability preliminary study. In: 11th annual International Conference on Education and New Learning Technologies – EDULEARN 2019 (2019)
6. Rocha, T., Nunes, R.R., Martins, P., Barroso, J.: Using Game-based technology to enhance learning for children with learning disabilities: a pilot study. In 3rd International Conference on Education and E-Learning – ICEEL 2019 (2019)
7. Gee, J.P.: What Video Games Have to Teach Us About Learning and Literacy. Palgrave Macmillan (2003)
8. Jenkins, H.: Game theory: how should we teach kids newtonian physics? Simple, play computer games. Technol. Rev. **3** (2002). http://www.technologyreview.com/articles/wo_jenkins032902.asp
9. Kebritchi, M., Hirumi, A.: Examining the pedagogical foundations of modern educational computer games. Comput. Educ. **51**(4), 1729–1743 (2008)
10. Squire, K.: Changing the game: what happens when video games enter the classroom? Innov. J. Online Educ. **1**(6) (2005)
11. Rosas, R., et al.: Beyond Nintendo: design and assessment of educational video games for first and second grade students. Comput. Educ. **40**(1), 71–94 (2003)

12. Csikszentmihaliy, M.: Flow: The Psychology of Optimal Experience. Harper & Press, New York (1990)

13. Provost, J.A.: Work, Play and Type: Achieving Balance in Your Life. Consulting Psychologist Press, Palo Alto (1990)

14. Rogoff, B.: Aprendices del pensamiento. El desarrollo cognitivo en el contexto social. Paidós, Barcelona (1993)

15. Griffiths, M.: The educational benefits of videogames. Educ. Health **20**(3), 47–51 (2002)

16. Horn, E., Jones, H.A., Hamlett, C.: An investigation of the feasibility of a video game system for developing scanning and selection skills. J. Assoc. People Severe Handicaps **16**, 108–115 (1991)

17. Masendorf, F.: Training of learning disabled children's spatial abilities by computer games. Zeitschrift Padagogische Psychol. **7**, 209–213 (1993)

18. Hollingsworth, M., Woodward, J.: Integrated learning: explicit strategies and their role in problem solving instruction for students with learning disabilities. Except. Child. **59**, 444–445 (1993)

19. Okolo, C.: The effect of computer-assisted instruction format and initial attitude on the arithmetic facts proficiency and continuing motivation of students with learning disabilities. Exceptionality **3**, 195–211 (1992)

20. Bierre, K., Chetwynd, J., Ellis, B., Hinn, D.M., Ludi, S., Westin, T.: Game not over: accessibility issues in video games. In: 11th International Conference on Human-Computer Interaction – HCII 2005. Lawrence Erlbaum Associates, Inc. (2005)

21. Westin, T., Bierre, K., Gramenos, D., Hinn, M.: Advances in game accessibility from 2005 to 2010. In: Stephanidis, C. (ed.) UAHCI 2011, Part II. LNCS, vol. 6766, pp. 400–409. Springer, Heidelberg (2011). https://doi.org/10.1007/978-3-642-21663-3_43

22. Yuan, B., Folmer, E., Harris, F.C.: Game accessibility: a survey. Univ. Access Inf. Soc. **10**, 81–100 (2011)

23. Atkinson, M.T., Gucukoglu, S., Machin, C.H.C., Lawrence, A.E.: Making the mainstream accessible: redefining the game. In: Sandbox 2006: Proceedings of the 2006 ACM SIGGRAPH Symposium on Videogames, pp. 21–28. ACM, New York (2006)

24. Bierre, K., Ellis, B., Hinn, M., Ludi, S., Westin, T.: Whitepaper: game not over: accessibility issues in video games (2005). http://www.igda.org/accessibility/hcii2005_gac.pdf

25. Grammenos, D.: Game over: learning by dying. In: CHI 2008: Proceeding of the 26th Annual SIGCHI Conference on Human Factors in Computing Systems, pp. 1443–1452. ACM, New York (2008)

26. Bierre, K., et al.: Accessibility in games: motivations and approaches (2004)

27. Grammenos, D., Savidis, A., Georgalis, Y., Stephanidis, C.: Access invaders: developing a universally accessible action game. In: Miesenberger, K., Klaus, J., Zagler, Wolfgang L., Karshmer, Arthur I. (eds.) ICCHP 2006. LNCS, vol. 4061, pp. 388–395. Springer, Heidelberg (2006). https://doi.org/10.1007/11788713_58

28. Kultima, A.: Casual game design values. In: Proceedings of the 13th International MindTrek Conference: Everyday Life in the Ubiquitous Era, pp. 58–65. ACM, September 2009

29. Blackmon, M.H., Polson, P.G., Muneo, K., Lewis, C.: Cognitive walkthrough for the web. In: CHI 2002, vol. 4, no. 1, pp. 463–470 (2002)

30. Papadakis, S.: Evaluating pre-service teachers' acceptance of mobile devices with regards to their age and gender: a case study in Greece. Int. J. Mob. Learn. Organ. **12**(4), 336–352 (2018)

31. Vidakis, N., Barianos, A.K., Trampas, A.M., Papadakis, S., Kalogiannakis, M., Vassilakis, K.: Generating education in-game data: the case of an ancient theatre serious game. In: CSED, no. 1, pp. 36–43 (2019)

32. Papadakis, S., Trampas, A.M., Barianos, A.K., Kalogiannakis, M., Vidakis, N.: Evaluating the learning process: the "ThimelEdu" educational game case study. In: CSEDU, no. 2, pp. 290–298 (2020)
33. Papadakis, S., Kalogiannakis, M.: Using gamification for supporting an introductory programming course. The case of classcraft in a secondary education classroom. In: Brooks, A., Brooks, E., Vidakis, N. (eds.) Interactivity Game Creation, Design Learning and Innovation, pp. 366–375. Springer, Cham (2017). https://doi.org/10.1007/978-3-319-76908-0_35
34. Papadakis, St., Kalogiannakis, M.: A research synthesis of the educational value of self-proclaimed mobile educational applications for young age children. In: Papadakis, S., Kalogiannakis, M. (eds.) Mobile Learning Applications in Early Childhood Education, pp. 1–19). IGI Global, Hershey (2020). https://doi.org/10.4018/978-1-7998-1486-3.ch001
35. Papadakis, S.: Evaluating a game-development approach to teach introductory programming concepts in secondary education. Int. J. Technol. Enhanc. Learn. 12(2), 127–145 (2020)
36. Connolly, T.M., Boyle, E.A., MacArthur, E., Hainey, T., Boyle, J.M.: A systematic literature review of empirical evidence on computer games and serious games. Comput. Educ. 59(2), 661–686 (2012)
37. Camilleri, M.A., Camilleri, A.C.: The students' readiness to engage with mobile learning apps. Interact. Technol. Smart Educ. 17(1), 28–38 (2019)
38. Marcelino, I., Barroso, J., Cruz, J.B., Pereira, A.: Elder care architecture. In: Proceedings - The 3rd International Conference on Systems and Networks Communications, ICSNC 2008 - Includes I-CENTRIC 2008: International Conference on Advances in Human-Oriented and Personalized Mechanisms, Technologies, and Services, pp. 349–354, 4693695 (2008)
39. Gonçalves, C., Rocha, T., Reis, A., Barroso, J.: AppVox: an application to assist people with speech impairments in their speech therapy sessions. In: Rocha, Á., Correia, A.M., Adeli, H., Reis, L.P., Costanzo, S. (eds.) WorldCIST 2017. AISC, vol. 570, pp. 581–591. Springer, Cham (2017). https://doi.org/10.1007/978-3-319-56538-5_59
40. Reis, A., et al.: Designing autonomous systems interactions with elderly people. In: Antona, M., Stephanidis, C. (eds.) UAHCI 2017. LNCS, vol. 10279, pp. 603–611. Springer, Cham (2017). https://doi.org/10.1007/978-3-319-58700-4_49

Improve Students' Learning Experience in General Chemistry Laboratory Courses

Yinghong Sheng[(✉)] and Fan Zhao

Florida Gulf Coast University, Fort Myers, FL 33965, USA
ysheng@fgcu.edu

Abstract. The current shift from a traditional classroom laboratory to a partial remote virtual lab is mainly due to COVID-19 pandemic. This pedagogical change is forcing academic institutions to rethink and redesign their lab courses. VR is promising technology to support this change. This study reviews current literature of the VR systems applied in higher education, clarifies some technical terms related to VR technology, and identifies the strengths and weaknesses of this technology. After a semi-interview with faculty members and students in the Chemistry department at a US university, we propose a new hybrid lab design with VR technology based on the literature review and interview results.

Keywords: Virtual reality · Chemistry lab · Education

1 Introduction

Effective and efficient chemistry education offers reliable knowledge transformation to next generation improving students' problem solving and critical thinking skills in Chemistry. One of the most important components in chemistry education is the laboratory experience. Chemistry labs are design to help students enhance acquired theoretical knowledge and support practical training through various learning resources [1]. Adequate chemistry lab training is critical to ensure desired learning outcomes through the chemistry education. However, there are always some challenges faced by most of the chemistry departments in the higher education as follows: (1) insufficient laboratory space to arrange enough chemistry lab courses [3]; (2) special restrictions on attendance, such as students with disabilities [2]; (3) insufficient faculty members to teach chemistry lab courses [3]; (4) expensive lab equipment and materials (some of them may not be accessible by small schools) [4]; (5) fatal experiments with certain chemical materials [3]; (6) dangerous results due to students' operating mistakes [3]. With increasing demands in chemistry lab courses but the lack of budget, real classroom space, and experienced faculty, changing trend of teaching with technologies becomes a need to enhance higher education learning outcomes. Additionally, the COVID-19 pandemic promoted more virtual education and forced less physical chemistry labs in classrooms. This transition expanded the above challenges to current chemistry lab courses. In this context, more and more computer-based simulation tools are developed to engage the chemistry

© Springer Nature Switzerland AG 2021
X. Fang (Ed.): HCII 2021, LNCS 12790, pp. 72–83, 2021.
https://doi.org/10.1007/978-3-030-77414-1_7

education and assist to improve students' learning performance. The simulation tools with virtual reality (VR) is the most promoted one adopted by many universities.

Pedagogical use of VR simulations has been adopted in various education areas such as healthcare [5–7], construction [8], military [9], and other higher education majors [10–12] to improve training effectiveness and avoid potential training risks. The success of VR applications in education depends on the users' feeling of "sense of presence", which gives the users a "real world" sensation and deceives the users' feeling on human behavioral parameters with the effects of 3D immersive environment [13]. In recent years, VR technology shows overwhelming advantages in training programs and education, such as schedule flexibility by self-learning, not limited to certain training locations, repeatedly and individually experiment practices, etc. [14–16]. It becomes an innovative method to provide a unique educational supplement to the in-class lectures and strengthen the students' inquired-based learning experiences, especially in laboratory education [17].

For decades, the chemistry lab course was offered in a physical laboratory. With the growth of computer and internet technologies, the use of simulation training has become an integral part of chemistry education. In respect to the experiments in a chemistry lab, it is widely admitted that VR has shown a great potential in enhancing students' theoretical knowledge and practically experimental skills [18–20]. However, although VR applications in chemistry labs has increasingly received educators' attention, in many academic studies during past decade, definitions of VR and VR related terms such as augmented reality (AR) simulation, immersed simulation/VR, 2D/3D VR are not clear, which caused some misunderstanding and misleading results about VR applications. Additionally, to deal with the future disaster situations such as the COVID-19 pandemic, there is a need to seek a better pedagogical solution for chemistry lab courses under multiple realistic limitations.

The purpose of this study is to briefly compare several common terms used in VR and shed the light on these terms and definitions of VR and other terms related to VR. Additionally, this study is trying to propose a hybrid teaching method with VR technology in chemistry lab education.

2 Literature Review of VR Applications

2.1 Virtual Reality

Computer based simulation technology, such as VR, plays an important role in current higher education. VR has been described as the learning and education supportive technology of the new century [21]. VR uses graphic systems combined with various interface devices to give the effect immersion in an interactive virtual environment [22]. Presence in a virtual environment gives users a feeling of being in a virtually mediated location similar to the real location. Users' feeling or sense of this presence is a critical factor linking their perceptions, intentions and actions in the virtual environment. The level of this presence determines the engagement of the users in the VR. VR technology has a variety of unique properties along with different terms that users are utilizing.

From dimensional perspective, it could be 2D, 3D VR technology. From immersive perspective, it could be non-immersive or immersive technology. From image or animation perspective, it could be AR, VR, and Mixed Reality (MR).

The initial VR simulation tools adopt conventional 2D technology which does not give depth to the objects, such as flight simulations games developed two decades ago. The advantages of 2D VR simulation include low-cost, mature technology, convenience to the users, and compatible to most of the current computers and mobile devices. 3D technology creates spatial depth off the 2D screen with 3D pop-up visualizations which makes some objects appeared closer and touchable to the users.

Immersion is a new term in VR describing the level of users' involvement experiences in the virtual environment [21]. Immersive VR (IVR) technology tends to "disconnect" users from the real world and replace the real world with the virtual world created in the virtual environment. From a user's perspective, immersive VR excludes the physical real world and provides an isolated perception of his/her sense from the reality by changing surrounding environment [23]. The typical immersive VR is mediated through head mounted displays (HMD), such as HTC glasses or Oculus Rift, allowing users to experience the desired degree of immersion. Combining with dimensions of VR, the effectiveness of 2D immersive VR can only show images and 2D videos to the users which is lack of depth perception. Therefore, current trend of VR technology is to adopt 3D technology with immersion giving users more realistic and immersive feelings in the virtual world.

Along with VR, there are two other similar technologies named AR and MR. In both AR and MR, real world is not isolated but mixed with the virtual world. In AR, users mainly interact with the real world and the virtual objects are the adds-on to the real world. A typical example of AR is the game Pokemon Go. Players of this game can see the real world plus the Pokemon as the virtual object. MR is more advanced technology combining both real world and virtual environment allowing users to interact with both worlds [24].

2.2 Laboratory Education Methods

According to the experiential learning theory, experience is one of the critical factors in the learning process [25, 26]. Practice under simulation scenarios allows users to enroll to the activities, reflect on the experience, observe the differences, identify crucial skills, and actively experiment gaining the knowledge to shape future practice [27]. Therefore, chemistry lab courses are important to support students with their operational skills and understand thoroughly with theoretical knowledge they learned in lectures.

There are typically four pedagogical methods to teach chemistry lab courses. The face-to-face method is the traditional classroom teaching that students sit the classroom for the lectures and practice their operational skills in a physical laboratory. With demand of teaching and learning efficiency, instructional videos were added to the traditional teaching method as a supplementing teaching method. Instructors can spend more time preparing the videos with more systematic and logical teaching philosophy, and students have more flexibility to watch the videos repeatedly at anytime and anywhere. This method reduces students' in-class pressure and encourages their learning preferences [28]. Research of recent years indicates the success of this method in higher education as useful pedagogical tools in engaging students in learning [29]. Both of these methods are teacher-centered and require passive learning by the students. To improve students' engagement with the knowledge and provide student-centered learning activities, 2D & 3D simulation tools were invented for lab courses. Lab simulations include multimedia instructions and visual guidelines, which allow students to independently analyze the lab information, construct their knowledge framework, and practice repeatedly on their lab skills [30]. Lately, immersive VR is actively being incorporated as an efficient teaching and learning tool in the lab education [31]. Students complete most of the lab activities in the VR world with instant feedbacks from the system. More and more educators are considering to embed VR into a regular laboratory education, especially for remote lab education [2].

2.3 VR in Higher Education

There are numerous academic studies exploring the potential benefits of VR application in higher education [2, 3, 8]. To some special subjects, such as medical, geographical, chemistry, biology, etc., VR technology allows students to visit some environments either hard or impossible to approach or unobservable phenomena due to various limitations [32–34]. Yu and Mann [35] indicates the usefulness of VR technology in nursing training program, especially for some emergency scenarios, such as neonatal resuscitation. Field trip is another example to adopt VR technology in class to visit different locations at the same time [14]. Additionally, VR technology provides flexibility in virtual training and education system modifications, which allows student to easily and quickly experiment with various systems that typically cannot be changed in laboratory or industrial conditions [36].

From learners' perspective, students are reported to feel more confident, open, participatory, creative, and understanding toward the knowledge they learned through VR technology [37–40]. VR systems enable students to complete training experiments independently and repeatedly at any time. This gives students more time to practice and understand the knowledge and skills. Moreover, VR systems guarantee the safety of students in the experiments involving some exceptionally dangerous chemical or unusual working conditions [41]. Lastly, all students have equal chance to practice in a VR educational system. Since it is virtual, a VR system gives all students equal and flexible access without limitations, especially for those disabled students, students with temporary restrictions on class attendance, such as pregnant or injured, or students who want makeup the labs at different time.

From learning and teaching perspectives, VR education systems attract students' attention [16], bring more learning engagement and enjoyment [42], enhance students' understanding of scientific concepts [15], and support inquiry-based learning [17]. Especially in chemistry lab education, Davenport et al. [43] demonstrate that VR chemistry lab improves students' problem solving skills. This result is in line with the work of Winkelmann et al. [20] which indicates that VR can be effective for teaching chemistry experiments.

Despite the clear advantages of VR technology in education, there are a number of challenges identified by Alalwan et al. [44] from a semi-structured interview of 29 science teachers. Technically, VR technology is still in its preliminary stage. Therefore, from both software design and hardware functionality perspectives, VR is limited to show its full capabilities in education, such as lack of competency of the VR systems, limited instructional design, not enough parental control support to K-12 students, requiring more time and practice to master the VR devices, and limited resources to support the fulfillment of VR functions. Besides the technical concerns, the potential negative health and mental impact of using VR for long periods, such as dizzying, uncomfortable feeling, higher cognitive load, eyestrain, pedophobia and cyber addiction, is revealed by some research [45–48]. Budget is another challenge to adopt VR technology in education covering the initial cost of the VR software and hardware, such as VR glasses and special training programs, and on-going cost including device maintenance, staff hiring, and training [46]. In addition, from a learning perspective, a few studies found negative effect on students' learning outcomes through VR learning environment, despite students' higher interest, motivation and engagement in the learning process [49, 50]. The authors argue that this can be reasoned by the complex design in the VR system which distracted students' attention. This results is in line with the discussion of Alalwan et al. [44] with recommendations of simplified VR software design.

This study focuses on the current chemistry lab teaching dilemma on a University in south USA. Our purpose is to develop an efficient and effective teaching and learning method to provide better lab education to our students in chemistry classes.

3 Chemistry Lab and Proposed Design with VR Technology

3.1 Current Solution

The Department of Chemistry offers 14 labs in General Chemistry I laboratory course (CHM1045L) and 13 labs in General Chemistry II laboratory course (CHM1046L) each semester. Due to the classroom space limitation, all the labs were performed in laboratory with a duration of 100 min, each session capped with 24 students.

Due to the large enrollment of General Chemistry I and II, the only two laboratory classrooms are reserved throughout the week, with more than 20 CHM1045L sessions and 14 CHM1046L sessions.

During the outbreak of COVID-19 in 2020 the department had to switch to online instruction and all lab sessions were taught virtually in the spring semester of 2020. Instructors gave an online lecture on the background and procedure of labs, then provided lab data for students to finish their lab reports. Students had no opportunity to obtain hands-on laboratorial training experiences.

Starting 2020 Fall semester, the department made some changes in order for students to get some laboratory experiences while still maintain the social distancing. In General Chemistry I laboratory course (CHM1045L), half of the students performed the wet lab in the laboratory, while the other half students conducted "Dry Experiments" using Labster simulations on computers. The next week, these two groups of students switched. Similarly, in General Chemistry II laboratory course (CHM1046L) students are split into two groups, they take turn to attend in-person lab, while the other group stayed virtual and use Zoom or FaceTime to watch their lab partners perform labs.

3.2 Concerns of Current Solutions

There are great concerns in the abovementioned solutions.

- Due to 100 minutes laboratory time limitation, some labs had to be modified, and reduced lab procedures are provided to students. For instance, Experiment #3 in General Chemistry II laboratory course "What is the Activation Energy of the Formation of a Chromium (III) EDTA complex?", requires students to collect a series experimental data at 8 different temperature settings. However, during the 100 minutes laboratory meeting time each group students could only get experimental data at most 3 different temperature settings. Therefore, the department modified the procedure and assigned all groups to obtain experimental data cooperatively. This helped to get "a complete set" of experimental data for students to calculate the activation energy of the reaction under study. However, the results had been often ruined by all sorts of errors and mistakes from different groups which hindered the students to obtain an accurate value of the reaction activation energy. On some occasions, instructors had to provide data for students to complete the post lab reports.
- We thought to open the laboratories 24/7 so that students can go anytime without time limit to perform their labs. This also raise two major concerns: (1) For safety reason it is impossible to open the laboratories to students without the supervision of lab managers or instructors; (2) This would dramatically increase the lab managers and instructors' working loads.
- The current lab teaching schedule can only allow students conduct half of the wet labs originally scheduled. Therefore, students only received half training opportunity.
- For those students who are online, the current alternating lab schedule makes it hard for them to understand the labs. Students did not have first-hand experience to know the details of the labs, they had to rely on their lab partners on screen to get an understanding of the lab.
- Instructors also received complaints from students about their lab partners, either their lab partners did not contact them, or not communicate in a timely manner, and had to rush to complete their lab reports in the last minutes. Good students don't want their grades negatively impacted by their weak lab partners, or their lab partners did not do correctly.
- Current lab simulations don't provide students hands-on experience, such as getting definitive results, accurate measuring, and any real time troubleshooting. The simulated labs aren't a full replacement for the entire class, though simulations are just fine if not every student can attend in-person lab sessions.

Below are some feedbacks from students on the current simulation used.
Advantage of Simulation:

- "It's great because you get the ability to restart just one portion of the lab when you make a mistake rather than redoing the entire lab".
- "I learned a lot from the process, and it was similar to the in person lab".
- "The simulation lab is definitely helpful because it helps me understand how the actual lab would have gone and it is easier because it automatically does the correct amount of solutions and things like that".

– "I love the simulation lab and I feel like I learn more than in lab. This is because I am able to answer questions as I do it, and all resources and help I could need are easily available to me, where as there is only one professor to several students that can help in lab".

– "One thing that I would like more of is the pre labs being a simulation instead of report. I feel the simulation better prepares you for the lab since you can see it not just read it".

Disadvantage of Simulation:

– "My only issue is that it can be a little laggy and take a minute to comprehend what you are doing".

– "My only complaint is sometimes, it can be glitchy and difficult to navigate".

– "I feel fine towards the simulation lab. Although I can definitely feel a difference when it comes to learning and understanding what the lab is trying to teach when it is in person, compared to when it is a simulation".

3.3 Expectations of Future Systems

Our future system should meet the following expectations:

1. The lab simulations should synchronize with our lab sequence and simulations would be as close as possible to the actual labs. This would allow online students to receive the lab training similar to the actual labs.
2. There would be embedded quiz questions throughout the simulations that are open note within the simulation.
3. Use simulation to provide a platform for students to learn the detail procedure of labs before they come to the lab. Students are evaluated by the embedded quiz questions. This would allow students get acquainted with the lab procedure and perform actual labs more efficiently in laboratory even with the 100 minutes limitation.
4. Students can rework the simulation for a higher score and could repeat the simulation as many times as they want.
5. Simulation would be mobile friendly so that students could work on simulations on their laptop, desktop or mobile devices.
6. Simulations have a module on how to use of equipment such as LabQuest Spectrophotometer before the lab even begins so that students could get a good idea how to use it.

3.4 Possible Solutions

Educators are looking for possible solutions for the current dilemma in chemistry lab education. Kelley [3] compares three chemistry lab teaching formats from conducting labs at school to completing experiments remotely at home with either school-provided or home-purchased lab supplies and concludes that in-person labs at school results in the best lab performance and learning outcomes. This results can be explained by better face-to-face instruction with instant feedback at school, higher class engagement with cooperative communications at school, and trusted lab safety supervision by the teachers at school.

Technically, to support remote experiment education at home, Zhou et al. [51] propose a method combining both AR and VR in a biological lab design. This design partially simplifies the simulation design by promoting students' theoretical knowledge learning through an AR system and improving students' experimental skills with a VR system.

3.5 Proposed Study

According to the literature review and interview information collected from our faculty members and students in the Chemistry department, we believe chemistry labs adopting VR technology is promising, especially for the remote lab course. Therefore, propose a new hybrid design for our current chemistry lab courses:

1. At the beginning of the semester, the first lab will be hold in the school laboratory.
   a. In a VR system, although students can see the 3D structure of all the lab equipment, they do not have a physical feeling/touch of the equipment. Therefore, we want students to cognitively feel and recognize all the experimental equations in the lab before they use the VR system;
   b. Safety instruction will be explained during this first class;
   c. Both hardware and software of the VR system for the lab will be introduced to the students.
2. Students complete required lab experiments through the VR system at home until the middle of the semester.
3. At the middle of the semester, students come back to the school laboratory. Previous studies suggest that engagement and learning are encouraged by personal, authentic, inquiry-based experiences [52–54]. Therefore, both physical and virtual lab experiments should offer in the lab course to complement each other efficiently supporting students' practical learning [20].
   a. Review all the labs they completed before;
   b. Complete an experiment in the school lab, which will help students comparing the differences between a real physical lab and a virtual lab;
   c. Reinforce the safety instruction;
   d. Q&A of the VR system.
4. Students complete required lab experiments through the VR system at home until the end of the semester.
5. At the end of the semester, students come back to the school laboratory for the last class.
   a. Review all the labs they completed before;
   b. Complete an experiment in the school lab, which will help students comparing the differences between a real physical lab and a virtual lab;
   c. Reinforce the safety instruction;
   d. Q&A of everything they learned during the semester.

4   Conclusions

Traditional classroom laboratory course design is insufficient for the current remote experimental education needs. VR technology has incredible potential to improve the students' learning outcomes in higher education [21]. Chemistry lab courses in school labs trains the students with highly practical and experiential skill-based learning. However, COVID-19 pandemic forced most universities shift from in-classroom labs to hybrid labs, which reduces students' practicing time in the lab. This study reviews current VR technology applications in higher education and proposes a new hybrid lab course design based on both the literature review and results from a semi-structured interview with faculty members and students in the Chemistry department at a US university. Our next step is to purchase and set up the VR hardware and software for a few chemistry labs and test the efficiency and effectiveness of this new hybrid lab design.

References

1. Bretz, S.L., Fay, M., Bruck, L.B., Towns, M.H.: What faculty interviews reveal about meaningful learning in the undergraduate chemistry laboratory. J. Chem. Educ. **90**(3), 281–288 (2013)
2. Dunnagan, C.L., Dannenberg, D.A., Cuales, M.P., Earnest, A.D., Gurnsey, R.M., Gallardo-Williams, M.T.: Production and evaluation of a realistic immersive virtual reality organic chemistry laboratory experience: infrared spectroscopy. J. Chem. Educ. **97**, 258–262 (2019)
3. Kelley, E.W.: Reflections on three different high school chemistry lab formats during COVID-19 Remote learning. J. Chem. Educ. **97**(9), 2606–2616 (2020)
4. Bruck, A.D., Towns, M.: Development, implementation, and analysis of a national survey of faculty goals for undergraduate chemistry laboratory. J. Chem. Educ. **90**(6), 685–693 (2013)
5. Shetty, V., Suresh, L.R., Hegde, A.M.: Effect of virtual reality distraction on pain and anxiety during dental treatment in 5 to 8 year old children. J. Clin. Pediatr. Dent. **43**(2), 97–102 (2019)
6. Scapin, S., Echevarría-Guanilo, M.E., Junior, P.R.B.F., Goncalves, N., Rocha, P.K., Coimbra, R.: Virtual Reality in the treatment of burn patients: a systematic review. Burns **44**(6), 1403–1416 (2018)
7. Arane, K., Behboudi, A., Goldman, R.D.: Virtual reality for pain and anxiety management in children. Can. Fam. Physician **63**(12), 932–934 (2017)
8. Wang, P., Wu, P., Wang, J., Chi, H.L., Wang, X.: A critical review of the use of virtual reality in construction engineering education and training. Int. J. Environ. Res. Public Health **15**(6), 1204 (2018)
9. Ahir, K., Govani, K., Gajera, R., Shah, M.: Application on virtual reality for enhanced education learning, military training and sports. Augmented Human Research **5**(1), 1–9 (2020)
10. Radianti, J., Majchrzak, T.A., Fromm, J., Wohlgenannt, I.: A systematic review of immersive virtual reality applications for higher education: design elements, lessons learned, and research agenda. Comput. Educ. **147**, 103778 (2020)
11. Degli Innocenti, E., et al.: Mobile virtual reality for musical genre learning in primary education. Comput. Educ. **139**, 102–117 (2019)
12. Johnston, E., Olivas, G., Steele, P., Smith, C., Bailey, L.: Exploring pedagogical foundations of existing virtual reality educational applications: a content analysis study. J. Educ. Technol. Syst. **46**(4), 414–439 (2018)
13. Kober, S., Kurzmann, J., Neuper, C.: Cortical correlate of spatial presence in 2D and 3D interactive virtual reality: an EEG study. Int. J. Psychophysiol. **83**, 365–374 (2012)

14. Fung, F.M., et al.: Applying a virtual reality platform in environmental chemistry education to conduct a field trip to an overseas site. J. Chem. Educ. **96**, 382–386 (2019)
15. Potkonjak, M.T., Lin, Y.W., She, H.C.: Learning through playing virtual age: exploring the interactions among student concept learning, gaming performance, in-game behaviors, and the use of in-game characters. Comput. Educ. **86**, 18–29 (2015)
16. Wang, C.Y., et al.: A Review of research on technology-assisted school science laboratories. Educ. Technol. Soc. **17**(2), 307–320 (2014)
17. Lee, E.A., Wong, K.W.: Learning with desktop virtual reality: low spatial ability learners are more positively affected. Comput. Educ. **79**, 49–58 (2014)
18. Jang, S., Vitale, J.M., Jyung, R.W., Black, J.B.: Direct manipulation is better than passive viewing for learning anatomy in a three-dimensional virtual reality environment. Comput. Educ. **106**, 150–165 (2017)
19. August, S.E., Hammers, M.L., Murphy, D.B., Neyer, A., Gueye, P., Thames, R.Q.: Virtual engineering sciences learning lab: giving stem education a Second Life. IEEE Trans. Learn. Technol. **9**, 18–30 (2016)
20. Winkelmann, K., Keeney-Kennicutt, W., Fowler, D., Macik, M.: Development, implementation, and assessment of general chemistry lab experiments performed in the virtual world of second life. J. Chem. Educ. **94**(7), 849–858 (2017)
21. Jensen, L., Konradsen, F.: A review of the use of virtual reality head-mounted displays in education and training. Educ. Inf. Technol. **23**(4), 1515–1529 (2017). https://doi.org/10.1007/s10639-017-9676-0
22. Pan, Z., Cheok, A.D., Yang, H., Zhu, J., Shi, J.: Virtual reality and mixed reality for virtual learning environments. Comput. Graph. **30**, 20–28 (2006)
23. Slater, M., Wilbur, S.: A framework for immersive virtual environments: Speculations on the role of presence in virtual environments. Teleoper. Virtual Environ. **6**(6), 603–616 (1997)
24. Kaplan, A.D., Cruit, J., Endsley, M., Beers, S.M., Sawyer, B.D., Hancock, P.A.: The effects of virtual reality, augmented reality, and mixed reality as training enhancement methods: a meta-analysis. Hum. Factors 0018720820904229 (2020)
25. Kolb, D.A.: Experiential Learning: Experiential Learning: Experience as the Source of Learning and Development. Prentice-Hall, Englewood Cliffs (1984)
26. Kolb, D.A., Boyatzis, R.E., Mainemelis, C.: Experiential learning theory: previous research and new directions. Perspect. Think. Learn. Cogn. Styles **1**(8), 227–247 (2001)
27. Poore, J.A., Cullen, D.L., Schaar, G.L.: Simulation-based interprofessional education guided by Kolb's experiential learning theory. Clin. Simul. Nurs. **10**(5), 241–247 (2014)
28. Eick, C.J., King, D.T., Jr.: Nonscience majors' perceptions on the use of YouTube video to support learning in an integrated science lecture. J. Coll. Sci. Teach. **42**, 26–30 (2012)
29. Lin, L., Atkinson, R.K.: Using animations and visual cueing to support learning of scientific concepts and processes. Comput. Educ. **56**, 650–658 (2011)
30. Liou, H.H., Yang, S.J., Chen, S.Y., Tarng, W.: The influences of the 2D image-based augmented reality and virtual reality on student learning. J. Educ. Technol. Soc. **20**(3), 110–121 (2017)
31. Radianti, J., Majchrzak, T.A., Fromm, J., Wohlgenannt, I.: A systematic review of immersive virtual reality applications for higher education: design elements, lessons learned, and research agenda. Comput. Educ. **147**, 103778 (2019)
32. De Jong, T. Instruction based on computer simulations and virtual laboratories. In: Mayer, R.E., Alexander, P.A. (eds.) Handbook of Research on Learning and Instruction, 2nd edn., pp. 502–521. Routledge, New York (2017)
33. Makransky, G., Lilleholt, L., Aaby, A.: Development and validation of the multimodal presence scale for virtual reality environments: a confirmatory factor analysis and item response theory approach. Comput. Hum. Behav. **72**, 276–285 (2017)

34. Merchant, Z., Goetz, E.T., Cifuentes, L., Keeney-Kennicutt, W., Davis, T.J.: Effectiveness of virtual reality-based instruction on students' learning outcomes in K-12 and higher education: a meta-analysis. Comput. Educ. **70**, 29–40 (2014)

35. Yu, M., Mann, J.S.: Development of virtual reality simulation program for high-risk neonatal infection control education. Clin. Simul. Nurs. **50**(C), 19–26 (2021)

36. Potkonjak, V., et al.: Virtual laboratories for education in science, technology, and engineering: a review. Comput. Educ. **95**, 309–327 (2016)

37. Loureiro, A., Bettencourt, T.: The use of virtual environments as an extended classroom–a case study with adult learners in tertiary education. Proc. Technol. **13**, 97–106 (2014)

38. Cai, S., Chiang, F., Sun, Y., Lin, C., Lee, J.: Applications of augmented reality-based natural interactive learning in magnetic field instruction. Interact. Learn. Environ. **25**(6), 778–791 (2017)

39. Pellas, N., Fotaris, P., Kazanidis, I., Wells, D.: Augmenting the learning experience in primary and secondary school education: a systematic review of recent trends in augmented reality game-based learning. Virtual Reality **23**(4), 329–346 (2019)

40. Paxinou, E., Panagiotakopoulos, C., Karatrantou, A., Kalles, D., Sgourou, A.: Implementation and evaluation of a three-dimensional virtual reality biology lab versus conventional didactic practices in lab experimenting with the photonic microscope. Biochem. Mol. Biol. Educ. **48**(1), 21–27 (2020)

41. Winkelmann, K.: Virtual worlds and their uses in chemical education. In: Suits, J., Sanger, M. (eds.) Pedagogic Roles of Animations and Simulations in Chemistry Courses. ACS Symposium Series, vol. 1142, pp. 161–179. American Chemical Society, Washington, DC (2013)

42. Cikajlo, I., Potisk, K.P.: Advantages of using 3D virtual reality based training in persons with Parkinson's disease: a parallel study. J. Neuroeng. Rehabil. **16**(1), 1–14 (2019)

43. Davenport, J., Rafferty, A., Yaron, D.: Whether and how authentic contexts using a virtual chemistry lab support learning. J. Chem. Educ. **95**(8), 1250–1259 (2018)

44. Alalwan, N., Cheng, L., Al-Samarraie, H., Yousef, R., Alzahrani, A.I., Sarsam, S.M.: Challenges and prospects of virtual reality and augmented reality utilization among primary school teachers: a developing country perspective. Stud. Educ. Eval. **66**, 100876 (2020)

45. Park, W.D., Jang, S.W., Kim, Y.H., Kim, G.A., Son, W., Kim, Y.S.: A study on cyber sickness reduction by oculo-motor exercise performed immediately prior to viewing virtual reality (VR) content on head mounted display (HMD). Vibroeng. Proc. **14**, 260–264 (2017)

46. Al-Ghareeb, A.Z., Cooper, S.J.: Barriers and enablers to the use of high-fidelity patient simulation manikins in nurse education: an integrative review. Nurse Educ. Today **36**, 281–286 (2016)

47. Fraser, K., Ma, I., Teteris, E., Baxter, H., Wright, B., Mclaughlin, K.: Emotion, cognitive load and learning outcomes during simulation training. Med. Educ. **46**(11), 1055–1062 (2012)

48. Macy, R., Schrader, V.: Pediophobia: a new challenge facing nursing faculty in clinical teaching by simulation. Clin. Simul. Nurs. **4**(3), 89–91 (2008)

49. Parong, J., Mayer, R.E.: Learning science in immersive virtual reality. J. Educ. Psychol. **110**(6), 785–797 (2018)

50. Makransky, G., Terkildsen, T.S., Mayer, R.E.: Adding immersive virtual reality to a science lab simulation causes more presence but less learning. Learn. Instr. **60**, 225–236 (2019)

51. Zhou, X., Tang, L., Lin, D., Han, W.: Virtual & augmented reality for biological microscope in experiment education. Virtual Reality Intell. Hardw. **2**(4), 316–329 (2020)

52. McDonnell, C., O'Connor, C., Seery, M.K.: Developing practical chemistry skills by means of student-driven problem based learning mini-projects. Chem. Educ. Res. Pract. **8**, 130–139 (2007)

53. Cartrette, D.P., Miller, M.L.: Purposeful design of formal laboratory instruction as a springboard to research participation. J. Chem. Educ. **90**, 171–177 (2013)
54. Mio, M.J., Benvenuto, M.A.: The unsafe lab practical. J. Chem. Educ. **98**(1), 243–245 (2021)

A Study on Serious Game Practice to Improve Children's Global Competence

Jingying Wang[1], Jia Li[2(✉)], Qianru Song[3], Xiaomei Ping[1], Dengbo Zhang[4], Qizhong Hu[3], and Shoubao Gao[3(✉)]

[1] Faculty of Education, Beijing Normal University, Beijing 100875, China
[2] College of Chemistry, Central China Normal University, Wuhan 430079, Hubei, China
amberlee1117@163.com
[3] School of Physics and Electronics, Shandong Normal University,
Jinan 250358, Shandong, China
gaoshoubao@sdnu.edu.cn
[4] Department of Education, Southwest University, Chongqing 400715, China

Abstract. With the acceleration of globalization, global competence has become an important competence for children to adapt to the future. In order to enable factoary and middle school students to master certain knowledge and skills, develop and improve their global competence during the learning process, a serious game app called "Global Adventure" is designed to promote children's knowledge, skills, attitudes and values of global competence in the game. The game has the best effect on the improvement of the skills which achieving three-level skills development of "perception"-"conformation"-"production". The development of the knowledge is followed by realizing four-level knowledge development of "conceptualization"-"comprehension"-"application"-"evaluation". The frequency of developing young people's attitudes and values is relatively less, but achieving five-level emotional development of "receiving"-"responding"-"valuing"-"believing"-"behaving". The four games all involve 8–9 domains of the four global competence factors, but the educational value they play is different. The game environment under the cooperative mode improves children's global competence better than the game environment under the single player mode. The audio-visual game mode can further promote the improvement of children's global competence. Global environmental issues play the most significant educational value.

Keywords: Global competence · Serious games · Primary and middle school students

1 Introduction

Since the 21st century, global competence has become an important dimension of the talent competence framework proposed by major international organizations and many countries and regions. The Organization for Economic Co-operation and Development (OECD) has planed to include global competence in the PISA test in 2018 to measure

© Springer Nature Switzerland AG 2021
X. Fang (Ed.): HCII 2021, LNCS 12790, pp. 84–102, 2021.
https://doi.org/10.1007/978-3-030-77414-1_8

the knowledge, skills, attitudes and values of young people on global issues in nearly 80 countries around the world, so as to enable them to prepare for a digitally-connected communities [1]. Global competence is based on the perspective of globalization, and comprehensively considers the cognitive concepts of world members with diverse cultural backgrounds. it aims to cultivate the capacity to analyse global and intercultural issues critically and from multiple perspectives, to understand how cultural differences affect perceptions, judgements, and ideas of self and others, and to engage in open, appropriate and effective interactions with others from different backgrounds on the basis of a shared respect for human dignity [2]. How to help children master certain knowledge and skills before school, develop and improve their global competence in the learning process has become a hot issue in the academic circle. Among them, it is a feasible way to improve students' global competence through serious games increasing children's immersive experience.

Serious games are electronic games which fully integrate educational and entertaining features by taking education as the main purpose and entertainment as a means. Compared with traditional educational methods, serious games are more acceptable and popular, with a broader target audiences. In 2003, the Woodrow Wilson International Scholars Center in Washington launched the "Serious Games Project" supporting serious games to form an organized industry and using cutting-edge entertainment technology to solve problems in multiple fields. Since then, there is a significant integration of serious games and education, and serious game products emerge in endlessly. It can be seen that the use of serious games to improve children's global competence has academic value and practical guidance. This article takes pre-school and low-level primary school students as the research objects, designs serious game APP to promote children's knowledge, skills, attitudes and values of global competence, and monitors the changes of children's global competence levels based on multi-modal data of activity performance in games, so as to explore the influence mechanism of serious games on global competence. Optimize the function of digital game APP in promoting the development of children's global competence and offer evidence-based suggestions for the teaching and management decision-making on global competence.

1.1 Literature Review

In 1993, Schechter [3] put forward the connotation of global competence for the first time. He believes that global competence aims to enable students to acquire global knowledge and skills for employment in a global environment, and develop the ability to appreciate cultural differences and intercultural sensitivity. Olson et al. [4] provides an operative definition of global competence. He believes that students must master enough substantive knowledge of language, culture and world issues, possess perceptual understanding such as open-mindedness, complexity of thinking and perspective consciousness, as well as intercultural communication skills of adaptation, empathy, and intercultural awareness in order to effectively interact in an interdependent world, which gives global competence higher practical guidance value. Hunter et al. [5] further expanded the working definition for the term of global competence which is having an open mind while actively seeking to understand cultural norms and expectations of others, leveraging the gained knowledge to interact, communicate and work effectively outside one's environment. In 2016, the OECD released the "Global Competency For an Inclusive World" report, proposing to conduct a global competence assessment in the 2018 International Student Assessment Project (PISA). This is the first time that global competence has been included in a large international assessment project. The framework integrates the research results of many scholars, gives a deeper and broader meaning to global competence, and forms a global competence assessment framework that includes four factors: knowledge, skills, attitudes, and values (as shown in Fig. 1 below). The framework consists of two layers. The first layer is the four main dimensions of global competence assessment: examining local, global and intercultural issues; understanding and appreciating the perspectives and world views of others; engaging in open, appropriate and effective interactions across cultures; taking actions for collective well-being and sustainable development. The second layer is specific knowledge, skills, attitudes and values that the each dimension builds on. In view of the fact that the global competence framework has measured the status of young people's knowledge, skills, attitudes and values on global issues in nearly 80 countries around the world, and has high authority and global applicability, this article uses this framework as the assessment system. Global competence is defined as the knowledge, skills, attitudes, and values that citizens in the context of globalization have to master when meeting with the opportunities and challenges brought about by globalization, and the practical actions putting these knowledge, skills, attitudes and values into reality (Table 1).

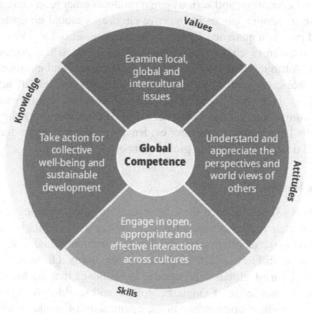

Fig. 1. Global competence framework

Table 1. Factors and domains of global competence

Factor	Domain	Content
Knowledge	Culture and intercultural relations	Awareness of one's own cultural identity; Understand the similarities and differences between different cultures; Protection of cultural differences and diversity; Identify a variety of complex identities
	Socio-economic development and interdependence	Studying development patterns in different regions of the world; Social and economic interdependence and linkages; Analysis of various forms of globalization issues
	Environmental sustainability	Promoting and supporting environmentally sustainable development; Complex systems and policies surrounding the demand and use of natural resources
	Global institutions, conflict and human rights	The establishment of global institutions such as the United Nations; Global governance in a world of highly unbalanced power relations; Causes and solutions of conflicts between States, ethnic or social groups; The positive role, responsibility and power of youth in society
Skills	Information retrieval and reasoning ability	Obtaining and inferring information from multiple sources; Determine information needs independently and select information sources; Check for information connections and discrepancies; Evaluate the value, validity, and reliability of information

(*continued*)

Table 1. (*continued*)

Factor	Domain	Content
	Intercultural communication skills	Express your ideas clearly and confidently; Respecting different expectations, views and needs, and respecting differences; Master multiple languages, check the meaning of words and phrases; Be an active listener; Be an effective speaker, make a point, persuade others, etc.
	Ability to analyze problems from multiple perspectives	Put yourself in the shoes of others and recognize and accept often conflicting points of view; Understanding the interconnection of different viewpoints; Understand the differences between groups, etc
	Conflict resolution ability	Analyze key issues, needs and benefits; To identify the causes of the conflict and the perspectives of the parties to the conflict; Identify areas of agreement and disagreement; Reconstruct conflicts; Manage the emotions of oneself and others; Consider needs and goals, identify possible compromise conditions, etc.
	Ability to adapt	Adapt to the new cultural environment and deal with culture shock; Building long-term relationships with people from other cultures in a constantly changing environment
Attitude	Open	Be sensitive, curious, and willing to communicate and understand other people and other views of the world; Accept and actively seek opportunities for intercultural communication; Other cultural points of view, language, behavior habits; Equal contact, cooperation and interaction

(*continued*)

Table 1. (*continued*)

Factor	Domain	Content
	Respect cultural differences	The dignity of all people and their right to choose their own affiliations, beliefs, opinions or practices is inalienable; Do not ignore cultural differences, do not need to adopt other people's beliefs; Respect does not violate principles; Distinguish between respect and tolerance, etc
	The global consciousness	Caring for others, moral responsibility; Care for future generations, protect the environment; Critical awareness of other people's viewpoints; Face up to differences and strive to create space for different lifestyles
Values	The dignity of the person	Refusing inhuman treatment, humiliation or indignity; Ensure self-selection, self-satisfaction, and self-actualization; To protect the identity of the group, to protect the culture; To meet the basic needs of everyone to create conditions, etc.
	Cultural diversity	A positive attitude towards cultural diversity; Regard cultural diversity as a social asset and ideal goal for the future; Take practical actions to protect the diversity of cultural heritage, etc.

Extant studies have explored influencing factors including the subject category, gender, learning motivation, foreign language level, contact style and personality characteristics of the individual [6]. It also includes family parenting styles, maternal depression [7], the type of school, national curriculum and international education [8]. In addition, social factors such as geography, intercultural exchanges, teacher professional standards, immigration, and mass media also have a certain impact on global competence [9].

It has been recognized by the academic community that intercultural communication can promote the global competence of students [6, 10, 11]. OECD [1] further pointed out that intercultural communication can promote global attitudes and skills, and intercultural exchange experience can enhance students' self-confidence when facing intercultural issues and strengthen the willingness to contact and learn foreign cultures. Meng et al. [6] found that students from Beijing reported higher global competence than students from Nanjing and Changchun, and the important reasons are the differences in the opportunities for intercultural exchange activities provided by universities in different regions. The study by Kang et al. [11] found that early exposure to global mass media will have a negative impact on college students' intercultural communication skills and knowledge. A large-scale immigration environment is conducive to the improvement of intercultural communication skills, but has a negative impact on global attitude. Early exposure to the global mass media will cause students to realize the differences between themselves and foreign cultures in advance, and reduce their comfort in communicating with foreigners, which will have a negative impact on the global competence of college students [5].

Serious games originated in the United States. In 2002, the U.S. Army's "U.S. Army" became the world's first well-designed and successfully operated serious game, which attracted widespread public attention and made the academic community began to realize the huge potential of video games, thus serious games ushering in a good development prospect. Throughout the entire development process, serious games mainly focus on the design or application from psychology, pedagogy, or purely technical perspectives. Granic et al. [12] proposed the influence of games on the internal psychological mechanism of individuals from the perspective of psychology, which proved the benefits of games. The effects of games on psychology are mainly focused on four main domains: cognitive (such as attention) and motivational (such as re-adaptation when facing failure), emotional (e.g. emotional management) and social (e.g. pro-social behavior), which provide a theoretical basis for studying the influence mechanism of serious games on people's psychology. Arnab et al. [13] abstracted from literature on game studies and learning theories and proposed the Learning Mechanics-Game Mechanics (LM-GM) model which includes a set of pre-defined game mechanics and pedagogical factors. This model became the important theoretical basis of the later serious game design and evaluation tools, which makes up for the lack of integration of "pedagogy" and "gameplay" principles in game design. *The Self-explanation and digital games: Adaptively increasing abstraction* published by Clark et al. [14] focused on the analysis of the self-explanation functionality, which can be interpreted as the content-related expression of students in learning activities and effectively support learning in the game environment, providing technical and theoretical support for using games for ability development and assessment. It can be seen that using serious games to promote students' abilities and literacy has become a mature technology, and the "pedagogical" and "entertainment" features of serious games have reached a dynamic balance. However, although serious games are proven to serve as educational tools, there is a lack of reliable, automated and repeatable methodologies that measure their effectiveness: What do players know after playing serious games? Do they learn from them? [15] Existing research shows that the vast majority of serious games are assessed by using questionnaires. This summative methodology of accessing is one-sided and cannot well measure learning outcomes. It can be seen that the assessment of the learning outcomes in serious games should not ignore the formative evaluation. Because the game itself is carried out through network equipment, a large number of users' input and game feedback behaviors occur in this process which generated a wealth of interaction data. Through the analysis of interaction data during the game, we can explore how users play the game and understand how they learn in games. Serious game evaluation should focus on multiple results, such as usability, participation, and motivation. In order to solve this problem, this article has developed a game product titled "Global Adventure", in which embeds various types of games such as action, role-playing, adventure, and simulation. This game can not only achieve the educational functions such as "understanding global and intercultural issues, engaging in open, appropriate and effective interactions with others from different backgrounds on the basis of a shared respect for human dignity, understanding and appreciating different cultures and values of the own country and foreign countries, thinking about issues with a global mindset, and respecting human dignity and cultural differences". Moreover, it can provide immediate feedback and real-time monitoring during the game process, using the multi-modal data collected during the experiment to monitor the changes of global knowledge, skills, emotions, and values. Text analysis of interview and audio materials, learning analysis of multi-modal data, model construction and other methods are used to explore the impact mechanism of serious games on global competence.

2 Method

2.1 Design Concept

On the basis of criticizing and inheriting Bloom's taxonomy of educational objectives, American scholar Hauenstein [16] put forward Hauenstein's taxonomy of educational objectives based on constructivism. It presents the integrity of human behavior, reflects the fact that individuals are learning as a whole individual, and highlights the process. It divides all educational objectives into four domains: cognitive, affective, psychomotor and behavioral. Each domain reduces 5 levels of educational objectives, and each level of educational objectives is divided into 2 to 4 subcategories, as shown in Table 2. The cognitive domain is on the development process of knowledge and mental abilities and skills; the affective domain is about the influence of emotions, values and beliefs on individual behavior; the psychomotor domain is about to develop movements, abilities and skills of the body; the behavioral domain is a composite domain that integrates cognitive, affective and psychomotor domains as a unified composite one. Hauenstein's taxonomy of educational objectives provides a guidance framework for serious games design to improve global competence, and provides theoretical support to use diversified evaluation methods to access the development of children's global competence during the game.

The viewpoint of embodied cognition holds that cognitive processes are deeply rooted in the body's interactions with the world: (1) cognition is situated; (2) cognition is time-pressured; (3) we off-load cognitive work onto the environment; (4) the environment is part of the cognitive system; (5) cognition is for action; (6) offline cognition is body based [17]. Therefore, in the learning of global competence, it is necessary to provide clear task goals, context, real-time interaction between the body and environment, etc.

The American psychotherapist Knud Illeris developed the concept of "meaningful learning", which includes "a change in the self as a learning context" and "the whole

Table 2. The theoretical framework of Hauenstein's taxonomy of educational objectives

domain / level	cognitive domain	affective domain	psychomotor domain	behavioral domain
1.0	Conceptualization identification/definition/ generalization	Receiving awareness/willingness/ attentiveness	Perception sensation/recognition/ observation/predisposition	Acquisition receiving/perception/ conceptualization
2.0	Comprehension translation/explanation/ extrapolation	Responding acquiescing/complying/ assessing	Simulation activation/imitation/ coordination	Assimilation responding/comprehension/simulation
3.0	Application clarification/solution	Valuing accept/preferring/confirm	Conformation integration/standardization	Adaptation valuing/application/ conformation
4.0	Evaluation analysis/qualification	Believing trusting/committing	Production maintenance/accommodation	Performance believing/evaluation/ production
5.0	Synthesis hypothesis/resolution	Behaving Demonstrating/modifying	Mastery origination/perfection	Aspiration behaving/synthesis/ mastery

individual, including his emotions and cognition, is involved in the learning". Only when a person faces a situation or challenge beyond what he can handle and cannot avoid it, but still have to overcome it to move forward, will he invest in meaningful learning [18]. Therefore, in the cultivation of global competence, understanding the similarities and differences between different cultures, recognizing and understanding the differences between different viewpoints and groups require constantly creating multicultural contexts to trigger and realize the "meaningful learning" of global competence.

Under the guidance of the theoretical framework of Hauenstein's taxonomy of educational objectives, embodied cognitive theory and meaningful learning theory, the serious game "Global Adventure" is designed based on real, global, and intercultural issues, uses dialogues, videos, etc. as material presentation methods, and includes four parts: "Snake Battle", "You Say One, I Say Two", "First Meet" and "Animals Go Home". Children from a first-person perspective, participate in the game according to the audio-visual prompts on the game interface and in accordance with the rules of the game, feel and experience global or intercultural issues in real situations, and improve children's ability to analyse global and intercultural issues critically and from multiple perspectives, to understand how cultural differences affect perceptions, judgements, and ideas of self and others, and to engage in open, appropriate and effective interactions with others from different backgrounds on the basis of a shared respect for human dignity.

2.2 The Snake Battle

Taking the dimension of "analyzing local, global and cultural issues" as the core concept of game design, the serious role-playing intelligence test game-"Snake Battle" was designed. The corona-virus pandemic is sweeping the world. The anti-virus measures adopted by countries and the effects are global and intercultural issues that have attracted much attention. Taking the corona-virus pandemic as the starting point, the game demonstrated in the form of "snakes eating apples" to test basic knowledge of corona-virus, precautions for epidemic prevention, the characteristics of prevention policies of different countries, and the nature of the country, political systems, governance models, and ideologies reflected.

A series of question scenarios are set up in the game and each scenario contains a question. The correct answer corresponds to a nutritious apple, and the wrong answer corresponds to a poisoned apple, as shown in Fig. 2. In the game, the child becomes a little greedy snake. By eating the nutritious apples scattered in the scene, the body of snake grows longer and longer. If it accidentally eats poisoned apples, the game ends. The length of the little snake's body will be used to judge the children's ability to analyze local, global, and intercultural issues.

Through the process of playing the game, in terms of the knowledge, children understand the causes of the various impacts that corona-virus pandemic made on different countries, objectively examine the anti-COVID policies of different countries, infer the cultural characteristics of each country, analyze the impact of economic development on anti-COVID measures, evaluate the macro-control role of the WHO and other national institutions in the pandemic, and realize the advanced learning from "comprehension" to "evaluation". In terms of skills, children read the information presented in the problem scene, identify key information, analyze and integrate relevant information of different countries, judge the differences in political systems, governance models, and ideologies between countries, and realize advanced learning from "perception" to "conformation". In terms of attitude, based on the understanding of basic information such as cultural characteristics, ideologies and political systems of different countries, children tolerantly treat and evaluate the anti-COVID measures of different countries and the choices made by individuals based on ethnic beliefs and dignity. In terms of values, on the basis of understanding the origins of different COVID-19 situations appeared in different countries, children can objectively evaluate the impact of policies that different countries made on human dignity, and achieve advanced emotional learning from "receiving" to "responding".

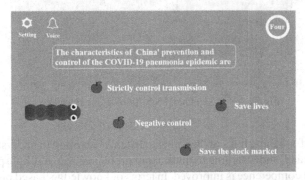

Fig. 2. "Snake Battle" game interface

2.3 You Say One, I Say Two

Taking the dimension of "understanding and appreciating viewpoints and worldviews of others" as the core concept of game design, the role-playing parent-child serious games-"You Say One, I Say Two" was designed. In order to better realize the effective communication and collision between different viewpoints, the game is developed in the form of parent-child interaction. Parents are the participants and instructors of children in the game. On the one hand, it can enhance the fun of the game through the interaction between parents and children; on the other hand, it can reduce the psychological burden and pressure so that children can devote themselves to games; at the same time, the game can also help parents to take more targeted measures to carry out family education and realize the expansion and extension of the educational value of serious games.

According to the characteristics of children's cognitive development levels at different stages of education, scenarios with gradients of difficulty are designed. Parents choose the corresponding section according to their children's grade, education level and other aspects. After selecting the corresponding section, the system will randomly select the corresponding situation from the question bank of the section. The situation type involves the content in life, technology, history, frontier and other fields. After the system randomly distributes scenarios according to the selected section, the participants play the game according to the game rules and tasks displayed on the interface. In the process of the four links, parents give immediate feedback on the children's comments, and decide whether to enter the next link according to the quality of children's comments, and complete the four links in turn (Fig. 3).

Fig. 3. "You Say One, I Say Two" game interface

Through the four game links of "learning to listen", "learning to understand", "learning to communicate" and "learning to think about problems from multiple perspectives", children's global competence is improved. In terms of knowledge, based on the objective understanding of different viewpoints, children could fully understand the connotation of "environmental sustainability" and "social interdependence" of the global knowledge, actively play their active role in society, and make their own contribution to the solution of globalization issues, so that realize the advanced learning from "comprehension" to "application". In terms of skills, children start from their own experience and cognition, through effectively communicating with others and making scientific reviews based on different perspectives, continuously strengthen the global awareness and at the same time cultivate them to form a higher level of intercultural communication ability to provide solutions to global problems, achieving the advanced learning from "conformation" to "production". In terms of attitude, based on the contextual materials involved in globalization issues on the viewing and listening interface, children make a comprehensive collection of the characters and opinions involved in the contextual materials, empathize with others in an attitude of openness and respect for different cultural differences, thereby comment on the views of others from a more objective perspective, and at the same time put forward their own views, achieving the advanced emotional learning from "responding" to "valuing". Finally, in terms of value, through the three processes of listening to others' opinions, understanding the rationality of others' opinions, and developing effective communication with others, children can fully consider the influence of different opinions on human dignity when communicating with others or encountering similar situations, as well as constantly question and deepen their own views, so as to make more comprehensive and mature comments.

2.4 First Meet

Taking the dimension of "engaging in open, appropriate and effective interaction with people from different cultural backgrounds" as the core concept of game design, the serious game "First Meet" was designed. In the game, people from different cultural backgrounds conduct contextual conversations and choose the correct behaviors. Although there are cultural differences, it can not stop achieving mutual communication, and also can not stop choosing cultural behaviors which respect each other more.

The first step of the game is to choose characters from different countries, such as Japan, Arabia, Germany and South Korea.The second step is to enter the situation. For example, the situation in the following picture is the first time a Japanese and an Arab meet, game players are allowed to choose their own way of greeting each other, which may lead to embarrassing scenes of the first meeting and causing cognitive conflicts in intercultural communication. The bubble box in the game will prompt the more appropriate communication way for the people when meeting for the first time (Fig. 4).

In terms of knowledge, the game involves people from different cultural backgrounds to make contextual exchanges, which is intended to let players understand the similarities and differences between different cultures, choose behaviors corresponding to cultural backgrounds, and achieve the advanced learning from "conceptualization" to "evaluation". In terms of skills, players treat and analyze different behaviors under different cultural backgrounds from multiple perspectives, so that they could understand and accept cultural differences and quickly adapt to the collisions between different cultures in the new environment, realizing the advanced learning from "conformation" to "production". In terms of attitude, players could choose to actively communicate with people from different cultural backgrounds and respect cultural differences. In terms of values, those who accept cultural diversity will enhance the tolerance of culture and realize the advanced emotional learning from "receiving" to "believing".

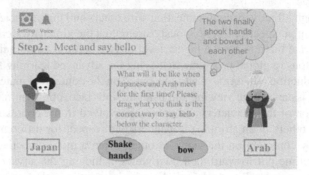

Fig. 4. "First Meet" game interface

2.5 Animals Go Home

Taking the "action for collective well-being and sustainable development" dimension as the core concept of game design, the serious game "Animals Go Home" was designed. The global ecological environment is closely related to human well-being. The environmental problems of different countries and regions are universal and common in nature. It has become a consensus to explore and strengthen global environmental protection. This game uses common environmental problems as the carrier, designs multiple animal images, and creates different scenarios related to ecological and environmental issues. Using the form of small animals finding new homes in the game tests the comprehension level of middle school students on major environmental issues the world is facing, including the causes, hazards and preventive measures.

In the game, the first step is to select animals such as polar bears, salmons, swallows, and then the system presents different ecological and environmental problems according to the choices. Students need to answer all the questions correctly before the animals can successfully reach their new homes. Figure 5 shows the game that polar bear finds iceberg. Global warming makes the Arctic sea ice gradually recede. Polar bears need to face a serious survival crisis. In order to reach distant glaciers, they need to choose safe floating ice according to 5 issues related to global warming. If they choose the wrong one, the floating ice will melt and the game is over.

This game uses ecological and environmental issues as a carrier, and mainly examines the ability of students to take actions for collective well-being and sustainable development. In terms of knowledge, students learn about global institutions related to environmental protection, analyze the main environmental problems the world is facing, answer the causes and protection measures of environmental problems, and realize the advanced learning from "conceptualization" to "evaluation". In terms of skills, because each type of game situation presents the dilemma faced by animals, students can identify the ecological and environmental problems behind them from the animal's perspective and choose universal environmental protection policy based on the economic, political, and cultural characteristics of each country and according to the actual needs, realizing the advanced learning from "perception" to "production". In terms of attitude, students develop global awareness in the process of playing the game, believe that their own behavior plays an important role in environmental protection, and can objectively view

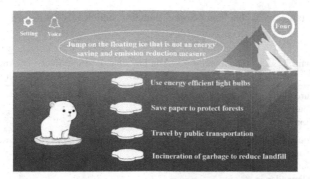

Fig. 5. "Polar Bear Finds Iceberg" game interface

the impact of different cultures on the environment. In terms of values, students have a deep understanding of the obstacles in various ecological and environmental issues to the protection and inheritance of culture, and can actively take actions to maintain the diversity of cultural heritage, achieving the advanced emotional learning from "receiving" to "behaving".

3 Results

The following four serious games are designed according to the four dimensions of global competence: analyzing local, global and intercultural issues-Snake Battle; understanding and appreciating viewpoints and worldviews of others-You Say One, I Say Two; engaging in open, appropriate and effective interaction with people from different cultural backgrounds-First Meet; action for collective well-being and sustainable development-Animals Go Home. The theoretical framework of global competence mainly includes four factors—knowledge, skills, attitudes and values, and 14 domain indicators. The four factors are divided into five advanced levels with reference to Hauenstein's taxonomy of educational objectives. In order to understand the level of each factor and domain under this framework, the content of the four designed serious games was encoded as follows.

According to Table 3 and Fig. 6, the serious game "Global Adventure" has a significant effect on improving the global competence of young people, especially best on the improvement of the skills which achieving three-level skill development of "perception"-"conformation"-"production". The second is the development of the knowledge, achieving the four-level development of "conceptualization"-"comprehension"-"application"-"evaluation". The frequency of cultivating young people's attitudes and values is relatively less, but achieving the five-level emotional development of "receiving"-"responding"-"valuing"-"believing"-"behaving". It is worth noting that the development level of information retrieval and reasoning abilities in the four serious games is relatively low, mainly at the "perception" level. The frequency of adaptability is designed less, with only one design at "conformation" level, which needs to be further improved.

According to Table 3 and Fig. 7, the four games all involve 8–9 domains of the four factors of global competence, but the educational value they play is different: the game "Snake Battle" highlights the knowledge of global competence; The game "You Say

Table 3. Coding table of global competence domains and levels contained in the "Global Adventure"

Factor	Domain	The Snake Battle	You Say One, I Say Two	First Meet	Animals Go Home
Knowledge	Culture and intercultural relations	Comprehension	–	Evaluation	–
	Socioeconomic development and interdependence	Evaluation	Comprehension	–	Evaluation
	Environmental sustainability	–	Comprehension	–	Application
	Global institutions, conflict and human rights	Evaluation	Application	–	Conceptualization
Skills	Information retrieval and reasoning ability	Perception	–	–	Perception
	Intercultural communication	–	Production	Conformation	–
	Ability to analyze problems from multiple perspectives	Conformation	Production	Production	–
	Conflict resolution ability	–	Conformation	–	Production
	Ability to adapt	–	–	Conformation	–
Attitudes	Open	Receiving	–	Valuing	–
	Respect cultural differences	Responding	Responding	Responding	Receiving
	The global consciousness	–	Valuing	–	Believing
Values	The dignity of the person	Responding	Responding	Receiving	–
	Cultural diversity	–	–	Believing	Behaving

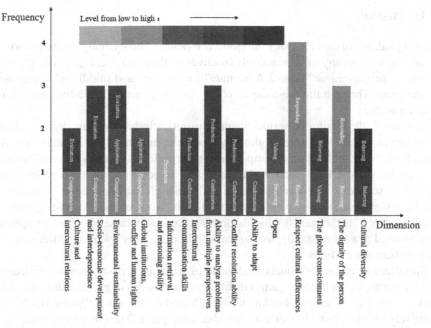

Fig. 6. The level statistics chart of the "Global Adventure" in enhancing 14 domains of global competence

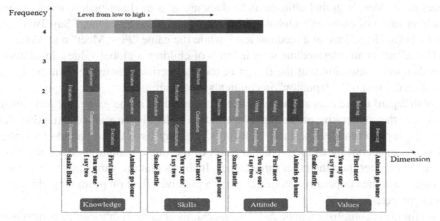

Fig. 7. The level statistical chart of the "Global Adventure" in enhancing the four factors of global competence

One, I Say Two" is more prominent in the improvement of young people's global skills, and also better in the attitude and knowledge; the "First Meet" game has a better role in young people's global skills and values; the game "Animals Go Home" plays a more balanced role in enhancing the knowledge, skills, attitudes and values of young people's global competence.

4 Discussion

With the guidance of experts, using the global competence theory analysis framework and Hauenstein's taxonomy of educational objectives as the theoretical guidance for game design, the serious game "Global Adventure" for primary and middle school students was designed. Through the pre-analysis of the serious game APP, the following points are summarized:

In general, the design of serious games theoretically has the function of promoting the development of children's global competence, and the effect is better. The four games have the best effect on the improvement of children's global skills and maintain at a high level, especially excel in the "analyzing issues from multiple perspectives" dimension; secondly, the development of children's global knowledge is also maintained at a high level, among which the promotion of "socioeconomic development and interdependence" is the best; finally, children's attitude and value of global competence are developed at a moderate degree, so that children are fully aware of differences and diversity between cultures.

Specifically, as for the educational value of the four serious games, children are differently affected by the four games in different dimensions of global competence.The development of children's global knowledge affected by the game "Snake Battle" is at a relatively high level and higher than the other three game. The other three games have a medium-level impact on global competence; the game "You Say One, I Say Two" improves children's global skills best, followed by the "First Meet" game, but the other two games do not have significant improvement in this factor; the effects of the four games on children's global attitude and values are at a medium or low level, among which, in terms of children's global attitude, the game "You Say One, I Say Two" and "Animals Go Home" are at a medium level, while the game "First Meet" and "Animals Go Home" are at an intermediate level in terms of children's global values. In addition, it needs special attention that the design of the four serious games seldom exerts the educational effect of "adaptation" in children's global attitude.

With regard to the educational effectiveness embodied in the game, the game environment in the cooperative mode improves children's global competence better than that in the single player mode. The game "You Say One, I Say Two" uses a parent-child interaction mode, according to the predicted result of the implementation effect, the score of which is higher than the other three games. It shows that the game environment and atmosphere in the cooperative mode can plays a positive effect on promoting children's global competence.

As for the accomplishment of various dimensions of global competence corresponding to the context presentation, the game mode that combines audio and video can promote children's global competence significantly. In the game of "You Say One, I Say Two", the video and audio settings increase the players' immersion in the game, which is conducive to improving the quality of interaction between game players and the game, so that the game itself can give full play to its educational effects. The predictive analysis results can further explain that improving the players' gaming experience by using diversified methods can promote the improvement of children's global competence.

As regards the educational value exerted by the characteristics of the context itself, the educational value exerted by global environmental issues is the most significant. In the context settings of the four games, the contexts set in "You Say One, I Say Two" and the "Animals Go Home" are based on current environmental issues, aiming to strengthen children's related abilities of global competence through improving children's perception and awareness of intercultural and global issues.

5   Limitation

Although the serious game APP has been rigorously designed by experts and researchers, there are still some shortcomings in the specific operation and promotion of applications. First, the influence of factors such as children's culture and ethnicity on the results was not considered. The research only designed games for students of Han nationality in the Chinese background, and did not consider how children from Chinese ethnic minorities or other countries would perform in games. It will be a challenging but meaningful work for future research to take the culture of each country all round into consideration to improve and perfect the game. Secondly, it has not designed and developed different game interfaces and contents suitable for children of different genders. From the global competence report, it can be seen that girls all outperformed boys in the comprehension of global issues, receiving foreign cultures, interest in foreign cultures, awareness of intercultural communication, the level of foreign language skills and the number of foreign languages they master. While boys are more capable of taking actions than girls. In the future, the serious game APP can be designed for children of different genders to achieve personalized education; in addition, except for the serious game "You Say One, I Say Two" which is designed in the form of parent-child interaction, the other three games are for single-player participation. The state of participation in the game and the performance that children participate in the form of peer participation or teacher-student participation need to analyze further. Finally, whether the conclusions reached through qualitative analysis are scientific and whether they have promotion value need to be verified by more empirical data. When conducting empirical research, it is also necessary to consider the impact of the participants' prior knowledge and experience, the length of time they participate in the game, the presented form and other factors on the experimental results.

Funding. National Natural Science Foundation of China (72074031) and the Key Project of Hubei Education Science Planning (2020GA011).

References

1. PISA 2018 Results (Volume VI): Are students ready to thrive in an interconnected world? PISA, OECD Publishing, Paris. https://doi.org/10.1787/d5f68679-en. Accessed 07 Feb 2021
2. Guillén-Nieto, V., Aleson-Carbonell, M.: Serious games and learning effectiveness: the case of It's a deal! Comput. Educ. **58**(1), 435–448 (2012)
3. Schechter, M.: Internationalizing the university and building bridges across disciplines. In: Cavusgil, S.T. (ed.) Internationalizing Business Education: Meeting the Challenge, pp.129–140. Michigan State University Press, Lansing (1993)
4. Olson, C.L., Kroeger, K.R.: Global competency and intercultural sensitivity. J. Stud. Int. Educ. **5**(2), 116–137 (2001)

5. Hunter, B., White, G.P., Godbey, G.C.: What does it mean to be globally competent. J. Stud. Int. Educ. **10**(3), 267–285 (2006)
6. Meng, Q., Zhu, C., Cao, C.: An exploratory study of Chinese university undergraduates' global competence: effects of internationalisation at home and motivation. High. Educ. Q. **71**(2), 159–181 (2017)
7. Moody, C.T., Rodas, N.V., Norona, A.N.: Early childhood predictors of global competence in adolescence for youth with typical development or intellectual disability. Res. Dev. Disabil. **94**, 1–13 (2019)
8. Kedia, B.L., Englis, P.D.: Transforming business education to produce global managers. Bus. Horiz. **54**(4), 325–331 (2011)
9. The OECD PISA Global Competence Framework–Preparing our youth for an inclusive and sustainable world. http://www.oecd.org/pisa/Handbook-PISA-2018-Global-Competence. pdf?utm_content=buffer396eb&utm_medium=social&utm_source=twitter.com&utm_cam paign=buffer. Accessed 07 Feb 2021
10. Semaan, G., Yamazaki, K.: The relationship between global competence and language learning motivation: an empirical study in critical language classrooms. Foreign Lang. Ann. **48**(3), 511–520 (2015)
11. Kang, J.H., Kim, S.Y., Jang, S.: Can college students' global competence be enhanced in the classroom? The impact of cross- and inter-cultural online projects. Innov. Educ. Teach. Int. **55**(6), 683–693 (2018)
12. Granic, I., Lobel, A., Engels, R.C.M.E.: The benefits of playing video games. Am. Psychol. **69**(1), 66–78 (2014)
13. Arnab, S.S., et al.: Mapping learning and game mechanics for serious games analysis. Br. J. Edu. Technol. **46**(2), 391–411 (2015)
14. Clark, D.B., Virk, S.S., Barnes, J., Adams, D.M.: Self-explanation and digital games. Comput. Educ. **103**, 28–43 (2016)
15. Serrano-Laguna, Á., Manero, B., Freire, M., Fernández-Manjón, B.: A methodology for assessing the effectiveness of serious games and for inferring player learning outcomes. Multimedi. Tools Appl. **77**(2), 2849–2871 (2017). https://doi.org/10.1007/s11042-017-4467-6
16. Hauenstein, A.D.: A Conceptual Framework for Educational Objectives: A Holistic Approach to Traditional Taxonomies. University Press of America, Lanham (1998)
17. Wilson, M.: Six views of embodied cognition. Psychon. Bull. Rev. **9**(4), 625–636 (2002)
18. Illeris, K.: How We Learn: Learning and Non-learning in School and Beyond, pp. 45–46. Routledge, London (2007)

JomGames: Creating a Motivating Learning Environment

W. L. WilliamCheng[1], P. S. JosephNg[1(✉)], H. C. Eaw[2], and K. Y. Phan[3]

[1] Institution of Computer Science and Digital Innovation, UCSI University, UCSI Heights, 56000 Cheras, Kuala Lumpur, Malaysia
1001850428@student.ucsiuniversity.edu.my,
josephng@ucsiuniversity.edu.my
[2] Faculty of Business and Management, UCSI University, UCSI Heights, 56000 Cheras, Kuala Lumpur, Malaysia
eawhc@ucsiuniversity.edu.my
[3] Faculty of Information and Communication Technology, Universiti Tunku Abdul Rahman, Kampar, Perak, Malaysia
kyphan@utar.edu.my

Abstract. Games have played an impactful life in our current generation brimming with technological advancement. Not only has it become the main source of entertainment for people to enjoy, but it has also transitioned to becoming a learning experience for others. With our current repetitive standards and methods of teaching and learning in schools, the mind of many students has dulled their creativities as well as developing the extrinsic motivation to study at all. However, the implementation of game learning can be developed into modern-day teaching and be used as a tool for students to grasp their potentials and be motivated to learn level more using games. From the mix mode research conducted, many tertiary students would rather replace their conventional studying methods with a game learning experience. The player will be able to understand, develop listening skills and verbal communication skills towards other people to understand when it is necessary to be assertive in an environment. Moreover, this game will tackle the understanding of real-life decision-making skills that mimic real-life situations for players to adapt to. With that said, JomGear Grind Games aims to help students learn various skills such as creative thinking and interpersonal skills.

Keywords: Creative problem-solving · Gamification · Game learning · Videogames · Games · Strategic problem solving · Interpersonal skill

1 The Behavioural Effects of Games on Students

The technological world has advanced so far beyond what people have comprehended. This has created a surge of innovations within the minds of many in this technological time [1]. These advancements have improved social media platforms that allow for messaging services for worldwide use to get information from various places in the world. For example, Instagram or Twitter would be a famous social media platform [2].

© Springer Nature Switzerland AG 2021
X. Fang (Ed.): HCII 2021, LNCS 12790, pp. 103–112, 2021.
https://doi.org/10.1007/978-3-030-77414-1_9

Adolescents and children who are still in school use this as a place of talking to new people and sharing their stories and info online. However, they have to overuse these social media platforms and have created a concern towards the media and parents for this addiction. This has become a problem to the world as these people are usually using this as a type of procrastination over their duties when the duties have been given and the responsibilities are ignored [3].

Having a creative mind that can also think strategically within a university student mind nowadays is no easy feat [4]. Skills such as having a mind to think outside the box and also have a strategic mind are sought out in workplaces and has become well-needed skills to have [5]. Within refinement of the skills, research and development will be able to have a greater impact on society and bring forth new modes of innovations from many young minds [6]. Moreover, talking with others is an essential skill to have when working with a group or with other people, with interpersonal skills coming into the mind [7]. Working together with greater efficiency is the first step in the success of a project or goal as it creates a bond and trustful relationship amongst the team [8]. Many university students come off as shy and socially awkward which deters to social and communication skills. Traumatic events or lack of human interaction and love during their early life could be a major factor in this [9]. Almost all student levels from primary to tertiary education have played games and can be hooked into getting their sole attention in understanding the concept of sand outcomes of the games [10]. It is also a fact that not only boys play video games, but girls equally do it as well which shows that there is a gender variety of video game players [11].

Self-efficacy can also be better leant and developed from video games in our current modern era as well as researched from studies [12]. It is also said that video games how developed more violent tendencies from the player due to negative habits and outcomes found within the game that tampers with the real-life behaviours of the young people that have tread a problem in the society of gaming [13, 14]. Be that as it may, positivity can be given from video games as well that helps benefit and give motivations to the player in developing interests within the game's theme and world [15].

2 Legacy and Related Works of Game Learning and Gamification

There are elements within a game which can provide a sense of learning experience and enjoyment towards gamer and it is known as gamification [16]. Conventional studying methods towards students nowadays are not going to work as they do feel enjoyment in using a textbook method to learn the outcomes of a subject and their respective skills as it may feel boring especially when technology can play a big role [17]. Because of this, university students only learn and study for a test for the sake of getting over with it and progressing in their course, this is where gamification helps in providing an intrinsic motivation to study and learn a certain course [18]. This brings forth many avenues for video games to become a platform for learning where the elements of gamification play a vital role in greater developing the motivation for the university student to learn skills [19]. User engagement can also be obtained in the form of prizes and game achievements which boosts the players desired outcome towards the goal [20]. From a study, heuristics design within the game's levels has brought forward greater refine towards the algorithm of gamification to this day [21] as shown in Table 1.

Table 1. Similar gaming application comparisons table

Gaming characteristics and features	Gear grind games	Logic master	Logical test	Skills
Creativity	/	/	/	–
Design	/	/	/	/
Strategic skill	/	/	/	/
Interactive quests	/	–	–	–
Achievements	/	–	–	–
Games	/	–	/	/
scoreboards	/	–	/	–
Level Building	/	/	/	/
tasks system	/	–	–	–
Communication and dialogue	/	–	–	–

Problem Statement, Question and Objective

The certain characteristics and features of the game will emphasize the development of interpersonal, creative and strategic problem-solving skills in a game learning setting and using gamification elements to enhance the experience to the students. From the study, heuristics design within the game's levels has brought forward greater refine towards the algorithm of gamification to this day [21–24] as shown in Table 1.

Table 2. Research questions

RQ1: Can university students grasp the understanding of creative and strategic problem solving from video games?
RQ2: Can interpersonal skills be greatly developed with the help of game learning and gamification?
RQ3: Can game learning and gamification replace the traditional studying methods in universities and provide students with intrinsic motivation to learn from games?

The questions from Table 2 will be defined and determined from the scope of the research. The Scope of the project will mainly be university students of any field related using interpersonal, creative, and strategic problem-solving skills. The age range should be around 17–24 for typical university student ages and will take place in selected universities like Monash University, Sunway University, UCSI University, University Malaya, Asia pacific University and Tunku Abdul Rahman University College. The research questions will be answered by the research objectives below in Table 3.

Figure 1 shows the highlighted key points of the research which are displayed within the research model to further explain the game design aspect of the game, the software required for the game will be done by the Godot Game Engine with the usage of the Microsoft visual studio for the C# language incorporation and coding design. The main game art will be mainly done with the inspiration of pixel art games such as Games like

Table 3. Research objectives

RO1: To create a video game that emphasized the values of creative and strategic problem-solving skills.
RO2: To help university students to develop better interpersonal skills to make friends and increase teamwork via gamification.
RO3: Using game learning and gamification to intrinsically make students motivated to study traditional studying methods

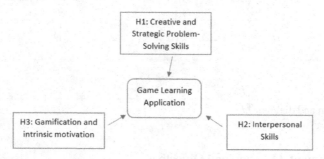

Fig. 1. Hypothesis research model

Fire Emblem and Undertale for the retro feel of the game overall. Figma will be greatly used to test the prototyping for the game where the outline will be copied and enhance when the game undergoes user interface and world design. The game will allow the development of key skills within the research which are interpersonal skills, creative and strategic problem-solving skills within the game application to further enhance students ability to communicate and to adapt to new situations creatively while also providing an intrinsic motivation for them to learn said skills.

3 Methodology

This research will be applying the usage of mixed-mode research of surveys and interviews to gain both qualitative and quantitative data. From Fig. 2 below, a mixed-mode method of surveys and interviews will be handed off to university students that like games and are interest in gamification to obtain both qualitative and quantitative data collections. A trial will be done with 5 survey respondents and 3 interview respondents. This is to check the efficiency of questions and check for amendments if questions are not understandable or appropriate. Random students will be selected for the research to ensure the data is not faked and the data set is qualitative.

4 Results and Findings

From the results that have been recorded from the research, the improvement of games on the creative and strategic problem solving of university students has been widely agreed on in both the preliminary and technical data collection.

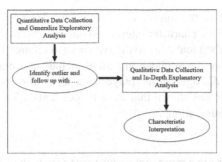

Fig. 2. Sequential design [25–37]

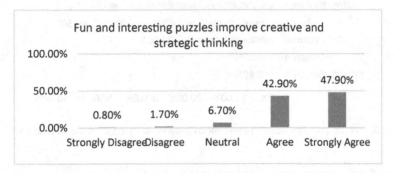

Fig. 3. Post-test results of fun puzzles improve creative & strategic thinking.

From Fig. 3, a lot of the responses showed an agreement that games can help university students improve upon their creative and strategic problem-solving skills and more than 90% of the respondents widely accept that puzzles can help in the improvement of creative and strategic thinking. This suggests that the game application should include more interesting puzzles that can help stimulate the thinking process of university students. Meanwhile, Fig. 4 summarized the effect of game interaction dialogue on university students.

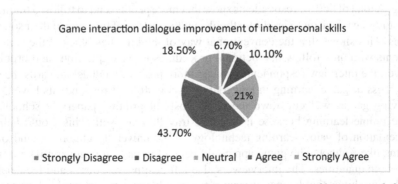

Fig. 4. Post-test results of game interaction dialogue improvement of interpersonal skills

From the data given in the figure, 43.7% of respondents agreed that the dialogue shown within games and the character interaction have helped in increasing the interpersonal skills of university students due to the realism and relatability of the conversation in games. This means that the application should include non-player characters (NPC) to include interactional dialogue to the player as a sense of communication. From the interview respondents, it has shown that most respondents agree that it is known as a source of indirect communication.

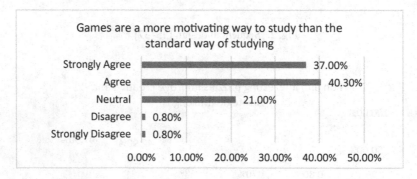

Fig. 5. Games post-test result a more motivating of studying than the standard way

Figure 5 can summarize that using games to study which leans towards game learning is better for university students as it creates more motivation for them to study compared to the usual textbook and lecture slide method. This could also motivate the lecturers at the university to use a hand on game learning method to teach students in a class so they can grasp the feel of games as an instrument of learning and also help them get more motivated to teach students as well. According to the interview results, most respondents responded with it being more fun and engaging way for students to learn while others state that games are new and not expected to the community of university students which suggests that people want more new inventive ways of studying instead of repetition.

Based on the interview and survey results of the research, most respondents agree upon the fact that most university students show a lack of creativity in out-of-the-box thinking. A total of 66% of respondents show that more people tend to follow a traditional way of studying which includes the textbook method instead of thinking of their solutions to things. This shows that the conventional way of thinking has blocked the creativity of students who only follow instructional procedures to most questions and problems. Moreover, the interview respondents showed more positive feedback towards the cost-effectiveness of game learning in universities. About 46% of respondents have agreed that having games will cut down the paper costs of printing papers in schools and promote online learning because it can save travelling as well. This would help the implementation of game learning technology in the university classroom and online platforms like Kahoot. The game app could be sold in large for universities for a low price in high quantities. The interviewers also left positive responses and feedback for remembering things that happen in games than study notes which could show that the interactivity and enjoyment of a game. Moreover, 63% of respondents agree that it helps due to the interesting features and plots of the game and it helps the brain function more due to less stress. The rest of the responses indicate that it is more visually aesthetic while books are more static in terms of memorability. This could suggest that the game application to include more interesting plot points where the learning applications are the key factors of the game at that point. Based on the responses and feedback from the data collection, the game's main menu features of the game application on a mobile and desktop mode. It includes a play option, settings option, quit option, and achievement option. Figure 6 below further illustrates the game application's main menu screen.

Fig. 6. Achievement screen of the game application

The achievement screen shows the allocated information of the student playing the game such as their full name, student ID, and their current lecturer in charge of the class. These points will be allocated from communication points that relate to the interpersonal skills gained in the game, creativity points that relate to the out-of-the-box thinking done in-game, and lastly the strategy points which show the tactful methods used in the game. Furthermore, the bottom part of the screen includes reward tiers that can be obtained soon which will increase the motivation factor of the students to accumulate more points to reach the hidden threshold to obtain the rewards which is a gamification factor of the game learning process.

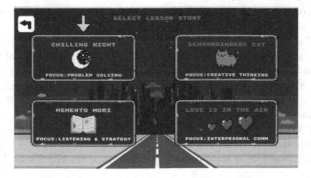

Fig. 7. Story selection of the game application

As shown above, Fig. 7 displays the game story selection which features multiple game story modes that can be chosen by the student to play based on the focus that they want to learn. The main focuses are shown at the bottom of each story selection so that the student will be shown a rounded-up emphasis on what they are going to get into once they select game mode. Each game mode can be played without order to give the freedom of choice to the player and the game modes can be revisited to relearn left out items and points of the story. Each story also contains its unique dialogue and to-do lists for the student to be involved in and complete. The guided storyline aims to provide a motivating environment to entice learning [38].

5   Conclusion, Limitation, and Future Work

In conclusion, JomGear Grind Games can help improve the learning habits and drive of University Students to further enhance their communication skills and out-of-the-box thinking using gamification elements that can be grasped from the game. Also, the scoreboard and rewards system help seek the encouragement of students and motivate them to try harder and more competitively as well as the storyline that lets them envelop into the game world. The limitations during the research that were found were the lack of time on how to research and the limited resources available for it. The game may be something to motivate the students to study but it is their capabilities and work that will benefit them. In the future, we seek to understand the extra benefits of the addition of AR and VR into the game for people to experience. This may benefit them even more as new technologies tend to sway the minds of people and their learning potential.

References

1. Griffy-Brown, C., Earp, B.D., Rosas, O.: Technology and the good society. Technol. Soc. **52**, 1–3 (2018)
2. Shu, M.T., Yaw, Y.W., Chih, M.W.: A study on digital games internet addiction, peer relationships, and learning attitude of senior grade of children in elementary school of Chiayi county. J. Educ. Learn. **9**(3), 2020 (2020)
3. Danah, H., et al.: Creativity and technology in education: an international perspective. Technol. Know. Learn. **23**, 409–42 (2018)
4. Leela, R.: Cooperative learning is a constructivist strategy in tertiary education. Int. J. Educ. Res. **6**(12) (2018)
5. Kang, C.M., et al.: A study on integrating penetration testing into the information security framework for Malaysian higher education institutions. In: International Symposium on Mathematical Science & Computing Research, Malaysia, pp. 156–161 (2015)
6. AdrianChin, Y.K., et al.: JomDataMining: learning behaviour affecting their academic performance, really? In: IEEE 6th International Conference on Engineering Technologies and Applied Science, Malaysia (2020)
7. AdrianChin, Y.K., et al.: JomDataMining: academic performance and learning behavior dubious relationship. Int. J. Bus. Inf. Syst. (Forthcoming 2020)
8. Lim, L.J., et al.: ScareDuino: smart farming with IoT. Int. J. Sci. Eng. Technol. **6**(6), 207–210 (2017)

9. Gerard, J.P., Cyndi, B., Selcuk, A., Jo, A.Y., Molly, H., John, F.C.: Creative problem-solving in small groups: the effects of creativity training on idea generation, solution creativity & leadership effectiveness. J. Creat. Behav. **52**(2), 25–36 (2018)

10. Matthew, B.: Student attitudes to games-based skills development: learning from video games in higher education. Comput. Hum. Behav. **80**, 283–294 (2018)

11. Frank, B., Janet, B., Michelle, Q., Peter, J.A., Shelley, B.B., Josh, S.: A clinical educator's experience using a virtual patient to teach communication and interpersonal skills. Australas. J. Educ. Technol. **34**(3) (2018)

12. Rowan, H.B.: Developing teamwork skills in undergraduate science students: the academic perspective and practice. In: Proceedings of the Australian Conference on Science and Mathematics Education, Monash University, 27–29 September 2017, pp. 137–148 (2019)

13. Daphne, B., Shawn, C.G.: Enhancing attentional control lessons from action video games. Neuron **104**, 147–163 (2019)

14. Fonseca, D., Villagrasa, S., Navarro, I., Sánchez, A.: Urban gamification in architecture education. Adv. Intell. Syst. Comput. **571**(1), 335–341 (2017)

15. Polo-Pena, A.I., Frias-Jamilena, D.M., Fernandez-Ruano, M.L.: Influence of gamification on perceived self-efficacy: gender and age moderator effect. Int. J. Sports Mark. Spons. (2020). ahead-of-print

16. Kühn, S., Kugler, D., Schmalen, K., et al.: Does playing violent video games cause aggression? A longitudinal intervention study. Mol. Psychiatry **24**, 1220–1234 (2019)

17. Lei, W., Kunter, G., Ramesh, S., Joseph, P.: Impact of gamification on perceptions of word-of-mouth consumers. Manag. Inf. Syst. **44**(4), 1–33 (2020)

18. Devin, J.M., Marina, M., Jessica, M., Nancy, L.H.: Exploring the pull and push underlying problem video game use: a self-determination theory approach. Personality Individ. Differ. **135**, 176–181 (2018)

19. Rapp, A., Hopfgartner, F., Hamari, J., et al.: Strengthening gamification studies: current trends and future opportunities of gamification research. Int. J. Hum. Comput. Stud. **126**, 1–6 (2018)

20. Lin, C.-J., Hwang, G.-J., Fu, Q.-K., Chen, J.-F.: A flipped contextual game-based learning approach to enhancing EFL students' English business writing performance & reflective behaviors. Educ. Technol. Soc. **21**(3), 117–131 (2018)

21. Waweru, B.W., et al.: Gamesy: how videogames serve as a better replacement for school? In: IEEE Student Conference on Research and Development, pp. 10–15 (2020)

22. Toda, A.M., Klock, A.C.T., Oliveira, W., et al.: Analysing gamification elements in educational environments using an existing gamification taxonomy. Smart Learn. Environ **6**(16), 18–32 (2019)

23. Mohd Hishamuddin, A.R., Ismail, Y.P., Noor Anida, Z.M.N., Nor Syazwani, M.S.: Gamification elements and their impacts on teaching and learning-a review. Int. J. Multimed. Appl. (IJMA) **10**(6), 37–46 (2018)

24. Knutas, A., van Roy, R., Hynninen, T., et al.: A process for designing algorithm-based personalized gamification. Multimed. Tools Appl. **78**, 13593–13612 (2019)

25. JosephNg, P.S., Loh, Y.F., Eaw, H.C.: Grid Computing for MSE during Volatile Economy. In: International Conference on Control, Automation and Systems, IEEE Explore, Busan, Korea, pp. 709–714 (2020)

26. JosephNg, P.S., et al.: EaaS: available yet hidden infrastructure inside MSE. In: 5th International Conference on Network, Communication, and Computing, ACM International Conference Proceeding Series, Kyoto, Japan, pp. 17–20 (2016)

27. JosephNg, P.S., Kang, C.M., Choo, P.Y., Wong, S.W., Phan, K.Y., Lim, E.H.: Beyond cloud infrastructure services in medium-size manufacturing. In: International Symposium on Mathematical Sciences & Computing Research, IEEE Explore. Ipoh, Malaysia, pp. 150–155 (2015)

28. JosephNg, P.S., Choo, P.Y., Wong, S.W., Phan, K.Y., Lim, E.H.: Malaysia SME ICT during economic turbulence. In: International Conference on Information & Computer Network, Singapore, pp. 67–71 (2012)
29. JosephNg, P.S., Yin, C.P., Wan, W.S., Nazmudeen, M.S.H.: Energizing ICT infrastructure for Malaysia SME during economic turbulence. In: Student Conference on Research and Development, IEEE Explore, Cyberjaya, Malaysia, pp. 328–322 (2011)
30. JosephNg, P.S., Eaw, H.C.: Making financial sense from EaaS for MSE during economic uncertainty. Adv. Intell. Syst. Comput. (Forthcoming 2021)
31. JosephNg, P.S., Eaw, H.C.: Still technology acceptance model? Reborn: exostructure as a service model. Int. J. Bus. Inf. Syst. (Forthcoming 2021)
32. JosephNg, P.S.: EaaS infrastructure disruptor for MSE. Int. J. Bus. Inf. Syst. 30(3), 373–385 (2019)
33. JosephNg, P.S.: EaaS optimization: available yet hidden information technology infrastructure inside medium-size enterprises. J. Technol. Forecast. Soc. Change 132(July), 165–173 (2018)
34. JosephNg, P.S., et al.: Exostructure services for infrastructure resources optimization. J. Telecommun. Electron. Comput. Eng. 8(4), 65–69 (2016)
35. JosephNg, P.S., Moy, K.C.: Beyond barebone cloud infrastructure services: stumbling competitiveness during economic turbulence. J. Sci. Technol. 24(1), 101–121 (2016)
36. Joseph, N.P.S., Mahmood, A.K., Choo, P.Y., Wong, S.W., Phan, K.Y., Lim, E.H.: Barebone cloud IaaS: revitalization disruptive technology. Int. J. Bus. Inf. Syst. 18(1), 107–126 (2015)
37. Joseph, N.P.S., Mahmood, A.K., Choo, P.Y., Wong, S.W., Phan, K.Y., Lim, E.H.: IaaS cloud optimization during economic turbulence for Malaysia small and medium enterprise. Int. J. Bus. Inf. Syst. 16(2), 196–208 (2014)
38. Mitchell, R., Schuster, L., Jin, H.S.: Gamification and the impact of extrinsic motivation on needs satisfaction: defining gamification. J. Bus. Res. 3(2), 323–330 (2018)

Multicraft: A Multimodal Interface for Supporting and Studying Learning in Minecraft

Marcelo Worsley[1]([envelope]) [ORCID], Kevin Mendoza Tudares[1], Timothy Mwiti[1],
Mitchell Zhen[2], and Marc Jiang[1]

[1] Northwestern University, Evanston, IL, USA
`marcelo.worsley@northwestern.edu`, {`KevinMendozaTudares2022`,
`MarcJiang2021`}`@u.northwestern.edu`
[2] University of California, Berkeley, Berkeley, CA, USA
`mitchellzhen@berkeley.edu`

Abstract. In this paper, we present work on bringing multimodal interaction to Minecraft. The platform, Multicraft, incorporates speech-based input, eye tracking, and natural language understanding to facilitate more equitable gameplay in Minecraft. We tested the platform with elementary, middle school students and college students through a collection of studies. Students found each of the provided modalities to be a compelling way to play Minecraft. Additionally, we discuss the ways that these different types of multimodal data can be used to identify the meaningful spatial reasoning practices that students demonstrate while playing Minecraft. Collectively, this paper emphasizes the opportunity to bridge a multimodal interface with a means for collecting rich data that can better support diverse learners in non-traditional learning environments.

Keywords: Games · Constructionism · Spatial reasoning · Data mining

1 Introduction

Interest and participation in video games continues to grow. Recent reports note that three out of four Americans play video games and an estimated 2.7 billion gamers around the globe [1]. While part of this growth in video games is fueled by the COVID-19 pandemic [2, 3], researchers have long discussed the important role that games can play for learning and socialization [4–7]. This opportunity for learning and socialization can have particular positive benefits for students who are disabled by inaccessible, physically collocated, game-based learning experiences. However, to be effective, virtual gaming environments must also be intentional about considering questions of accessibility. Technological developments like the Xbox Adaptive Controller provide an important step towards accessible gaming experiences. Nonetheless, the goals of accessible gaming experiences should also consider equitable play and identify ways that students' game-based practices demonstrate student knowledge development and expertise. Regarding equitable play, it is not sufficient to simply replace the input modality. Additional steps

© Springer Nature Switzerland AG 2021
X. Fang (Ed.): HCII 2021, LNCS 12790, pp. 113–131, 2021.
https://doi.org/10.1007/978-3-030-77414-1_10

should be taken to develop comparable gaming experiences for all participants. Furthermore, beyond including novel interfaces for supporting participation, there is an important opportunity to utilize different modalities to chronicle student learning.

In this paper we describe our efforts to combine these ideas in a platform called Multicraft. Multicraft is a collection of multimodal interfaces that allow students to use speech, gaze, text, or any combination of these modalities to play Minecraft. The platform also includes built-in features that can accelerate game play and a method for storing multimodal data that researchers can use to study student in-game computational thinking and spatial reasoning practices.

The next section highlights prior research that informs our work and situates Multicraft relative to this prior work. We then present a quick summary of the design principles and technical architecture for Multicraft. We also highlight some of the core features of the platform. This is followed by a short presentation of user feedback on different elements of the platform. After describing the platform and user feedback, we transition into a high-level presentation of some of the research that we have conducted using multimodal data. We particularly focus on ways that eye-tracking and video data have allowed us to study various complex spatial reasoning practices that students exhibit while playing Minecraft. We conclude with a discussion of future work and suggestions for overarching objectives for this type of work.

2 Prior Literature

2.1 Autcraft

Autcraft is a user community and user-generated modification of Minecraft that was specifically developed for learners with Autism and their families [6, 8, 9]. Across this work Ringland emphasizes how a Minecraft community, when appropriately designed, can be an important space for autistic youth and their families. Ringland [10] specifically describes how families configure and navigate the physical, liminal, and virtual spaces needed to successfully participate in Minecraft. Many of the core features of Autcraft are achieved through the rich community of people, and the custom Minecraft mods that govern how students are permitted to interact within the game. The design of Multicraft takes a similar approach of configuring an open-source server that users can customize and deploy as needed. Additionally, the inclusion of multiple possible input modalities speaks to a recognition of the varying liminal spaces that families configure. Moreover, Multicraft also includes features that try to adapt to the user, as opposed to requiring the user to conform to standardized methods of input. Our adoption of this strategy is an attempt to utilize ability-based design (ABD) [11], which we describe in the following section.

2.2 Ability Based Design

ABD is a set of tenets for guiding computer scientist as they create accessible interfaces. A central tenet of ABD is to embed adaptation into the design of the interface, as opposed to requiring the user to carry the burden of using their own adaptive technologies and tools. Moreover, interfaces should be designed to be utilized with a variety of input modalities. While Multicraft still has several limitations in terms of the abilities that are supported, our goal is to integrate features that reflect the diverse set of abilities that human possess.

2.3 Multimodal Learning Analytics

The use of multimodal data also provides a means to leverage techniques from Multimodal Learning Analytics (MMLA) [12]. MMLA is a collection of strategies that can support real-time and post-hoc analysis of learners in non-traditional learning environments. Historically MMLA has involved a broad set of modalities that frequently include video, audio, gesture tracking, eye tracking, affect detection, and electro-dermal activation [13, 14]. Multicraft utilizes multimodal fusion of text, speech, and gaze data to provide an accurate and naturalistic input modality. Beyond that, however, the multimodal data provides an opportunity to carefully chronicle student learning and knowledge development within the Minecraft game. In looking at student game play using multimodal data, we will mostly explore work on student spatial reasoning skills, which we quickly summarize in the next section.

2.4 Spatial Reasoning Skills

Spatial reasoning refers to a variety of skills that generally pertain to one's ability to perceive, utilize, and store different types of spatial information [15]. This might include the ability to perform navigation tasks using a map, mentally folding a piece of paper, or rotate an object in one's mind. A variety of spatial reasoning tests have been developed to measure these skills in laboratory contexts, but a growing body of research advocates for researchers to examine spatial reasoning in less restricted contexts [16, 17]. Video games have also been a context where researchers have studied spatial reasoning skills [18–20]. Hence, one of the contributions that we explore alongside the development of a multimodal interface is the opportunity to analyze student data, particularly eye-tracking and video data, to better understand and acknowledge the ways that students practice spatial reasoning in Minecraft. This approach follows in a traditional of psychological research that studies mental rotation using eye tracking data during standardized spatial reasoning tests [21–23].

2.5 Summary

There is a broad collection of prior and relevant work that relates to this project. An important distinction that we emphasize with Multicraft is the goal of supporting equitable play and using multimodal data to discern student learning practices. Bringing together these different ideas is novel relative to the prior work in these domains.

3 Multicraft

Multicraft is a platform designed to support multimodal interaction in Minecraft. The current platform integrates speech-based input, eye tracking and natural language understanding and reflects a set of design principles that is informed by hundreds of hours observing elementary and middle school students play Minecraft. These observations include working with students with a variety of physical, visual, and neurological impairments. For example, our team has watched students with cerebral palsy effectively disconnect from the Minecraft experience because of an inaccessible interface. We have seen students on the autism spectrum experience significant anxiety and frustration when they incorrectly execute a command and are unable to easily undo that action. And we have generally seen how novice Minecraft players have struggled to be accepted into a classroom Minecraft community because they have not yet learned the syntax of the platform. These types of observations and others contribute to the design principles that we have incorporated into the Multicraft platform.

3.1 Design Principles

Our design principles center on equitable play, taking a pluralistic approach, allowing for natural language input, facilitating collaboration, and easy version control.

Equitable play is a goal that we believe is sorely missed within prior work. Many of the existing accessible interface look to simply replace the keyboard and mouse with other input modalities but do nothing to ensure that the overall experience is equitable. We enact this principle by seamlessly embedding some computer programming into the platform. For example, students can request to build a house with certain dimensions, instead of having to manually place every block for said house. Students can also easily clone existing objects, create large ravines, and quickly create entire cities.

Pluralistic approach refers to allowing users to complete the same action using a variety of modalities and commands [24, 25]. Given the Constructionist orientation of Minecraft it seems appropriate to also ensure that our platform supports multiple forms of engagement and execution. Concretely, we achieve this by permitting users to complete the same action using a variety of modalities. This goal is also an acknowledgement of the diversity and intersectionality present within disability communities. Users bring many different abilities and preferences, hence, Multicraft aims to support as many of those abilities and preferences as possible.

Allowing natural language input speaks to our desire for Multicraft to adapt to the language and syntax of our users, as opposed to requiring users to learn a specific syntax. The inclusion of a Natural Language Understanding (NLU) Engine advances this principle.

Facilitating collaboration is a central component of the Minecraft platform in that players can collaboratively build, mine, and battle within shared virtual worlds. Players can also share materials with one another. However, Minecraft does not allow players to easily share entire built structures with one another. Multicraft adds this functionality by allowing players to name their built structures which subsequently lets other players to easily re-use them.

Version control refers to the player's ability to easily undo and redo executed commands. Minecraft natively allows students to add and destroy blocks, however, many students have trouble undoing previous actions (e.g., using a command to create a $10 \times 10 \times 15$ house). Not being able to undo or redo command-based build actions inadvertently discourages students from using different commands.

3.2 System Technical Architecture

In the current version, users may speak simple commands to the game, such as "build a ten by twenty-two wall of stone" or "move forward fifteen blocks". The user can also use eye tracking commands like "track my eyes and build a ten by ten by ten building of quartz". This command will start the eye tracker and build the desired structure where the user looks. These commands are executed instantaneously, speeding up the process of building compared to placing blocks individually or using the more complicated built-in Minecraft commands. We achieve these types of interactions by integrating several technical components (Fig. 1). The overall technical architecture can be split into three layers: User Devices, the Multicraft Client and the Multicraft Server.

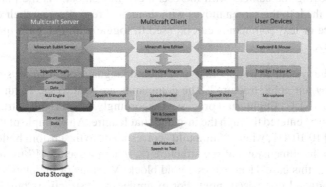

Fig. 1. Technical architecture of Multicraft

User Devices. Users have the option of using any number of input modalities. We emphasize an eye tracker and microphone, because these are the two multimodal inputs that we have explicitly integrated and tested with participants. However, many of the capabilities also work for participants who may be playing Minecraft with a keyboard, mouse, or touch screen.

Multicraft Client. The Multicraft Client interface includes capabilities for communicating between the User Devices and the Multicraft Server. This includes handling text, speech, and eye tracking data, and sending instructions to the Multicraft server.

Audio Processing. For users that elect to use speech-based input, we have included Speech-to-Text capabilities for converting the audio information into transcriptions. This component consists of a Python program that uses web sockets to communicate with a speech recognition engine. While this piece is customizable, our current implementation uses the IBM Watson Speech-to-Text service. Because of the atypical vocabulary used within Minecraft, and because we wanted to optionally include "Multicraft" as a custom trigger word, we utilize a custom language model and augment the standard dictionary with Minecraft specific words like "redstone" and "ender pearl".

Eye Tracking Module. Gaze interaction is implemented through a C# program that utilizes a Tobii Eye Tracker 4C and the Tobii Interaction Library Beta API. This program collects 2D gaze point data in real time and subsequently uses that data to adjust the player's in-game camera. This eye tracker-based movement results in the current fixation location moving to the center of the computer screen. This capability can be optionally toggled on or off through a voice command (e.g., "start tracking my eyes") or using text. There are three ways of interacting with the eye tracker. The first is for building and allows the user to determine where to build a structure that they request via voice command. The second is for navigation and allows the user to focus and move their character forward. By dwelling at the center of the screen (±50 pixels) for three seconds, their avatar begins to walk forward, and continues to walk until they change their gaze. The third is for moving the camera with the user's eye movement. As the player looks to the right or to the left, the screen moves with them, and re-centers on their current gaze location. Voice or text commands can be used to toggle with eye gaze mode the user wishes to utilize.

Text Input. The system also supports typed natural language commands, such as "build a ten by ten by ten gold structure". The commands are sent to the Natural Language Understanding (NLU) Engine and processed accordingly. More rigidly structured commands can also be entered through the in-game chat feature. An example of this would be "/mmbuild 10 10 10 41", where "/mmbuild" corresponds to the custom build command, "10 10 10" to the dimensions of the structure (x, y, and z), and "41" to the Minecraft material ID - in this case 41 indicates a gold block. Versions of the platform have also supported shorthand text-based input. For example, the instruction "build a 10 by 10 by 10 gold structure", could be written in shorthand as "b 10 10 10 41". One reason for including a shorthand notation is because entering "hacks" is already part of the Minecraft culture. Additionally, it eliminates the need for the additional hardware or client-side software used with speech recognition.

Multicraft Server. The main server side component is a Minecraft Bukkit server with a SpigotMC plugin. Bukkit is a free, open-source software for running and extending Minecraft servers. SpigotMC is a high-performance Minecraft server API. The SpigotMC plugin handles executing Multicraft-specific commands and passing those instructions to Minecraft. Multicraft depends on a NLU Engine that we briefly described in the next section.

NLU Engine. The understanding engine produces a semantic representation of the audio transcripts (or text-based commands) using SpaCy [26]. It subsequently operationalizes those requests into actions within the Minecraft game. Beyond this, the NLU engine incorporates some unique features.

Synonym Detection and Keyword Extraction: We use WordNet [27] to ensure that synonyms are mapped to supported game-based actions. This allows us to support a larger set of commands than simply "build", "move" and "track," for example. Currently, the system can execute commands for building structures, placing blocks, and moving the player along cardinal directions. It also supports activating eye tracking to be used for building or navigating, adjusting the camera, adding items to the user's inventory, and saving, naming, and cloning previously built structures. Finally, as we describe in more detail later, it also supports undo and redo capabilities. In addition to identifying synonyms for actions, the platform can also identify synonyms for cardinal directions and different in-game materials. After identifying the appropriate synonyms, the engine performs keyword extraction. It identifies numbers, material types, cardinal directions, and certain parts of speech. Together, synonym and keyword detection allow players more freedom in how they issue commands.

Error Detection and User Feedback: Error detection and feedback provide a player with information on why an error has occurred if a command is not executed. For example, if a build command is issued without dimensions, a message is displayed on the screen that informs the player that the command requires dimensions.

Saving and Naming of Structures: Building in Minecraft can involve a lot of repetition. Multicraft provides a simple way of accomplishing repeated building by allowing players to name their structures after they have built them. Once a player builds a structure, they can name it (e.g., "home"), move to a new position and issue the command, "/mclone home" and a replica will be built. The system also supports sharing objects with others. The structures that the user names are available for all other users on that Minecraft server to utilize.

Undoing and Redoing: The server implementation also includes the ability to undo and redo items within a user's build history. For example, if a student issues a command to "build a fifteen by eight by nine brick house" and subsequently decides that they no longer want that structure, they can simply say "undo" and the structure will be removed. Similarly, they can say "redo" or type "/mredo" to recreate the structure.

Simplification of Existing Minecraft Commands: The server-side implementation also includes simplifications of built-in Minecraft commands. For example, Minecraft has existing commands for filling a space with blocks or cloning an existing structure. To use these capabilities, students need to remember the Cartesian coordinates for the bottom front, and upper rear portions of the space to be filled or cloned. Multicraft includes text or speech commands that can be used to store these values for the user and subsequently allow them to issue a command to fill or clone the space.

4   Part 1: User Experiences with Multicraft

Throughout the platform development process, we have conducted user studies with different groups of participants. Within this section, we will discuss three groups of user studies. The first were middle school students participating in one-week long summer Minecraft camps. The second group of participants were middle school student participating through Minecraft clubs. The third group were K-2nd graders.

4.1   Overview

Each group of participants experienced a slightly modified set of tasks. These differences were due to our ongoing development of the Multicraft platform. They were also influenced by the COVID-19 pandemic, which interrupted significant portions of our data collection. The summer camp students tested Multicraft's capabilities, but without eye tracking. Instead, we focused on examining how students would make use of the speech-based natural language input. The middle school Minecraft club participants tested the combined speech and eye-tracking interface. The elementary school students primarily tested the text-based input interface, with a select few also testing speech-based capabilities in Minecraft.

4.2 Participants

The summer camp participants included ten students that identified as boys, and 1 that identified as a girl. None of them identified as frequent Minecraft users, and all were between 12 and 14 years old. The middle school Minecraft club participants included three students that identified as girls and 7 students that identify as boys. All students ranged in age from 12–14 years old. All the students identified as having prior experience with Minecraft. The elementary school participants included four students that identify as girls and five that identify as boys. All students were between kindergarten and 2nd grade. Only two of the students had prior experience with Minecraft. One student in each of the programs was on the autism spectrum, however, our observations will not be based solely on those students.

4.3 User Testing Tasks

As previously noted, each group completed a different set of tasks. However, consistent across each group was a researcher-led demonstration of the basic capabilities of the platform. The summer camp participants were asked to use the platform while engaging in free play and also given pictures of buildings to recreate. The Minecraft club participants completed three specific tasks. First, they were asked to use the eye tracker to move around the world. This involved adjusting their gaze to the desired location and dwelling in the middle of the screen to move forward. Next, they tested text input commands. Here they could follow the example to construct a building of one-hundred cubic blocks or create something of their own choosing. They then tried a slightly modified way to build the same structure. Finally, they tested out building with the eye tracker activated.

Elementary school students were given two tasks to complete. The first task involved trying two different approaches for building a 100 cubic feet structure in Minecraft. The second tasks asked them to build that same structure but also create copies of that structure. They completed these two tasks using native Minecraft features and Multicraft features. We also had some of the students test our speech-based input alongside using text-based input.

4.4 Data Collection

Our data collection with the summer camp participants was the most extensive. During the program, the research team collected audio and video data of each student using Open Broadcaster Software (OBS) on the respective participant laptops. OBS also enabled us to capture a video of the screen. In addition to the individual videos, we also collected whole room video, and conducted some informal interviews and surveys with the students about Multicraft. Informal interviews asked students their views on the utility of the platform. We did not explicitly ask them if they did or did not like the platform because the authors had previously interacted with some of the students, and we thought their stated perceptions might be biased. Hence, a large portion of the analysis is based on what we observed students do, and less about what students explicitly said.

For the middle school Minecraft club participants, our data collection included observations and informal interviews. Individual students tested the platform, one-at-a-time. After they finished their tasks, a research team member asked a few questions about the accessibility of the areas of improvement for future iterations, overall enjoyment with Multicraft, and ease of use.

Finally, for the elementary school students, we conducted informal interviews and observed as students used the platform. Specifically, we asked students (and their parents) about the relative ease of use between Minecraft commands, and our custom Multicraft commands.

4.5 Data Analysis

Members of the research team, namely the authors, individually and collectively watched videos of student game play. The research team took note of different observations and discussed these notes with other team members to get their assessment and interpretation of the different episodes. We also consulted our field notes and debrief notes from the different sessions. The surveys from students were also looked at qualitatively to get a general picture of student perceptions. The pieces of data that we selected for this analysis serve as exemplars for some of the design elements that we wish to highlight with this platform. In this way, the analysis is not intended to suggest absolute causality, or universality. Instead, they are indications of potential interpretations of student behaviors and utterances.

4.6 Observations and Findings

Through the observations, surveys, and interviews we were able to identify some important information about Multicraft and its potential to enhance the Minecraft gameplay experience. We also uncovered some challenges with the platform and potential future developments. We will organize the results based on modalities. Specifically, we will begin with observations and student comments associated with text-based input, then speech-based input, and, finally, gaze-based input. We then touch on some key ideas from student interviews.

Text-Based Input. Text-based input proved to be quite difficult for several of the students that we tested with. This was true across the novice middle school students and elementary school students. None of the students knew how to type, with most students trying to type with two or three fingers. This meant that their attempts to enter different commands were hampered by being slow and inaccurate. This resulted in them having to re-enter the same commands a second, and, at times, a third, or fourth time. The shorthand text input, on the other hand, provided a seamless interaction for both middle school and elementary school students. One of the current realities is that many children who are growing up in the age of touch screen and audio assistants, do not have much experience typing. However, only having to type a single letter and a handful of numbers seem to be appropriate for the different users that we observed. The biggest challenge in the case of shorthand text input was the need for students to know the numeric code for the block types that they wanted to use. The numeric codes offered both advantages and disadvantages. Using a number was easier than knowing how to spell words like "acacia", but it also meant that students needed a way to look up the correct material codes. To address this, students found a webpage that includes a full list of block types and their codes, and kept that webpage open so that they could toggle to it as needed. In later versions of this platform, we introduced the ability to use the numbers and material names interchangeably. Apart from this, students seemed to find that the shorthand text input approach worked as expected. Moreover, the young students were particularly appreciative of the ability to name structures and quickly clone them. They also expressed a preference for Multicraft's commands over the Minecraft text commands because the Multicraft required fewer words.

For the middle school students with prior Minecraft experience, using text-based input appeared to be the most natural form of interaction. They already had experience using different Minecraft commands through coding activities in their Minecraft clubs. The students reported that the Multicraft commands made constructing large structures much easier, and many users stated they preferred using the commands over placing the individual blocks. The one deviation from this was that students do not always know exactly what they want to build. In those instances, they did not find much utility in the Multicraft text-based input modality which requires users to state the dimensions of their desired structure.

Speech-Based Input. For many of the students, the prospect of using speech-based input offered a welcome alternative to having to type. They also liked the idea of natural language input because remembering a specific syntax for the various functions that Minecraft makes available was challenging for many of the students. However, in practice, some students found the speech recognition accuracy to be unreliable. Because of this, some students had to repeat their requests several times before getting it to successfully build. We believe that this is due to poor quality acoustic models for adolescents and because many of our participants spoke other languages at home. Once the requests were properly processed, students expressed amazement that the structure was created so quickly. Their amazement and excitement generated social interactions among their peers, as they eagerly shared their creations with other students. Students also appeared to be comfortable talking to the computer and did so using their normal speech cadence and tone. Another challenge was that students expressed uncertainty about what kinds of instructions they could issue, a common challenge within multimodal interfaces [28]. We have since developed a cheat sheet that users can utilize as they interface using Multicraft. We have also improved the speech recognition by executing some additional code-based customizations.

Despite these challenges, the elementary school students that we observed preferred speech-based input to typing. In fact, some of the students even tried to use speech-based input within the Minecraft inventory because they were not sure how to spell the name for several of the materials. At times they would start typing a word incorrectly and subsequently become unable to find the block-type of interest. When facilitators were present, they would ask for spelling assistance, but in the absence of adult involvement, it is unclear how they would be able to build their structures as envisioned. This challenge, on the part of students, exemplifies a primary challenge we want to overcome. Students may have complex and intricate ideas in their minds, but lack the computer knowledge, or Minecraft experience to enact that idea.

Eye Tracking Input. Of the three modalities, eye tracking was the one that students found to be most intriguing. Many students had interfaced with systems that used speech recognition, or seen people use them on smartphones. Eye trackers, on the other hand, were a novelty. For the experienced Minecraft users that tested the eye tracking system, there was a noticeable learning curve to navigating the game with their eyes. It generally took students between five and ten minutes to get to the point where they were comfortable using their eyes to navigate and build in Minecraft. Additionally, one of the most frequent comments about the eye tracking feature was that moving the camera with eye movement at first felt unnatural. We also observed that it took time for them to learn the mapping of gaze position to camera movement speed. However, with some practice, students became quite proficient integrating this additional modality into their game play.

Interviews. In addition to observations, we also conducted informal interviews with students about the Multicraft interface. Some of the questions raised were based on observations that we made. Other questions were focused around how socially acceptable it would be to use this platform when playing with friends, and what additional functionality the students would like to see added to the platform. Here, we focus on questions of social acceptability because that is of primary consideration for our goal of equitable play.

The question around student perceptions of using Multicraft during general multiplayer games was met with mixed reviews. Many students saw no problem with using Multicraft in creative mode (the game mode where students freely build and create). To them, Multicraft fit into their existing schema of Minecraft hacks. In fact, many students came to refer to the shorthand text-based input "Tim [Mwiti]'s Hack" because he had introduced it to them and showed them how it worked. However, students were less keen about using Multicraft in survival mode (a mode where players have limited resources and need to mine and hunt to survive), as they likened it to cheating. When further probed about why it was cheating, a student described that the current implementation does not use any of your inventory items, meaning that when using Multicraft you have an unlimited supply of resources. This would be unfair in survival mode. Other students agreed with this assessment and suggested that while in survival mode, the user should only be able to use items in their inventory. Students were also concerned with the social stigma associated with using Multicraft in multiplayer survival. Because some of the text commands are entered through the chat terminal, some players' Multicraft actions may be visible to others. In our ongoing development, we are working to address these concerns with social stigma and acceptability.

5 Part 2: Multimodal Analyses of Minecraft Gameplay

Alongside the utility that Multicraft provides for users, we are also interested in ways that the multimodal data used in the Multicraft platform can be help us better understand and chronicle students' growing competencies. In this section we present data from a laboratory-based study and two Minecraft summer camp-based studies.

5.1 Overview

The summer camp-based studies included students completing build challenges as well as open-builds. Within these camps we were interested in the spatial reasoning practices that students exhibit across different building contexts. The summer camps lasted for approximately 15 h.

The laboratory-based study included undergraduate and graduate students who completed a mental rotation test and three specific build challenges. This study was undertaken to look at the ways that mental rotation practices that students employ on standardized spatial reasoning tasks might mirror onto the practices students use in Minecraft. It was also an opportunity to explore development of automated techniques for studying spatial reasoning in Minecraft. As students completed the one-hour long build challenges, eye tracking and screen recordings were captured.

5.2 Participants

The summer camp-based studies include the same one that was discussed in Sect. 4. In addition to those students, the data in this section also includes an additional summer camp with 12 middle school students. This group included four females, and eight males. All but one of the students had prior experience with Minecraft.

As previously noted, the laboratory-based study included 19 undergraduate and graduate students. Fifteen students identified as males, while the remaining four identified females. Sixteen of the students were undergraduates, while the remaining three were pursuing graduate degrees. One of the students is on the autism spectrum.

5.3 User Testing Tasks

Within the summer camp studies, students completed various build challenges. One of the structures that students created can be seen in Fig. 2.

Within the laboratory-based study, students were asked to complete a mental rotation test [29] and then to use in-game reference images (e.g., Fig. 3) to recreate the three structures pictured in Fig. 4, 5 and 6.

5.4 Data Collection

Across the different studies, we collected eye-tracking and screen recordings of student gameplay. The eye-gaze data was captured using the Tobii 4C eye tracker, which was collecting data at 90 Hz. The screen recordings were created using the Social Signal

Fig. 2. Sample structure that students recreated in Minecraft

Fig. 3. Picture of in-game reference images with eye tracking data overlay (green dots). (Color figure online)

Fig. 4. Structure A   **Fig. 5.** Structure B   **Fig. 6.** Structure C

Interpretation (SSI) framework [30] or OBS. We also collected whole room audio, individual audio, and server logs of student game-based actions using the LogBlock plugin. The eye-tracking data and screen recordings are the focal portion of these analyses, though the game-based log data did inform portions of the analyses.

5.5 Data Analysis

The summer camp-based analysis heavily relied on human annotation of the video data. Because the total collection of videos included more than 100 h of data, we elected to use some simple data mining to help with the video selection process. Computational analysis was used on the log data to look for sessions that showed noticeable differences in the number of blocks that students placed and based on differential performance on the mental rotation test. Based on this information, we were able to select a small collection of videos to human code. The research team collectively watched and coded the videos for different spatial reasoning practices. A subset of these observations is presented in this paper.

The data analysis process for the laboratory-based study used computer vision- based contour detection and synchronous eye tracking data to identify salient features and gaze patterns on the different mental rotation test questions. Contour detection is an approach that allows a computer program to label contiguous shapes within a given image. The contours can be hierarchical, such that a given contour can contain several other contours. Figure 7 contains three contours from a mental rotation test question.

For the eye gaze data, we computed fixations and saccades following research conventions. A fixation was recorded when any set of successive data points was no more than 25 pixels apart from one another, and when the collection of gaze points represented

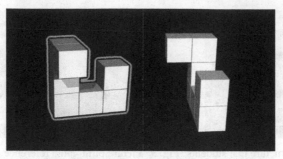

Fig. 7. Picture of hierarchical contours outlined in yellow, green, and blue. (Color figure online)

at least 50 ms. The resultant features were used for human observation of common gaze patterns and are also supplied to different machine learning algorithms to highlight correlations between different features and student performance on the mental rotation test.

5.6 Observations and Findings

Summer Minecraft Clubs: The summer camp-based analysis helped surface several ways that student exhibit spatial reasoning practices while playing Minecraft. Broadly speaking, several of the ideas connect to work on using visual anchors to help students make sense of a given design [22, 31]. Some of these practices include choosing a starting point, frequently a corner of a structure, or the middle, and subsequently counting along a single dimension. In some videos students can be heard verbally counting, or moving their mouths as they pass over the different blocks. Viewers can also see the eye gaze trace jump from block to block within the screen recordings.

Another common approach was students looking at a structure from a specific perspective. This perspective was often chosen to match the angle of the reference picture and simplifies their ability to draw a correspondence between the reference image and the structure that they are building.

One specific instance of perspective taking is taking a bird's-eye view of a structure. Frequently, students would fly above their current build so they could see the entire structure. When looking from above, students would scan over the relative dimensions and look for symmetries or other obvious discontinuities.

Perhaps the most intriguing use of the bird's-eye view was in conjunction to students creating their own attentional anchors. We see in example of them when students try to recreate a mushroom tower (Fig. 8). While they are working on the bottom part of the mushroom top, they need to create an oval that will go around the center column that they have created. When the students take a bird's-eye view, they see that the surrounding oval is not quite right (Fig. 9). To fix this, they voluntarily create a rectangular scaffold (Fig. 10), which is used to more easily construct the oval. This represents a fairly complex spatial practice that the student spontaneously uses to fix this build.

Collectively, we see students using several different strategies to spatially reason about structures in Minecraft. The summer camp-based studies helped us surface some

Fig. 8. Mushroom tower image

Fig. 9. Failed design for mushroom rim (the dark portion)

Fig. 10. Scaffold created by students to anchor mushroom rim

of these practices as inferred from computer-informed video selection, and subsequent human analysis. The laboratory study that we conducted was an attempt to explore some of these patterns using more automated techniques and regarding a validated mental rotation test [29].

Laboratory Study: The laboratory-based analysis is still a work in progress. Thus far we have been able to successfully combine computer vision derived features, automated detection of fixation points, and machine learning to discern differential gaze patterns among students that exhibit different mental rotation ability. As a sample output from the mental rotation test portion of the video, see Fig. 11.

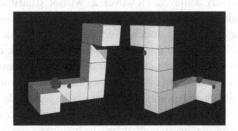

Fig. 11. Aggregated frequent fixation points for laboratory-based study

In Fig. 11 we can see the most common gaze points across all participants, as overlaid on a static image of the mental rotation test image (note: detecting this static image in the different frames of the video required using ORB feature detection as students could scroll up and down on the screen, a process that we do not describe here in the interest of brevity). When we aggregate across the fixation points within the reference images that students looked at to inform their builds, we can see what students are and are not paying attention to. We think that this type of analysis can translate to the Minecraft gameplay data by specifically examining which parts of a reference Minecraft building students are and are not paying attention to when trying to replicate a structure.

Our analysis of correlations between different features and student performance on mental rotation tasks has also demonstrated some promise [32]. For example, previous analysis found that a decision tree trained on a broad selection of contour-based, fixation, and saccade features can be used to accurately model student mental rotation performance. Our interest in doing this type of analysis was to explore a good research methodology for studying student spatial reasoning using computer vision and eye tracking data. We see this computational approach being something that we can translate into our analyses of Minecraft video game play and presumably detect some of the complex spatial reasoning practices that we observed in the summer camp-based Minecraft analysis.We might also use these features as a way to look at how individual students' spatial reasoning practices change over time relative to themselves.

6 Discussion

The overarching objective of the featured studies and analyses was to describe our current efforts to couple a multimodal interface that promotes equitable play with opportunities to use MMLA to delve into the complex spatial reasoning practices that students demonstrate while playing Minecraft. The user feedback from elementary and middle school students suggests that there are several aspects of the Multicraft platform that they find to be compelling and useful for different groups of users. Several students found the speech and gaze-based input modalities to be a welcomed change from the standard approach to building in Minecraft. These different modalities were adopted based on our observations from working with hundreds of elementary and middle school students play Minecraft, and particularly informed by observed experiences of students with disabilities. The results that we have gathered so far suggest that many of the objectives around using multimodal input were achieved. However, as we noted earlier in this paper, simply providing alternate modalities for input is insufficient. Instead, we want to afford a more equitable gaming experience where students feel equipped to participate alongside their peers regardless of abilities. In one respect, the student feedback that using Multicraft during multiplayer survival seemed unfair is an acknowledgement that Multicraft can offer noticeable benefits in executing different commands and actions faster. At the same time, however, this feedback also points to potentially larger challenges about the social stigma of accessible interfaces that aim for equitable experiences. The students' primary concerns were about players having access to resources outside of their inventory, which is something that we can easily correct in future iterations of the platform, but some social stigma may persist.

Our ongoing analyses using multimodal data also hint at some promising opportunities to chronicle the knowledge and reasoning strategies that students evidence while playing Minecraft. Our human analysis of video data keyed in on several common spatial reasoning practices, while also noting the ways that students might be intentionally creating visual anchors to help them better recognize symmetries and other visual elements. Additionally, the computational analysis that we briefly described that combines computer vision, fixation detection, and machine learning during mental rotation tests is a first step in automatically mining student game play data for different spatial reasoning-relevant practices. We suggest, however, that this is just one example of what we can accomplish using techniques from MMLA in game-based learning contexts. Though we did not describe it in detail, our work also involves looking at student computational thinking in Minecraft using student game-play videos and eye tracking data.

To date, we have successfully used computer vision to detect how much time students spend using the coding interface in Minecraft Education Edition. Detecting these video clips has helped us focus our human video analysis process by automatically selecting clips where students are actively programming. It also can help elucidate the design prompts and activity structures that successfully lead to students doing more programming in Minecraft. Moving forward, we intend to build out more of the techniques from laboratory studies to utilize on data derived from more ecological settings.

7 Limitations

A major limitation of this work is that it was conducted with small groups of students who self-selected into the programs. Additionally, these studies were completed with multiple groups of participants who had interacted with one of the authors on previous occasions. This may have made the students less likely to share their true opinions. Another potential limitation is that we tested different elements of the platform with different populations. While we had planned for a more systematic study during the first quarter of 2020, the COVID-19 pandemic made this infeasible. Finally, while some students with disabilities were present in our different groups of users, neither the data collection nor the analysis identified them. On the one hand, that these students were able to participate alongside other students seems to be a positive observation. However, we recognize that this work should be tested with more students with disabilities, especially in recognition of the diversity and intersectionality that exists across the different disability communities. Nonetheless, we believe that the insights gathered thus far are still beneficial for considering the design of multimodal interfaces for equitable play. We intend to address these limitations within our on-going studies and as we continue to develop the platform. As we think more about the future development of this work, we also want to speak to an important consideration in thinking about using MMLA. Prior research in MMLA has involved the use of various multimodal sensors that can proxy for everything from arousal, to cognitive load, to mind wandering, to fine motor gesticulations. We must be careful not to use the analytics in ways that are normative and overlook the diversity that exists among and within different populations. One approach for addressing this is to look at ways that students' data deviates from their typical behaviors. Hence, even in thinking about ways that we look at student eye tracking data and examining the visual spatial anchors that they may be references, simply looking at aggregate behaviors across groups should be conducted with caution.

8 Conclusion

This project began because of our motivation to make Minecraft more accessible for students with disabilities. However, more important than simply making Minecraft more accessible, we wanted to promote a game play and social experience that would be equitable. Through our user studies, we found that the platform helps fulfill some of those goals by providing capabilities that can spur on amazement and excitement among traditional Minecraft users and novices. We also find that many of the multimodal components, while not immediately intuitive for users, proved to be preferred modes of game play. In this sense, we feel that this tool is moving in the right direction in terms of the system capabilities that it provides. Our analyses also point to the meaningful ways that multimodal data can be used to study student learning in these game-based environments, and free students from standardized testing and learning experiences. As we iterate on this platform, we look forward to creating a more robust solution that we will test among students with disabilities, and among mixed ability groups, since our goal is to support inclusive learning experiences for all students.

References

1. NPD: Across All Age Groups, U.S. Consumers are Investing More of Their Entertainment Participation, Time and Money on Video Games, Reports The NPD Group (2020). https://www.npd.com/wps/portal/npd/us/news/press-releases/2020/across-all-age-groups-us-consumers-are-investing-more-of-their-entertainment-participation/
2. Nielsen Media: 3, 2, 1 GO! Video gaming is at an all-time high during covid-19, 03 June 2020. https://www.nielsen.com/us/en/insights/article/2020/3-2-1-go-video-gaming-is-at-an-all-time-high-during-covid-19/. Accessed 19 Dec 2020
3. Clement, J.: Increase in video game sales during the coronavirus (COVID-19) pandemic worldwide as of March 2020 (2021). https://www.statista.com/statistics/1109977/video-game-sales-covid/. Accessed 02 Feb 2021
4. Plass, J.L., Homer, B.D., Kinzer, C.K.: Foundations of game-based learning. Educ. Psychol. 50(4), 258–283 (2015)
5. Stevens, R., Satwicz, T., McCarthy, L.: In-game, in-room, in-world: reconnecting video game play to the rest of kids' lives. Ecol. Games Connect. Youth Games Learn. 9, 41–66 (2008)
6. Ringland, K.E., Boyd, L., Faucett, H., Cullen, A.L.L., Hayes, G.R.: Making in minecraft: a means of self-expression for youth with autism. In: Proceedings of the 2017 Conference on Interaction Design and Children, pp. 340–345 (2017)
7. Granic, I., Lobel, A., Engels, R.C.M.E.: The benefits of playing video games. Am. Psychol. 69(1), 66–78 (2014). American Psychological Association, Granic, Isabela: Developmental Psychopathology Department, Behavioural Science Institute, Radboud University Nijmegen, Montessorilaan 3, Nijmegen, Netherlands, 6525 HR, i.granic@pwo.ru.nl
8. Ringland, K.E., Wolf, C.T., Boyd, L.E., Baldwin, M.S., Hayes, G.R.: Would you be mine: appropriating minecraft as an assistive technology for youth with autism. In: Proceedings of 18th International ACM SIGACCESS Conference on Computers and Accessibility - ASSETS 2016, pp. 33–41 (2016)
9. Ringland, K.E., Wolf, C.T., Dombrowski, L., Hayes, G.R.: Making "safe" community-centered practices in a virtual world dedicated to children with autism. In: Proceedings of the 18th ACM Conference on Computer Supported Cooperative Work & Social Computing, pp. 1788–1800 (2015)
10. Ringland, K.E.: A place to play: the (dis)abled embodied experience for autistic children in online spaces. In: Proceedings of the 2019 CHI Conference on Human Factors in Computing Systems, pp. 1–14 (2019)
11. Wobbrock, J.O., Kane, S.K., Gajos, K.Z., Harada, S., Froehlich, J.: Ability-based design: concept, principles and examples. ACM Trans. Access. Comput. 3(3), 1–36 (2011)
12. Blikstein, P., Worsley, M.: Multimodal learning analytics: a methodological framework for research in constructivist learning. J. Learn. Anal. 3(2), 220–238 (2016)
13. Sharma, K., Giannakos, M.: Multimodal data capabilities for learning: what can multimodal data tell us about learning? Br. J. Educ. Technol. e13280 (2020)

14. Worsley, M.: Multimodal learning analytics' past, present, and, potential futures. In: Companion Proceedings of the 8th International Conference on learning Analytics & Knowledge (2018)
15. Uttal, D., Cohen, C.A.: Spatial thinking and STEM education. When, why, and how? Psychol. Psychol. Learn. Motiv. - Adv. Res. Theory **57**, 147–181 (2012)
16. Ramey, K.E., Stevens, R., Uttal, D.H.: Steam learning in an in-school makerspace: the role of distributed spatial sensemaking. In: Proceedings of International Conference of the Learning Sciences, ICLS 2018, vol. 1, no. 2018-June, pp. 168–175 (2018)
17. Ramey, K.E., Uttal, D.: Making sense of space: distributed spatial sensemaking in a middle school summer engineering camp. J. Learn. Sci. **26**(2), 277–319 (2017)
18. Green, C.S., Bavelier, D.: Action-video-game experience alters the spatial resolution of vision: Research article. Psychol. Sci. **18**(1), 88–94 (2007)
19. Wauck, H., Xiao, Z., Chiu, P.-T., Fu, W.-T.: Untangling the relationship between spatial skills, game features, and gender in a video game. In: Proceedings of the 22nd International Conference on Intelligent User Interfaces - IUI 2017 (2017)
20. Nguyen, A., Rank, S.: Spatial involvement in training mental rotation with minecraft. In: Proceedings of the 2016 Annual Symposium on Computer-Human Interaction in Play Companion Extended Abstracts, pp. 245–252 (2016)
21. Fitzhugh, S., Shipley, T.F., Newcombe, N., McKenna, K., Dumay, D.: Mental rotation of real word Shepard-Metzler figures: an eye tracking study. J. Vis. **8**(6), 648 (2008)
22. Just, M.A., Carpenter, P.A.: Eye fixations and cognitive processes. Cogn. Psychol. **8**(4), 441–480 (1975)
23. Xue, J., Li, C., Quan, C., Lu, Y., Yue, J., Zhang, C.: Uncovering the cognitive processes underlying mental rotation: an eye-movement study. Sci. Rep. **7**(1), 10076 (2017)
24. Resnick, M., et al.: Design Principles for Tools to Support Creative Thinking. Science (80-) **20**(2), 25–35 (2005)
25. Turkle, S., Papert, S.: Epistemological pluralism and the revaluation of the concrete. J. Math. Behav. **11**(1), 1–30 (1992)
26. Spacy. http://spacy.io
27. Miller, G.A., Beckwith, R., Fellbaum, C., Gross, D., Miller, K.J.: Introduction to wordnet: an on-line lexical database. Int. J. Lexicogr. **3**(4), 235–244 (1990)
28. Tse, E., Greenberg, S., Shen, C., Forlines, C.: Multimodal multiplayer tabletop gaming. Comput. Entertain. **5**(2), 12 (2007)
29. Ganis, G., Kievit, R.: A new set of three-dimensional shapes for investigating mental rotation processes: validation data and stimulus set. Figshare, June 2014
30. Wagner, J., Lingenfelser, F., Baur, T., Damian, I., Kistler, F., André, E.: The social signal interpretation (SSI) framework: multimodal signal processing and recognition in real-time. In: Proceedings of the 21st ACM International Conference on Multimedia, pp. 831–834 (2013)
31. Abrahamson, D., Shayan, S., Bakker, A., Van Der Schaaf, M.: Eye-tracking Piaget: capturing the emergence of attentional anchors in the coordination of proportional motor action. Hum. Dev. **58**, 218–244 (2016)
32. Worsley, M.: Seeing spatial reasoning. In: Companion Proceedings of 11th International Conferenece on Learning Analytics and Knowledge (LAK) (2021)

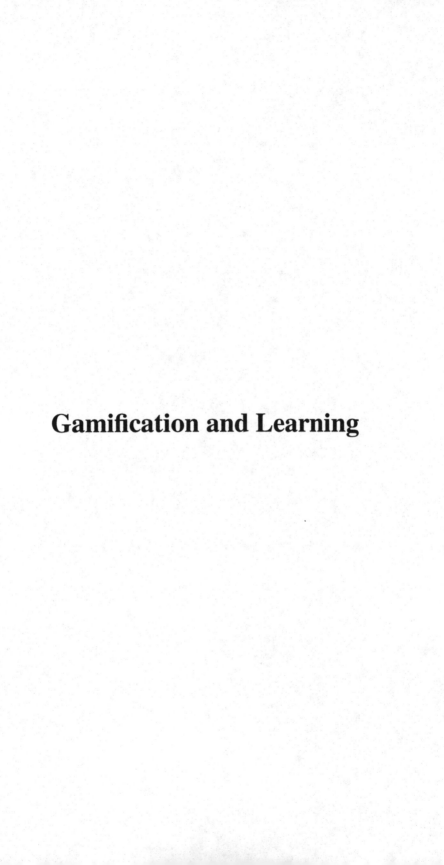

Gamification and Learning

Understanding the Impact on Learners' Reading Performance and Behaviour of Matching E-Learning Material to Dyslexia Type and Reading Skill Level

Weam Gaoud Alghabban[1,3](✉) [iD], Hadeel Mohammed Al-Dawsari[2,3] [iD], and Robert Hendley[3] [iD]

[1] Computer Science Department, Alwajh University College, University of Tabuk, Tabuk, Saudi Arabia
walghabban@ut.edu.sa
[2] Department of Computer Sciences, Princess Nourah Bint Abdulrahman University, Riyadh, Saudi Arabia
hmalateeq@pnu.edu.sa
[3] School of Computer Science, University of Birmingham, Birmingham, UK
{wga814,hma776,R.J.Hendley}@cs.bham.ac.uk

Abstract. Dyslexia is a universal reading difficulty where each individual with dyslexia can have a different combination of underlying reading difficulties. For instance, errors in letter identification or omissions or transpositions within or between words. Nowadays, adaptive e-learning and gamification have become more common. Different learner characteristics have been used when adapting e-learning systems, such as the user's learning style or knowledge level. However, little attention has been directed towards understanding the benefits of using dyslexia type or reading skill level when adapting systems for learners with dyslexia. This, despite dyslexia type and reading skill level being significant factors in their education and learning. This paper reports on research which aims to improve this understanding through empirical studies designed to evaluate the benefits of adaptation with native Arabic speaking children with dyslexia. A mixed-methods approach was used. In the first experiment the focus is on a qualitative understanding of the effects of adaptation based on dyslexia type. The second experiment provides a quantitative analysis of the effects of adaptation based upon the reading skill level of learners with dyslexia. Findings revealed that the majority of learners are motivated when adapting learning material to dyslexia type. Analysis of the results indicated that adapting based on reading skill level does achieve improved learning gain and lead to greater learner satisfaction compared to a non-adaptive version. Implications of these experiments are discussed.

Supported by University of Tabuk and Princess Nourah Bint Abdulrahman University, Saudi Arabia.

W. G. Alghabban and H. M. Al-Dawsari—Both authors contributed equally to this research.

X. Fang (Ed.): HCII 2021, LNCS 12790, pp. 135–154, 2021.
https://doi.org/10.1007/978-3-030-77414-1_11

Keywords: Dyslexia type · Skill level · Arabic · Adaptation · E-Learning

1 Introduction

Reading is one of the most important basic linguistic skills [29]. The majority of readers are able to understand written text automatically and easily. However, many readers face difficulties and have to apply conscious effort when reading. This can, in turn, lead to social and educational exclusion [29]. These readers are known as people with dyslexia.

Dyslexia has been defined by the main international classification, ICD-10 [44] as "a specific and significant impairment in the development of reading skills, which is not solely accounted for by mental age, visual acuity problems, or inadequate schooling". Typical symptoms include inaccurate and/or slow word recognition, comprehension, misspelling and poor decoding abilities [44].

E-learning can support the development of learners' knowledge and skills without the constraints of time and place [16]. However, traditional e-learning systems have several drawbacks compared to real-life teaching [19]: they provide the same learning experience to all learners. This decreases the effectiveness of the learning and can lead learners to become dissatisfied and demotivated [37].

Adaptive e-learning systems and gamification aim to improve learners' experience by making the learning process more effective, and increasing their satisfaction and engagement [31,34]. These systems can adapt the learning content and presentation based upon different characteristics of learners [15]. For learners with dyslexia, dyslexia type and reading skill level are significant factors in their education [20,22]. The dual-route model for single word reading predicts different types of dyslexia, each resulting from different underlying causes [21]. The reading skill level of a learner is also a significant characteristic that should be considered [27]. There is, therefore, a strong argument that such an e-learning environment should apply different teaching approaches based on these two characteristics, rather than treating all learners the same.

This research aims to investigate the impact of adapting learning material based on dyslexia type and reading skill level in a computer-based training system for Arabic. There is very limited research that explores teaching learners with dyslexia to read Arabic [7], despite it being a widely spoken language [30] with a high rate of dyslexia [11]. A mixed-methods approach, using qualitative and quantitative methods, is used to collect and analyze data. An evaluation, in terms of learning performance and learners satisfaction, is presented.

The remainder of this paper is organized as follows. Section two presents some important background upon which the studies are built. Sections three & four present the experimental procedures in detail, followed by the discussion in Section five. Finally, Section six draws some conclusions and points to future work.

2   Background

This section covers the theoretical foundation behind this research: features of Arabic orthography relevant to dyslexia, dyslexia types in Arabic based on the dual-route model for single word reading, adaptation in e-learning and further related work.

2.1   Dyslexia in Arabic

Dyslexia is sensitive to language. The differences in language orthography and structure have a large impact on the difficulties that the readers face. Unfortunately, there are few studies that explore dyslexia in Arabic. This research targets training young, native Arabic speaking learners with dyslexia.

Arabic is the fifth most spoken language. Over 200 million individuals speak Arabic as their first language. It is also used as a second language by millions of Muslims [30]. The Arabic orthography is different from that of English. Therefore, the manifestation of dyslexia [6] is also different [18]. For instance:

- The cursive nature of the Arabic language (where the letters are joined to form a word or sub-word).
- The use of dots to distinguish between different letters.
- Different letter forms depending on the position within a word.
- The use of non-vowelized text (a non-transparent orthography) [18].

Types of Dyslexia in Arabic. Helmer Myklebust, was the first person to suggest classifying developmental dyslexia into different types [21]. There have been several proposals for classifying dyslexia in order to develop a better understanding and thus to provide better support [8,21]. Dyslexia has been classified based on 'symptoms' (Ingram's classification) [8] and also by using the dual-route model for single word reading [21]. Here, Friedmann and Coltheart [21] suggested using that model in order to predict the different 'symptoms' of different types of dyslexia. The dual-route model has proved effective and is widely used [9]. Consequently, this is the approach adopted in this research.

In order to understand the types of dyslexia based on the dual-route model for single word reading, understanding the process is essential (see Fig. 1).

The reading process can be summarized in the following stages:

- The **orthographic-visual analysis system** analyzes the target word to identify its letters, encode each letter's position within the word and bind these letters to that word.
- The result from the previous stage is stored in the **orthographic input buffer** that decomposes the word to its stem. For instance, decomposing the word "birds" into "bird".
- The lexical-phonological route is used for reading familiar words (known written words stored in the reader's lexicon) quickly and accurately. This is achieved by passing the word to the **orthographic input lexicon**:

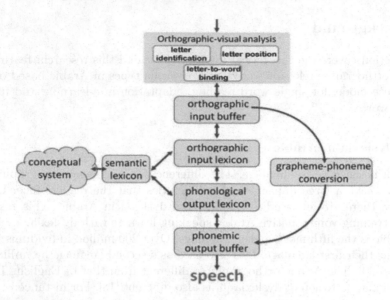

Fig. 1. Dual-route model for a single word reading [21].

- The **phonological output lexicon** will write to the **phonemic output buffer**.
- The corresponding entry in the **conceptual-semantic system** is activated to access the word's meaning.
- The sub-lexical-phonological route is used for reading unfamiliar words. This is accomplished by passing the written word to the **grapheme-to-phoneme conversion** component. It analyzes the letters into either letters or groups of letters (graphemes) that form a single phoneme. Finally, this information is passed to the **phonemic output buffer**.

As seen in the previous stages, each component of the dual-route model is essential and performs an important task in the reading process. A deficit in any component will cause a reading impairment and thus a type of dyslexia.

Dyslexia in Arabic is classified into seven types based on the deficit in the dual-route model [22]. This research focuses on only two frequent types; **Letter Position Dyslexia (LPD)** and **Vowel letter Dyslexia (VD)** [22].

LPD arises from an inability to encode the order of the letters within the word due to a reading deficit in the orthographic-visual analyser stage, specifically the function that is responsible for encoding the relative position of letters within the word [21,22]. They migrate letters within words especially the middle ones [21,22].

On the other hand, VD suffers from omitting, transposing, substituting and adding vowel letters (such as reading the word "bit" as "but" or even "boat") due to a specific deficit in the sub-lexical route which impairs the way the vowels are processed [21,22]. Such errors appear only with the vowel letters during reading and not with vowel phonemes during speech production [21].

In the Arabic orthography, three aspects should be considered [22]:

- Each vowel letter identifies a single long vowel.
- There is a difference between long and short vowels. Long vowels are encoded orthographically, while short ones are usually eliminated from written words.
- A vowel letter has different forms depending on its position.

Friedmann and Haddad-Hanna [22] found that VD occurs more frequently, with typical errors including: vowel additions, migrations, omissions, and substitutions. Vowel addition is indicated by the elongation of a short vowel, while vowel omission is indicated by shortening a long vowel.

2.2 Adaptation in the E-Learning Domain

The emergence of e-learning has enabled the wider learner community to have access to educational content. However, such wider access has raised concerns with respect to the delivery of appropriate learning experience to different learners, since most e-learning systems do not adapt material to meet the needs of the individual learner [19]. Research aims to find ways in which the specific needs of a learner can be identified, and material adapted to suit those needs [19].

Another challenging task in e-learning is motivating learners to use such systems in order to enhance their learning gain. Gamification has proved to increase learners motivation, engagement, and to support them through their interaction with material [34].

In the context of e-learning systems, adaptation is defined as a procedure for tailoring the educational environment to these differences [14] with the aim of improving learning outcome [31]. Different learner characteristics can be considered such as knowledge level [32] and learning styles [35]. Learners with dyslexia, like everyone, are different in their needs, preferences, and their skill level. These parameters must also be considered in adaptive e-learning systems. Therefore, this research focuses on types of dyslexia and their reading skill level.

Skill Level. According to Self [38], "a student model is what enables a system to care about a student". Different learners' data and characteristics can be represented in a learner model as sources for providing adaptation [19]. These characteristics can be classified into affective (motivation and emotions), cognitive (knowledge level, skill level), and conative (learning style and goals) [39]. Data can be collected implicitly, explicitly or a combination of both. Implicit techniques involve feedback generated from the system that monitors user activity like page scrolling, time spent on a page and page visits [23]. Explicit techniques involve feedback generated from the user like tests and questionnaires [23].

One of the most common learner modelling techniques in adaptive e-learning systems is the overlay model [40]. The overlay model is often used to represent the learner's knowledge [16]. The key idea of the overlay model is that the learner model is a subset of an idealised domain model based on the assumption that a learner may have correct but incomplete knowledge of the domain [16]. The domain is decomposed into a set of elements and the overlay model is a set of masteries over those elements. The overlay model, in its simplest form, assigns a Boolean value (yes or no) to each element in the domain, indicating whether a learner knows or does not know that element. It can also use qualitative values (poor, average, good) or a quantitative measure (the probability that the learner knows the concept) [15]. Although the overlay model is used extensively due to its representation of learner knowledge for each concept independently, one drawback is that it does not represent incorrect knowledge or misconceptions. In addition, it cannot represent other characteristics such as learners' behaviour, personality and preferences [16]. For this reason, many adaptive e-learning systems use a combination of other learner modelling approaches with the overlay model.

Among learner characteristics, learners' knowledge level is recognized as a fundamental factor [20], when presenting learning materials to the learner [19]. It describes the extent to which a learner understands, applies and recalls specific information related to a particular topic [35]. Learners' knowledge level is one of the most commonly used adaptive parameters. For example, SQL-Tutor [33] and ELM-ART [43] both consider learners' knowledge level in order to adapt learning content. Also, ActiveMath adapts mathematical content to learners' knowledge level, goals and media preferences [32].

In this research, we refer to skill level rather than knowledge level. Knowledge is learning principles of a subject, while skill is the ability to apply that knowledge in a context. According to Sun and Peterson [41], individuals learn generic and declarative knowledge first and then, through practice, turn such knowledge into specific, usable procedural skill. This research targets training young learners in reading skills. The learners already have the basic, formal knowledge and by practising they develop it into specific skills which can be applied subconsciously rather than through conscious reasoning.

2.3 Related Work

Some e-learning systems have been developed to teach Arabic learners with dyslexia. Some of these systems adapt based on learner characteristics while others do not.

In terms of adaptivity, Alghabban et al. [3] investigated how personalizing learning material based on dyslexia type affects children's satisfaction. An adaptive e-learning system was implemented to help children in elementary schools to practice their reading skill. The system was evaluated by a controlled experimental study. The results showed that children with dyslexia were more engaged with their learning experience when matching the learning content to their dyslexia type. However, the learning performance and effectiveness were not considered.

Other research has considered the learning style of learners with dyslexia as one characteristic in adaptive e-learning systems. For example, Benmarrakchi et al. [12] developed a framework for an adaptive m-learning system to support children with dyslexia. The proposed system aimed to enhance the students' fundamental skills such as reading, comprehension, writing, concentration, short-term memory and Arabic orthography. However, the evaluation methodology was not presented, leading to difficulty in understanding its effectiveness. Similar work has been done by Alghabban et al. [2] by developing a cloud-based m-learning tool for learners with dyslexia in primary schools. The proposed tool enabled manual adaptation of the interface and different modalities of input and output based on learning styles of learners with dyslexia. The tool was evaluated using pre- and post-tests and demonstrated an increase in reading skills after three months use. However, again, the design methodology was not presented, which makes it difficult to evaluate the effectiveness.

Overall, there is very little research which draws upon the theoretical understanding of dyslexia and which uses this to derive adaptive learning. Where this has been investigated, the evaluation of its effectiveness is very limited. Therefore, in this research we seek to build upon existing research into the causes and effects of dyslexia and understand whether and how this can be used to derive adaptation of learning to improve the learners' experience.

3   Experiment 1: Dyslexia Type Adaptivity

This experiment aims to understand the impact of adapting learning material based on dyslexia type, on the behaviour of learners with dyslexia. A between-subject experiment was conducted. A mixed-methods approach was used to collect and analyze the data. The quantitative data, in term of learning gain and learner satisfaction scores, is reported in [1].

3.1   Data Collection

Data was gathered by using: a dyslexia type diagnostic test, a pre-reading test and taking notes when observing learners. The dyslexia type diagnostic test was used to determine learner's dyslexia type. It is based on the standardized tests approved by the Ministry of Education in Saudi Arabia. The test was validated by a number of special education experts and refined to produce the final version. The pre-reading test was used to determine the learner's reading skill level.

3.2   DysTypeTrain System

The Dyslexia Type Training system (*DysTypeTrain*) was designed and implemented to support this experiment. It is a dynamic web-based e-learning system. It trains learners with dyslexia via eight different reading activities, each one containing ten training exercises, giving a total of 80 exercises. The difficulty of these activities gradually increases. In each training exercise, a word is pronounced and an image is displayed along with three choices. Each choice displays a different word.

Figure 2 shows an example of a training exercise. The learner listens to the target word and chooses the correct answer from the three choices. If the learner chooses the correct word then verbal, encouraging, motivational feedback is given [11], and they gain a point. Otherwise, remedial feedback is given. The total point score is presented at the top left corner of the screen. Feedback on training progress is provided as a training exercise number (between 1 and 10) in the top of the screen. The learner can re-play the target word, as many times as they want, by clicking on the audio icon presented in the middle right of the screen and use the image displayed underneath as a hint. Once the activity is completed, a motivational message is displayed. The experience of success was a natural reward which was controlled computationally [28]. The learner should achieve 80% through each activity [28] to unlock the next level. Otherwise, they will repeat it [5]. The incorrect words were chosen to target VD difficulties.

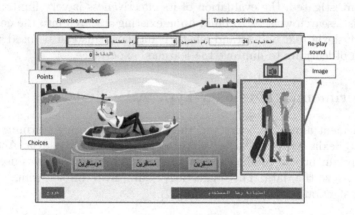

Fig. 2. A screenshot of one of the DysTypeTrain system training exercises.

The training material was chosen from the primary school curriculum to target VD. It combines short vowels (fat-ha (/a/), kasra (/i/) and dammah (/u/)), and long ones (alef (a), yaa (i), waw (u)), progressing from simple words (i.e. three-letters words with only fat-ha short vowel & alef long vowel) to advanced ones (i.e. five or six-letters words with a mix of all short and long vowels).

3.3 Method

Originally, this experiment targeted VD and LPD due to their frequency [22]. In practice, LPD was not found in the target population and another common reading difficulty was used. This is the difficulty in distinguishing between Short Vowels. It is named by the researcher as Short Vowel Dyslexia (SVD). Therefore, this experiment targeted SVD and VD rather than of LPD and VD.

The experiment took place in Riyadh, Saudi Arabia. Consent was obtained from both schools and learners' parents/guardians. The learners were welcomed and introduced to the objectives of the experiment. Then, their demographic information was collected, and their dyslexia type was determined. The pre-reading test was conducted to assess their initial reading skill level. Learners were divided randomly into two groups, balanced by age, grade, and their prior reading performance. Both the matched (VD) group and mismatched (SVD) group used the same version of the *DysTypeTrain*. The learning material of the website matched the matched group while mismatched the other one.

The experiment took place in person with guidance from the experimenter, in a quiet room, within the learner's school. Nobody was in the room except the learner and the experimenter. The learner sat in front of a desk with a laptop while the experimenter sat next to them observing and solving any technical problems. Learners worked individually. There were eight experimental sessions: two sessions per learner per week. Each session had a duration of approximately 35 min and the total duration of the study was one month. At the beginning of the first session, the experimenter explained the *DysTypeTrain* layout. During each session, the experimenter observed the learners and took notes about their interaction with the system and facial expressions. Neither the learner nor the experimenter was aware of the experimental condition to which the learner had been allocated.

3.4 Participants

Originally, 20 female, native Arabic speaking learners, already diagnosed with dyslexia, were recruited from different elementary schools. Due to the Coronavirus pandemic (COVID-19), this number dropped down to 16 who completed the experiment. The learners were aged from 9–14 years (Grades 4 to 6). All had previous experience with electronic devices. The learners were assigned either to the mismatched group (n = 8) or the matched group (n = 8). Learners had approximately the same prior reading skill level, with no statistically significant difference between the groups. Thirteen of 16 learners completed the experiment in school. The remaining three completed it remotely via Zoom meetings due to the closure of schools (COVID-19).

3.5 Findings

Participant Observations. Based on the schools' policy, the sessions were not video recorded. Learner observations were collected using structured notes taken by the experimenter. These data were analyzed using Thematic Content Analysis [13]. In this method, codes (and sub-codes if necessary) are generated from all data collected. Then the codes are synthesized into themes (and sometimes sub-themes) and theoretical concepts. These codes should be related to each other within a theme and the themes should also relate to each other and to the entire data set.

When observing the learners during their interaction with the system, several findings were noted in terms of study mode, learners, choices and training activities. In term of **study mode**, 13 learners were able to complete the study in person while the remaining three completed the study remotely using Zoom meetings. In both groups the online mode affected both the clarity of the system's audio and the ability to observe the learner's facial expressions. In the online mode, learners were not always able to hear the system's audio clearly ("The sound is not clear", or they physically brought their ears close to the device) and the experimenter had to re-pronounce the target word to enable them to proceed.

In term of **learners**, a majority of learners in both groups were engaged and motivated. They reported that the system was "better than the textbook" and cited reasons such as "because it has audio", "because it has audio and I can choose", "I liked it because there is a challenge to win and better than the textbook because it has audio", "because it let me know my mistakes". Therefore, the audio feature was the dominant reason for their engagement and motivation towards the system. However, later sessions were affected negatively. For instance, one learner was tired and demotivated because the session was conducted almost at the end of the school day. Another learner was also demotivated because the session took place during the school's play-time.

In addition, two findings were noted in term of **choices**:

- All learners in both groups (except one in the mismatched group) tried to figure out the correct choices by both concentrating on the spoken target word and spelling it out. Removing the short vowel from the last letter of the target word was a surprising way which one of the learners followed to help her figure out the correct choice. Using their finger to spell out the target word on the table was another method used. Two learners (one learner from each group) benefited from the displayed image.
- Five learners in each group insisted that their wrong choices were correct or they lost focus on the task.
- Three learners in the mismatched group and one in the matched group realised their errors before completion. They completed the remaining exercises quickly and randomly in order to start afresh.
- One learner in the mismatched group focused on points and became happy each time she gained one.
- One learner in the matched group faced difficulty in choosing the correct choice and complained "The choices are too similar".

Finally, in term of **training activities**, none of the learners in either group was able to complete all of the eight activities on the first attempt. They repeated some of these activities many times until they succeeded. This repetition had both positive and negative effects:

- *Positive Effects*: Three learners in each group increased their focus in later attempts in order to succeed. In addition, one learner in the matched group was able to recall their mistakes and thus avoid repeating them. Three learners in the mismatched group and five in the matched one were able to memorize their correct choices and thus re-choose them quickly and without re-listening to the target word. However, one of the learners from the mismatched group fell into the trap of memorizing the position of the correct choice instead of the choice itself without noticing that the position of the choices changes each time.

- *Negative Effects*: Four learners in the mismatched group and five in the matched one became bored during some of their sessions. Three learners in the mismatched group and two in the matched one lost their focus and switched to choosing their answers randomly – perhaps to either waste time or to win by chance. Some of them required more than one experimental session to complete a single training activity. As a result, five learners in each group were not able to complete all eight training activities during the eight experimental sessions. One learner (in the matched group) completed half of the activities while the others completed between six to eight activities.

One learner (in the mismatched group) reported that "it is hard and I prefer to use paper". This learner also took breaks in the sessions and was agitated.

4 Experiment 2: Reading Skill Level Adaptivity

This experiment aims to understand the impact on reading performance of adapting learning material based on the reading skill level of learners with dyslexia. The effect on satisfaction of learners with dyslexia is also presented.

4.1 Experiment's Questions and Hypotheses

This experiment addresses the following questions:

Q1: **Does adapting learning material based on reading skill level of learners with dyslexia improve reading performance compared to non-adapted material?**

Q2: **Does adapting learning material based on reading skill level of learners with dyslexia achieve a higher level of learner satisfaction compared to non-adapted material?**

Two hypotheses were formulated for this experiment:

- *H1:* Adapting learning material to the reading skill level of learners with dyslexia achieves significantly better learning gain compared to non-adapted material.
- *H2:* Adapting learning material to the reading skill level of learners with dyslexia achieves significantly better learner satisfaction compared to non-adapted material.

4.2   Measurements and Data Collection

Two measurements were used in this experiment. Reading performance was assessed directly after finishing the experiment to derive the learning gain. Learner satisfaction was also measured.

Data was gathered using several tools: reading skill level diagnostic tests, reading tests (pre- and post-tests) and a satisfaction questionnaire. The reading skill level tests were used to determine the reading skill level of the learner.

Three basic tests were used to determine the reading skill level of learners: reading letters with the different short vowels (S1), reading words with Sakin letter(s) (S2) and reading words with short vowels and Sakin letter(s) (S3).

Pre- and post-tests are commonly used to derive learning gain. Here, these included different vowelized words from the curriculum and were validated by special education experts. Each learner was asked to read these words aloud to measure their performance. The pre-test was applied at the start of the study to balance the experimental conditions. At the end, the same test was used to re-assess the learner's performance (post-test). The learning gain is the difference between the pre-test score and the post-test score.

Learner satisfaction was measured using a reliable and validated tool, the E-Learner Satisfaction (ELS) questionnaire [42]. ELS measures overall satisfaction of learners with e-learning systems [42]. The test uses ten questions adapted to a 5-point scale using the Smileyometer [3], a widely-used instrument which matches children's cognitive abilities with these scales (awful, not very good, good, really good and brilliant) [36].

4.3   DysSkillTrain System

The Dyslexia Skill Level Training system (*DysSkillTrain*) was designed to support the aim of this experiment. It is a dynamic, web-based e-learning system. There are two versions to support the two experimental conditions. The adaptive version of the system matches training material to reading skill level, and the non-adaptive version provides a combination of training material at all reading skill levels. Both versions of the system were identical; the only difference is the curriculum.

The system provides six different reading sessions each with 20 training activities (a total of 120). The difficulty gradually increases in both versions. The content of the training material was drawn from the school curriculum to target the three skills (S1, S2, S3). For S1, the reading material includes reading letters with the different short vowels progressing from the simple short vowel (fat-ha (/a/)), (kasra (/i/)) to the advanced short vowel (dammah (/u/)). For S2, the reading material includes reading words with Sakin letter(s) progressing from simple words (with one Sakin letter at the end of two-letter words) to advanced ones (i.e. two Sakin letters in the middle or at the end of three- and four-letters words). A Sakin letter is a letter with a sukun on top of it (indicated by a small circle) which is a letter with no vowel. For S3, the reading material includes reading words with short vowels progressing from simple words (i.e. words of three letters with only the fat-ha short vowel) to advanced ones (i.e. words of three- and four-letters with a mix of all three short vowels and Sakin letters).

Figure 3 shows an example of a training session for S1. It follows the same procedure as *DysTypeTrain* in presenting the question, target word and its audio icon, three choices (one correct) and the training progress bar. Motivational feedback is presented, if they choose the correct answer, and remedial feedback in the case of choosing a wrong answer. Additionally, motivational messages and the total point score are presented after completing the activities. The training sessions' layout for S2 and S3 is consistent with those for S1; that is keeping the question, target word and its audio icon and the choices in the same place. The only difference is the training material for each skill.

Fig. 3. A screenshot of one of the DysSkillTrain system training sessions.

4.4   Method

The experiment took place in Jeddah, Saudi Arabia. Before conducting the experiment, learners were welcomed and introduced to the objectives of the experiment. Their demographic information was collected, their reading skill level was determined and their initial reading performance was assessed by the pre-test. The learners were divided into two groups, balanced by age, grade, and pre-test score. The control group used the non-adaptive version of the system, while the adaptive group used the adaptive version.

The experiment took place in person, in a quiet room, within the learner's school. Neither the learner nor the experimenter was aware of the experimental condition to which the learner had been allocated. The learner sat in front of a desk with a laptop with the experimenter next to them. The experimenter explained the *DysSkillTrain* layout. Learners worked individually. There were six sessions: two sessions per learner per week. Each session had a duration of approximately 30 min. After finishing the experiment, the post-test and ELS tool were administered.

4.5   Participants

Originally, 44 female, native Arabic speakers, already diagnosed with dyslexia, were recruited. Due to the closure of schools (COVID-19), this number dropped down to 41, who completed the experiment. Learners were aged from 7–10 years (Grade 2 to 4). They had previous experience with electronic devices. The learners were assigned to the control group (n = 21) or the adaptive group (n = 20) balanced by age and grade. All learners had approximately the same prior reading skill level with no statistical difference between groups (mean score of pre-test for the adaptive group = 3.9, SD = 1.74, mean for the control group = 4.19, SD = 1.99).

4.6   Results

Both adaptive and control groups were homogeneous in terms of gender, language, age and pre-test. The data were analyzed using the IBM SPSS statistical software.

Learning Gain. Hypothesis 1 about learning gain was tested. As shown in Fig. 4, the post-test and learning gain of the adaptive group were higher than the control group. The findings indicate that there was generally a positive effect in adapting learning material to the reading skill level of learners with dyslexia. The significance of the learning gain was tested. The data deviated from a normal distribution, as assessed by Shapiro-Wilk's test ($p < 0.05$), so an independent sample Mann-Whitney U test was used to determine if there were differences between the groups. The results indicate that the learning gain for the adaptive group (mean ranks = 29.18) were statistically significantly higher than the control group (mean ranks = 13.21), $U = 373.5$, $p = 0.000017 \approx 0.00$, $Z = 4.307$. Therefore, the first hypothesis is confirmed, and it can be concluded that adapting learning material to the reading skill level of learners with dyslexia yields significantly better learning gain than in the non-adaptive condition.

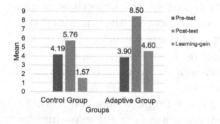

Fig. 4. Results of pre-test, post-test and learning gain of the control and adaptive groups.

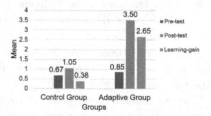

Fig. 5. Results of unseen words pre-test, post-test and learning gain of the control and adaptive groups.

Additional Findings. The previous subsection demonstrated the benefit of training learners with dyslexia when reading known words. Whether this can be generalised to unseen words is investigated in this subsection. Figure 5 shows that the mean scores for unseen words in the post-test is higher in the adaptive group. As the data deviated from the normal distribution, as assessed by Shapiro-Wilk's test ($p < 0.05$), an independent sample Mann-Whitney U test was used to determine if there were differences between the groups. The results indicate that the scores for the adaptive group (mean rank $= 29.75$) were statistically significantly higher than for the control group (mean rank $= 12.67$), $U = 385$, $p = 0.000002 \approx 0.00$, $Z = 4.714$.

Learner Satisfaction. Based on the analysis of the learners' satisfaction, shown in Table 1, the adaptive group (Mean $= 4.77$, SD $= 0.13$) had a larger mean satisfaction score than the control group (Mean $= 4.22$, SD $= 0.44$), indicating that there was a positive effect on learner satisfaction when learning material was adapted to their reading skill level.

Table 1. Satisfaction scores of learners with dyslexia.

ELS components	Satisfaction of control group		Satisfaction of adaptive group	
	Mean	SD	Mean	SD
Learning content	4.20	0.91	4.63	0.59
System personalization	4.68	1.23	5	0
System interface	4.24	0.88	4.76	0.47
General satisfaction	4.22	0.44	4.77	0.13

As the learner satisfaction score distributions of both adaptive and control groups were normally distributed (Shapiro-Wilk's test $p > 0.05$), an independent-sample t-test was used to investigate if there were statistically significant differences in satisfaction score between the two groups. Results indicated that the learner satisfaction score for the adaptive group, $t(23.37) = 5.38$, $p = 0.000017 \approx 0.00 < 0.05$, was statistically significantly higher than the control group. Therefore, the second hypothesis is confirmed and it can be concluded that adapting learning material to the reading skill level of learners with dyslexia yields significantly better learner satisfaction than in the non-adaptive condition.

5 Discussion

This research was affected by COVID-19. It decreased the number of learners and negatively affected the process of observing the learners.

The observation showed that learners were engaged and motivated to learn. This is consistent with the high learners' satisfaction scores with the *DysType-Train* system [1]. There is a strong relationship between learners' motivation and satisfaction [26]. Almost all learners followed the same method in figuring out the correct choice by concentrating on the spoken target word and decoding it.

The repetition feature embedded within the system enhanced the short-term memory of the learner through their memorizing the correct choices. This is in line with previous studies where repetition is shown to be useful for learners with dyslexia [5] and increases learning effectiveness and can be used along with prior knowledge and time spent as strong predictors for good results [25].

In addition, this research confirms that adapting to learner's reading skill level is one factor that can enhance learning. This is in line with previous studies, which have argued that learners' knowledge and skill level should be considered [19, 27, 43]. This study differs from existing work targeting dyslexia, which either lacks formal evaluation [4, 10, 11] or where the size of the sample is small [11].

Finally, the results follow the argumentation of Kangas et al. [26] that there is a strong relationship between learners' motivation and satisfaction, where satisfaction is influenced by the learning content. This experiment showed that learners with dyslexia were more satisfied when adapting learning material according to their reading skill level. This is in line with a previous study [3]. The system interface was identical between the two conditions, but the interface component in the ELS was rated more highly in the adaptive condition, as well as the learning and system personalization components. It is a useful way to assess how well the learning matches the learners' needs. While they may not be able to explicitly assess this match, they are, at least subconsciously, aware of it and this will be reflected in their assessment of aspects of the system that do not change between conditions.

6   Conclusion and Future Work

This research investigated the impact of adaptation based on learners' dyslexia type and reading skill level. Adaptation of learning material according to these two important characteristics of learners with dyslexia [21, 27] is still a significant gap in existing research, especially in Arabic [2, 12]. Arabic dyslexia was targeted in this research since there are few studies in this language [11, 30]. This research also addressed the lack of rigorously designed and controlled experimental evaluations in previous studies [4, 11]. One experiment targeted learners' dyslexia type and the other learners' reading skill level. A mixed-methods approach of qualitative and quantitative analysis was used.

The first experiment aimed to investigate the impact on the behaviour of learners with dyslexia, when adapting learning material based on dyslexia type. It was conducted with 16 Arabic learners with dyslexia. The qualitative findings of this experiment revealed that the majority of learners were motivated and engaged. This is consistent with the learner's satisfaction with the *DysTypeTrain* presented in [1]. There is a strong relationship between learners' motivation and satisfaction [26]. In addition, presenting the target word in different modes (audio and visual) was beneficial. Many learners insisted on the correctness of their errorful answers and it might be useful to add audio feedback to remedy this. It was also clear that many learners had additional problems that affected their ability to study. Despite the positive results of this experiment, there are several limitations. One is the small number of learners. Therefore, it is not possible to generalize the findings.

The second experiment aimed to investigate the impact on reading performance of adapting the learning material based on the reading skill level of learners. It was conducted with 41 Arabic learners with dyslexia. The quantitative results of this experiment revealed that adaptation based upon learners' reading skill level leads to a significant improvement in learning gain and satisfaction. This is in line with classroom practice [17] where, once the learner's reading level has been determined, teachers select the most appropriate materials for each learner [17]. Moreover, the current findings indicated that learners' reading performance showed the greatest degree of generalization when learning materials were matched to the learners' reading skill level. More importantly, in contrast to previous research [11], this experiment is one of the few studies which consider a combination of learning effectiveness and learners' satisfaction as metrics with a significant number of learners.

Reading speed is a good indicator of reading fluency. In the future we will include reading speed, as one important metric. A limited number of reading skills are covered in this study. This was an appropriate decision but in the future, we will extend the research to cover, for instance, long vowels and sentence level reading. Further investigation of other metrics, such as reading speed, as mentioned, is also required.

The complex co-morbidities of many learners with dyslexia suggests that adaptation based on other factors (e.g. learning style or personality) would be valuable. Similarly, in this work there are a limited number of gamification elements and these are fixed across each experimental condition. Adapting the gamification elements to match the, often complex, needs of individuals in this population is an important area of future research [24].

References

1. Al-Dawsari, H., Hendley, R.: The effect of matching learning material to learners' dyslexia type on reading performance. In: 2020 World Congress in Computer Science, Computer Engineering, and Applied Computing (2020, in press)
2. Alghabban, W.G., Salama, R.M., Altalhi, A.H.: Mobile cloud computing: an effective multimodal interface tool for students with dyslexia. Comput. Hum. Behav. **75**, 160–166 (2017). https://doi.org/10.1016/j.chb.2017.05.014
3. Alghabban, W.G., Hendley, R.: The impact of adaptation based on students' dyslexia type: an empirical evaluation of students' satisfaction. In: Adjunct Publication of the 28th ACM Conference on User Modeling, Adaptation and Personalization, UMAP 2020, pp. 41–46. Adjunct, Association for Computing Machinery, New York (2020). https://doi.org/10.1145/3386392.3397596
4. Alghabban, W.G., Salama, R.M., Altalhi, A.: M-learning: effective framework for dyslexic students based on mobile cloud computing technology. Int. J. Adv. Res. Comput. Commun. Eng. **5**(2), 513–517 (2016)

5. Aljojo, N., et al.: Arabic alphabetic puzzle game using eye tracking and chatbot for dyslexia. Int. J. Interact. Mob. Technol. (iJIM) **12**(5), 58–80 (2018)
6. AlRowais, F., Wald, M., Wills, G.: An Arabic framework for dyslexia training tools. In: 1st International Conference on Technology for Helping People with Special Needs (ICTHP-2013) (19/02/13–20/02/13), pp. 63–68, February 2013
7. AlRowais, F., Wald, M., Wills, G.: Developing a new framework for evaluating Arabic dyslexia training tools. In: Miesenberger, K., Fels, D., Archambault, D., Peñáz, P., Zagler, W. (eds.) ICCHP 2014. LNCS, vol. 8548, pp. 565–568. Springer, Cham (2014). https://doi.org/10.1007/978-3-319-08599-9_83
8. Alsobhi, A.Y., Khan, N., Rahanu, H.: Toward linking dyslexia types and symptoms to the available assistive technologies. In: 2014 IEEE 14th International Conference on Advanced Learning Technologies, pp. 597–598. IEEE (2014). https://doi.org/10.1109/ICALT.2014.174
9. Annett, M.: Laterality and types of dyslexia. Neurosci. Biobehav. Rev. **20**(4), 631–636 (1996). https://doi.org/10.1016/0149-7634(95)00076-3
10. Benmarrakchi, F.E., Kafi, J.E., Elhore, A.: User modeling approach for dyslexic students in virtual learning environments. Int. J. Cloud Appl. Comput. (IJCAC) **7**(2), 1–9 (2017). https://doi.org/10.4018/IJCAC.2017040101
11. Benmarrakchi, F., Kafi, J.E., Elhore, A.: Communication technology for users with specific learning disabilities. Procedia Comput. Sci. **110**, 258–265 (2017). https://doi.org/10.1016/j.procs.2017.06.093. 14th International Conference on Mobile Systems and Pervasive Computing (MobiSPC 2017)/12th International Conference on Future Networks and Communications (FNC 2017)/Affiliated Workshops
12. Benmarrakchi, F.E., El Kafi, J., Elhore, A., Haie, S.: Exploring the use of the ICT in supporting dyslexic students' preferred learning styles: a preliminary evaluation. Educ. Inf. Technol. **22**(6), 2939–2957 (2016). https://doi.org/10.1007/s10639-016-9551-4
13. Braun, V., Clarke, V.: Using thematic analysis in psychology. Qual. Res. Psychol. **3**(2), 77–101 (2006). https://doi.org/10.1191/1478088706qp063oa
14. Brusilovsky, P.: Adaptive hypermedia for education and training. In: Durlach, P.J., Lesgold, A.M. (eds.) Adaptive Technologies for Training and Education, pp. 46–66. Cambridge University Press. https://doi.org/10.1017/cbo9781139049580.006
15. Brusilovsky, P., Millán, E.: User models for adaptive hypermedia and adaptive educational systems. In: Brusilovsky, P., Kobsa, A., Nejdl, W. (eds.) The Adaptive Web. LNCS, vol. 4321, pp. 3–53. Springer, Heidelberg (2007). https://doi.org/10.1007/978-3-540-72079-9_1
16. Chrysafiadi, K., Virvou, M.: Student modeling approaches: a literature review for the last decade. Expert Syst. Appl. **40**(11), 4715–4729 (2013). https://doi.org/10.1016/j.eswa.2013.02.007
17. Dolgin, A.B.: How to match reading materials to student reading levels. Soc. Stud. **66**(6), 249–252 (1975). https://doi.org/10.1080/00220973.1943.11019435
18. Elbeheri, G.: Dyslexia in Egypt. In: Smythe, I., Everatt, J., Salter, R. (eds.) The International Book of Dyslexia: A Guide to Practice and Resources, pp. 79–85. Wiley, Hoboken (2005)
19. Essalmi, F., Ayed, L.J.B., Jemni, M., Kinshuk, Graf, S.: A fully personalization strategy of e-learning scenarios. Comput. Hum. Behav. **26**(4), 581–591 (2010). https://doi.org/10.1016/j.chb.2009.12.010
20. Felder, R.M., Silverman, L.K.: Learning and teaching styles in engineering education. Eng. Educ. **78**(7), 674–681 (1988)

21. Friedmann, N., Coltheart, M.: Types of developmental dyslexia. In: Bar-On, A., Ravid, D. (eds.) Handbook of Communication Disorders: Theoretical, Empirical, and Applied Linguistics Perspectives, pp. 1–37. De Gruyter Mouton, Berlin (2016)
22. Friedmann, N., Haddad-Hanna, M.: Types of developmental dyslexia in Arabic. In: Saiegh-Haddad, E., Joshi, R.M. (eds.) Handbook of Arabic Literacy. LS, vol. 9, pp. 119–151. Springer, Dordrecht (2014). https://doi.org/10.1007/978-94-017-8545-7_6
23. Gauch, S., Speretta, M., Chandramouli, A., Micarelli, A.: User profiles for personalized information access. In: Brusilovsky, P., Kobsa, A., Nejdl, W. (eds.) The Adaptive Web. LNCS, vol. 4321, pp. 54–89. Springer, Heidelberg (2007). https://doi.org/10.1007/978-3-540-72079-9_2
24. Ghaban, W., Hendley, R.: Can we predict the best gamification elements for a user based on their personal attributes? In: Fang, X. (ed.) HCII 2020. LNCS, vol. 12211, pp. 58–75. Springer, Cham (2020). https://doi.org/10.1007/978-3-030-50164-8_4
25. Harandi, S.R.: Effects of e-learning on students' motivation. Procedia Soc. Behav. Sci. **181**, 423–430 (2015)
26. Kangas, M., Siklander, P., Randolph, J., Ruokamo, H.: Teachers' engagement and students' satisfaction with a playful learning environment. Teach. Teach. Educ. **63**, 274–284 (2017). https://doi.org/10.1016/j.tate.2016.12.018
27. Klašnja-Milićević, A., Vesin, B., Ivanović, M., Budimac, Z.: E-learning personalization based on hybrid recommendation strategy and learning style identification. Comput. Educ. **56**(3), 885–899 (2011). https://doi.org/10.1016/j.compedu.2010.11.001
28. Lyytinen, H., Erskine, J., Kujala, J., Ojanen, E., Richardson, U.: In search of a science-based application: a learning tool for reading acquisition. Scand. J. Psychol. **50**(6), 668–675 (2009). https://doi.org/10.1111/j.1467-9450.2009.00791.x
29. M. Mastropavlou, V.Z.: Integrated intelligent learning environment for reading and writing d3. 2 - learning strategies specification report (2013)
30. Mahfoudhi, A., Everatt, J., Elbeheri, G.: Introduction to the special issue on literacy in Arabic. Read. Writ. **24**(9), 1011–1018 (2011). https://doi.org/10.1007/s11145-011-9306-y
31. Maravanyika, M., Dlodlo, N., Jere, N.: An adaptive recommender-system based framework for personalised teaching and learning on e-learning platforms. In: 2017 IST-Africa Week Conference (IST-Africa), pp. 1–9 (2017). https://doi.org/10.23919/ISTAFRICA.2017.8102297
32. Melis, E., et al.: ActiveMath: a generic and adaptive web-based learning environment. Int. J. Artif. Intell. Educ. (IJAIED) **12**, 385–407 (2001)
33. Mitrovic, A.: An intelligent SQL tutor on the web. Int. J. Artif. Intell. Educ. **13**(2–4), 173–197 (2003)
34. Osipov, I.V., Nikulchev, E., Volinsky, A.A., Prasikova, A.Y.: Study of gamification effectiveness in online e-learning systems. Int. J. Adv. Comput. Sci. Appl. **6**(2), 71–77 (2015)
35. Papanikolaou, K.A., Grigoriadou, M., Kornilakis, H., Magoulas, G.D.: Personalizing the interaction in a web-based educational hypermedia system: the case of inspire. User Model. User-Adap. Inter. **13**(3), 213–267 (2003). https://doi.org/10.1023/A:1024746731130
36. Read, J.C., MacFarlane, S.: Using the fun toolkit and other survey methods to gather opinions in child computer interaction. In: Proceedings of the 2006 Conference on Interaction Design and Children, IDC 2006, pp. 81–88. Association for Computing Machinery, New York (2006). https://doi.org/10.1145/1139073.1139096

37. Schiaffino, S., Garcia, P., Amandi, A.: eteacher: providing personalized assistance to e-learning students. Comput. Educ. **51**(4), 1744–1754 (2008). https://doi.org/10.1016/j.compedu.2008.05.008

38. Self, J.: The defining characteristics of intelligent tutoring systems research: ITSs care, precisely. Int. J. Artif. Intell. Educ. (IJAIED) **10**, 350–364 (1998)

39. Self, J.A.: Formal approaches to student modelling. In: Greer, J.E., McCalla, G.I. (eds.) Student Modelling: The Key to Individualized Knowledge-Based Instruction, pp. 295–352. Springer, Heidelberg (1994). https://doi.org/10.1007/978-3-662-03037-0_12

40. Stansfield, J.L., Carr, B.P., Goldstein, I.P.: Wumpus advisor I. A first implementation of a program that tutors logical and probabilistic reasoning skills. AI memo 381 (1976)

41. Sun, R., Peterson, T.: A hybrid model for learning sequential navigation. In: Proceedings 1997 IEEE International Symposium on Computational Intelligence in Robotics and Automation CIRA 1997, pp. 234–239. Towards New Computational Principles for Robotics and Automation (1997). https://doi.org/10.1109/CIRA.1997.613863

42. Wang, Y.S.: Assessment of learner satisfaction with asynchronous electronic learning systems. Inf. Manag. **41**(1), 75–86 (2003). https://doi.org/10.1016/S0378-7206(03)00028-4

43. Weber, G., Brusilovsky, P.: ELM-ART – an interactive and intelligent web-based electronic textbook. Int. J. Artif. Intell. Educ. **26**(1), 72–81 (2015). https://doi.org/10.1007/s40593-015-0066-8

44. WHO: The ICD-10 classification of mental and behavioural disorders: clinical descriptions and diagnostic guidelines. World Health Organization (1992)

Scaffolding Executive Function in Game-Based Learning to Improve Productive Persistence and Computational Thinking in Neurodiverse Learners

Ma. Victoria Almeda[(✉)] [iD] and Jodi Asbell-Clarke [iD]

TERC, 2067 Massachusetts Avenue, Cambridge, MA 02140, USA
{mia_almeda,jodi_asbell-clarke}@terc.edu

Abstract. Computational Thinking (CT) and learning games both may have unique potential to engage a broad range of learners, including those with cognitively diverse needs. Many STEM interventions typically do not leverage the cognitive assets of learners [1] nor do these initiatives prioritize effective differentiated instruction and learning [2, 3]. The INFACT, Include Neurodiversity in Foundational and Applied Computational Thinking, project addresses this problem by leveraging two games, *NumberFactory* and *Zoombinis*, to build foundational CT practices in elementary and middle school learners. In this paper, we describe work in progress to design adaptive digital scaffolds that support a wide variety of learners' Executive Function (EF) often associated with neurodiverse needs. Providing adaptive game environments through these embedded EF scaffolds may play a critical role in the ability of all learners to productively persist in the context of mathematical problem-solving and computational thinking.

Keywords: Computational Thinking · Executive function · Neurodiverse learners · Productive persistence · Game-based learning

1 Computational Thinking (CT)

STEM (Science, Technology, Engineering, and Mathematics) learning is critical for a strong economy and a strong workforce [4–6]. Yet some of our most talented learners may underperform in school-based STEM because of neurodiverse conditions - those having special education needs dealing with cognition, such as attention deficit hyperactivity disorder (ADHD), autism spectrum disorders (ASD), dyslexia, anxiety disorders, and intellectual disabilities. Increasingly, STEM literacy includes Computational Thinking (CT), a term coined by Jeannette Wing [7] to describe the set of ideas and practices involved in problem-solving where solutions can be represented in a form that can be carried out by an information-processing agent, such as a computer. CT is now rapidly being introduced in K-12 education [8], and is thought to be a fundamental new skill for the workforce [9]. While an exact definition of CT is still nebulous, CSTA [10] and Shute, Sun, and Asbell-Clarke [11] identify four fundamental CT practices that form a foundation of CT. These are:

© Springer Nature Switzerland AG 2021
X. Fang (Ed.): HCII 2021, LNCS 12790, pp. 155–172, 2021.
https://doi.org/10.1007/978-3-030-77414-1_12

- **Problem Decomposition:** reducing the complexity of a problem by breaking it into smaller, more manageable parts.
- **Pattern Recognition:** seeing trends and groupings in a collection of objects, tasks, or information.
- **Abstraction:** making generalizations from observed patterns and making general rules or classifications about the objects, tasks, or information by discerning relevant from irrelevant information.
- **Algorithm Design:** establishing replicable solutions to a set of problems.

CT may be particularly advantageous for addressing inclusivity of neurodiverse learners in STEM learning, and ultimately in the future STEM workforce. CT may be conducive to the cognitive strengths of some neurodiverse learners. For instance, the rigid thought-patterns referred to as lack of cognitive flexibility for some learners with autism can also be seen as an asset when considering the systematic and detailed thought required for solving computational problems [12]. This asset view of neurodiversity is also consistent with hiring programs at many IT companies, including industry leaders such as Microsoft [13], who are seeking workers with autism and other neurodiverse conditions.

1.1 Engaging Neurodiverse Learners in CT Through Games

Our team has been studying how learners' develop CT practices through game-based learning, particulary in TERC's computer game called *Zoombinis* [14]. Digital games are argued to be less threatening for some neurodiverse learners [15] and improved learning in a game may create a snowball effect on learning in other areas [16]. Bridging, in which teachers provide activities and strategies to connect implicit learning in games to external classroom learning, can improve game-based learning [17].

In our previous studies using *Zoombinis* and related CT activities with students in grades 3–8, we demonstrated that *Zoombinis* is effective as both a support and a measure of students' CT practices. Our team was able to reliably and confidently detect CT practices within students' gameplay [18, 19]. Students who played more of the game, and who demonstrated more CT practices in the game, showed more improvement on external measures of CT outside the game [14]. During our previous research with *Zoombinis*, teachers reported that CT activities provided opportunities for students who typically struggled in other subjects to become more engaged and more productive - sometimes even emerging as CT leaders in the class. Teachers also noted that CT practices align remarkably well with strategies that special education teachers use to support problem-solving practices with students with IEP/504 plans. They explained the CT practices, such as problem decomposition, were exactly the problem-solving strategies they were teaching their students, but they never had such a clear way to describe them before.

[CT activities] added a lot more engagement because they understand the expectations. It made things more explicit. Like, ok, right now we're doing problem decomposition. We're going to break this down and figure out what we really need

to know. CT has made learning more accessible and more engaging for everybody, but especially for the kids who really need that. – 8th grade teacher [20].

One downfall to studying CT among neurodiverse learners is that we do not yet have an established set of measures of CT practices for elementary and middle school learners, particularly those who may struggle with extraneous factors of testing such as reading comprehension, ability to articulate their thinking, and anxiety. These factors may present particular barriers for many neurodiverse students, who may be highly skilled in CT but not in test taking [21].

Game-based learning assessments (GBLA) provide a promising solution to fill this gap. The idea of stealth assessment in games dates back to Shute [22] and Gee [23] who saw the potential of digital games not just for learning, but for natural, in situ assessment of learning. Combinations of methods such as Evidence-Centered Design [24] and Educational Data Mining have evolved over the past decade to create a vibrant field of research in GBLA. GBLA may provide tools to measure overall performance within a learning game on specified learning outcomes, and also inform what types of supports can help learners persist productively within games to achieve those learning outcomes.

2 Productive Persistence

Persistence plays a significant role in games, where players encounter progressive levels of difficulty [25]. However, not all persistence is uniformly beneficial, especially when the time struggling is not used effectively. Learning may not necessarily depend on a learner's ability to persist, but rather on his or her ability to distinguish when effort is productive or unproductive. Productive persistence occurs when effort yields some progress towards learning, whereas unproductive persistence occurs when effort yields little to no progress towards learning [26, 27].

Some researchers have already distinguished important differences between these modes of persistence, especially in the context of games where evidence suggests that unproductively struggling can be highly frustrating and can impede on learning [27, 28]. About 30 to 40% of high school students demonstrated unproductive persistence, in which they were unable to successfully complete a level after 8 or more attempts, in a 2D physics game called Physics Playground. Owen and colleagues [27] used educational data mining techniques to predict unproductive persistence from productive persistence in *Mastering Math*, a game-based adaptive learning system. They found model-derived student profiles that emerged from unproductively persistent behaviors and could provide insights about in-the-moment interventions. Recent research has shown that incentivizing productive persistence increased children's use of efficient strategies in an educational math game [29], and enticing productively persistent learners to engage more can potentially improve learning [30].

It is particularly important to distinguish between productive and unproductive persistence to support neurodiverse learners, as many students with cognitively diverse needs are likely to demonstrate persistence and to keep pursuing through challenging tasks [31]. Using the Weschler Intelligence Scale for Children-Revised (WISC) and district criteria to determine students with disabilities, average-achieving, and gifted, Montague and Applegate [32] found that middle school students with learning disabilities persisted just as long in math problem solving as average achievers. Despite their ability to persist, students with learning disabilities used significantly fewer problem-solving strategies and had lower math scores than average and gifted students without disabilities. This illustrates the tendency for neurodiverse learners to continue persisting in an unproductive manner with ineffective trial-and-error strategies (Montague & Applegate, 2000), and the need to assess persistence and provide interventions that support productive persistence for a wide range of learners.

Game-based learning environments offer an innovative way to measure and ultimately support productive persistence. We plan to embed stealth assessments within our games, building EDM models to analyze gamelog data so that we can assess whether a student is productively or unproductively persisting through their behaviors within the games themselves [25].

3   Executive Function

Our research is framed in the assumption that we can support the productive persistence of neurodiverse learners by addressing needs for executive function that may stand in the way of their engaging productively in CT learning tasks. We focus on EF because it underlies many neurodiverse conditions [33]. Executive function is the set of activities the brain coordinates when organizing and prioritizing information and tasks [34, 35]. These include processes conducted in goal-oriented tasks such as: setting goals; designing and implementing a plan to achieve those goals; and practicing metacognition to understand what has and has not been accomplished towards the goal [33]. When learners are attentive to a task at hand, they are more likely to be proficient at applying their EF skills [33]. Typically cognitively diverse students have different levels of attention and working memory when engaging in digital games, and Deater-Deckard, Chang and Evans [36] argue that studying how to best support each learner is an area for further research.

Neuroscience researchers sometimes distinguish the cognitive and emotional aspects of EF into what is called "cold" and "hot" EF [16]. Cold EF typically includes cognitive functions such as:

- **Working memory:** how well a learner retains information in the short term while completing a task
- **Cognitive flexibility:** how well a learner refines their ideas based on new information and experiences
- **Inhibitory control:** how well a learner can switch from one set of rules or ideas to another, thus inhibiting the tendency to only resort to a previous mental model

Hot EF typically includes self-regulation of emotion and self-discipline such as:

- **Persistence:** a learner's will and motivation to continue working at difficult tasks
- **Inhibitory control:** how well a learner ignores distractions and suppresses unproductive impulses

Two other highly related facets EF in the context of learning are:

- **Attention:** How well a learner can focus on one source of stimulation or information in the presence of others.
- **Metacognition** is the ability for a learner to know and articulate what he or she doesn't know.

In problem-solving this requires an overarching awareness of the task at hand, and what parts of the task have been completed, partially completed, or not yet started. Metacognition also requires the learners' ability to express their implicit thinking, making their thinking visible to themselves and to others.

3.1 Designing Supports for Neurodiverse Learners in CT through Games

The call to support neurodiversity through technology-related problem solving has led our team to study the intersection between Computational Thinking (CT), Persistence, and Executive Function (EF). Some of the dynamic processes between these areas of interest emerged as learners struggled with solving puzzles in our games. In our observations of *Zoombinis* gameplay, we noticed that players who continued to persist and were not successful in completing the puzzle did not use more efficient strategies that involved systematic testing. For instance, players who make repeated errors (duplicate pizzas or mudballs previously rejected in *Zoombinis*) were unlikely to solve the puzzle. We created digital scaffolds designed to target EF skills that could help learners with more effective decision making based on their prior moves, with the goal of eventually supporting their productive persistence and CT learning.

4 Overview of INFACT

The INFACT projects aims to design and study a comprehensive and inclusive CT program to support teachers and students for grades 3–8. INFACT leverages the cognitive strengths of neurodiverse learners and embeds flexible supports for learners with a wide variety of differences in attention and executive function.

INFACT includes a wide array of CT activities, including several digital puzzle games that will support learners' EF to help make their thinking visible and promote productive problem solving. One of these is a subset of the *Zoombinis* logic puzzles from the game we previously studied. Another is an elementary math interactive that our team co-designed with elementary math teachers called *NumberFactory*. *NumberFactory* focuses on place value and the construction of multi-digit numbers using CT. For INFACT, we have designed EF scaffolds embedded within both of these games that are intended to support students' Attention, Working Memory, Inhibitory Control, Cognitive Flexibility, and Metacognition while they are building CT practices in the games.

For the design research of the EF scaffolds, our team conducted initial interviews with 10 learners in grades 3–8, most of whom were neurodiverse learners, and all of whom were familiar with *Zoombinis* and/or *NumberFactory*. We used paper prototypes of UI designs alongside the functional interactive games to facilitate the design of supports that players said they needed to overcome cognitive barriers they encountered when playing with the games that were not directly attributed to CT. For example, sometimes players were not paying attention to a key piece of information on the screen. Sometimes they lost track of where they were in the puzzle or forgot the results of their previous moves. Our design research participants requested tools that would point out and highlight what they needed to know, and something to help them keep track of that pertinent information. Our design team balanced this wide array of requests with the simultaneous need to avoid overloading the user interface with too many distracters for students. Particularly for neurodiverse students, we wanted to keep the cognitive load of the interface low, while providing differentiable supports for executive function.

The embedded cognitive (cool EF) support tools we have designed include:

Flashlight tool: To support learners' attention in both *Zoombinis* and *NumberFactory*, we have built a tool that highlights relevant information that learners might not be attending to so that they can focus on the salient information in an activity.

Bookkeeping tool: To support learners' working memory in both *Zoombinis* and *NumberFactory* we have designed graphical organizers (i.e. interactive data tables) to help learners keep track of necessary information, removing the load on their working memory, and helping them organize the information in ways that help them decide their next move in the puzzles.

Expression tools: To support learners' working memory and metacognition in both *Zoombinis* and *NumberFactory* we have designed tools that help make learners implicit problem solving visible.

Representation supports: To support learners' cognitive flexibility in *NumberFactory* we have designed supports that help learners transition between one representation of a number and others.

The embedded emotional regulation (hot EF) support tools we have designed include:

Customized Pacing: To provide a motivating and non-threatening experience for each learner, the pacing of the learning puzzles is differentiated according to learners' performance in the current and previous puzzles.

Suggested Breaks: When learners are struggling, even with substantial scaffolding, the game will suggest a break rather than have the learner persist unproductively (wheel-spinning).

The next phase of the design research involves learning how to provide the right tool to each learner at the right time. We are designing adaptivity models that "trigger" the scaffolds based on patterns of players' behaviors within the game. For example, if a player consistently repeats a similar mistake or makes moves that are not consistent with the evidence provided, we would trigger an appropriate intervention. In the next sections, we present how we are designing adaptive EF scaffolds embedded within two existing STEM learning games.

4.1 Example 1: NumberFactory

NumberFactory is a prototype web-based learning game that was co-designed by TERC and math educators as part of a Research-Practice Partnership. The goal of *Number-Factory* is to engage neurodiverse elementary math learners in the practices required to have fluent understanding of place value, a concept core to mathematics learning [e.g., 37–39]. In *NumberFactory* players are asked to build numbers a set of unit blocks (see Fig. 1). Each puzzle in *NumberFactory* is only completed when the arrangement of unit blocks sums up to the number required. Otherwise the player is allowed to try again. Learners must coordinate three levels of units (i.e., a unit of "100" is composed of ten units of 10, each of which is, in turn, composed of ten 1s) to understand simultaneously how all three levels of units relate, and to abstract this concept to how units work in general [38].

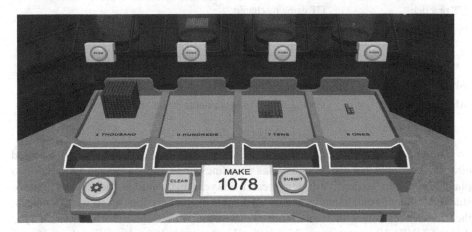

Fig. 1. Screenshot of *NumberFactory*

CT is embedded throughout the design of *NumberFactory* and the game mechanics for CT and place value are aligned (Table 1). *NumberFactory* is framed such that the act of breaking down a number into its units is an act of problem decomposition. Similarly, pattern recognition is required to identify unit blocks in groups to build a multi-digit num-ber. The generalization of those groups into units that can be coordinated (exchanged) is an act of abstraction, and by operationalizing these actions into a generalized "code" for a robot the players is engaged in algorithm design.

The cognitive flexibility learners need to work with mental models of numbers and units becomes particularly important as they move to problems with multi-digit numbers. Players may persist unproductively, or cease to persist, if confronted with unsupported EF challenges. Players' behaviors in *NumberFactory* can be categorized into 4 categories: 1) Successful puzzle completion; 2) Early errors (e.g. first or second error in the puzzle); 3) Repeated error; 4) Inactivity. The adaptivity models will generate different responses to each behavior. A successful completion will lead to the next puzzle (logging the number of tries to reach success). An early error will continue on, but count the number of errors toward the trigger. A repeated error will trigger certain scaffolds. Inactivity will trigger other scaffolds, in particular the Attention scaffold. This is outlined in Table 2.

Table 1. Overlap of CT practices and place value game mechanics in *NumberFactory*.

CT practice	CT game mechanic
Problem decomposition	Building one-digit numbers first and then build to multi-digit numbers
Pattern recognition	Explicitly identifying groups of unit blocks to build numbers
Abstraction	Exchanging unit blocks (e.g., change ten 1s for one 10 block)
Algorithm design	Coding a robot to make multi-digit numbers from unit blocks

The exact thresholds that define the boundary between early errors and repeated errors is a variable that can be adjusted as we refine our adaptivity models. Our team had planned to conduct extensive design research this year that would include observations of students' affect to understand when their frustration and boredom levels would indicate the need of a scaffold with *NumberFactory*. This observational research has been delayed due to COVID-19 so we are working with educators to help us determine the values of those thresholds for different students.

4.2 Example 2: *Zoombinis*

Zoombinis is a popular, award-winning, learning game that engages learners grades 3–8 in computational problem solving. The goal of *Zoombinis* is for players to guide packs of 16 zoombinis characters through 12 dynamic puzzles to safety in Zoombiniville. *Zoombinis* puzzles are based on logical decision making and require increasingly complex CT to solve. Our team's previous research on *Zoombinis* gameplay in classes showed that duration of game play and student CT practices exhibited within gameplay were predictors of students' CT learning [14]. Gameplay behaviors in each of the puzzles are consistent with implicit CT practices (see Table 3).

Our previous research demonstrated CT learning in three of the *Zoombinis* puzzles: Pizza Pass, Mudball Wall, and Allergic Cliffs, so we chose to use these three puzzles to design and test our EF scaffolding tools (see Figs. 2, 3, 4 and 5).

Table 2. Operationalization of scaffolds and triggers in *NumberFactory*

EF need	Scaffolding tool	Trigger	Tool description
Attention	Flashlight	Inactivity OR repeated errors	A "flashlight" highlights salient information, such as the 100-block button along with the 100 place value in the number being made
Working memory and metacognition	Bookkeeping and expression tools	Successful task initiation followed by repeated errors	A pop-up "spreadsheet" that shows explicitly how the numbers of blocks of each unit sum together to a number
Inhibitory control and persistence	Pacing and breaks	Repeated errors	The pacing of complexity of the puzzles for each player is determined by their performance in previous puzzles
Cognitive flexibility	Multiple representations of numbers (e.g. 1, one, 1-unit block)	Completed puzzle in one representation followed by repeated errors with different representation	Educators or students choose their preferred representations for initial puzzles and new representations are gradually transitioned in until fluency is demonstrated with new representations
Attention	Flashlight	Inactivity OR repeated errors	A "flashlight" highlights salient information, such as the 100-block button along with the 100 place value in the number being made

Table 3. Overlap of CT practices and game mechanics in *Zoombinis*.

CT practice	CT game mechanic
Problem decomposition	Figuring out the big problem to solve, and identifying what part of the problem to solve first
Pattern recognition	Collecting enough information to recognize any patterns in what has already been done
Abstraction	Identifying the general rule of the puzzle
Algorithm design	Applying strategies to use that help solve the puzzle

In Pizza Pass, players are challenged to figure out what type of pizza will satisfy Arno, the troll. Arno will only say whether he wants more toppings, does not like at least one of the toppings, or that the pizza is perfect. Players can efficiently solve the problem by demonstrating systematic testing - trying out one topping at a time - rather than randomly trying toppings or continuously trying the same toppings.

In Mudball Wall, players are challenged to figure how the colors and shapes correspond to the row and columns of the wall. When they hit the dotted cells on the wall, they are able to safely catapult their zoombinis onwards. Players must be able to recognize and abstract the patterns and colors and shapes into rows or columns of the wall.

In Allergic Cliffs, the challenge is for players to figure out which zoombinis can cross the bridge. The cliffs under the bridge are allergic to certain attributes of the zoombinis and when they sneeze it rejects the current zoombini. Each time a zoombini is sneezed off, a peg will spring loose, causing the bridge to be closer to collapsing. Efficient gameplay requires players to develop systematic methods to test their zoombinis, such as keeping multiple attributes constant over subsequent turns.

Similar to *NumberFactory*, designers considered the different types of behaviors that would suggest that learners are unproductively persisting through the games to design EF scaffolds for *Zoombinis*. Examples of this type of these behaviors are repeated errors, such as duplicate pizzas, duplicate mudballs, and duplicate zoombinis in Allergic Cliffs. Another example in Allergic Cliffs is the percentage of zoombinis exiting the level, with lower percentages indicating less efficient solutions to the puzzle. In our adaptive models, both these behaviors will trigger bookkeeping scaffolds designed to support their attention and working memory (see Figs. 2, 3 and 4). At the end of the round, learners will be provided with the expression tool designed to help them with their metacognition (see Figs. 5 and 6).

Attention Scaffold: Flashlight Tool

This interactive tool is designed to highlight salient information in the puzzle. For example, in Allergic Cliffs the player can select an attribute from a table and all the zoombinis with that attribute will be highlighted in the puzzle. Similarly, in Pizza Pass the player can select a topping and all previously played pizzas with that topping will be highlighted. The attention scaffold is triggered by repeated duplicates, which may indicate that the player is not attending to the previous results, so they are highlighted.

Working Memory Scaffold: Bookkeeping Tool

This interactive tool is designed to help players keep track of information in the puzzle.

In Allergic Cliffs, the bookkeeping tool is the same as the flashlight tool as the same tool serves both purposes. In Pizza Pass, the bookkeeping tool is a separate interactive that allows players to sort toppings in a table by accepted or rejected by each troll. The working memory scaffolds are triggered when the player is acting inconsistent with available evidence, particularly if they have succeeded in past puzzles and thus likely just need the EF boost. In Mudball Wall, the bookkeeping tool takes the form of labels on the rows and columns that help identify the information already available from the grid.

Metacognition: Expression Tool

At the end of each puzzle, there is an expression tool that allows the player to make their implicit thinking explicit. For example, at the end of Allergic Cliffs, a pop-up box asks players to complete the expression IF (select zoombini attribute) THEN (select bridge). This tool allows them to complete their thinking by articulating the rule they used. This tool is designed to support players' metacognition, while also serving as an embedded performance-based assessment tool during game-based learning research.

We have designed these EF scaffolds to blend seamlessly into the game by incorporating *Zoombinis* characters and images into these scaffolds. In the first iteration of our design research, we plan to keep these scaffolds on, with the option for players to turn these scaffolds off anytime throughout their gameplay. We also plan to investigate when it would be appropriate to trigger these scaffolds for different types of learners with various EF needs.

Fig. 2. Flashlight and Bookkeeping tool in Pizza Pass

Fig. 3. Bookkeeping tool in Mudball Wall

Fig. 4. Bookkeeping tool in Allergic Cliffs

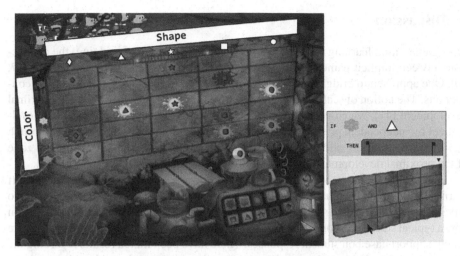

Fig. 5. Expression tool in Mudball Wall

Fig. 6. Expression tool in Allergic Cliffs

5 Discussion

Prior game-based learning research has shown the importance of bridging, the connection between implicit game-based learning and explicit learning in the classroom [17, 40]. One approach to bridging is providing scaffolding to help learners make these connections. The notion of scaffolding is related to Vygotsky's concept of zone of proximal development [41], which is described as the distance between a learner's actual development by independent problem solving and the level of potential development through assistance. Scaffolding allows learners to reach learning goals that are within the zone of the proximal development and may be difficult to achieve without support [42].

In the field of computer-based learning, scaffolding refers to digital tools that support learners in complex and challenging tasks. Brush and Saye [43] posit that there are two types of scaffoldings: hard scaffolds, static supports that are planned in advance based on how a typical student responds to a task and soft scaffolds, dynamic supports that require timely support based on student responses. There have been mixed results regarding the effects of hard scaffolds on learners' performance in computer-based learning environments. While some studies have reported positive impacts of hard scaffolds on learning [44, 45] other studies have found null effects when compared to soft scaffolds [46]. A potential reason why hard scaffolds may not always be effective is because they are not adaptable [47–49] and are less likely to address student's learning needs [50]. In contrast, soft scaffolds can provide spontaneous support that better facilitates the student's ability to regulate their learning [51].

In this paper we have described how we are designing adaptive scaffoleds for EF in game-based learning context. The INFACT project team is designing EF-based scaffolding by embedding soft supports that target cognition and emotion regulation across two of our games. In designing these different types of scaffolds, we take into account varied behaviors that are potentially indicative of a learner's unproductive persistence or wheel-spinning. In the case of *NumberFactory*, encountering a greater number of levels without achieving a gold bar reward is likely indicative of an unproductively persistent learner. For *Zoombinis*, we leverage game-based assessments of CT, specifically our detectors of *learning game mechanic*, which indicate a player's lack of understanding of the game, and *acting inconsistent with evidence*, which reveals that a player's moves are not consistent with the evidence provided from prior moves [52]. We examine these specific detectors for each of the three *Zoombinis* puzzles to identify which features significantly contribute to detecting *learning game mechanic* or *acting inconsistent with evidence*. The process of examining these detectors allows us to make evidence-based decisions about which features can be used as triggers to signal EF scaffolding within the game.

In addition to learning about players' negative and positive gaming experiences, observations from the usability testing sessions will provide insight about the adaptability of the game (Table 4). Instead of using arbitrary cut-offs to indicate when a student is struggling [28, 53], findings grounded from observations of user experiences can help inform when learners need digital scaffolding in their progression throughout their game. Importantly, it can help us determine meaningful features (e.g., thresholds for repeated mistakes or moves that are inconsistent with the evidence provided) that may be useful for building more accurate adaptive models for neurodiverse learners using

Table 4. Usability metrics for iterative design research.

Category	Game	Research question	Tasks
Test 1: Usability	*NumberFactory*	What is easy or difficult about playing the game with EF Scaffolding Tools?	Play *NumberFactory* for 30 min
	Zoombinis		Play *Zoombinis* for 30 min
Test 2: Findability	*NumberFactory*	Can learners easily turn off scaffolding tools in the game?	All scaffolding tools are automatically turned on. When you are frustrated with a specific scaffold, can you find a way to turn off that scaffold?
	Zoombinis		
Test 3: Adaptability	*NumberFactory*	What is the threshold in repeated errors that learners turn on our scaffolding tools?	All scaffolding tools are automatically turned off. Turn on a scaffolding tool when you feel it is appropriate
	Zoombinis		

educational data mining techniques. Specifically, we are building models to detect when students are likely to get overly frustrated or bored and their gameplay becomes no longer productive. As previously discussed, unproductive persistence or wheel-spinning can lead to disengagement [28] and potential learning loss [54]. By detecting the trigger points, in real-time just before wheel-spinning starts, we can intervene with a just-in-time support. Our two-step methodology is our approach to address each learner's level of engagement and potential wheel-spinning through iterative design research and automated data mining detectors, toward supporting individual learners' unique needs.

6   Conclusion

In line with the Universal Design for Learning (UDL) framework, INFACT focuses and designs for students with cognitively diverse needs to provide equitable, high-quality instruction for all learners. INFACT aims to unleash the potential of neurodiverse learners by developing a variety of activities that embed CT practices within STEM contexts. In this paper, we describe two digital games, *NumberFactory* and *Zoombinis*, which consist of problem-solving puzzles that engage learners in fundamental practices of CT. In each game, we provide digital scaffolding that aims to support students' EF skills related to working memory, cognitive flexibility, inhibitory control, attention, and metacognition. By analyzing data logs generated through gameplay, we can detect evidence of students' affect or persistence, including whether learners are productively or unproductively persisting through these puzzles. We can use this information to build adaptive models that differentiate the content and pacing of scaffolds for each unique student.

By ensuring that CT opportunities are equitable for learners in our games, INFACT has the potential to strengthen our workforce, including neurodiverse learners whose talents and strengths often are unrecognized and untapped in K-12 education. *Number-Factory* and *Zoombinis* offer innovative digital solutions to broaden STEM participation, highlighting the assets of cognitively diverse students and promoting differentiated STEM instruction and learning in today's modern classrooms.

References

1. Callinan, S., Theiler, S., Cunningham, E.: Identifying learning disabilities through a cognitive deficit framework: can verbal memory deficits explain similarities between learning disabled and low achieving students? J. Learn. Disabil. **48**(3), 271–280 (2015)
2. Immordino-Yang, M.H., Darling-Hammond, L., Krone, C.: The brain basis for integrated social, emotional, and academic development. National Commission on Social, Emotional, and Academic Development, Washington DC (2018)
3. Prast, E.J., Van de Weijer-Bergsma, E., Kroesbergen, E.H., Van Luit, J.E.: Differentiated instruction in primary mathematics: effects of teacher professional development on student achievement. Learn. Instr. **54**, 22–34 (2018)
4. National Research Council: Committee on Prospering in the Global Economy of the 21st Century: An Agenda for American Science and Technology, Committee on Science, Engineering, and Public Policy. National Academy Press, Washington DC (2007)
5. Langdon, D., McKittrick, G., Beede, D., Khan, B., Doms, M.: STEM: Good Jobs Now and for the Future. ESA Issue Brief# 03–11. US Department of Commerce (2011)
6. Carnevale, A.P., Smith, N., Melton, M.: STEM: Science Technology Engineering Mathematics. Georgetown University Center on Education and the Workforce (2011)
7. Wing, J.M.: Computational thinking, 10 years later. Microsoft Research Blog (23) (2016)
8. Barr, V., Stephenson, C.: Bringing computational thinking to K-12: what is Involved and what is the role of the computer science education community? ACM Inroads **2**(1), 48–54 (2011)
9. Vergara, C.E., et al.: Aligning computing education with engineering workforce computational needs: new curricular directions to improve computational thinking in engineering graduates. In: 2009 39th IEEE Frontiers in Education Conference, pp. 1–6 (2009)
10. CSTA. https://www.csteachers.org/page/standards. Accessed 19 Feb 2021
11. Shute, V.J., Sun, C., Asbell-Clarke, J.: Demystifying computational thinking. Educ. Res. Rev. **22**, 142–158 (2017)
12. Schmidt, M., Beck, D.: Computational thinking and social skills in Virtuoso: an immersive, digital game-based learning environment for youth with autism spectrum disorder. In: Allison, C., Morgado, L., Pirker, J., Beck, D., Richter, J., Gütl, C. (eds.) iLRN 2016. CCIS, vol. 621, pp. 113–121. Springer, Cham (2016). https://doi.org/10.1007/978-3-319-41769-1_9
13. Microsoft: Autism Hiring Program (2019). https://www.microsoft.com/en-us/diversity/inside-microsoft/cross-disability/hiring.aspx. Accessed 19 Feb 2021
14. Asbell-Clarke, J., et al.: The development of students' computational thinking practices in elementary- and middle-school classes using the learning game, Zoombinis. Comput. Hum. Behav. **115** (2021)
15. Saridaki, M., Gouscos, D., Meimaris, M.: Digital games-based instructional design for students with special education needs: practical findings and lessons learnt. In: Proceedings of the 4th European Conference on Games-Based Learning: ECGBL2010, p. 343. Academic Conferences Limited (2010)
16. Semenov, A.D., Zelazo, P.D.: The development of hot and cool executive function: a foundation for learning in the preschool years. In: Executive Function in Education: From Theory to Practice, pp. 82–104 (2018)

17. Asbell-Clarke, J., Rowe, E., Bardar, E., Edwards, T.: The importance of teacher bridging in game-based learning classrooms. In: Farber, M. (ed.) Global Perspectives on Gameful and Playful Teaching and Learning, pp. 211–239. IGI Global, Pennsylvania (2020)
18. Rowe, E., et al.: Assessing implicit science learning in digital games. Comput. Hum. Behav. **76**, 617–630 (2017)
19. Rowe, E., Asbell-Clarke, J., Almeda, M.: Computational thinking in Zoombinis: results from a national implementation study. Poster Presented at the Technology, Mind, and Society Conference, Washington D.C. (2010)
20. Barchas-Lichtenstein, J., Brucker, J.L., Nock, K., Tietjen, L., Norlander, R.: CodePlay: Year 2 Fall Semester Process Evaluation Brief. NewKnowledge Publication #NSF.051.432.02 (2019)
21. Munoz, R., Barcelos, T.S., Villarroel, R.: CT4All: enhancing computational thinking skills in adolescents with autism spectrum disorders. IEEE Lat. Am. Trans. **16**(3), 909–917 (2018)
22. Shute, V.J.: Stealth assessment in computer-based games to support learning. Comput. Games Instr. **55**(2), 503–524 (2011)
23. Gee, J.P.: What video games have to teach us about learning and literacy. Comput. Entertainment (CIE) **1**(1), 20 (2003)
24. Mislevy, R.J., Haertel, G., Riconscente, M., Rutstein, D.W., Ziker, C.: Evidence-centered assessment design. In: Mislevy, R.J., Haertel, G., Riconscente, M., Rutstein, D.W., Ziker, C. (eds.) Assessing Model-Based Reasoning Using Evidence-Centered Design. SS, pp. 19–24. Springer, Cham (2017). https://doi.org/10.1007/978-3-319-52246-3_3
25. Ventura, M., Shute, V., Small, M.: Assessing persistence in educational games. Des. Recommendations Adapt. Intell. Tutoring Syst. Learn. Model. **2**(2014), 93–101 (2014)
26. Beck, J.E., Gong, Y.: Wheel-spinning: students who fail to master a skill. In: Chad Lane, H., Yacef, K., Mostow, J., Pavlik, P. (eds.) AIED 2013. LNCS (LNAI), vol. 7926, pp. 431–440. Springer, Heidelberg (2013). https://doi.org/10.1007/978-3-642-39112-5_44
27. Owen, V.E., et al.: Detecting wheel-spinning and productive persistence in educational games. In: International Educational Data Mining Society, pp. 378–383 (2019)
28. Beck, J., Rodrigo, M.M.T.: Understanding wheel spinning in the context of affective factors. In: Trausan-Matu, S., Boyer, K.E., Crosby, M., Panourgia, K. (eds.) ITS 2014. LNCS, vol. 8474, pp. 162–167. Springer, Cham (2014). https://doi.org/10.1007/978-3-319-07221-0_20
29. O'Rourke, E., Haimovitz, K., Ballweber, C., Dweck, C., Popović, Z.: Brain points: a growth mindset incentive structure boosts persistence in an educational game. In: Proceedings of the SIGCHI Conference on Human Factors in Computing Systems, pp. 3339–3348 (2014)
30. Strother, S., Van Campen, J., Grunow, A.: Community College Pathways. Carnegie Foundation for the Advancement of Teaching, Stanford (2013)
31. Armstrong, T.: Neurodiversity: Discovering the Extraordinary Gifts of Autism, ADHD, Dyslexia, and Other Brain Differences. Da Cappo Press, Cambridge (2010)
32. Montague, M., Applegate, B.: Middle school students' perceptions, persistence, and performance in mathematical problem solving. Learn. Disabil. Q. **23**(3), 215–227 (2000)
33. Meltzer, L., Dunstan-Brewer, J., Krishnan, K.: Learning differences and executive function: understandings and misunderstandings. In: Meltzer, L. (ed.) Executive Function in Education: From Theory to Practice, pp. 109–141. The Guilford Press, New York (2018)
34. Brown, S.W.: Timing and executive function: bidirectional interference between concurrent temporal production and randomization tasks. Mem. Cognit. **34**(7), 1464–1471 (2006)
35. Diamond, A.: Executive functions. Annu. Rev. Psychol. **64**, 135–168 (2013)
36. Deater-Deckard, K., Chang, M., Evans, M.E.: Engagement states and learning from educational games. New Dir. Child Adolesc. Dev. **139**, 21–30 (2013)
37. Battista, M.: Cognition-Based Assessment Teaching of Multiplication and Division: Building on Students Reasoning. Heinemann, Portsmouth (2012)
38. Norton, A., Boyce, S.: Provoking the construction of a structure for coordinating n+1 levels of units. J. Math. Behav. **40**, 211–232 (2015)

39. Wright, R.J., Ellemor-Collins, D., Tabor, P.D.: Developing Number Knowledge: Assessment, Teaching and Intervention with 7–11 Year Olds. Paul Chapman Publications/Sage, London (2011)

40. Rowe, E., Bardar, E., Asbell-Clarke, J., Shane-Simpson, C., Roberts, S.J.: Building bridges.: In: Russel, D., Laffey, J. (eds.) Handbook of Research on Gaming Trends in P-12 Education, pp. 442–468. IGI Global, Pennsylvania (2015)

41. Vygotsky, L.: Interaction between learning and development. Read. Dev. Child. 23(3), 34–41 (1978)

42. Wood, D., Bruner, J.S., Ross, G.: The role of tutoring in problem solving. J. Child Psychol. Psychiatry 17(2), 89–100 (1976)

43. Brush, T.A., Saye, J.W.: A summary of research exploring hard and soft scaffolding for teachers and students using a multimedia supported learning environment. J. Interact. Online Learn. 1(2), 1–12 (2012)

44. Demetriadis, S.N., Papadopoulos, P.M., Stamelos, I.G., Fischer, F.: The effect of scaffolding students' context-generating cognitive activity in technology-enhanced case-based learning. Comput. Educ. 51(2), 939–954 (2008)

45. Papadopoulos, P.M., Demetriadis, S.N., Stamelos, I.G., Tsoukalas, I.A.: The value of writing-to-learn when using question prompts to support web-based learning in ill-structured domains. Educ. Technol. Res. Dev. 59(1), 71–90 (2011). https://doi.org/10.1007/s11423-010-9167-0

46. Vreman-de Olde, C., de Jong, T.: Scaffolding learners in designing investigation assignments for a computer simulation. J. Comput. Assist. Learn. 22(1), 63–73 (2006)

47. Bulu, S.T., Pedersen, S.: Scaffolding middle school students' content knowledge and ill-structured problem solving in a problem-based hypermedia learning environment. Educ. Tech. Res. Dev. 58(5), 507–529 (2010)

48. Chen, C.H., Wu, I.C., Jen, F.L.: Designing online scaffolds for interactive computer simulation. Interact. Learn. Environ. 21(3), 229–243 (2013)

49. Xun, G.E., Land, S.M.: A conceptual framework for scaffolding Ill-structured problem-solving processes using question prompts and peer interactions. Educ. Tech. Res. Dev. 52(2), 5–22 (2004)

50. Chen, C.H., Law, V.: Scaffolding individual and collaborative game-based learning in learning performance and intrinsic motivation. Comput. Hum. Behav. 55, 1201–1212 (2016)

51. Azevedo, R., Cromley, J.G., Seibert, D.: Does adaptive scaffolding facilitate students' ability to regulate their learning with hypermedia? Contemp. Educ. Psychol. 29(3), 344–370 (2004)

52. Rowe, E., et al.: Assessing implicit computational thinking in Zoombinis puzzle gameplay. To appear in a Special Issue of Computers and Human Behavior on Learning Analytics and Assessment (in press)

53. Palaoag, T.D., Rodrigo, M.M.T., Andres, J.M.L., Andres, J.M.A.L., Beck, J.E.: Wheel-spinning in a game-based learning environment for physics. In: Micarelli, A., Stamper, J., Panourgia, K. (eds.) ITS 2016. LNCS, vol. 9684, pp. 234–239. Springer, Cham (2016). https://doi.org/10.1007/978-3-319-39583-8_23

54. Kai, S., Almeda, M.V., Baker, R.S., Heffernan, C., Heffernan, N.: Decision tree modeling of wheel-spinning and productive persistence in skill builders. J. Educ. Data Min. 10(1), 36–71 (2018)

A Framework of Gamified Learning Design Targeting Behavior Change and Design of a Gamificated Time Management Training Manual

Beixian Chen, Weitse Wang, and Linlin Shui[✉]

Communication University of China, Beijing, China
cucsll@cuc.edu.cn

Abstract. In recent years, more attention has been paid to the application of gamification in the field of education. Previous research suggests that gamification in education can strengthen motivation and provide fun and engaging experiences. This research suggests a framework with game design element based on the behavior change model of TTM and SNAP. Consequently, with reference to this, a gamificated manual that trains primary school students' time management skill is designed. This manual has been put into use and it has obtained rather positive primary feedback. Moreover, empirical research is conducted using this project in order to explore the impact of contemplation staged gamification in the model. The results suggested that the addition of game design elements at this stage increase the primary school students' willingness to use the manual instead of their willingness to learn about time management. However, gamification elements do exhibit various effects as for the short-term storage of knowledge. The following explanation is then provided based on the experimental results and the framework raised: in educational gamification design with behavior modification as its aim, gamification can interfere and have a positive impact even before the action of behavior change; however, not all addition of gamification elements will lead to a positive result and the relative decision should be made carefully. The future research direction of educational gamification design aimed at behavior modification shall be discussed.

Keywords: Gamification · Education · Behavior change

1 Introduction

The concept of gamification was born in as early as the 00s [1] though only being paid extensive attention in 2010s [2, 3]. The widely accepted definition of gamification currently is the one raised in 2011: gamification refers to the use of game design elements within non-game contexts [2].

The smallest design unit of gamification in specific application is called game design elements. Dicheva et al. [4] divided game elements into two parts: gamification design principles and game mechanics. There are 11 gamification design principles in total,

© Springer Nature Switzerland AG 2021
X. Fang (Ed.): HCII 2021, LNCS 12790, pp. 173–188, 2021.
https://doi.org/10.1007/978-3-030-77414-1_13

including goals/challenges, personalization, rapid feedback, visible status, unlocking content, freedom to choice, freedom to fail, storyline/ new identities, onboarding, time restrictions and social engagement, while there are six game mechanics: points, badges, levels, leader boards, virtual goods and avatars. This definition of game design elements is adopted in this paper.

There has already been rather widespread application of gamification in the field of education, serving various functions in different subdivisions. Game mechanism is used to excite the interest of students during the learning process [5]; gamified environment can improve the quality of teaching [6]; during lessons and cultivation of soft skills, gamification helps inspire students, thus improving the efficiency of learning [7]; in terms of the transformation of life attitude, gamification training program has exhibited positive results [8]. Due to the difference between the goals of gamification in different cases, there exists huge discrepancy between the game design elements adopted in the research, ways to measure the results (e.g. questionnaire for participants or direct measurement of behavior data) as well as the kinds of results measured (e.g. transformation of attitude, preservation of knowledge, improvement of experience). The viewpoint of this paper will be focused on the gamified learning process targeted at the cultivation of behavior habits. It presents a manual that cultivate the time management awareness and ability of primary school students and conducts experimental research on some of the segments.

2 Behavior Change Model

In order to achieve the goal of behavior change, we need to first establish a behavior change model, whose efficiency will be improved by adding game design elements into the suitable segments.

2.1 TTM and SNAP Model

Filippou et al. [9] integrated the TTM and SNAP models which formed the framework of behavior change used to guide the choice of intervention point when guiding students to change their behavior habits.

Transtheoretical Model (alternatively referred to as the 'Stages of Change' model) gives an overview of the stages experienced when individuals try to modify their behavior. These stages include: pre-contemplation, contemplation, preparation, action, maintenance and termination [10].

At pre-contemplation stage, an individual is unaware of the need to change hence there is no intention to change his behavior. At contemplation stage, the individual starts thinking about his behavior. Subsequently, at the preparation stage, the individual starts to formulate a plan to change his behavior. Before behavior change takes place, the individual will enter the maintenance stage, in which the individual will often try to prevent relapse of his behavior until it is completely altered after entering the termination stage (Fig. 1).

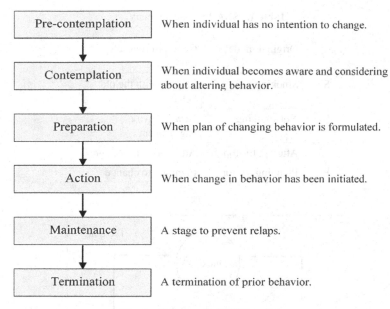

Pre-contemplation	When individual has no intention to change.
Contemplation	When individual becomes aware and considering about altering behavior.
Preparation	When plan of changing behavior is formulated.
Action	When change in behavior has been initiated.
Maintenance	A stage to prevent relaps.
Termination	A termination of prior behavior.

Fig. 1. Six stages of TTM model.

This model is insufficient in that it fails to take the situation where an individual may alter his behavior due to unpredictable reasons and leap between stages at any moment into consideration. Furthermore, some stages in the model were criticized as useless definitions that are subjective and arbitrary. However, in educational gamification aimed at behavior change, this model is highly consistent with the process of students receiving information and altering behavior, hence is worthy of use as a reference.

In order to offset the shortage of TTM, Filippou added the SNAP model of motivation to better explain the transformation between the preparation and action stages. The SNAP model views the change of motive in behavior modification as a dynamic process [11]. The basic precondition for this model is that one must set an ideal behavior which he hopes to adhere to, e.g. 'I wish to quit smoking'. Then the individual will experience fluctuation across the four different stages. Because this model was initially created as a model to help quit smoking, these stages are written according to this specific situation. However, this model can also be applied to scenarios unrelated to smoking [12]. The following table outlines the two versions of the acronym definition (Table 1 and Fig. 2).

Table 1. SNAP model summary

	Original model	General-propose model
S	Smoking	Staying with the old behavior
N	Not smoking	New behavior engagement
A	Attempt to stop	Attempting to change
P	Planning to stop	Planning to change

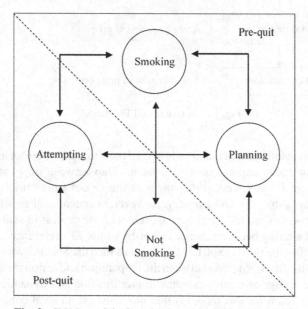

Fig. 2. SNAP model of motivation (for quitting smoking).

Under this model, an individual could jump across the four stages due to any reasons. Transformation between stages is an outcome of the dynamic change and confrontation between the two motives, namely, the feeling of wanting to do something and the feeling that they ought to change their behavior.

Filippou et al. combined the TTM and SNAP models, forming a new model shown as follows (Fig. 3):

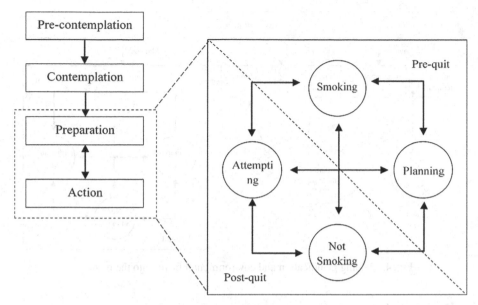

Fig. 3. Combining TTM and SNAP model.

When behavior change exists as the goal of learning, game design elements could interfere at multiple stages of the model in order to achieve the goal of promoting this learning process. Firstly, at the contemplation stage, it requires external information for the individual to generate the idea of behavior change. Game design elements can play a positive role in this stage. When the individual transfers from the preparation stage to action stage, the game design element can act as a trigger making this transformation smoother. Moreover, the promotion of multiple game design elements for motive is proved in the paper by Sailer et al. [13], hence at the maintenance stage of the model, the interference of game design elements has the potential to have a positive impact on maintaining behavior change.

The TTM and SNAP models are models based on the self-initiated process of behavior change, hence more external factors need to be taken into consideration when applying it to achieve educational goals. Students' motive of behavior change may require guidance from family members and school who will also play supporting roles in subsequent stages. Therefore, the environmental factor is added based on the existing model (Fig. 4).

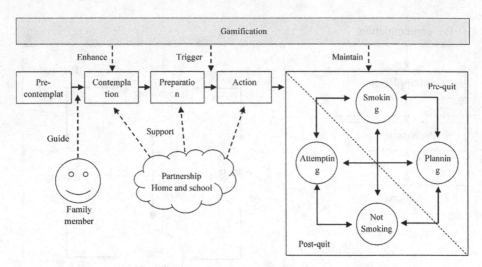

Fig. 4. Adding gamification and environmental factor into the model.

3   Design

3.1   Background of Design

When the COVID-19 pandemic broke out, social restrictions were implemented with Wuhan as a representative and people were forced to stay at home. We observed that due to quarantine, parents and children were able to spend more time together hence more conflicts occurred during the pandemic. In the past, children had teachers supervising them and their study plans in schools. As schools were shut down during the pandemic, life and learning environment of students were combined into one, challenging the time management ability of students.

Under the background of global pandemic, this research conducts in-depth family interviews regarding environmental background, gains insight into the pain point of families in quarantine, conducts toll design based on the previously mentioned model and explores the model and theory raised using experiments. This research will utilize gamification design to develop a course and tool for students' time management ability training. It will also include teaching and tool designs based on research outcome regarding time management training by front-edge literature and combined with the gamification and behavior change model raised in this paper.

We conducted family interviews for children aged 10 to 15 in Wuhan, China. We found out through in-depth interviews of 10 families and learned some facts. firstly, all family members desire high-quality family interaction during quarantine, wishing to ease family relationship through more games; secondly, children do not repel long-distance learning but still require supervision from parents in terms of planning and arrangement of learning; thirdly, parents are worried that students' vision could be harmed due to long duration of usage of electronic products hence parents tend to choose more paper games for entertainment, e.g. board games and poker.

3.2 Content of Design

A clear goal for action-driven time management behavior is to reduce conflicts of targets, to formulate suitable strategy and to turn target into action as well as the effective surveillance of progress towards the target [14], and more control over time means higher level of happiness and working efficiency [15]. Time management behavior is also very closely linked to time perception [16], we also found out through previous interviews that time perception of primary school students is weak and highly unspecific. According to Häfner and Stock, time management consists of eight important parts: 1. Confirmation of priority ranking and goal setting; 2. Strategy making; 3. Design of how to apply and use the strategy in daily life; 4. Feedback on the execution of strategy; 5. Reward setting; 6. Behavior analysis; 7. Ability to identify time management issue; lastly, test result [17]. As mentioned above, this research will use front-edge literature as the design basis of time management tool and is divided into six parts: time perception, goal setting, goal division, strategy making, execution and feedback, as shown in the following Fig. 5.

The most difficult part of time management is strategy making, which is even more difficult for primary school students with weak time perception. It also remains a problem to completer one's study and homework with high efficiency and to maintain the corresponding quality. Many research pointed out that duration of work is linked to productivity. Researchers of Geneva International Labor Office pointed out that the link between the two is related to the biological level [18]. They proposed a solution strategy to find out one's most suitable working duration and allow one to start working at high physiological energy level. The optimal productivity time (OPT) method of time management was raised by the Stamford University which suggests one to execute the most energy-consuming activity when his physiological energy level is the highest. This means that when one is the most energetic from 10 to 12am, he should be arranged to do work that requires the most attention and thinking [19]. This research applies the OPT time management method at the strategy making stage so that students can set their goals in a more straightforward manner.

3.3 Gamification of Design

As time management training is a kind of behavior change, front-edge literature proves that gamification has some positive effects in terms of behavior modification. This research further combines time management training with gamification design to motivate the motive and behavior change of the participant to some extent. There were no clear definition of game design elements by any researchers in the past, until Deterding [2] divided game design elements into five levels in 2011: 1. Game interface design patterns; 2. Game design patterns and mechanics; 3. Game design principles and heuristics; 4. Game models; 5. Game design methods. Dicheva et al. made new arrangements based on the framework raised by Deterding and analyzed as well as confirmed the principles of educational gamification design. They also proposed corresponding suitable gamification mechanism including points, badges, levels, progress bars, leaderboards, virtual currency, and avatars etc. [4].

The behavior change model proposed in this research corresponds to the time management training stage; the time perception stage is the pre-contemplation stage while

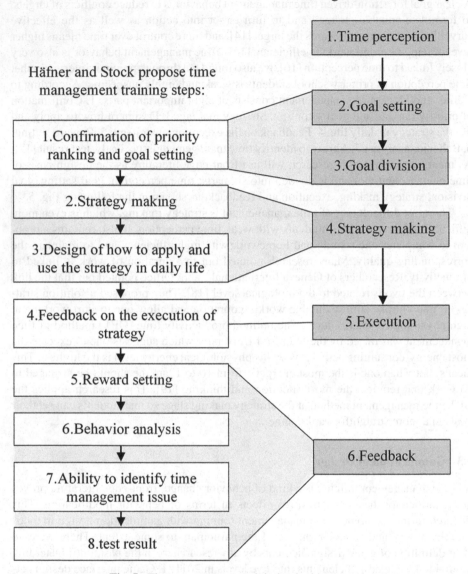

This study propose time management training steps:

Häfner and Stock propose time management training steps:

1.Time perception

2.Goal setting

3.Goal division

1.Confirmation of priority ranking and goal setting

2.Strategy making

3.Design of how to apply and use the strategy in daily life

4.Strategy making

4.Feedback on the execution of strategy

5.Execution

5.Reward setting

6.Behavior analysis

6.Feedback

7.Ability to identify time management issue

8.test result

Fig. 5. Time management tool design in this research

goal setting and goal division belong to the contemplation stage. Strategy making, execution and feedback is one continuous cycle of action. People realize the missing parts in their strategies through feedback, or their improvement. These act as feedback for people and motivates them to continue their action. Gamification design can provide a motive of behavior change for the participants. In the time perception stage, storytelling, avatars and challenging elements are used to give students a specific image of time, they can image time as a strong monster. Students can turn themselves into little warriors facing the challenge to defeat the monster. Once they have a clear goal, they can start arranging their plans. The cooperation element is used to allow students to have company. Social interaction can increase their executive power for action at the final feedback stage, during which they can obtain rewards once they achieve their goals successfully. The game design elements used in time management training based on the behavior change model is as shown in the following Table 2.

Table 2. The game design elements used in time management training based on the behavior change model.

Behavior change model		Time management training stage	Gamification design elements
	Pre-contemplation	Time perception	• Storytelling • Challenges
	Contemplation	Goal setting	• Challenges • Strategy
		Goal division	
Maintenance	Preparation	Strategy making	• Rewards • Partner
	Action	Execution	• Partner
		Feedback	• Immediate feedback • Points • Badges • Progress bar

Finally we came up with a 8-page time management training manual called *the Time Monster Manual*.

4 Application

4.1 Environment

Under strict quarantine policies, family environment was confronted by the issue of work-school overlap. At the same time, parents and students also generate conflicts due their multiple roles under the same roof. All these factors contribute to the generation of family conflict and contradictions as well as low quality of parent-child interaction. During the pandemic, the role of parents becomes increasingly important for students. We cooperated with the Wuhan Education Bureau. We also chose this area which was shut down for one month for our interviews. Gamified time management training courses are conducted to promote the time management manual and called for the participation of local primary school teachers, students and their parents.

4.2   Application of the Manual

Limited by the pandemic, we conducted our gamified time management training courses online. The time management manual and explanatory videos were shared using cloud space which could be freely printed by the participants. The duration of the course was one hour and the participants were local primary school teachers, students and their parents in Wuhan. In the course, we educated students about the importance of time management and raised their awareness of time in a gamified manner. We then passed them out tool of time management, the Time Monster manual. During the process, we made sure that the parents and children learned about the tool and planned their family strategy to combat the monster through interaction across participants on the online platform. In the interactive process of the course, we noticed that the students were the most excited when preparing to make plans with their parents. After the course, families get the time management manual for long-term trial.

4.3   Discussion

After putting the manual into use for a month, we conducted questionnaire surveys and interviews with the participants. Most of the participants considered the manual helpful in time management. Compared with the past, they found study plans arranged more clearly and lives changed as well.

During the interviews, more than half of the students expressed that they were excited to have their parents accompanied when learning the manual in class. Some also preferred to implement the plan accompanied by parents after class. On the other hand, some parents mentioned that their children's time management skills have improved when using the manual. These feedbacks support our theoretical model well: 1. Parents plays an important role in the early stages of behavior modification, especially contemplation, preparation and action stage; 2. Accompanying and cooperating parts in gamification designs help students get cognition inspiration, and strengthen the execution and maintenance of behaviors.

We noticed that many participants emphasized the effect of online courses when describing how their motivation changes. On the other hand, results of questionnaire surveys also indicate that participants of online courses have continued to use the manual for longer time compared to those who download the manual directly. Due to the limitation of survey, we would rather consider the appearance a tendency than a significant statistical result. But it does prompt that courses may have significant effect in the early stages of behavior modification, as well as the gamification designs. Therefore, the next step of our research is to design a further experiment, to verify whether the manual provided independent effects and how these effects would be achieved.

5   Experiment

In order to explore the impact of the teaching part of the manual on students' motive and outcome of usage, we simulated this part for further research. We conducted questionnaire survey before and after the experiment to examine the effect of game design elements when added into the contemplation and preparation stage of behavior change.

5.1 Questions and Hypothesis

We came up with the following research questions and hypothesis.

RQ1. What is the impact of the addition of game design elements in teaching part on the attitude of the participants towards learning time management tools?

Considering the contemplation stage of the course in the entire gamified manual, at this stage, the participants start to generate ideas about behavior change. We hope that the addition of gamification elements into the course can help promote the generation of students' willingness towards taking action in time management. This led to our following hypothesis:

H1. The addition of game design elements can help promote the participants' attitude towards learning time management methods.

RQ2. What is the impact of the addition of game design elements in teaching part on the willingness of participants to use the manual?

We hope that the course can stimulate the participants' motive to use the manual and start changing their behavior. This led to our following hypothesis:

H2. The addition of game design elements can help promote the participants' willingness to use the manual.

RQ3. What is the impact of the addition of game design elements in teaching part on the understanding and memory preservation of the course content?

H3. The addition of game design elements can strengthen the understanding and memory preservation of the course content.

5.2 Method

Course Simulation. In order to prove the above hypothesis, we designed a course to simulate the teaching part. In the course, the teacher first introduced why time management is essential for learning, then introduced two methods. One is about goal management, the other is about understanding the change of energy level in a day using energy curve to arrange schedule. Lastly the gamified time management manual including the two methods was introduced.

The participants were divided into the experimental group and the controlled group. The two groups receive the same knowledge information. The controlled group was taught by the normal method while game design elements were added into the course of the experimental group. It was pointed out in Kapp's [20] paper that storytelling in gamified learning improves engagement. Since storytelling matches the course content well in this case, we chose it as the game design element added. The teaching of the experimental group used the story of a warrior combating the monster of time trying to fit students into role of warrior. When teaching the time management methods, some terms used in time management tools were substituted by elements in the story. The teaching content of the controlled group was completely the same except for the gamified way of narration (Fig. 6).

Fig. 6. Course video and the manual.

Due to the preventive measures during the pandemic, the researchers were unable to gain access to school, hence the course was recorded and played by the teachers instead.

Participants. We randomly chose two Grade 5 classes in the Affiliated Primary School of Xicheng Foreign Language School for the test. The educational levels of students across the students in this class are similar to that of each other with the same courses taken and no time management related courses being conducted in school. The participants do not know the groupings they are in. 38 were in the experimental group, with 19 boys and 19 girls; 40 were in the controlled group, with 21 boys and 19 girls.

Measurement. The students were asked to fill in an anonymous questionnaire both before and after the course. In the pre-test questionnaire, students were asked to score their willingness to do time management, and their willingness to learn a time management tool like schedule books. After the course, students were asked to fill in a post-test questionnaire which includes subjective questions relating to knowledge mentioned in the course to test whether the students have understood or memorized the knowledge well. At the end of the post-test questionnaire, students could apply for the manual (Fig. 7).

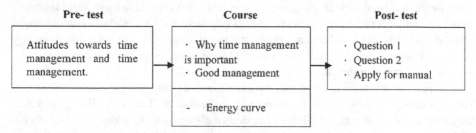

Fig. 7. Process of the experiment.

To Compare the effect of the control condition and experiment condition, the one-sample Kolmogorov–Smirnov test has been employed to test the distributions of data. The data which correspond to normal distribution were analyzed using independent-samples t test, while others using independent-samples Mann-Whitne U test. All analyses were performed using SPSS 20.0 (IBM Corp., Armonk, NY).

5.3 Results

There are in total 35 effective questionnaires collected from the experimental group and 38 from the controlled group (Table 3).

Table 3. Results

	Variable	Control Condition (n = 38)		Experimental condition (n = 37)		Test		p
		Mean (SD)	Median	Mean (SD)	Median	t^a	Z^b	
Pre-test	Attitude towards time management	4.16 (1.13)	4.50	4.16 (0.80)	4.00		−0.724	0.469
	Attitude towards using a time management tool	4.18 (1.43)	5.00	3.81 (1.29)	4.00	1.187		0.239
Post-test	Attitude towards time management	12.53 (2.38)	13.00	12.68 (1.99)	12.00		−0.152	0.879
	Question 1	1.68 (1.23)	2.00	0.73 (1.04)	0.00		−3.258	**0.001***
	Question 2	3.26 (1.48)	3.00	3.86 (1.21)	4.00		− 1.813	**0.070***

[a]Independent-samples t test, t value; [b]Independent-samples Mann-Whitne U test, Z value; $*p < 0.1$; $**p < 0.05$; $***p < 0.01$

RQ1. Regarding to attitude towards time management, there was no significant effect of participation between control condition ($M = 4.16$, $SD = 1.13$) and experimental condition ($M = 4.16$, $SD = 1.13$) in pre-test ($Z = -0.724$, $p > 0.1$), nor between the two conditions in post-test($Z = -0.724$, $p > 0.1$). H1 could not be confirmed.

RQ 2. Regarding to attitude towards using a time management tool, there is no significant difference between the two conditions ($t = 1.187$, $p < 0.239$) before taking the course. The number of participants who applied for the manual turned to be different. 31.6% (12 of 38) of participants in control condition applied for the manual while 57.1% (20 of 35) participants in experimental condition did so. Thus, hypothesis 2 was supported.

RQ 3. Concerning impact of game design elements on the understanding and memory preservation of knowledge, for question 1, there was a significant difference between the two conditions ($Z = -3.258$, $p < 0.01$). The score of control condition ($M = 1.68$, $SD = 1.23$) is higher than experimental condition ($M = 0.73$, $SD = 1.04$). For question 2, the result was opposite. There was a marginal significant difference between the two conditions $(Z = -1.813, p < 0.1)$. The score of control condition $(M = 3.26, SD = 1.48)$ is lower than experimental condition $(M = 3.86, SD = 1.21)$. Hypothesis 3 was not supported and further discussion is needed.

5.4 Discussion

The above experimental results verify that the application of game design elements has a positive effect on the course, leading to students' significant interest in the manual. According to the theory of landers et al. [21, 22], gamification affect learning via a mediating process wherein gamification alters a psychological characteristic that itself affects an outcome of interest (see Fig. 8; D → C → B). Therefore, we can infer that the game design elements introduced in the teaching process of this experiment can indirectly affect the learning effect of subsequent behavior change stages by influencing the students' attitude towards the manual.

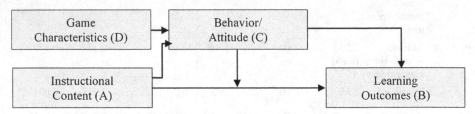

Fig. 8. Theory of gamified learning.

Furthermore, it can be observed from the experimental results that the specific selection of game design elements will affect memory preservation. The most obvious fact is that when the original nouns are changed by storytelling elements, it may cause students' understanding obstacles and even lead to confusion of similar concepts, suggesting that we should be more cautious in the selection and use of game design elements. We will conduct further research in the future.

Another problem that needs further study is the influence of curriculum form. In the actual promotion of the manual, online video courses will be more commonly used instead of live teaching. Therefore, we need to study dependence of the game design elements introduced in the course on communication and interaction between teachers and students, and make optimization.

6 Conclusion

In this paper, we suggested a framework for gamification based on behavior change model. In this framework, we used TTM model to divide each stage of behavior change, and added game design elements and environmental factor in the appropriate stage. With reference to this, a gamification tool manual is designed to train primary school students' time manage skill at home. In the follow-up after use, we found that, consistent with the framework, the participation of parents and other environmental factors can promote students' motivation. In addition, in the contemplation stage and preparation stage of the framework, the gamified teaching of manual content promotes the motivation of subsequent manual use. In the additional experiment, we found that Gamification of teaching improved the motivation of students to use the manual, but the intrinsic motivation of time planning was not produced.

We got the enlightenment that in gamification design of teaching tools aimed at behavior change, the process of introducing and teaching the tools should also be considered as part of the tool, and needs to be designed properly, as contemplation and preparation are critical stages to behavior change process.

In future studies, we will focus on the role of gamification in other stages of behavior change and the effects of other game design elements in the early stages of behavior change. The framework of this article will continue to be improved.

References

1. Marczewski, A.: Gamification: a simple introduction & a bit more-tips, advice and thoughts on gamification. Self-published via kdp.amazon.co.jp. (2012). http://amazon.com/
2. Deterding, S., Dixon, D., Khaled, R., Nacke, L.: From game design elements to gamefulness: defining "gamification". In: Proceedings of the 15th international academic MindTrek conference: Envisioning future media environments, pp. 9–15. ACM, New York (2011). https://doi.org/10.1145/2181037.2181040
3. Werbach, K.: (Re)defining gamification: a process approach. In: Spagnolli, A., Chittaro, L., Gamberini, L. (eds.) PERSUASIVE 2014. LNCS, vol. 8462, pp. 266–272. Springer, Cham (2014). https://doi.org/10.1007/978-3-319-07127-5_23
4. Dicheva, D., Dichev, C., Agre, G., Angelova, G.: Gamification in education: a systematic mapping study. J. Educ. Technol. Soc. 18(3), 75–88 (2015)
5. Hew, K.F., Huang, B., Chu, K.W.S., Chiu, D.K.: Engaging Asian students through game mechanics: findings from two experiment studies. Comput. Educ. 92, 221–236 (2016)
6. Barna, B., Fodor, S.: An empirical study on the use of gamification on IT courses at higher education. In: Auer, M.E., Guralnick, D., Simonics, I. (eds.) ICL 2017. AISC, vol. 715, pp. 684–692. Springer, Cham (2018). https://doi.org/10.1007/978-3-319-73210-7_80
7. Lam, Y.W., Hew, K.F., Chiu, K.F.: Improving argumentative writing: effects of a blended learning approach and gamification. Lang. Learn. Technol. 22(1), 97–118 (2017)
8. González, C.S., et al.: Learning healthy lifestyles through active videogames, motor games and the gamification of educational activities. Comput. Hum. Behav. 55, 529–551 (2016). https://doi.org/10.1016/j.chb.2015.08.052
9. Filippou, J., Cheong, C., Cheong, F.: Improving study habits using a behaviour change framework incorporating social motivation and gamification. In: Pacific Asia Conference on Information Systems, p. 264. AIS, Chengdu (2014)
10. Prochaska, J.O., Velicer, W.F.: The transtheoretical model of health behavior change. Am. J. Health Promot. 12(1), 38–48 (1997)
11. West, R.: The multiple facets of cigarette addiction and what they mean for encouraging and helping smokers to stop. COPD: J. Chronic Obstr. Pulm. Dis. 6(4), 277–283 (2009)
12. West, R.: The challenge of behaviour change. University College London [ppt] (2009). http://www.rjwest.co.uk/downloadfile.php?filename=uploads/090209challengeofhealthbehavchnge2.ppt

13. Sailer, M., Hense, J.U., Mayr, S.K., Mandl, H.: How gamification motivates: an experimental study of the effects of specific game design elements on psychological need satisfaction. Comput. Hum. Behav. **69**, 371–380 (2017). https://doi.org/10.1016/j.chb.2016.12.033
14. Macan, T.H.: Time management: test of a process model. J. Appl. Psychol. **79**(3), 381–391 (1994). https://doi.org/10.1037/0021-9010.79.3.381
15. Claessens, B.J.C., Van Eerde, W., Rutte, C.G., Roe, R.A.: Planning behavior and perceived control of time at work. J. Organ. Behav. **25**(8), 937–950 (2004). https://doi.org/10.1002/job.292
16. Pinneker, L., Häfner, A., Stock, A., Oberst, V.L.: How to get control of your time. In: Poster Session Presented at the 14th European Congress of Work and Organizational Psychology. EAWOP, Santiago de Compostela (2009)
17. Häfner, A., Stock, A.: Time management training and perceived control of time at work. J. Psychol. **144**(5), 429–447 (2010). https://doi.org/10.1080/00223980.2010.496647
18. The Optimal Amount of Time to Spend Working Each Day. https://fourpillarfreedom.com/the-optimal-amount-of-time-to-spend-working-each-day-according-to-research/. Accessed 11 Jan 2021
19. Seven time management tips for happier days. https://bewell.stanford.edu/seven-time-management-tips-for-happier-days/. Accessed 11 Dec 2021
20. Kapp, K.M.: Games, gamification, and the quest for learner engagement. Train. Dev. **66**(6), 64–68 (2012)
21. Landers, R.N., Landers, A.K.: An empirical test of the theory of gamified learning. Simul. Gaming **45**(6), 769–785 (2014). https://doi.org/10.1177/1046878114563662

Can Games and Gamification Improve Online Learners' Outcomes and Satisfaction on the Madrasati Platform in Saudi Arabia?

Wad Ghaban[✉]

Ministry of Education, Riyadh, Saudi Arabia

Abstract. Because of the recent COVID-19 pandemic, the Saudi Arabian government established a new online learning platform to help students in primary and high schools continue their learning from home. This study aims to examine the effects of online learning on teachers and students. For that, we asked 40 teachers and 123 students about their user experiences with the new platform. Most of the teachers and students were satisfied with their experience. However, they both claimed that a lack of motivation and engagement and missing interactions with peers and teachers were the greatest shortcomings of online learning. To compensate for this, teachers aimed to use different tools and provide games and gamification elements in their online lessons to motivate and engage students.

Keywords: Online learning · Motivation · Games · Gamification · Satisfaction

1 Introduction

During the emergency and crisis, governments around the world responded quickly to adapt to the new situation. For example, during the novel coronavirus pandemic that started in Wuhan, China and spread quickly throughout the world, most governments set strict rules to protect the public [9]. Because the virus was new and unknown, most countries closed schools, universities, shops and most other places. As these places can be a common place to spread the virus in public [12]. However, it was hard to keep children away from school. For that reason, most countries made accommodations to let children learn from home. Saudi Arabia is one of the first countries to take this first step during the lockdown, as Saudi Arabia closed schools beginning on the 9th of March 2020. Then, the Saudi Arabian government and the Ministry of Education established a new online learning platform called Madrasati. The new platform allows teachers and students to do their online lessons and to submit materials, assignments and exams.

© Springer Nature Switzerland AG 2021
X. Fang (Ed.): HCII 2021, LNCS 12790, pp. 189–200, 2021.
https://doi.org/10.1007/978-3-030-77414-1_14

In this paper, we want to highlight the features provided by the platform and to examine whether the platform is beneficial for teachers and students. We start by providing a questionnaire for teachers about their experiences, struggles and challenges. As a result, most of the teachers argue that a lack of motivation and engagement is the main issue [2]. To address this, teachers are regularly using gamification elements and integrating games into their lessons [5]. This paper also tried to determine if online learning has a positive effect on learners' satisfaction and outcomes. We did this by asking learners to fill in a pre-test related to the computer curriculum. Then, three months after using the online learning platform, we asked learners to fill in a post-test, which was similar to the pre-test. We did this to find out if there was any improvement in learners' knowledge. In addition, we asked learners to fill in an e-learner satisfaction tool (ELS) [16] to measure learners' satisfaction, and asked other open questions to query learners about what they liked and did not like during their experience of online learning.

The results showed that learners enjoyed their experience, and they improved in their outcomes. However, many learners still miss their traditional schools and miss the physical interactions between their friends and teachers.

2   Background

The recent virus COVID-19 caused the death of millions of people [15]. Most countries took quick action to protect the public by closing public places and cancelling major events, such as shopping malls, cinemas and museums [15]. In addition, most countries closed schools and universities to protect teachers and students. According to UNESCO, almost 1.2 billion students were away from the school during the pandemic [12]. Countries started to guide students to learn at home by publishing materials every week and having parents be responsible for taking care of children's learning. However, other countries have used online learning platforms to deliver efficient learning.

The idea of online learning is not a new concept and has been used before in other crises. For example, [13] show that during the SARS and H1N1 outbreaks in 2002 and 2008, many places in China used online learning for students. However, there has been no research showing the effect of online learning on students.

Different research studies have shown that online learning can be as beneficial to learners as traditional learning. In addition, these studies show that the performance of learners in online learning is the same as that of traditional learning. In online learning, learners can have their lessons at any time in any place at an extra cost for travel and accommodation [1]. However, some other studies have claimed that online learning cannot be the same as traditional learning. This kind of learning can be anxiety-provoking and boring for some learners [10]. Learners can feel isolated during online learning. So, different online platforms are integrated with games and gamification elements, such as Khan Academy and massive open online courses (MOOCs) [11].

2.1 Games and Gamification Elements

Different techniques have been used to motivate students in online learning and to make the learning process more enjoyable. For example, [5] show that integrating online courses with verbal and physical rewards can help to motivate students. Further, as [14] pointed out, considering the social interaction between learners is important for engaging students. For example, competition between learners is essential to improving students' knowledge and motivation. Another important technique is the use of games and gamification [4]. Different kinds of games can be used, for example, educational games where the whole lesson is designed as a game for a specified learning goal to allow learners to accomplish the goals. Further, these kinds of games can provide students with quick feedback [5].

Gamification is considered to be another technique that can be used to motivate and engage students [4]. Gamification can be defined as the use of game elements, such as points and badges, in non-game contexts, such as learning [3]. Unlike games, in gamification, the lesson is not changed to a game, but gamification elements can be added. For example, if the student provides a correct answer, he/she will receive a point. After collecting five points [7], for instance, learners will receive a badge. Different research studies have shown the positive effect of gamification on students' performance and enjoyment [6].

3 The Madrasati Platform

By March 2020, the World Health Organization (WHO) announced that the COVID-19 virus had become a global pandemic. As a result, schools and universities were closed, and students began to study at home.

Saudi Arabia was among the earliest countries to close its schools. The Saudi government and the Ministry of Education have created a special platform for use by students in primary and high schools. Figure 1 shows a screenshot of the platform, Madrasati, which enables students to check their online school schedules, lessons and curricula assigned to them. Students can also use this platform to submit their homework, contact their teachers and peers, take exams, and see their grades after submitting their homework exams.

Fig. 1. The home page for Madrasati platform

The Madrasati platform enables teachers to prepare their lessons and publish all learning materials associated with them. The platform is linked with Microsoft Teams, so after each lesson is prepared, a link is created to an online meeting for that lesson, where both teacher and students can be in a live online meeting at the same time. Students can also see a recorded version of the lesson at any time they like. Teachers can also send homework and exams to students (Fig. 2). To motivate and engage students in online classes, teachers can offer badges, points and motivational phrases.

Fig. 2. The schedule and the lesson in Madrasati platform

Unfortunately, as the literature points out, online learning has shortcomings, including the fact that online students may feel bored and isolated from their peers and teachers. To counter this, the Madrasati platform enables students and teachers to communicate with each other using conversations or email, both of which the platform includes

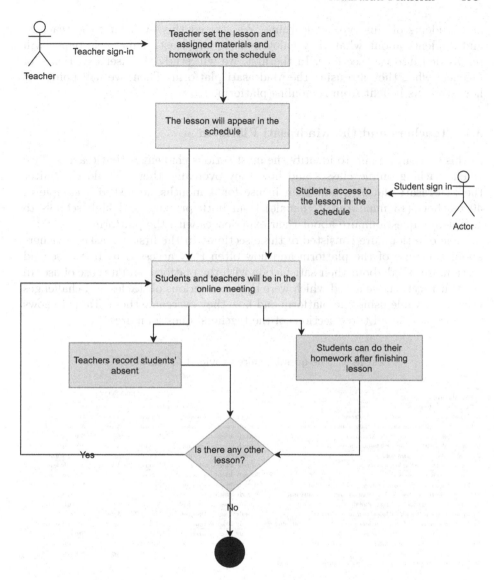

Fig. 3. The flow of the students and the teachers in Madrasati platform

Teachers prepare their lessons on the platform by assigning materials, homework and extra resources to enrich students' learning. As mentioned, after each lesson is assigned, it appears to students as a link. When they click it, students are directed to the synchronous online lesson, during which the teacher and students are live at the same time on Microsoft Teams and can benefit from all its features, including chat and voice calls. Figure 3 shows the flow of a lesson on the Madrasati platform.

Online learning is a new experience for both teachers and students. In this study, we aimed to identify the benefits and shortcomings for both teachers and students of this type of learning. We started this by asking the teachers and students about what they enjoyed most and least. Thus, this paper will be divided into two sections. In the first, we will study the user experience of teachers when they are using the Madrasati platform. Then, we will point out how students benefit from the online platform.

3.1 Teachers and the Madrasati Platform

In this section, we aim to identify the most serious challenges that teachers face when teaching online classes and how they overcame them. To do this, after the Madrasati platform had been in use for 4 months, we asked a sample of 40 teachers (13 male and 27 female) from both primary and high schools to complete a questionnaire about their experiences with the platform.

The questionnaire consisted of three sections. In the first, we asked teachers about their use of the platform and how often they accessed it. In the second section, we asked about their satisfaction with the platform and its ease of use. In the third section, we asked which were the most serious obstacles and challenges they faced while using the platform and how they overcame them. Table 1 shows the questions in all three sections of the teachers' questionnaires.

Table 1. The questionnaire provided to teachers

Questions	Response				
1. I use Madrasati platform	Yes			No	
2. I access to Madrasati platform	Never	Once a month	Once a week	Once a day	More then once daily
3. I am satisfied with my experience in Madrasati	Strongly disagree	Disagree	Normal	Agree	Strongly agree
4. I am satisfied with the arrangement of the icons in Madrasati	Strongly disagree	Disagree	Normal	Agree	Strongly agree
5. I am satisfied with colours used in Madrasati	Strongly disagree	Disagree	Normal	Agree	Strongly agree
6. I am satisfied with the features integrated in Madarasati	Strongly disagree	Disagree	Normal	Agree	Strongly agree
7. I can find what ever I want quickly	Strongly disagree	Disagree	Normal	Agree	Strongly agree
8. I can access to my online lesson easily	Strongly disagree	Disagree	Normal	Agree	Strongly agree
9. I can follow my students easily	Strongly disagree	Disagree	Normal	Agree	Strongly agree
10. I am using gamification elements integrated in Madrasati	Strongly disagree	Disagree	Normal	Agree	Strongly agree
11. The gamification elements in Madrasati are enough for students	Strongly disagree	Disagree	Normal	Agree	Strongly agree
12. I choose to change my lessons into games	Strongly disagree	Disagree	Normal	Agree	Strongly agree
13. I prefer to use tools with my lesson to motivate students	Strongly disagree	Disagree	Normal	Agree	Strongly agree
14. I think it is important to integrate lesson with tools to motivate students	Strongly disagree	Disagree	Normal	Agree	Strongly agree
15. I think games and gamification can motivate students	Strongly disagree	Disagree	Normal	Agree	Strongly agree
16. I think adding games and gamification may distract students	Strongly disagree	Disagree	Normal	Agree	Strongly agree
17. I am satisfied with online learning	Strongly disagree	Disagree	Normal	Agree	Strongly agree
18. Do you think there is any issues with online learning? Mention them?					

Results. The results showed that the teachers were committed to using the platform. In fact, 73% of the teachers said they accessed the platform daily, and nearly 27% accessed it more than once a day. The teachers noted that they needed to check regularly on whether students had asked questions, as well as mark students' assignments (Fig. 4).

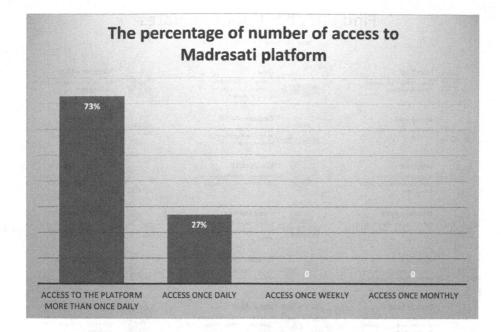

Fig. 4. The flow of the students and the teachers in Madrasati platform

The results also showed that 90% of the teachers were satisfied with the platform. They reported that it was easy to find what they wanted and commented favourably on its colours and design. However, some teachers noted that during the first two months of using the platform, due to their lack of training, they found it difficult to add extra resources and information for their students. They also noted a problem with homework not appearing for some students.

The most serious challenge that the teachers reported was students' lack of motivation. Regarding this, one questionnaire item asked about the tools that teachers used to motivate and engage their students, and 77% of teachers responded that they used the badges, points and motivational phrases integrated into the Madrasati platform. Also, 85% of teachers mentioned that they integrated their lessons with other tools to change a lesson or part of one into a game. The tools they used to accomplish this included Wordwall, Liveworksheets and Quizizz.

Wordwall.net. Wordwall.net enables teachers to create custom activities for students. For example, a teacher can customise learning resources like games, including hangman, word match, balloon pop, open the box and random wheel. On the Wordwall website, teachers can create their own activities or search by lesson title for activities that have been used by other teachers. Figure 5 shows various activities provided by Wordwall. Another Wordwall feature enables students to check their answers after submitting them.

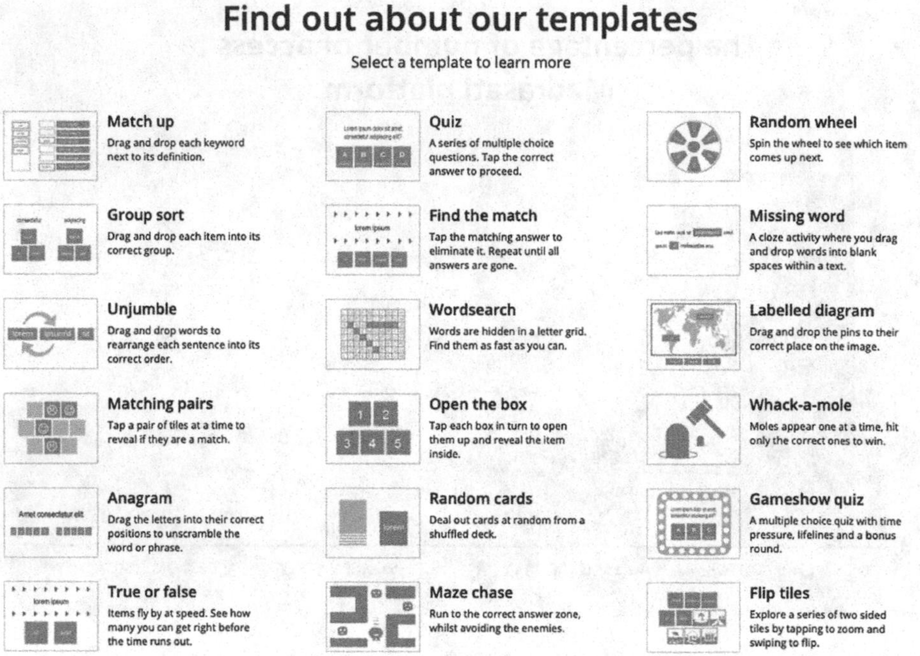

Find out about our templates

Select a template to learn more

Match up
Drag and drop each keyword next to its definition.

Quiz
A series of multiple choice questions. Tap the correct answer to proceed.

Random wheel
Spin the wheel to see which item comes up next.

Group sort
Drag and drop each item into its correct group.

Find the match
Tap the matching answer to eliminate it. Repeat until all answers are gone.

Missing word
A cloze activity where you drag and drop words into blank spaces within a text.

Unjumble
Drag and drop words to rearrange each sentence into its correct order.

Wordsearch
Words are hidden in a letter grid. Find them as fast as you can.

Labelled diagram
Drag and drop the pins to their correct place on the image.

Matching pairs
Tap a pair of tiles at a time to reveal if they are a match.

Open the box
Tap each box in turn to open them up and reveal the item inside.

Whack-a-mole
Moles appear one at a time, hit only the correct ones to win.

Anagram
Drag the letters into their correct positions to unscramble the word or phrase.

Random cards
Deal out cards at random from a shuffled deck.

Gameshow quiz
A multiple choice quiz with time pressure, lifelines and a bonus round.

True or false
Items fly by at speed. See how many you can get right before the time runs out.

Maze chase
Run to the correct answer zone, whilst avoiding the enemies.

Flip tiles
Explore a series of two sided tiles by tapping to zoom and swiping to flip.

Fig. 5. The homepage of the Wordwall

Live Worksheet. This website enables teachers to create interactive worksheets that include various types of questions: matching, multiple-choice and fill-in-the-blank. When students finish their worksheets, they can have them auto-marked and sent directly to their teachers. Figure 6 shows an example of Liveworksheets.

Quizizz. Quizizz can be used as either an application or a web-based tool and adds an element of gamification: competition. In Quizizz, teachers write questions in multiple-choice format. Then, using a code, students can compete to provide the most correct answers, which are presented on the leader board.

3.2 The Effect on Learners of Integrating Games and Gamification into Learning

In this section, we review the effects of using games and gamification on students, and we measure students' outcomes and satisfaction with the Madrasati platform. To do so, we first obtained ethical agreement from 123 students (50 boys and 73 girls) aged 16–18 years who attended various schools in Saudi Arabia. We ensure that students and their parents are aware that their data will be encrypted and securely saved. Students and their parents were free to choose to drop out of the study, in which case their data would not be used.

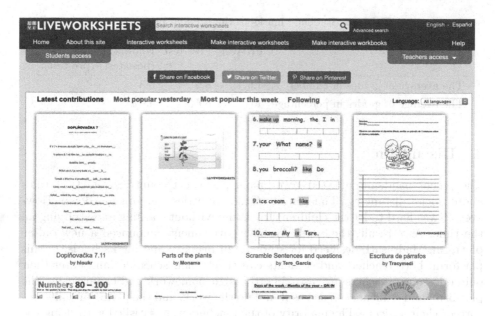

Fig. 6. The homepage of the live worksheet

Before beginning to use the Madrasati platform, teachers asked their students to complete a pre-test evaluation containing 10 items related to the computer curriculum that they would be studying during the term. Then, the students used the Madrasati platform daily five days a week, from 9 am to 2 pm Most teachers used gamification elements integrated into the platform as well as other fun ways to present their lessons. At the end of the three-month term, we asked the students to complete a post-test evaluation that contained 10 items, such as those on the pre-test evaluation. We measured the learning outcomes by subtracting the students' pre-test scores from their post-test scores. To measure their satisfaction, we asked the students to complete an ELS.

The results of comparing the pre-and post-test scores showed that students benefitted from participating in the online classes, with most students receiving higher post-test marks than pre-test ones. Table 2 shows the results of students' pre-and post-tests. When asked about their satisfaction, 96% of students said they noticed no difference between learning online and doing so in a traditional school. Furthermore, they enjoyed the flexibility of online schools, as they could attend their lessons anywhere, including, for example, in the car or even in the hospital. Some students noted that the online lessons were helpful when they caught the COVID-19 virus, including one student who did so and experienced mild symptoms but never stopped attending school online. He described the online classes as helpful during his isolation, as he was able to talk with his teacher and socialise with friends. Despite being able to do these things, 81% of students noted that they missed being in school and seeing their friends.

Table 2. Students' marks in the pre-and post-test

	Pre-test	Post-test	Knowledge gain (post-test)-(pre-test)
The average of grades in number	4.6	8.9	5.3
The average of grades in percentage	46%	89%	43%

4   Discussion

The recent pandemic affected governments, as most countries set strict rules about social distancing. Thus, most of the countries were on lockdown. However, it was hard to let the children stay home without learning and studying all the time. As a result, the Saudi Arabian government announced a new online platform, Madrasati, designed for students in primary and high schools. In this platform, both teachers and students can check their schedules and enter their online lessons. Teachers are also able to assign homework and exams using the platform, and students can access it and do the work, and the platform will auto-correct their answers. The majority of the teachers were satisfied with using the platform, and they found it easy to deal with. However, some of the teachers complained about the platform freezing in some cases, especially on the first day of school and the first day of the final exams. However, they accepted this and mentioned that it is acceptable if we look to the huge number of students who accessed the platform at the same time using the same features, such as completing an exam, for instance. Teachers also complained about issues that occurred with some students. For example, in some cases, homework did not appear to all students. They also mentioned that the motivational phrases and gamification elements integrated with the platform are not enough. Students need more techniques to motivate them. For example, assigning badges for students who do a significant amount of homework and another badge for students who access the platform regularly. Teachers also mentioned that there must be an announcement page that can be presented to all students and staff within the school. This confirmed what [7] pointed out, as points and badges are not enough to motivate students in online learning. Further, some teachers complained about the cost of the internet. They also mentioned that the tools used to make the lessons more fun are not free. They can do only three to five lessons, and then they need to buy a subscription.

In the same manner, the students were satisfied with their experience in online learning. They found it was really easy, and it helped them to be more focused, which was reflected in their grades, as we saw an improvement in their results on the post-test.

However, most students showed that they really wanted to be back in school. As they mentioned, they miss their friends and they miss the feeling of being in school. Further, some of the students described online learning as good if it was two to three hours daily. However, they attend their online school from 9 am to 2 pm with only five-minute breaks between sessions. Students pointed out that digital interaction between their peers and other teachers is not enough. They said that they wanted to be with their friends face-to-face. This confirmed what [8,13] pointed out' that the interaction via technology can be described as cold and cannot replace physical interaction.

In conclusion, we point out that online learning can be as good as traditional learning, even for learners in primary and high schools. However, students and teachers faced some issues at the beginning because it was a new situation for everyone. However, by the end of the term, students and teachers had gotten used to the platform, and they found it easy to deal with. Further, most of the teachers argued that students' marks from online learning are the same as those from traditional learning. For that, we aim to collect more data about students' marks on traditional learning and compare their scores from online learning to examine if there is a significant difference between students' progress in online and traditional learning. Although online learning can still be beneficial, even if in-person school is resumed, for example, in the case of heavy rain or snow.

5   Conclusion

Because of COVID-19, Saudi Arabia set rules to lockdown and guide people to social distance. However, it was hard to keep children away from school, as there was the potential to waste a year of children's education. For that, the Saudi Arabian government and the Ministry of Education established an online learning platform for students in primary and high schools. By using this platform, students and teachers were able to organise an asynchronous online classroom. They could also complete and submit homework and exams. This paper tried to determine the benefits and shortcomings of this platform.

Most of the teachers and students were satisfied with their experience with the platform after three months of using it. Teachers and students claimed that it was hard to accept this kind of learning and the new situation in the first few weeks. However, they quickly dealt with it effectively. Further, some of the teachers and students enjoyed their experience with online learning. However, students mentioned a lack of social connection with their peers and teachers. While most teachers claimed that the main issue with online learning is the lack of motivation and engagement. As a result, most teachers and students integrate their lessons with games and gamification elements using several tools. Using these techniques had a positive effect on students, as the teachers showed that students started to attend regularly and became more active in the lessons.

References

1. Anderson, T., Elloumi, F.: The Theory and Practice of Online Learning, 2nd ed. Athabasca University, Athabasca (2008). Accessed 3 Mar 2009
2. Chen, K.C., Jang, S.J.: Motivation in online learning: testing a model of self-determination theory. Comput. Hum. Behav. **26**(4), 741–752 (2010)

3. Dichev, C., Dicheva, D., Angelova, G., Agre, G.: From gamification to gameful design and gameful experience in learning. Cybern. Inf. Technol. **14**(4), 80–100 (2014)
4. Dicheva, D., Dichev, C., Agre, G., Angelova, G., et al.: Gamification in education: a systematic mapping study. Educ. Technol. Soc. **18**(3), 75–88 (2015)
5. Filsecker, M., Hickey, D.T.: A multilevel analysis of the effects of external rewards on elementary students' motivation, engagement and learning in an educational game. Comput. Educ. **75**, 136–148 (2014)
6. Ghaban, W., Hendley, R.: Investigating the interaction between personalities and the benefit of gamification. In: Proceedings of the 32nd International BCS Human Computer Interaction Conference, p. 41. BCS Learning & Development Ltd. (2018)
7. Ghaban, W., Hendley, R.: How different personalities benefit from gamification. Interact. Comput. **31**(2), 138–153 (2019). https://doi.org/10.1093/iwc/iwz009
8. Ghaban., W., Hendley., R., Fleck., R.: Investigating how social elements affect learners with different personalities. In: Proceedings of the 11th International Conference on Computer Supported Education - CSEDU, vol. 2, pp. 416–423. INSTICC, SciTePress (2019). https://doi.org/10.5220/0007732404160423
9. Irawan, A.W., Dwisona, D., Lestari, M.: Psychological impacts of students on online learning during the pandemic COVID-19. KONSELI Jurnal Bimbingan dan Konseling (E-Journal) **7**(1), 53–60 (2020)
10. Keller, J., Suzuki, K.: Learner motivation and e-learning design: a multinationally validated process. J. Educ. Media **29**(3), 229–239 (2004)
11. Simões, J., Redondo, R.D., Vilas, A.F.: A social gamification framework for a k-6 learning platform. Comput. Hum. Behav. **29**(2), 345–353 (2013)
12. Suryaman, M., et al.: COVID-19 pandemic and home online learning system: does it affect the quality of pharmacy school learning? Syst. Rev. Pharm. **11**, 524–530 (2020)
13. Swan, K., Shih, L.F.: On the nature and development of social presence in online course discussions. J. Asynchronous Learn. Netw. **9**(3), 115–136 (2005)
14. Udvari, S.J., Schneider, B.H.: Competition and the adjustment of gifted children: a matter of motivation. Roeper Rev. **22**(4), 212–216 (2000)
15. Unger, S., Meiran, W.R.: Student attitudes towards online education during the COVID-19 viral outbreak of 2020: distance learning in a time of social distance. Int. J. Technol. Educ. Sci. (IJTES) **4**(4), 256–266 (2020)
16. Wang, Y.S.: Assessment of learner satisfaction with asynchronous electronic learning systems. Inf. Manag. **41**(1), 75–86 (2003)

Methodological Considerations for Understanding Students' Problem Solving Processes and Affective Trajectories During Game-Based Learning: A Data Fusion Approach

Maya Israel[1](✉), Tongxi Liu[1], Jewoong Moon[2], Fengfeng Ke[2],
and Ibrahim Dahlstrom-Hakki[3]

[1] University of Florida, Gainesville, FL 32611, USA
`misrael@coe.ufl.edu`
[2] Florida State University, Tallahassee, FL 32306-4453, USA
[3] TERC, Cambridge, MA 02140, USA

Abstract. This paper describes methodological considerations for fusing data sources in understanding both affective and problem solving states of students as they engage in computational thinking (CT) game-based learning. We provide both a theoretical and empirical rationale for using data including facial recognition and students' logfile data to gain a more robust explanation of why students may experience emotions such as frustration during CT game-based learning activities. We showcase illustrative examples using data from individual learners to highlight the methodological approaches that we have taken. Finally, given the complexities of understanding constructs such as affect and problem solving, we provide a rationale for using a data fusion methodological approach.

Keywords: Game-based learning · Gameplay · Facial expression · Data fusion

1 Introduction

There is growing momentum for increasing young learners' exposure to computational thinking (CT) practices in K-12 instructional settings [52]. Although there is still debate about the definition of CT, it is broadly considered as systematic problem solving process (either with or without the use of computers) that involves decomposing complex problems into sub-problems, solving the sub-problems with sequential and planned steps, and finally abstracting and generalizing the solutions [38]. The rationale for focusing on CT includes its affordances for promoting innovative and imaginative thinking [7], logical problem solving [27], and developing the full set of mental tools to solve complex problems effectively [25]. Thus, there is a growing need to explore effective ways of introducing CT into K-12 educational environments [8].

One approach to introduce young learners to CT is through game-based learning. Game-based learning environments were developed to facilitate students' domain specific knowledge and skill acquisition, in which the game content is typically designed

© Springer Nature Switzerland AG 2021
X. Fang (Ed.): HCII 2021, LNCS 12790, pp. 201–215, 2021.
https://doi.org/10.1007/978-3-030-77414-1_15

with problem solving tasks and challenges. These environments have been shown to motivate students' engagement and perceived achievement with attractive story lines and interesting tasks [30]. Game-based learning has been shown to increase motivation and interest [26, 31, 47] and support implicit learning (i.e., problem solving skills) within STEM related literacies [13].

When students interact with game-based learning environments, students experience a wide range of cognitive and affective states [18], which may influence their learning in problem solving tasks [35]. For example, Sankaran and Bui [34] found that students with higher motivation and positive emotion displayed better performance during their learning processes, while Wine and colleagues [49] found a negative linear relationship between cognitive anxiety and learning. Thus, tracking and responding to these cognitive and affective states is a core aim of adaptive game-based learning environments that seek to foster increased motivation and improved learning. In addition to understanding learners' cognitive and affective states during game play, it is also critical to understand how and to what extent learners employ problem solving strategies as their knowledge and expertise increases. This knowledge can help researchers and designers gain a deeper understanding of how learners solve problems and when they need additional scaffolds (both from within the game and from external inputs such as teachers) to move forward.

Research on emotion in game-based learning environments presents several methodological limitations. For example, most previous research has relied on annotating students' learning and affect manually [36]. Moreover, because learning processes are implicit, it is difficult to monitor and track students' learning progression [20]. Learning analytics informed by multimodal data hold significant promise for deeper understanding of students' interactions in game-based learning environments. Such methodologies include sensor-based technologies (e.g., facial expression analysis) and data mining techniques such as sequential pattern mining [17]. Using multimodal data to interpret students' learning strategies, emotions and other learning related performance has implications for improving adaptive interventions and scaffolding that support students' cognitive, affective and metacognitive aspects of learning [17].

2   Research Context and Purpose

The purpose of this paper is to present methodological approaches to study both students' problem solving and emotional responses using multimodal data collection and analysis. Our aim is to provide suggestions for approaches to fusing multiple data approaches with the goal of better understanding students' affective and problem solving strategies. More specifically, we are interested in detecting both emotions and problem solving processes and detecting trigger moments wherein students' problem solving or emotions shifts from one state to another state. For example, students may transition from engagement to frustration as well as transition from systematic testing to unproductive approaches such as trial and error.

2.1 Data Sources and Participants

We primarily focus on the integration of students' log file data and facial expression to predict students' learning processes and affective trajectories within a game-based learning environment called *Zoombinis* [5]. *Zoombinis* is an award-winning game (zoombinis.con) originally designed as a puzzle game situated in the problems of database design, allowing ample scaffolded problem solving for young learners [33]. It includes 12 puzzles wherein learners work through logic problems involving bringing characters to safety by figuring out problems involving sorting, matching, and sequencing attributes of the *Zoombinis*.

Fig. 1. Example images of *Zoombinis* puzzles (top left going clockwise): Allergic Cliffs, Bubblewonder Abyss, Mudball Wall, and Pizza Pass [5]

Data were collected from 30 students who played research versions of four Zoombinis puzzles. The research versions of these puzzles were the same as those in the commercial game except that it was free to participants and included data logging. The four puzzles (see Fig. 1) studied were:

– **Allergic Cliffs**: In this puzzle, Zoombinis can only cross one of two bridges. The player must discover which attributes allow each Zoombini to cross which bridge.
– **Bubblewonder Abyss**: In this puzzle, Zoombinis must move through a maze that has junctions and switches triggered by Zoombini attributes.
– **Mudball Wall**: In this puzzle, players must figure out how the color and shape of each mudball corresponds to a position on the wall.

- **Pizza Pass**: In this puzzle, the player must find the combination of pizza (and at higher level ice cream) toppings desired by a troll blocking the Zoombinis' path.

In this study, we explored how separate and combined modalities of data (e.g., facial expression and gameplay behaviors) depict and predict students' learning and affect while playing *Zoombinis*.

3 Approaches to Multimodal Data Collection and Analysis

Multimodal learning analytics using machine learning has shown promise in unpacking patterns in behaviors [6, 28, 29]. In educational research, this approach provides new insights into learning in game-based tasks in which students have different probability to generate unique, personalized learning processes and affective trajectories [9]. Multimodal data collection and analysis can be leveraged to understand students' learning behaviors and model students' interactions or outcomes. For instance, in order to examine knowledge acquisition and assess implicit learning, a range of data channels such as facial expressions [22, 44], gameplay behaviors [2, 3, 43], self-reports [12], and eye gaze [14, 23, 46] have been used in game-based learning environments. Few of these studies, however, have used multimodal approaches such as combining facial expressions and gameplay behaviors to draw the pictures of students' learning progressions.

The following sections provide both a summary of literature and example using Zoombinis to show how different data sources can be used to examine students' problem solving and affective states.

3.1 Emotion from Facial Expression

As stated above, emotions are closely related and intertwined with students' cognitive performance in game-based learning settings. Negative emotions can result in reduced focus [37] while positive emotions may facilitate increased focus [19]. Thus, understanding the relationship between learners' emotional states during gameplay can provide a critical lens into identifying their engagement and learning. One approach to study motion detection is through the studies of facial expressions [22, 24]. For instance, Bosch and colleagues [10] developed an automated detector of affective states based on students' facial features when they interacted with a physics educational game system. Another study examined the relationship among students' facial behavior, emotions, and learning via an automatic facial expression recognition system [51]. Taub [44] contextualized students' facial expressions by integrating these data with their gameplay analysis, which suggested a relationship between facial expressions, students' learning strategies, and learning performance. For example, brow raising could predict when a student was confronted with obstacles and lip tightening and pressing may have been evidence of students' engagement in a task where needed to process more information. Despite the promising trajectories of such studies in attempting to establish models of detecting and interpreting students' facial expressions to better understand their learning process, these studies also unearth significant limitations. That is, to what extent can one data source (i.e., facial expression) be an accurate predictor of something as complex as emotion detection?

3.2 Emotion from Gameplay Sequence

A learning trajectory is defined as the "paths by which learning might proceed" (p. 135) when students progressed towards their intended learning goals [39]. Similarly, affective trajectories are defined as a sequence of affective states over time in a complex learning context [16]. Because of the range of learner experiences as well as the fact that individual students' learning pathways are not known in advance, learning and affective trajectories are considered hypothetical in educational research [41]. However, understanding the general learning and affective trajectories students may experience may provide insight in how to support them. In game-based learning, for example, sequences of affective states are related to students' gameplay events; unproductive trials may be associated with frustration, cuing the need for hints and supports from the learning system or external intervention [11]. Thus, analyzing transitions between affect and interaction patterns in students' learning processes and can provide insight into the complex interplay between students' affect and learning.

3.3 Multimodal Data Fusion Between Facial Expression and Gameplay Data

Analyzing both facial expressions and gameplay patterns is useful to estimate students' affective and learning trajectories, which will provide multimodal data to clearly demonstrate students' learning state. Humans use multiple modalities in interactions, and a single channel of data won't fully capture the learning interactions [15]. In particular, in digital game-based learning, students interact with both the digital game world and the external learning environment (e.g., peers and the facilitator). As such, it is warranted to explore and conduct multimodal data fusion that integrates a sentimental analysis with students' facial expressions and the sequence mining with the logged gameplay behaviors.

Research on fusing data between students' emotions and gameplay events is emerging. Andres and colleagues studied how students' in-game actions can denote either boredom or confusion in gameplay [4]. Through sequence mining of middle school students' gameplay logs, they computed frequent gameplay sequences and then conducted correlation analysis to identify a significant association between gameplay sequences and negative emotions. Taub and Azevedo [42] examined how students' gameplay sequence is associated with their emotional states. They used IMotions to capture the facial expressions of six emotions (joy, anger, surprise, contempt, confusion, and frustration) and then categorized two student groups based on the gameplay efficiency and emotion levels (high and low). They then conducted differential sequence mining to demonstrate how sequence patterns of students' gameplay differed across two groups. These previous studies focused on a cross validation between students' gameplay sequences and emotional states to investigate students' learning processes. They appear limited to tracking the ongoing dynamics of in-game actions together with the evolving emotional states. It remains murky as to how players refine their in-game strategies in relation to changed emotional states. Therefore, it is important to conduct fine-grained data analysis to fully capture the dynamics between students' gameplay strategy and emotional states changed across time.

4 Multimodal Data Fusion of *Zoombinis* Gameplay Data

To illustrate our data fusion approach, we attempted to fuse two data resources (facial expression and gameplay data) to understand a student's in-game learning states in *Zoombinis* gameplay. In this section, we introduce our data wrangling procedure of multimodal data fusion, and illustrate how we concatenate emotion recognition results with sequence mining. Specifically, we demonstrate a data fusion example based on students' in-game strategy and emotion data from the Mudball Wall puzzle. The goal of the Mudball Wall puzzle is to launch mudballs onto the cells with dots. Each mudball a student has launched is related to either the shapes or the colors. If a mudball hits specific cells with dots, a stepping boulder will move Zoombinis up to the cliff. During gameplay, students are required to identify hidden patterns of either shapes or colors aligned with mud ball positions.

4.1 Data Wrangling Procedure

The multimodal data analysis in this case consists of three data wrangling steps:
(1) collecting students' physical and digital behavior data, (2) yielding individuals' emotion recognition and gameplay strategy mining results in each gaming round, and (3) concatenating and then visualizing two different data sources (i.e., gameplay sequence and emotion state) in a time series format. Figure 2 displays the data wrangling steps of *Zoombinis* gameplay data for multimodal data fusion.

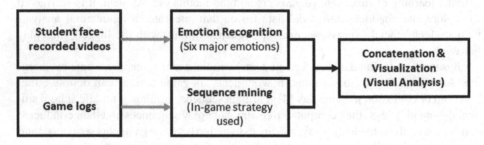

Fig. 2. Data wrangling steps of *Zoombinis* gameplay data

First, we collected students' physical and digital behavior data—their facial expressions recorded with the web camera, and a log of their gameplay activities—in *Zoombinis*. We then used the open-source python package to process students' face recorded videos and conduct facial expression analysis. This package was designed using a convolutional neural network-a deep learning technique specialized in processing a large set of high-resolution images. The associated emotion detection model was trained with the Facial Expression Recognition 2013 (FER-2013) open-source dataset shared by the data repository of [50]. The reported accuracy of emotion detection in the package is above 65%. This package computed the likelihood of major six emotions (i.e., angry, disgust, scared, happy, sad, and surprised) based on multi class classification. Human coders with expertise iteratively reviewed and coded the video recorded facial expressions as a cross validation of the machine computed emotion recognition results. At the same time, the researchers coded students' enactment of various gameplay strategies with the game logs based on a predefined coding scheme [1]. There are five in-game strategies for the Mudball Wall puzzle: (a) color or shape constant, (b) 2D pattern completer, (c) maximizing dots, (d) try all combinations of colors shapes, and (e) alternating color and shape. Table 1 shows the details of each strategy in the puzzle.

Table 1. Strategy types and definitions in the Mudball Wall puzzle

Strategy	Definition
Color or shape constant	A player holds either color (e.g., blue) or shape (e.g., square) constant, while testing the other to find the pattern of a row or column
2D pattern completer	A player aims at completing the entire row and column to identify the entire hidden pattern
Maximizing dots	A player targets dots. The strategy only applies when players have completed either row or column rules and players need to be in the implementation phase
Try all combinations of colors & shape	A player tests all shape and color pairs. A player alternates both attributes between moves and does not try repetitive shape or color
Alternating colors/shape	Players systematically change between color and shape constants to finish either a row or column of the grid

We then concatenated two different data sources, integrated and visualized them in a time series format. Figure 3-A and Fig. 3-B are illustrative examples of the multimodal data fusion. These are time series graphs depicting how a student's in-game strategies with emotional states emerged in both early (A) and later gameplay (B) grounds. The graph basically contains three different data types: gameplay strategy used (bar graph), emotional states (line graph), and in-game performance (line graph with square markers).

Visual Analysis of Time Series. We conducted a visual analysis to compare two time series graphics displaying a student's gameplay strategy uses and emotional states in early and later gameplay rounds. The time series data can be explained using the following indices: level, trend, and variability (Gast Spriggs, 2009). As demonstrated by Fig. 3, the student showed a high level of positive emotional states in the early gameplay round, in comparison to that of the later round. The student experienced a lower enjoyment state during the later stage of the gameplay round. Correspondingly, his gameplay strategies switched more frequently during the later gameplay round (8th to 16th attempt in graph B). This finding suggests that the student was likely to undergo challenges and frustration during this period. Moreover, the student's enjoyment state in the early gameplay round shows a slightly increasing trend. In comparison, that of the enjoyment state in the later round appeared decreasing. In terms of variability, the student's enjoyment state

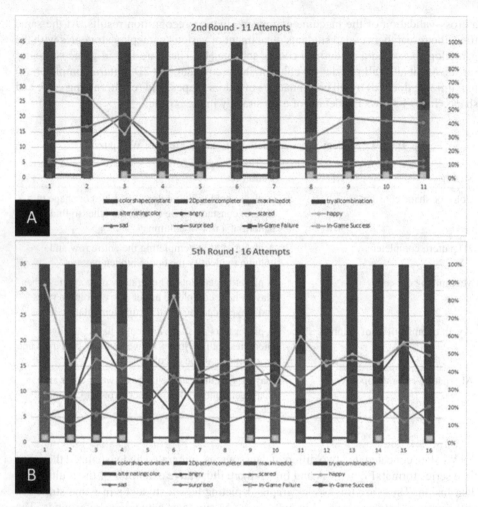

Fig. 3. Time series graphs displaying the gameplay strategies, emotional states, and in- game performance of a single subject (A = Early gameplay round, B = Later gameplay round)

appears moderate and consistent. In the earlier gameplay round, the student's enjoyment decreased at the third attempt and increased again to the highest point at the sixth attempt. Interestingly, the student switched the gameplay strategy after the 3rd gameplay attempt when experiencing the lowest enjoyment state. After maintaining a successful game performance continuously over the next three attempts, the student's enjoyment then reached the highest level. Later on, his enjoyment state again gradually decreased until the end of this gameplay ground, in spite of a four-time straight success. This pattern suggests that the student may have been under challenged and bored. In the later gameplay round, the student's enjoyment state fluctuated. Correspondingly, he used a more dynamic combination of in-game strategies than in the earlier round. In this example, the visual analysis findings with multimodal data fusion in our approach provided a better understanding of the interactions between in-game performance, game-based problem solving strategies, and emotion states.

4.2 Modeling Students' Problem Solving Process with Hidden Markov Models

When learners interact with game-based learning environments, they exhibit game play actions that suggesting a wide range of in-game problem solving sequences. These gameplay actions can indicate students' implicit learning process in problem solving tasks [35]. Multiple theories of problem solving hypothesize that there are distinct qualitative phases exhibited during effective problem solving [48]. Exploration of how learners both employ problem solving strategies and advance in their use of these strategies can provide critical information not only about how learners solve problems, but when learners could benefit from external scaffolding. From this perspective, understanding how and why learners engage in problem solving is a pressing challenge. When learners interact with game-based learning environments, the problem solving process is invisible; we only have access to gameplay actions by behavioral evidence, such as that generated from their login file data. Thus, studying problem solving within game-based learning environments presents several challenges. First, it is difficult to identify an individual learner' implicit problem solving process. Second, although the literature recognizes that problem solving processes are not static, there is only limited research investigating when and why transitions between problem solving phases occur.

In game-based learning environments, one method for providing detailed information for ascertaining learners' potential problem solving states is through data captured from real time actions [21]. Revealing these states can help us investigate learner's problem solving progress and what actions might promote these transitions (e.g., seeking help, finding a pattern, or adopting a different perspective). However, as stated above, categorizing individuals' gameplay actions as problem solving phases can be challenging; as such, they are considered "hidden" [45]. One approach to identify hidden states is through the application of Hidden Markov Model (HMM - [32]), which could generate probabilistic models of learners' transitions between hidden states with data mining [40]. Through this approach, we can examine patterns in learners' transitions among problem solving phases, which can be time-consuming through qualitative analysis alone, especially at a large scale.

Illustrative Example from *Zoombinis*. In our example, Mudball Wall, students were asked to complete a multidimensional grid with painting balls of various shapes and colors [5]. In a specific puzzle, students attempt to launch paintballs of colors and shapes and hit targeted cells with dots through multiple attempts. Students' gameplay logs generated many features for each attempt (e.g., how many correct features of colors and shapes selected by the student to correspond to rows or columns or both of them, how much time spent on this attempt).

1) Coding students' gameplay behaviors. Establishing a granularity of the gameplay behaviors data was needed, which allowed us to better understand and delineate students' problem solving process. Based on the previous description of students' interaction with Mudball Wall, we chose to look at the events when students launched their specific mud-ball with different colors and shapes (denoted in the logs as LAUNCH MUDBALL); this

state provided us insights into students' processes for exploring strategies and solutions. By leveraging students' previous attempts in the same game round, we could examine more complex relationships between their current attempt and previously made attempts. We then automatically coded each students' LAUNCH MUDBALL events using binary codes (see Table 2).

Table 2. Strategy types and definitions in the Mudball Wall puzzle

Marker	Code	Description
Did this attempt succeed?	S/F	S denotes success while F denotes fail
Are there any strategies used in this attempt?	U/N	U denotes some strategies used while N denotes no strategies used (e.g., trying all combinations of colors and shapes, alternating colors)
Is there a correct attribute that always exists in the following attempts?	E/A	E denotes exist while A denotes absent
Are any unique combinations of colors and shapes selected in this attempt?	Y/W	Y denotes some unique toppings selected while W denotes no unique toppings selected

2) Coding students' problem solving behaviors. Previous work with *Zoombinis* has resulted in definitions for specific, iterative phased of problem solving when students engaged in Mudball Wall Puzzles (Rowe et al., 2017; Rowe et al., 2019):

- **Trial and Error**: students show no evidence of employing strategies, their actions are random and independent of prior actions.
- **Systematic Testing**: students employ some strategies to test the mudball attributes (e.g., test one attribute at each attempt, isolate one mudball attribute to columns or rows).
- **Implementing Solution**: students identify one or more common attributes that are in the same columns or rows.
- **Generalizing Solution**: this phase has two scenarios: students generalize mudball values to attributes, for instance, rows are indicative of colors; a sequence of behaviors is repeated across multiple game rounds.

Based on previous coded descriptions of each attempt created by students, we tried to use Hidden Markov Model (HMM) to identify the nature and transition of problem solving phases a student demonstrated in during the problem solving process. In order to achieve this goal, two researchers of our team discussed and identified specific patterns which indicated students' problem solving processes. Students' behaviors were coded as **Trial and Error** when there was no evidence indicating that they performed the tasks in an ordered, planned way. Random trials occurred in several attempts, seen as a sequence of the codes **FNAW, FNAY, FNAW**.

A Systematic Testing phase was coded when there was observable evidence of strategies (denoted by U) used in one attempt by the student. Table 2 provides strategies which were used frequently in Mudball Wall puzzles. For example, if a student tried different strategies to solve the puzzles even without proper answers, seen as a sequence of **FNAW, FUAY, FUAY**, which seemed to indicate that the student tried new combinations of various colors and shapes for a mudball with some systematic strategies, his/her behaviors were also coded as Systematic Testing.

Similarly, when a student recognized one specific attribute was in the same column or row, the sequence of **FURY, FURY, SURW** was observed. This sequence might indicate that the student attempted to consider new solutions to hit other empty grids while keeping the correct attributes. Hence, we coded this behavior as **Implementing Solution** because of evidence that the student had already understood partial solutions or full solutions of this puzzle.

Since we did not examine multiple game rounds, the **Generalizing Solution** phase was not considered in this illustrative example. Hence, a student might be in one of three problem solving phases in one round. To account for students who were not familiar with playing Mudball Wall puzzles, we did not code any first attempt in each game round; thus, these first attempts were aimed to give students a chance to better understand the goals of Mudball Wall.

3) Illustrative Example Results.

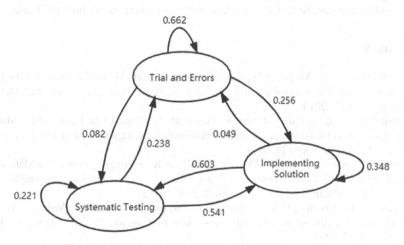

Fig. 4. HMM for problem solving phases for one student

We used Python's HMMLEARN package to create our HMM. Different initial transition table values were set up in order to eliminate the limitation of local optima when calculating the probabilities of transitions between different hidden phases. Results from one student showed that our HMM stably converged to the following transition table finally (Fig. 4).

5 Discussion and Implications

This study sets the stage of methodological approaches that involve fusion of multiple data sources to understand problem solving process and emotional states as students engage in game-based computational thinking (CT) activities. Our exploration in fusing the data of facial expressions and gameplay logs to identify the association between emotional states and game-based problem solving strategies suggests that multimodal data sources are cooperative in tracking or estimating the states of game-based computational problem solving. A visual and association analysis of the time series data of both data sources has provided a better understanding of the dynamics governing a learner's game-based problem solving strategies, in-game performance, and emotion states. The finding implies that the learner's cognitive and affective states during problem solving are highly interactive with each other and dynamically evolving. Efforts to scaffold the desirable cognitive and affective states to reinforce game-based problem solving performance should tackle the cognitive affective dynamics simultaneously, rather than focusing on an individual facet. Future research on multimodal data fusion on cognitive affective states during problem solving should integrate additional data sources, such as eye tracking and speech data. The process of data fusion, especially in terms of the associative data analysis with the sequence or time series data, should be further investigated. It is warranted to explore alternative and applicable state estimation methods in identifying, extracting, and congregating features from each data source for a common cognitive-affective state (e.g., frustration, boredom, or chanciness) during CT education.

References

1. Almeda, M.V., et al.: Modeling implicit computational thinking in zoombinis mudball wall puzzle gameplay. Paper submitted to the Technology, Mind, and Society conference, October, Washington D.C. (2019)
2. Alonso-Fernández, C., Calvo-Morata, A., Freire, M., Martinez-Ortiz, I., Fernández-Manjón, B.: Applications of data science to game learning analytics data: a systematic literature review. Comput. Educ. **141**, 103612 (2019)
3. Alonso-Fernández, C., Martínez-Ortiz, I., Caballero, R., Freire, M., Fernández-Manjón, B.: Predicting students' knowledge after playing a serious game-based on learning analytics data: a case study. J. Comput. Assist. Learn. **36**(3), 350–358 (2020)
4. Andres, J.M.L., Rodrigo, M.M.T., Baker, R.S., Paquette, L., Shute, V.J., Ventura, M.: Analyzing student action sequences and affect while playing physics playground. In: EDM (Workshops) (2015)
5. Asbell-Clarke, J., et al.: The development of students' computational thinking practices in elementary-and middle-school classes using the learning game, zoombinis. Comput. Hum. Behav. **115**, 106587 (2021)
6. Azevedo, R., Gašević, D.: Analyzing multimodal multichannel data about self- regulated learning with advanced learning technologies: issues and challenges (2019)
7. Barr, D., Harrison, J., Conery, L.: Computational thinking: a digital age skill for everyone. Learn. Leading Technol. **38**(6), 20–23 (2011)
8. Barr, V., Stephenson, C.: Bringing computational thinking to K-12: what is involved and what is the role of the computer science education community? ACM Inroads **2**(1), 48–54 (2011)
9. Blikstein, P.: Multimodal learning analytics. In: Proceedings of the Third International Conference on Learning Analytics and Knowledge, pp. 102–106 (2013)

10. Bosch, N., D'mello, S.K., Ocumpaugh, J., Baker, R.S., Shute, V.: Using video to automatically detect learner affect in computer-enabled classrooms. ACM Trans. Interact. Intell. Syst. (TiiS) **6**(2), 1–26 (2016)
11. Bosch, N., D'Mello, S.: The affective experience of novice computer programmers. Int. J. Artif. Intell. Educ. **27**(1), 181–206 (2017)
12. Cloude, E.B., Taub, M., Lester, J., Azevedo, R.: The role of achievement goal orientation on metacognitive process use in game-based learning. In: Isotani, S., Millán, E., Ogan, A., Hastings, P., McLaren, B., Luckin, R. (eds.) AIED 2019. LNCS (LNAI), vol. 11626, pp. 36–40. Springer, Cham (2019). https://doi.org/10.1007/978-3-030-23207-8_7
13. DeHaan, R.L.: Teaching creativity and inventive problem solving in science. CBE—Life Sci. Educ. **8**(3), 172–181 (2009)
14. Dever, D.A., Wiedbusch, M., Azevedo, R.: Learners' gaze behaviors and metacognitive judgments with an agent-based multimedia environment. In: Isotani, S., Millán, E., Ogan, A., Hastings, P., McLaren, B., Luckin, R. (eds.) AIED 2019. LNCS (LNAI), vol. 11626, pp. 58–61. Springer, Cham (2019). https://doi.org/10.1007/978-3-030-23207-8_11
15. Di Mitri, D., Schneider, J., Specht, M., Drachsler, H.: From signals to knowledge: a conceptual model for multimodal learning analytics. J. Comput. Assist. Learn. **34**(4), 338–349 (2018)
16. D'Mello, S., Graesser, A., et al.: Monitoring affective trajectories during complex learning. In: Proceedings of the Annual Meeting of the Cognitive Science Society, vol. 29 (2007)
17. Emerson, A., Cloude, E.B., Azevedo, R., Lester, J.: Multimodal learning analytics for game-based learning. Br. J. Edu. Technol. **51**(5), 1505–1526 (2020)
18. Grafsgaard, J., Wiggins, J., Boyer, K.E., Wiebe, E., Lester, J.: Predicting learning and affect from multimodal data streams in task-oriented tutorial dialogue. In: Educational Data Mining 2014 (2014)
19. Isen, A.M.: Some ways in which positive affect influences decision making and problem solving. Handbook Emot. **3**, 548–573 (2008)
20. Kang, J., Liu, M., Qu, W.: Using gameplay data to examine learning behavior patterns in a serious game. Comput. Hum. Behav. **72**, 757–770 (2017)
21. Krumm, A., Means, B., Bienkowski, M.: Learning Analytics Goes to School: A Collaborative Approach to Improving Education. Routledge (2018)
22. Lane, H.C., D'Mello, S.K.: Uses of physiological monitoring in intelligent learning environments: a review of research, evidence, and technologies. In: Parsons, T.D., Lin, L., Cockerham, D. (eds.) Mind, Brain and Technology. ECTII, pp. 67–86. Springer, Cham (2019). https://doi.org/10.1007/978-3-030-02631-8_5
23. Lee, J.Y., Donkers, J., Jarodzka, H., Van Merriënboer, J.J.: How prior knowledge affects problem solving performance in a medical simulation game: using game-logs and eye-tracking. Comput. Hum. Behav. **99**, 268–277 (2019)
24. Loderer, K., Pekrun, R., Lester, J.C.: Beyond cold technology: a systematic review and meta-analysis on emotions in technology-based learning environments. Learn. Instruct. 70 101162 (2018)
25. Lu, J.J., Fletcher, G.H.: Thinking about computational thinking. In: Proceedings of the 40th ACM Technical Symposium on Computer Science Education, pp. 260–264 (2009)
26. Mayer, R.E.: Computer games in education. Ann. Rev. Psychol. **70**, 531–549 (2019)
27. Mohaghegh, D.M., McCauley, M.: Computational thinking: the skill set of the 21st century (2016)
28. Ochoa, X., Worsley, M.: Augmenting learning analytics with multimodal sensory data. J. Learn. Analytics **3**(2), 213–219 (2016)
29. Oviatt, S., Grafsgaard, J., Chen, L., Ochoa, X.: Multimodal learning analytics: assessing learners' mental state during the process of learning. In: The Hand- book of Multimodal-Multisensor Interfaces: Signal Processing, Architectures, and Detection of Emotion and Cognition-Volume 2, pp. 331–374 (2018)

30. Plass, J.L., Homer, B.D., Kinzer, C.K.: Foundations of game-based learning. Educ. Psychol. **50**(4), 258–283 (2015)
31. Qian, M., Clark, K.R.: Game-based learning and 21st century skills: a review of recent research. Comput. Hum. Behav. **63**, 50–58 (2016)
32. Rabiner, L., Juang, B.: An introduction to hidden markov models. IEEE ASSP Mag. **3**(1), 4–16 (1986)
33. Rowe, E., Asbell-Clarke, J., Cunningham, K., Gasca, S.: Assessing implicit computational thinking in zoombinis gameplay: pizza pass, fleens & bubblewonder abyss. In: Extended Abstracts Publication of the Annual Symposium on Computer- Human Interaction in Play, pp. 195–200 (2017)
34. Sankaran, S.R., Bui, T.: Impact of learning strategies and motivation on performance: a study in web-based instruction. J. Instr. Psychol. **28**(3), 191 (2001)
35. Sawyer, R., Rowe, J., Azevedo, R., Lester, J.: Filtered time series analyses of student problem solving behaviors in game-based learning. Int. Educ. Data Mining Soc. (2018)
36. Schneider, B., Blikstein, P.: Unraveling students' interaction around a tangible interface using multimodal learning analytics. J. Educ. Data Mining **7**(3), 89–116 (2015)
37. Schwarz, N.: Feelings-as-information theory. Handbook Theories Soc. Psychol. **1**, 289–308 (2011)
38. Shute, V.J., Sun, C., Asbell-Clarke, J.: Demystifying computational thinking. Educ. Res. Rev. **22**, 142–158 (2017)
39. Simon, M.A.: Reconstructing mathematics pedagogy from a constructivist perspective. J. Res. Math. Educ. **26**(2), 114–145 (1995)
40. Sutton, R.S., Barto, A.G., et al.: Introduction to Reinforcement Learning, vol. 135. MIT press Cambridge (1998)
41. Sztajn, P., Confrey, J., Wilson, P.H., Edgington, C.: Learning trajectory based instruction: toward a theory of teaching. Educ. Res. **41**(5), 147–156 (2012)
42. Taub, M., Azevedo, R.: Using sequence mining to analyze metacognitive monitoring and scientific inquiry based on levels of efficiency and emotions during game-based learning. J. Educ. Data Mining **10**(3), 1–26 (2018)
43. Taub, M., Mudrick, N.V., Azevedo, R., Millar, G.C., Rowe, J., Lester, J.: Using multi-channel data with multi-level modeling to assess in-game performance during gameplay with crystal island. Comput. Hum. Behav. **76**, 641–655 (2017)
44. Taub, M., Sawyer, R., Smith, A., Rowe, J., Azevedo, R., Lester, J.: The agency effect: the impact of student agency on learning, emotions, and problem solving behaviors in a game-based learning environment. Comput. Educ. **147**, 103781 (2020)
45. Tissenbaum, M.: I see what you did there! divergent collaboration and learner transitions from unproductive to productive states in open-ended inquiry. Comput. Educ. **145**, 103739 (2020)
46. Tsai, M.J., Huang, L.J., Hou, H.T., Hsu, C.Y., Chiou, G.L.: Visual behavior, flow and achievement in game-based learning. Comput. Educ. **98**, 115–129 (2016)
47. Vlachopoulos, D., Makri, A.: The effect of games and simulations on higher education: a systematic literature review. Int. J. Educ. Technol. High. Educ. **14**(1), 1–33 (2017). https://doi.org/10.1186/s41239-017-0062-1
48. Wiltshire, T.J., Butner, J.E., Fiore, S.M.: Problem solving phase transitions during team collaboration. Cogn. Sci. **42**(1), 129–167 (2018)
49. Wine, J.: Test anxiety and direction of attention. Psychol. Bull. **76**(2), 92 (1971)
50. Wolfram: The facial expression recognition 2013 (fer-2013) dataset. The Wolfram Data Repository (2018)

51. Xu, Z., Woodruff, E.: Person-centered approach to explore learner's emotionality in learning within a 3D narrative game. In: Proceedings of the Seventh International Learning Analytics & Knowledge Conference, pp. 439–443 (2017)
52. Yadav, A., Hong, H., Stephenson, C.: Computational thinking for all: pedagogical approaches to embedding 21st century problem solving in k-12 classrooms. TechTrends **60**(6), 565–568 (2016)

Using Eye Tracking for Research on Learning and Computational Thinking

Fengfeng Ke[1](✉) (iD), Ruohan Liu[2], Zlatko Sokolikj[1], Ibrahim Dahlstrom-Hakki[3] (iD), and Maya Israel[2] (iD)

[1] Florida State University, Tallahassee, FL 32306-4453, USA
fke@fsu.edu
[2] University of Florida, Gainesville, FL 32611, USA
[3] TERC, Cambridge, MA 02140, USA

Abstract. This paper presents a conceptual discussion of the theoretical constructs and perspectives in relation to using eye tracking as an assessment and research tool of computational thinking. It also provides a historical review of major mechanisms underlying the current eye-tracking technologies, and a technical evaluation of the set-up, the data capture and visualization interface, the data mining mechanisms, and the functionality of freeware eye trackers of different genres. During the technical evaluation of current eye trackers, we focus on gauging the versatility and accuracy of each tool in capturing the targeted cognitive measures in diverse task and environmental settings—static versus dynamic stimuli, in-person or remote data collection, and individualistic or collaborative learning space. Both theoretical frameworks and empirical review studies on the implementation of eye-tracking suggests that eye-tracking is a solid tool or approach for studying computational thinking. However, due to the current constraints of eye-tracking technologies, eye-tracking is limited in acting as an accessible and versatile tool for tracking diverse learners' naturalistic interactions with dynamic stimuli in an open-ended, complex learning environment.

Keywords: Eye-tracking · Literature and technology review · Computational thinking

1 Introduction

Computational thinking (CT) refers to a notion of using algorithmic thinking and computational solutions to represent complex tasks, solve problems, and design systems [2, 6, 52, 56]. Prior research has conceptualized and studied CT as a) a problem-solving practice (e.g., algorithm design, testing, and debugging, or data organization and analysis), b) an assortment of computational concepts (e.g., sequence, parallelism, control), c) foundational cognitive processes related to algorithmic thinking (e.g., abstraction, pattern recognition and generalization), and d) dispositions and perspectives important for the enactment of the aforesaid elements (e.g., tolerance for ambiguity, persistence, collaboration). Despite emerging as an area of growing educational significance in K-12

© Springer Nature Switzerland AG 2021
X. Fang (Ed.): HCII 2021, LNCS 12790, pp. 216–228, 2021.
https://doi.org/10.1007/978-3-030-77414-1_16

education, conceptual and empirical research on CT education is still under-researched [3]. In particular, there is a need to explore effective methods and tools for assessing CT as a multifaceted competency developed and enacted during dynamic, contextualized practices. Recent research is starting to suggest the use of eye tracking for assessing or validating learning of CT, attitudes toward, cognitive engagement with, or processes and states of development in CT practices (e.g., [4, 39, 50]). However, this research approach is still emerging and is not yet a common practice.

Eye tracking has long been used in the field of cognitive psychology to study underlying cognitive constructs such as attention, memory formation, and processing difficulty [45, 46]. It has also long been considered one of the best measures of visual attention allocation [42], and hence a prominent approach for tracking learners' interaction with the external environment or stimuli. The use of eye tracking to study students' attention and explore their cognitive processes or efforts in authentic educational environments has been more limited but has garnered increasing interest in recent years [12]. Advances in both hardware and software based eye tracking solutions along with a reduction in their cost has made deployment of these solutions at scale possible [41, 55]. There is also an increasing need for a non-intrusive assessment or analysis tool that can track learners' engagement, cognitive processing patterns, and their cognitive-affective states in a personalized, highly interactive, or collaborative learning environment. In partnership with other multimodal or action-oriented data resources, eye tracking enables learning scientists to better study affordances of a learning environment along with learners' agency and conscientiousness.

Therefore, in this paper we intend to provide a conceptual discussion of the theoretical constructs and perspectives in relation to using eye tracking as a CT assessment tool. We will also survey the current eye-tracking technologies—freeware desktop, mobile, and web-based eye trackers—to present a technical evaluation of their set-up, data capture and visualization interface, data mining mechanisms, and functionality. During the technical evaluation of current eye trackers, we focus on gauging the versatility and accuracy of each tool in capturing the targeted cognitive measures in diverse task and environmental settings—static versus dynamic stimuli, in-person or remote data collection, individualistic or collaborative learning space, and neurodiverse learners.

2 Theoretical Constructs and Perspectives

Much of the prior work involving eye tracking and learning has focused on looking at memory formation with a focus on the cognitive processes involved. This has included looking at the visual attention, processing difficulty, working memory, and long-term memory aspects of simple tasks including sentence reading, visual search, category formation and list recall [46]. Prior research on eye tracking and learning have provided a great deal of understanding of the various cognitive elements that make up learning but have had limited impact on classroom learning [12]. In the following section, we provide a review of major theoretical perspectives and related constructs that should shed light on using eye tracking in the assessment and research of CT.

2.1 Eye-Mind Assumption (EMA) and Visual Attention

The relationship between eye movements and cognitive processes are based on two assumptions established by Just and Carpenter [23]: the immediacy assumption and eye-mind assumption. Assuming a linkage between a person's visual focus and cognitive focus, the immediacy and eye-mind assumption were often used as an operational basis for interpreting eye-tracking data. Just and Carpenter contended, "there is no appreciable lag between what is being fixated and what is being processed" and "the interpretations at all levels of processing are not deferred; they occur as soon as possible" (p. 331).

People's visual attention behavior involves two types of attention: overt attention and covert attention [14]. Overt attention is the act of intentionally directing one's attention towards visual stimuli, it happens when one selectively attends to one stimulus while others are ignored. Covert attention is a neural process, it happens when one attends to something without moving the eyes towards the object attended [15]. In the literature, eye-tracking methodology is emphasized to provide a direct and objective measure of overt attention by capturing the timing and location of participants' visual focus during visual studies [17]. Covert attention, however, cannot be directly measured via eye-tracking technology, but it can be inferred by integrating eye-tracking measures with other types of measures such as behavioral data and physiological data [14, 30].

Eye-tracking has become a focus of interest in computer-supported collaborative learning (CSCL) research. It is considered a promising technique to examine and support visual attention coordination, or joint attention, in collaborative learning environments [47]. Joint attention is the ability to coordinate one's focus of attention with that of another person during a social interaction; it is "crucial for the development of social communication, learning and the regulation of interpersonal relationships" ([10], p. 502). The literature suggests that eye gaze, earlier than language and pointing gestures, is typically the initial communicative channel one develops and relies on to experience joint attention in social interactions [43]. With the enhancement of the eye-tracking technology in measuring subtle changes in visual attention, eye-tracking becomes a robust method to detect joint attention (e.g., [34]).

Previous studies emphasized that the ability to establish joint attention is crucial for a group to establish a common mental model and empathy in collaborative problem solving (e.g., [48]). Joint attention was measured in multiple ways in these studies. For example, Papavlasopoulou et al. [38] compared eye fixations of participants in two different groups and examined the level of their gaze similarity (e.g., spatial dispersion). Schneider et al. [48] constructed a metric for joint attention by incorporating the captured gaze points with two additional parameters: latency and distance between gazes. Pietinen, Bednarik, and Tukiainen [44] developed a new joint visual attention metric using the number of overlapping fixations and fixation duration of overlapping fixation to examine the quality of collaboration.

2.2 Engagement

Engagement and its measurement have long been a focus of research in human-computer interaction [37]. Traditionally, engagement is measured through self-report instruments [16]. Eye-tracking can compensate for the weaknesses of self-report measures (e.g., honesty, sampling bias) and is gaining growing popularity in research of engagement. At a lower end, engagement can be measured by the act of paying attention [33]. O'Brien and Toms [36] argued that user engagement manifests through the observed interest and visual attention when the user interacts with a designated tool. Extending this view, Bassett and Green [7] concluded that visual attention provides an important lens to understand cognitive engagement. Based on the eye-mind assumption that people tend to engage with what they visually attend to, eye-tracking metrics such as fixation frequency and fixation duration are widely used to indicate the level of engagement in learning. Specifically, higher fixation frequency and longer fixation duration are linked to higher levels of engagement in learning. As an effective tool to measure micro-level engagement [33], eye-tracking has been utilized along with other types of measures (e.g., performance, self-report, and physiological measures) to capture and assess multifaceted engagement in learning (e.g., [24]).

2.3 Inferring Cognitive Processes, States, and Traits via Eye Tracking

Current eye-tracking technologies allow researchers to trace participants' eye movements with minimum intrusiveness, which makes the eye-tracking data a solid inference of the cognitive or information processing patterns, states, or traits [1, 54]. In the research of multimedia learning, eye-tracking is frequently used to study how learners visually process different formats of information. The literature has established a number of eye-tracking metrics that are commonly used to infer participants' cognitive processes during learning [22]. For example, the number of fixations overall is a widely used eye-tracking measure in HCI studies, it is thought to be negatively associated with participants' searching efficiency [19]. A greater number of fixations indicate lower searching efficiency which possibly due to the poor design of visual elements display [22]. Frequency of fixations on a specific area or element demonstrates the importance of the fixated area or element. Additionally, the time one spends gazing at a particular component of a visual scene designates the content he/she is visually engaged with [32].

Fixation duration is a commonly used metric to measure the level of processing difficulty in learning [51]. A longer fixation duration on a stimulus indicates greater processing difficulty associated with the stimulus (e.g., [35]). Saccades, the quick movements between fixations, is another cognitive measure related to eye-tracking [18]. Saccade is believed to relate to the change of focus in visual attention and interest in learning (e.g., [18]). Typical saccade-based metrics include number of saccades, saccadic amplitude (i.e. saccadic distance), saccade regressions, saccadic duration, or saccadic velocity [9]. Previous studies suggested that fewer saccades are associated with less mental effort during task performance (e.g., [39]). Saccade amplitude, specifically, is used to gauge the cognitive processes that involve planning and hypothesis testing [11].

2.4 Cognitive Load and Effort

Cognitive load is a commonly examined cognitive construct in eye-tracking research (e.g., [29]). The cognitive load theory implies that humans have a limited capacity and duration of working memory, and the amount of information one is able to process and temporarily store in working memory cannot exceed the limit of the capacity [53].

Fixation counts and fixation duration are typical metrics used to infer the mental effort participants exert or the cognitive load they experience during a task (e.g., [58]). According to Obaidellah et al. [35], low fixation time and counts link to less effort in mental processing, while long fixation time and high fixation counts indicate more effort is warranted for the task. In addition to these fixation-based measures, another important metric in identifying cognitive load is pupil size [32]. Pupil size has in recent years been used to examine the degree of cognitive load participants experience when accomplishing a task. Prior research found that pupil dilation increases when a task is perceived cognitively demanding (e.g., [21]).

3   Prior Eye-Tracking Reviews

A number of prior eye-tracking review studies have been conducted to provide an overview of eye-tracking methodology, how it connects to research of HCI, learning, and cognitive science, as well as the merits and challenges associated with using eye-tracking for educational and research purposes (e.g., [1, 8, 25, 31, 49]). In this section, we provide a synthesis of the major findings and discussions of these review studies.

Alemdag and Cagiltay [1], for example, conducted a systematic review of eye-tracking research in the domain of multimedia learning. This work revealed the popularity of temporal and count scales of eye-tracking measurements in multimedia research, providing three cognitive processes: selecting, organizing, integrating. The authors emphasized the necessity to bridge the current gap of eye-tracking studies with young participants, and advocated more effort to be invested in research in the K-12 contexts. Additionally, future studies should consider including qualitative analysis of eye movement measures to supplement and support quantitative eye-tracking measures.

Focusing on the application of eye-tracking methods in spatial cognition, Kiefer et al. [25] provided a review of recent literature and claimed that the potentials of mobile eye-trackers in real-world studies have only just started to be exploited. However, two main challenges of current mobile eye-tracking studies should be acknowledged: a) the processing of mobile eye-tracking data is labor-intensive; b) the real-world environment is hard to control. Therefore, the trade-off between internal and external validity is a particular challenge for eye-tracking studies in authentic environments. For future eye-tracking research in spatial cognition, the author suggests that more effort be devoted to advance the traditional eye-tracking analysis, beyond the classic fixation, saccade or scan-path measures, and consider deconstructing the complexity of the interplay between ambient and focal attention [27], and participants' switching patterns across areas of interest [28].

Blascheck et al. [8] performed a survey of 90 publications to examine visualization techniques used in eye-tracking studies. Overall, nine types of visualization techniques were identified while some existing challenges and unanswered questions were revealed. For example, capturing participants' interactions with dynamic stimuli still emerged as a major challenge in current eye-tracking studies. Given the growing trend of research involving multimodal data analysis, developing multimodal data visualization techniques (e.g., combining eye-tracking data with other sensor information from EEG devices, or skin-resistance measurements) can be a potential focus in future eye-tracking research.

3.1 Summary

Multiple salient and common themes have emerged from the findings of these previous eye-tracking review studies. First, the diversity and richness of quantitative metrics of eye-tracking as inferences of the aforementioned theoretical constructs on cognition and learning are unanimously reported by prior reviews. The parameters involved in these quantitative eye-tracking metrics are generally specified in the previous studies. On the other hand, an integral analysis with these eye-tracking metrics to infer on a comprehensive or multifaceted cognitive process, state, or trait of learners is still lacking. The previous reviews also reported a concern on the lack of cross-validation and in-depth analysis with the current quantitative eye-tracking data [1, 8, 25, 31, 49]. Second, even though eye-tracking has been frequently used to investigate the dynamics between a learner (user) and an interactive, computerized learning environment, the designated stimuli or areas of interest in such an environment are typically fixed, pre-defined, and constrained. Due to the limited functionality of current eye-trackers, eye tracking is generally used in a highly controlled lab setting and falls short of capturing and measuring the learners' interactions with dynamic or emerging stimuli in an open-ended learning space. Ultimately, prior research on how the implementation of eye-tracking will address the needs of neurodiverse users or learners with diverse cognitive or physiological characteristics is generally missing. As such, sampling bias is an innate issue in eye-tracking research.

4 A Survey and Evaluation of Existing Eye-Tracking Technologies

4.1 Introduction

From the onset of the 20th century, scientific research has been using basic eye movements such as saccadic suppression, saccade latency, and the size of the perceptual span to make deductions in the field of behavioral experimental psychology. The fast stream of technological development has allowed eye tracking to trickle into other fields of research, with hardware and software algorithms allowing researchers of different scientific fields to incorporate eye tracking into their scientific endeavors. In addition, the availability of eye tracking has made it present not only in scientific research but also in the commercial world. Initially, eye tracking relied on hardware specifically built for eye tracking, such as Charles Judd's eye movements camera [59]. However, the fast opportunities that eye tracking offered to the commercial world has pushed for faster development and a shift from the expensive, intrusive and specially built apparatus to software that works with any general webcam.

With the introduction of eye-tracking in both the commercial world and scientific research, a unique field of research has emerged to improve the accuracy of the eye tracking algorithms as well as the real-time information they provide. Various companies are interested in tracking the gaze of potential customers on their infomercials, while the scientific community develops a similar goal of pinpointing the gaze of a user of a specific platform. One way of estimating this gaze is using real-time images of certain facial features and specific interactions with a platform to estimate the part of the platform at which the user is looking. This appearance-based method does not require specific cameras and can be done using a regular webcams, but is limited by the computational power of the estimation algorithm. Conversely, a different method relies on a more technologically advanced camera to extract features not available to the naked, and runs specific models with these unseen features to estimate gaze. One such example of this model based method is an infrared camera that uses the IR glint of the eye to estimate the gaze. These methods may not be computationally expensive but require specific hardware to function.

The appearance-based method has opened up an interdisciplinary field of computational mathematics that aims to output the most accurate gaze estimation, given an input of images of specific facial features of a user and interactions of said user with the medium. This goal has been approached from all the different corners of computational mathematics and data mining. The model is generally a two-step process, consisting of an algorithm extracting facial features, such as the pupils of the eyes, and the gaze prediction algorithm, correlating those features with specific points of the screen. The simplest gaze prediction algorithm is the interpolation of interactions with a known gaze point to produce a curve from which the gaze point of other interactions can be estimated. The model is a good starting point as it makes certain assumptions about the user's interactions and has been used in certain papers where these assumptions are valid. In addition, this method is not computational expensive so therefore can be done on various platforms and mediums.

4.2   Evaluation of Freeware Eye-Trackers

WebGazer. An exemplary embodiment of the appearance based method is WebGazer [40] with the additional feature of data validation, in the form of data points acquired during specific mouse movements. WebGazer uses the facial recognition algorithms to identify the pupils in the image which chronologically corresponds to a specific mouse click. This facial recognition algorithm converts the pixels that make up the pupils into a 120D feature vector. Afterward, this feature vector, along with screen coordinates of the corresponding click, form the linear interpolation with which future gaze points are estimated. WebGazer does not require an initial calibration. The parameters of the linear interpolation are formed as the software is being used, meaning that it might take some time for the said parameters to stabilize around a specific value and consequentially for the program to make stable gaze predictions.

WebGazer algorithm is implemented in JavaScript, which can be included on the HTML side of any website. Therefore any activity that would require the use of WebGazer would have to be hosted on a specific website. WebGazer uses Clmtrackr for the facial recognition portion of the algorithms but has the option to incorporate other tools or libraries. Lastly, WebGazer has been designed with the anonymity of the website visitor in mind, therefore as it is being hosted on a website, it only records the estimated gaze coordinates of a website visitor and aggregates them with data collected of other users. This aggregated data provides a general overview of the estimated gaze of all visitors. This feature makes WebGazer ideal for discovering what captures the attention of most visitors of a website, but also makes WebGazer very difficult to use in applications where the gaze of a specific user needs to be tracked continuously and known at each time point.

PACE. The algorithm behind PACE [20] works in a similar manner as that of WebGazer: the gaze estimation algorithm is trained as the software is being used. It also uses the Clmtrackr to acquire the facial features, and packages them into 120D feature vectors, expanding the data collected to the whole face instead of being limited to the pupils. PACE also collects the corresponding gaze screen coordinates from mouse clicks and other mouse interactions. But before those mouse-click coordinates are used as part of the training data, they undergo a rigorous process that validates whether the position of the mouse matched the user's gaze at that moment through behavioral and data-driven validation. The first hundred validated data points, both screen coordinates and corresponding feature vectors are fed into a random decision forest to train the gaze prediction algorithms that estimates the gaze from then on. In conclusion, PACE, like WebGazer, does not require an initial calibration from the user but does not produce any gaze estimation until a specific amount of acceptable data has been gathered. Unlike WebGazer, PACE does not constantly retrain its algorithm and therefore the gaze estimation parameters stabilize conclusively. PACE is a standalone system that can extract data from both live webcam recordings and pre-recorded webcam videos, and therefore can easily be used in situations where the exact movement of the gaze of a specific user needs to be known.

TuckerGaze. Venturing further from the simple design of the gaze prediction with linear interpolation and random forest, there are other algorithms that use more complex mathematical methods but require a bit more computational power. This trade-o limits the applications and settings in which they could be used. Like the previously mentioned software, TuckerGaze [57] extracts facial features of images from its training data using Clmtrackr. However, the training data is not gathered throughout the use of the software; instead it is collected before the software is used, through an initial calibration. The collected training data is then trained on an algorithm with Ridge Regression and the resulting model is used for future gaze prediction. After its use online, TuckerGaze reevaluates its prediction model using SVC with Gaussian Kernel. TuckerGaze has been hosted on websites and has only been used for specific gamelike interactions, to produce gaze estimation during preordained stimuli. It does not have the variability of use as the aforementioned software, but presents an important evolutionary landmark in appearance based gaze estimation.

Gaze Capture. Another important evolutionary landmark in eye-tracking algorithm is the introduction of artificial neural networks. The recent widespread utilization of artificial neural networks (ANNs) in the computational world for the purposes of classification and regression has inspired attempts of incorporating ANNs in gaze estimation. The team behind Gaze Capture [26] built a training data set from collecting mobile phones camera face recordings of a large number of participants, following guided movements on screen. The cropped up images of faces and eyes from each recording and the assumed corresponding gaze point were used to train a neural network. This neural network is the basis for the gaze prediction software behind Gaze Capture. Such a setup, through its incorporation of mobile phones, allows for fast training of neural networks. But it does not translate into accurate predictions outside of the environment in which the training data was made. Therefore it may be unsuitable for gaze estimations in environments where the screen used is significantly larger than the screen of a mobile device or tablet.

OpenFace 2.2. While not specifically designed for eye tracking, OpenFace [5] is a popular open source toolkit that is capable of identifying eye location, eye landmarks, head orientation, and gaze direction. OpenFace is primarily designed for facial behavior analysis. The software can identify 68 facial landmarks and based on those landmarks can identify 12 facial Action Units (AUs). While it doesn't directly detect emotions the detected AUs can be mapped onto emotion states based on the Facial Action Coding System (FACS) [13].

OpenFace doesn't provide actual eye tracking, that is, it does not provide a direct estimate of what the subject is viewing on the screen. Instead of training a neural network to map visual input onto screen locations, OpenFace instead tries to model the eye itself and maps the visual data onto eyeball orientation. OpenFace is also estimates head location and head orientation which in combination with the eye orientation data should allow for an estimate of the gaze location on any surface relative to the camera location.

In order to assess the accuracy of OpenFace's gaze orientation algorithm, we collected data from four participants. All participants had normal vision. Two participants were adults and two were children ages 8 and 10. Participants were asked to sit two feet in front of a laptop computer running OpenFace. Participants were asked to perform the follow series of head and eye movements:

- Fixate the center of the left, right, top and bottom edges of the screen without moving their heads
- Move their heads up, down, left, and right while fixating the center of the screen

Changes in the magnitude and direction of their gaze was measured as they performed these actions. The results were consisted across all four participants, see Table 1 for details.

Table 1. Results of observed impact on detected gaze orientation in OpenFace 2.2 as eye and head orientation is manipulated independently.

Action	Prediction	Observation
Look left, head fixated	Gaze shifts to the left	Gaze shifts to the left
Look right, head fixated	Gaze shifts to the right	Gaze shifts to the right
Look up, head fixated	Gaze shifts up	Little to no shift in gaze
Look down, head fixated	Gaze shifts down	Little to no shift in gaze
Fixate center, head moves left	No change in gaze	Small gaze shift to the left
Fixate center, head moves right	No change in gaze	Small gaze shift to the right
Fixate center, head moves up	No change in gaze	Gaze shifts up
Fixate center, head moves down	No change in gaze	Gaze shifts down

The findings of our small assessment of the accuracy of gaze orientation detection in OpenFace 2.2 indicates that the software algorithm has a difficult time distinguishing between head and eye movements, even though it is able to detect each independently. This challenge is a common one in eye tracking research which is why most lab research involving eye tracking uses a protocol that eliminates head movement. More troubling however is that OpenFace was unable to detect vertical shifts in eye orientation if they were not accompanied by head movements. This makes OpenFace's algorithm only useful for very coarse estimates of visual attention allocation.

5 Conclusion and Implication

Both theoretical frameworks and empirical review studies on the implementation of eye-tracking suggest that eye-tracking is a solid tool or approach for not only capturing observed engagement behaviors or states (e.g., visual engagement and joint attention coordination), but also inferring covert cognitive processes or traits (e.g., information processing patterns, cognitive effort or commitment). A rich set of eye-tracking metrics have been delineated and infield tested as measures for these cognitive variables in the research of learning and HCI. All these prominent facets of eye-tracking apply to CT, a componential area of both learning and HCI. However, due to the current constraints of eye-tracking technologies, eye-tracking is limited in acting as an accessible and versatile tool for tracking diverse learners' naturalistic interactions with dynamic stimuli in an open-ended, complex learning environment. Such a limit imposes a conflict between eye-tracking and the current CT education that highlights an inclusive or adaptive design for neurodiversity as well as authentic, constructionism-oriented learning activities. Notably, the recent development of deep learning and data mining can potentially push the boundary of eye-tracking algorithms to enhance its accuracy and versatility in gaze capturing and prediction in a more naturalistic and versatile way. It is also warranted for cognitive and learning scientists to conduct more systematic research on the methods of data fusion and integral analysis that will enhance and cross-validate the interpretation of the eye-tracking data along with that of other multimodal behavioral and physiological data.

References

1. Alemdag, E., Cagiltay, K.: A systematic review of eye tracking research on multi- media learning. Comput. Educ. **125**, 413–428 (2018)
2. Anderson, N.D.: A call for computational thinking in undergraduate psychology. Psychol. Learn. Teach. **15**(3), 226–234 (2016)
3. Angeli, C., Giannakos, M.: Computational thinking education: issues and challenges (2020)
4. Arslanyilmaz, A., Corpier, K.: Eye tracking to evaluate comprehension of computational thinking. In: Proceedings of the 2019 ACM Conference on Innovation and Technology in Computer Science Education, p. 296 (2019)
5. Baltrusaitis, T., Zadeh, A., Lim, Y.C., Morency, L.P.: Openface 2.0: facial behavior analysis toolkit. In: 2018 13th IEEE International Conference on Automatic Face & Gesture Recognition (FG 2018). pp. 59–66. IEEE (2018)
6. Barr, D., Harrison, J., Conery, L.: Computational thinking: a digital age skill for everyone. Learn. Lead. Technol. **38**(6), 20–23 (2011)

7. Bassett, D., Green, A.: Engagement as visual attention: a new story for publishers. In: Publishing and Data Research Forum, London, pp. 17–20 (2015)
8. Blascheck, T., Kurzhals, K., Raschke, M., Burch, M., Weiskopf, D., Ertl, T.: State- of-the-art of visualization for eye tracking data. In: EuroVis (STARs) (2014)
9. Borys, M., Plechawska-Wójcik, M.: Eye-tracking metrics in perception and visual attention research. EJMT **3**, 11–23 (2017)
10. Caruana, N., et al.: Joint attention difficulties in autistic adults: an interactive eye- tracking study. Autism **22**(4), 502–512 (2018)
11. Cowen, L., Ball, L.J., Delin, J.: An eye movement analysis of web page usability. In: People and Computers XVI-Memorable Yet Invisible, pp. 317–335. Springer (2002). https://doi.org/10.1007/978-1-4471-0105-5_19
12. Dahlstrom-Hakki, I., Asbell-Clarke, J., Rowe, E.: Showing is knowing: the potential and challenges of using neurocognitive measures of implicit learning in the classroom. Mind Brain Educ. **13**(1), 30–40 (2019)
13. Ekman, R.: What the Face Reveals: Basic and Applied Studies of Spontaneous Expression using the Facial Action Coding System (FACS). Oxford University Press, Oxford (1997)
14. Ellis, N.C., Hafeez, K., Martin, K.I., Chen, L., Boland, J., Sagarra, N.: An eye- tracking study of learned attention in second language acquisition. Appl. Psycholinguist. **35**(3), 547–579 (2014)
15. Findlay, J.M., Findlay, J.M., Gilchrist, I.D., et al.: Active Vision: The Psychology of Looking and Seeing, vol. 37, Oxford University Press, Oxford (2003)
16. Fredricks, J.A., McColskey, W.: The measurement of student engagement: a compartive analysis of various methods and student self-report instruments. In: Handbook of Research on Student Engagement, pp. 763–782. Springer (2012). https://doi.org/10.1007/978-1-4614-2018-7_37
17. Godfroid, A.: Eye tracking. Routledge encyclopedia of second language acquisition, pp. 234–236 (2012)
18. van Gog, T., Jarodzka, H.: Eye tracking as a tool to study and enhance cognitive and metacognitive processes in computer-based learning environments. In: Azevedo, R., Aleven, V. (eds.) International Handbook of Metacognition and Learning Technologies. SIHE, vol. 28, pp. 143–156. Springer, New York (2013). https://doi.org/10.1007/978-1-4419-5546-3_10
19. Goldberg, J.H., Kotval, X.P.: Computer interface evaluation using eye movements: methods and constructs. Int. J. Ind. Ergon. **24**(6), 631–645 (1999)
20. Huang, M.X., Kwok, T.C., Ngai, G., Chan, S.C., Leong, H.V.: Building a personalized, auto-calibrating eye tracker from user interactions. In: Proceedings of the 2016 CHI Conference on Human Factors in Computing Systems, pp. 5169–5179 (2016)
21. Hyönä, J., Tommola, J., Alaja, A.M.: Pupil dilation as a measure of processing load in simultaneous interpretation and other language tasks. Q. J. Exp. Psychol. **48**(3), 598–612 (1995)
22. Jacob, R.J., Karn, K.S.: Eye tracking in human-computer interaction and usability research: ready to deliver the promises. In: The Mind's Eye, pp. 573–605. Elsevier (2003)
23. Just, M.A., Carpenter, P.A.: A theory of reading: from eye fixations to comprehension. Psychol. Rev. **87**(4), 329 (1980)
24. Kaakinen, J.K., Ballenghein, U., Tissier, G., Baccino, T.: Fluctuation in cognitive engagement during reading: evidence from concurrent recordings of postural and eye movements. J. Exp. Psychol. Learn. Mem. Cogn. **44**(10), 1671 (2018)
25. Kiefer, P., Giannopoulos, I., Raubal, M., Duchowski, A.: Eye tracking for spatial research: Cognition, computation, challenges. Spat. Cogn. Comput. **17**(1–2), 1–19 (2017)
26. Krafka, K., et al.: Eye tracking for everyone. In: 2016 IEEE Conference on Computer Vision and Pattern Recognition (CVPR), June 2016

27. Krejtz, K., Duchowski, A., Krejtz, I., Szarkowska, A., Kopacz, A.: Discerning ambient/focal attention with coefficient k. ACM Trans. Appl. Perception (TAP) **13**(3), 1–20 (2016)
28. Krejtz, K., et al.: Gaze transition entropy. ACM Trans. Appl. Perception (TAP) **13**(1), 1–20 (2015)
29. Kruger, J.L., Doherty, S.: Measuring cognitive load in the presence of educational video: towards a multimodal methodology. Australas. J. Educ. Technol. **32**(6) (2016)
30. Kulke, L.V., Atkinson, J., Braddick, O.: Neural differences between covert and overt attention studied using EEG with simultaneous remote eye tracking. Front. Hum. Neurosci. **10**, 592 (2016)
31. Lai, M.L., et al.: A review of using eye-tracking technology in exploring learning from 2000 to 2012. Educ. Res. Rev. **10**, 90–115 (2013)
32. Liu, H.C., Lai, M.L., Chuang, H.H.: Using eye-tracking technology to investigate the redundant effect of multimedia web pages on viewers' cognitive processes. Comput. Hum. Behav. **27**(6), 2410–2417 (2011)
33. Miller, B.W.: Using reading times and eye-movements to measure cognitive engagement. Educ. Psychol. **50**(1), 31–42 (2015)
34. Navab, A., Gillespie-Lynch, K., Johnson, S.P., Sigman, M., Hutman, T.: Eye- tracking as a measure of responsiveness to joint attention in infants at risk for autism. Infancy **17**(4), 416–431 (2012)
35. Obaidellah, U., Al Haek, M., Cheng, P.C.H.: A survey on the usage of eye-tracking in computer programming. ACM Comput. Surv. (CSUR) **51**(1), 1–58 (2018)
36. O'Brien, H.L., Toms, E.G.: What is user engagement? A conceptual framework for defining user engagement with technology. J. Am. Soc. Inform. Sci. Technol. **59**(6), 938–955 (2008)
37. O'Brien, H.L., Cairns, P., Hall, M.: A practical approach to measuring user engagement with the refined user engagement scale (UES) and new UES short form. Int. J. Hum Comput Stud. **112**, 28–39 (2018)
38. Papavlasopoulou, S., Sharma, K., Giannakos, M., Jaccheri, L.: Using eye-tracking to unveil differences between kids and teens in coding activities. In: Proceedings of the 2017 Conference on Interaction Design and Children, pp. 171–181 (2017)
39. Papavlasopoulou, S., Sharma, K., Giannakos, M.N.: How do you feel about learning to code? Investigating the effect of children's attitudes towards coding using eye- tracking. Int. J. Child-Comput. Interact. **17**, 50–60 (2018)
40. Papoutsaki, A., Sangkloy, P., Laskey, J., Daskalova, N., Huang, J., Hays, J.: Webgazer: scalable webcam eye tracking using user interactions. In: Proceedings of the Twenty-Fifth International Joint Conference on Artificial Intelligence, pp. 3839–3845 (2016)
41. Park, S., Aksan, E., Zhang, X., Hilliges, O.: Towards end-to-end video-based eye-tracking. In: Vedaldi, A., Bischof, Horst, Brox, T., Frahm, J.-M. (eds.) ECCV 2020. LNCS, vol. 12357, pp. 747–763. Springer, Cham (2020). https://doi.org/10.1007/978-3-030-58610-2_44
42. Peterson, M.S., Kramer, A.F., Irwin, D.E.: Covert shifts of attention precede involuntary eye movements. Percept. Psychophys. **66**(3), 398–405 (2004)
43. Pfeiffer, U.J., Vogeley, K., Schilbach, L.: From gaze cueing to dual eye-tracking: novel approaches to investigate the neural correlates of gaze in social interaction. Neurosci. Biobehav. Rev. **37**(10), 2516–2528 (2013)
44. Pietinen, S., Bednarik, R., Tukiainen, M.: Shared visual attention in collaborative programming: a descriptive analysis. In: Proceedings of the 2010 ICSE Workshop on Cooperative and Human Aspects of Software Engineering, pp. 21–24 (2010)
45. Rayner, K.: Eye movements in reading and information processing: 20 years of research. Psychol. Bull. **124**(3), 372 (1998)
46. Rayner, K.: The 35th sir frederick bartlett lecture: eye movements and attention in reading, scene perception, and visual search. Q. J. Exp. Psychol. **62**(8), 1457–1506 (2009)

47. Schneider, B., Pea, R.: Real-time mutual gaze perception enhances collaborative learning and collaboration quality. Int. J. Comput.-Support. Collab. Learn. **8**(4), 375–397 (2013). https://doi.org/10.1007/s11412-013-9181-4

48. Schneider, B., Sharma, K., Cuendet, S., Zufferey, G., Dillenbourg, P., Pea, R.: Leveraging mobile eye-trackers to capture joint visual attention in co-located collaborative learning groups. Int. J. Comput.-Supported Collab. Learn. **13**(3), 241–261 (2018)

49. Sharafi, Z., Soh, Z., Guéhéneuc, Y.G.: A systematic literature review on the usage of eye-tracking in software engineering. Inf. Softw. Technol. **67**, 79–107 (2015)

50. Sharma, K., Papavlasopoulou, S., Giannakos, M.: Coding games and robots to en- hance computational thinking: How collaboration and engagement moderate children's attitudes? Int. J. Child-Comput. Interact. **21**, 65–76 (2019)

51. Shojaeizadeh, M., Djamasbi, S., Trapp, A.C.: Density of gaze points within a fixation and information processing behavior. In: Antona, M., Stephanidis, C. (eds.) UAHCI 2016. LNCS, vol. 9737, pp. 465–471. Springer, Cham (2016). https://doi.org/10.1007/978-3-319-40250-5_44

52. Shute, V.J., Sun, C., Asbell-Clarke, J.: Demystifying computational thinking. Educ. Res. Rev. **22**, 142–158 (2017)

53. Sweller, J.: Cognitive load during problem solving: effects on learning. Cogn. Sci. **12**(2), 257–285 (1988)

54. Underwood, G., Radach, R.: Eye guidance and visual information processing: reading, visual search, picture perception and driving. In: Eye Guidance in Reading and Scene Perception, pp. 1–27. Elsevier (1998)

55. Valliappan, N., et al.: Accelerating eye movement research via accurate and affordable smartphone eye tracking. Nat. Commun. **11**(1), 1–12 (2020)

56. Wing, J.M.: Computational thinking. Commun. ACM **49**(3), 33–35 (2006)

57. Xu, P., Ehinger, K.A., Zhang, Y., Finkelstein, A., Kulkarni, S.R., Xiao, J.: Turkergaze: crowdsourcing saliency with webcam based eye tracking. arXiv preprint arXiv:1504.06755 (2015)

58. Zagermann, J., Pfeil, U., Reiterer, H.: Measuring cognitive load using eye tracking technology in visual computing. In: Proceedings of the Sixth Workshop on Beyond Time and Errors on Novel Evaluation Methods for Visualization, pp. 78–85 (2016)

59. Judd ,C.H.: Psychol. Rev. Monoh. Suppl. **VII**(35) (1907)

Evaluating the Use of Visual Prompts in Online Meeting Applications for Kindergarteners

Hira Naseem[✉] [iD] and Osama Halabi[✉] [iD]

Qatar University, Doha, Qatar
hn2000131@qu.edu.qa, ohalabi@qu.edu.qu

Abstract. The use of online meeting applications for educational purpose, has increased during pandemic. These meeting applications mostly use textual prompts as a way of communicating with the user, which might not be suitable for kindergarteners. To enhance the usability of meeting applications, Visual Prompts and visual cues are suggested to apply in this research for attaining better user experience, and the efficacy and efficiency is proved by the experiments and results of this study. A task-based user experiment was designed for kindergarten children, aged from three to seven, where they were asked to complete certain tasks based on three different Visual Prompt designs in the online meeting application interface. The Visual Prompts were designed using Unity software for Zoom application platform. The results were analyzed for task success rate and task completion time using SPSS statistical analysis software. The results showed high t-values of success rate ($t = 5.093$) and task completion time ($t = 10.093$), which indicates that the technical scaffolding, in the form of Visual Prompts, is more helpful to communicate the information for a given task. Moreover, it was concluded that the use of Visual Prompts enhanced the learnability of an online meeting application for young children, whereas the textual prompts lagged in performance due to underdeveloped language skills of the same age group.

Keywords: Visual prompts · Multi-touch interaction · Kindergarten children · Human computer interaction · Online teaching platforms

1 Introduction

Online education using video conferencing and online meeting applications have gained much popularity during the covid-19 pandemic situation globally [1], and most of educational institutes have opted for distance/online learning models or hybrid teaching models [2]. The sudden shift of teaching method of delivery from face-to-face to online meetings has infused the need to studying the currently available user interfaces for tablets, smartphones, and PCs. For the sake of this simplicity, this study is will evaluate the tablet interface only as studies have shown that input via touch screen is far more natural and intuitive as compared to other conventional input devices such as keypads [3]. Moreover, there is larger acceptance for multi-touch screen as compared to single touch in younger children [4].

© Springer Nature Switzerland AG 2021
X. Fang (Ed.): HCII 2021, LNCS 12790, pp. 229–244, 2021.
https://doi.org/10.1007/978-3-030-77414-1_17

As such, there has been some resistance in the learning process for children in kindergarten classes when using these electronic devices and online meeting applications for taking classes [3]. The popular and most used platforms for online meetings are Zoom, WebEx, MS Teams, and Google Meets. A typical online video conferencing platform from Zoom application is shown in Fig. 1. There are continuous textual instruction and pop-up demos for explaining the buttons and actions which is based on adult user interface design principles.

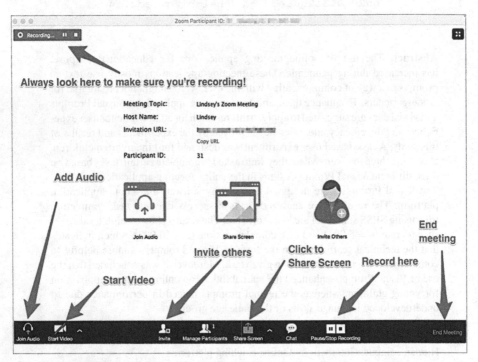

Fig. 1. Typical video conferencing application interface with red arrows for highlighting the buttons. Screenshot taken by author via Zoom Application PC Client [5]

With kindergarten children using the online meeting applications, mostly they require an adult to assist in the initial setup, but afterwards, they are mainly interacting with their teacher on their own. Mostly, the online meetings require the child to mute/unmute options, but there can be imbedded learning activities, which required the children to draw or choose options on the screen.

Previously, multiple studies have proven that demo in the form of short text and videos within the application will improve learnability, by guiding the user about performing simple operations until he fully understands the functionality of the product [6, 7]. But user interface designing process of online learning applications for children gets more challenging because of their verbal limitations [8, 9]. Special communication strategies such as technical scaffolding, are used in these devices now-a-days to overcome this issue [10, 11]. In support of this, many studies are also exploring the use of visual aid, and Visual Prompts to evaluate the efficiency and effectiveness in using these interfaces.

A study conducted in Spain, used Visual Prompt and cues to overcome the communication gap between application and younger children [12]. This test was conducted on a gaming application for kindergarteners and it proves the efficacy of simultaneous visuals prompts. The results confirmed that despite of their age, kindergarteners can interact using multiple gestures and were able to achieve the goal smoothly by the help of visual cues. However, this study only considered two visual aids at one point, and that too on a gaming-based learning application, as shown in Fig. 2.

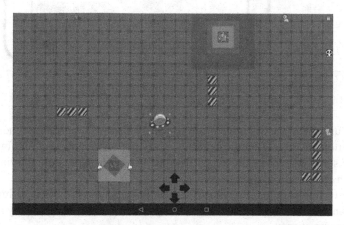

Fig. 2. Example of game with Visual Prompts for gestures [12]

Another study by the same research team, explored the Visual Prompts for directional awareness in kindergarten children, using a tablet user interface [13]. The study concluded that kindergarten children could complete a task with directional awareness with almost 100% accuracy. It was found that children were very efficient in interpreting and predicting the data from the Visual Prompts to anticipate the location of different objects outside of tablet screen virtual world. Again, this study also used a gaming interface for conducting this research, with single visual aids at one time, as shown in Fig. 3.

Since tablet games are very popular in children and are widely used these days for entertainment, the evaluation of Visual Prompts using game user interface can be questionable. Now-a-days, the same children have no option but to opt for online meeting platforms, which can be a very different user interface as compared to a game user interface.

Online meeting applications requires novel graphical strategies to enhance learnability of application. Instead of continuous demos and textual instruction, the online meetings interface should focus on having Visual Prompts, as they can help concentrating more on content learning, rather than getting the hold of available options. In addition, using visual cues can enable children to share information from their end and thus engaging in better collaborative learning with teacher as well as other students.

Meeting applications for online learning lacks the flavor of these special communication strategies and to the author's best knowledge, there no explorative study done to

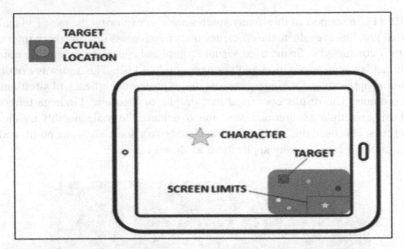

Fig. 3. Visual Prompts with directional clues [13]

improve the user interface of online meeting platforms for supporting online education for kindergarten children. Therefore, in this study, an online meeting platform will be used as case study, to explore the effect of using Visual Prompts in improving the user experience in an education setting.

The aim of this paper is to evaluate Visual Prompts as a solution to improve the usability of online meeting platforms for kindergarteners. This is achieved by addressing the following objectives:

1. Introduce appropriate graphical strategies such as Visual Prompts and visual cues to improve usability.
2. Enhancing the learnability and reducing technical scaffolding from the adults
3. Conducting high fidelity prototyping to test outcome of proposed solutions
4. Suggesting recommendations for improved UX design based on results.

The organization of this paper is given as; firstly, the introduction; secondly a literature review in accordance with Visual Prompts and user interface testing methods; thirdly a breakdown of research methods and steps taken to proceed with this study; fourth the results from experiments, and lastly a discussion on the results obtained, followed by a conclusion.

2 Literature Review

Many studies have been conducted in the previous two decades exploring the use of multi-touch display and to improve its usability for children. However, in the current situation of covid-19 pandemic, the use of touch devices has increased in the kindergarteners for educational learning [14]. Most of the online learning is taken place through online platforms, i.e., some institutes are using Zoom meeting client while other are opting for Microsoft Teams. However, the challenge is transfer of information to the young children aged between 2 to 4 years. While using these applications children need technical support from the adults for interactive sessions with instructors. Using touchscreens for gaming apps and other entertainment applications such as YouTube and video-players is not difficult for young children, which implies that the interface of online meeting clients lacks some basic Human Computer Interaction (HCI) principles to make it usable. In this paper we aim to deduce and evaluate a solution to improve the usability of these online meeting clients for kindergarteners.

In 2007, a study was conducted to improve the usability by giving instructions in the form of animation. It was found that the animated information proved itself to be useful if coupled with spoken instruction from the adult. However, it was effective for the children with age six and onwards and not for the younger children [15]. This posed a need for having an adult giving spoken instruction or recording audio messages, which can be a challenging task for different speaking dialects.

Another study by Kahkonen and Ovaska, proposed that instructions in the form of text or animation does not improve learnability, to overcome the limitations of textual information, audio messages coupled with animated video were evaluated [7]. It more explored that not only children but adults with novice knowledge about computer devices will perform better with this kind of graphical help. However, there were also limitations such as language barriers and vocabulary. Another study performed by Baloain et al. strongly agrees with the findings of previously mentioned study. It propose that young children aged 5 to 7 are ready for visual cues but they have issues with audio instructions [16].

In response to above mentioned challenges, there has been many attempts in the HCI research area to enhance usability of touch screen devices for young children. In 2019, a study propose that Visual Prompts are effective tool of communication for kindergarteners [13]. Young children were able to perform better in the gaming app environment with the help of visual cues and Visual Prompts. These graphical techniques prove themselves to be effective for communicating directional awareness. In the cited work, certain recommendations have been added for designer to choose appropriate type of prompt in accordance with the application.

Following to this, in 2020, an extension of this study conducted by same team, found that kindergarteners can comprehend Visual Prompts and visual ques effectively [12]. The use of appropriate prompts and ques will enhance the usability of a game app up to an extent where adult guidance is no longer needed. Moreover, these children can comprehend simultaneous Visual Prompts as well and they were able to achieve the goal efficiently by comprehending this graphical kind of help.

Another study concluded that, including Visual Prompts does not guarantee the usability improvement [17]. Poor design i.e., ignoring all the basic principles and guide-lines of HCI will not be successful. Appropriate Visual Prompts and Visual cues in accor-dance with the domain of application is needed i.e., environmental requirements, func-tional requirements, usability requirements, and user experience requirements should be considered.

In the current scenario of covid-19 pandemic, touch screens are also used for online learning. This online learning requires the use of online meeting clients. The following knowledge gaps have been identified by looking at the previous studies in this area:

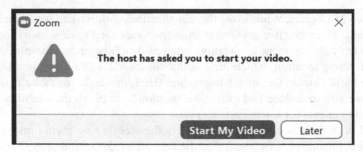

Fig. 4. Textual instruction. Screenshot taken by author via Zoom Application PC Client [5].

1. These online meeting applications failed to follow some of the basic principles and guidelines of HCI and Interface design.
2. The use of textual prompts, as shown in Fig. 1 and Fig. 4, failed to communicate information to the kindergarteners.
3. Limitations of language and vocabulary does not allow them effective use of these application.
4. There is a high dependability on learning scaffolding from the adults. These interruptions in the form of technical scaffoldings divert their attention and make them unable to focus on learning session.

Clearly, there is a need to design the user interface targeting the young children' audience, which will require new design tools and strategies to be applied in the online meeting platforms. Therefore, this research aims at exploring, proposing, and evaluating, an interface to enhance learnability through appropriate Visual Prompts and cues. Secondly, on basis of evaluation result, recommend improved UX design.

3   Methods

The evaluation methods will be exploring whether the kindergarten children are able to interact/play with application in which evaluation of three different types of Visual Prompts is carried out in a real application targeted to kindergarten children. Hence, the results obtained in this work should be a step forward in the process of obtaining effective semiotic systems understandable by kindergarten children that could be used in education.

The main aim of this study is to enhance the usability of the current online meeting applications for children. During this study, three types of Visual Prompts and cues will be designed and evaluated, and at the end, the best one will be selected. By the best one, it was meant that this type of Visual Prompt helped the children of kindergarten perform the task efficiently in given time. These prompts will be designed by keeping the mental model of children in consideration.

For evaluation, hypothesis (H-1) was defined as "Visual Prompts and cues will enhance the usability of online meetings applications in terms of efficiency". To counter argue the hypothesis (H-1), we define a null hypothesis (N-1) as "Visual Prompts and cues does not affect the usability of online meeting applications". In order, to prove the Null Hypothesis (N-1) wrong, a task-based experiment was conducted.

In addition, to observe the effects of Visual Prompts on the task accuracy, a second hypothesis (H-2) was defined as "Visual Prompts and cues enhance the accuracy of the input by a kindergartener". The counter argument of the second hypotheses (H-2) is the null hypothesis (N-2), which was defined as "Visual Prompts and cues does not affect the accuracy of input".

The target for the experiment can be defined as; design and analyze at least three different Visual Prompts and evaluate their usability in terms of effectiveness and efficiency for the kindergarteners. These evaluations were performed on children aged from 3 to 7 with both male and female genders. The maximum range in the children was kept 7 years of age, because the cognitive skills and the behaviors of these children are evolving and developing until the age of 7 [18]. As the goal is to explore how the designed Visual Prompts are effective for children and how their evolving cognitive skills affects their efficiency, we define four age groups for the children aged between 3–4, 4–5, 5–6 and 6–7.

Moreover, the research questions of this study can be formulated as; "can the Visual Prompt communicate the information to the young children for performing the desired task effectively?". To analyze the research question, tasks will be devised accordingly. The research question is about the appropriateness of visual cues to communicate information, i.e., it helps children to complete the task. In this study, the aim is to explore the possible answers to above mentioned question.

3.1 Participants

In this study, children aged from 3 to 7 years old, took part in the experiment. The mean (M) of their age was 46 months with a gender distribution of 4 males and 6 females. The children were grouped according to their age, and each group "A" consists of children aged "A+1".

Table 1. Age group of participants

Group	Age	Number of participants
2	3–4	2
4	4–5	3
5	5–6	3
6	6–7	2

The number of participants according to their age group is shown in Table 1. The 3 to 7-year age range was chosen to evaluate the usefulness of proposed Visual Prompts and Visual cues. The youngest users were children aged 3 years because after recent pandemic even young children are taking online learning sessions.

3.2 Equipment

The interactive framework was designed using in Vision studio and Unity for the experiment. The device used in this experiment was Lenovo IdeaPad flex 5, with 64-bit Windows 10 as operating system and another device Samsung Galaxy S10 with android 9.0 Pie with One UI 1.1. Both devices were equipped with multi-touch screens as well as fast operating systems capable of supporting most modern online meeting applications.

3.3 Tasks

In the experiment, firstly, the tasks will be defined and then evaluated for its effectiveness and efficiency by analyzing the time taken to complete the task. The task defined for this study are as follows:

Task 1: To turn off/on their mic in respond to a Visual Cue.
(Note that the instructor will be present online and sometime will not be able to make contact through speech. She/he will send a ping and a Visual Cue will be popped up.)
Task 2: To turn off/ on their video when a Visual Prompt is seen.
Task 3: To share their screen when a Visual Cue Popped up. .

The key task analyzed in this experiment is using the mic button. Children were asked to turn on and turn off the mic within their meeting application environment. By taping the mic icon, the task will be completed, and task completion time will be recorded.

Similarly, in task 2, the children are required to turn on and off their camera by pressing the button on the screen without any adult scaffolding. By taping the camera icon, the task will be completed, and the task completion time will be recorded.

To evaluate the usability of product in terms of HCI, statistical analysis will be performed [19]. The data collected during this study will be analyzed using *SPSS statistical analysis software.*

3.4 Procedures

The experiment will be carried out for three consecutive days on the participants with four iterations on each day. But there will be a new Visual Prompt or visual cue on each day.

Before the testing session of each day, an instructor will be guiding the children about the metaphors present on the different icons. He will be helping children to understand the task and the desired output. He will ensure that each child can identify different mic and camera and can differentiate between two of them. After these introductory explanations, no further adult scaffolding will be given during the testing phase of experiment. When the test begins, each child needs to perform three iteration for each task with a specific type of Visual Prompt and there will not be any intervention by the examiner. When the correct action is performed the task will end and the task completion time will be recorded but in case of wrong input the visual cues will keep on popping to grab the attention until correct completion of task. In this case task completion time and wrong inputs will be mapped in an Excel spreadsheet.

3.5 Design Implementation

Usually, the screen of the online meeting application has two main button icons, which are mic and camera, and they are most frequently used during an online meeting session. Three different types of Visual Prompts and cues were designed for these two buttons.

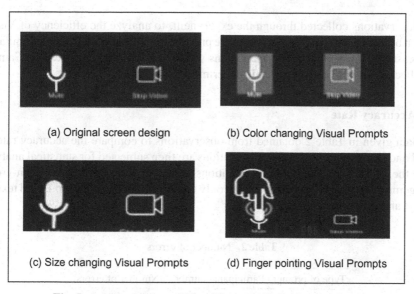

(a) Original screen design

(b) Color changing Visual Prompts

(c) Size changing Visual Prompts

(d) Finger pointing Visual Prompts

Fig. 5. Implementation of Visual Prompts (Color figure online)

As given in Fig. 5(a), the original the two said button icons are plain. However, in the Visual Prompt Fig. 5(b), the color of these buttons changes when it is requested by the host. The change in color prompts the user to perform some action. Thus, helping the host to communicate the desired action with the user which was otherwise difficult. In the second button design Fig. 5(c), the buttons re-sizes themselves into bigger and smaller icons. Thus, grasping the attention of user by changing its size. When the host wants to turn on/off the camera or mic for a certain user, he can send the request. At the user end, the request will be shown in the form if re-size Visual Prompt. In the third design of the visual cue Fig. 5(d), a hand appeared with a pointing finger towards specific button. This clearly gives a message to the user to tap this button. It not only grasps the attention of user but also drives user towards desired action.

3.6 Evaluation

To evaluate the usability of hypotheses, in terms of HCI, statistical analysis is performed. According to Hypothesis (H-1), we have one independent variable (Time of Task Completion) and two dependent variables (Textual Cues vs. Visual Cues), and the experiment strategy used to collect data was "With-in Group". Therefore, we will be using Paired Sample t-test for analyzing the collected data [19].

To measure the accuracy of Visual Prompts and cues another test with same setting will be conducted but this time the group organization will be between groups. To analyse the result, Independent Sample t-test will be applied.

4 Results

The observations collected through the experiment, to analyze the efficiency of Visual cues on basis of Task Completion Time were projected to Paired-Sample t-test. Similarly, for measuring the accuracy the observations were analyzed using Independent Sample t-test because of a slight difference in experiment arrangement.

4.1 Accuracy Rate

The data given in Table 2 obtained from observations to compare the accuracy rate of visual and textual prompts. These observations are then subjected for statistical analysis using the SPSS software. These observations were obtained through between-group arrangements. Each group was given with only one kind of prompt. Group 1 tried textual prompt and group 2 tried Visual Prompt.

Table 2. Number of errors

Type of prompt	Participants number	Number of errors
Textual	1	8
Textual	2	5
Textual	3	4
Textual	4	7
Visual	5	0
Visual	6	2
Visual	7	0
Visual	8	1

The readings obtained through this experiment were stored in Excel spreadsheets and later mapped into boxplot, as shown in Fig. 6.

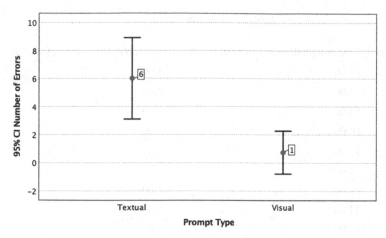

Fig. 6. Success rate results

An independent sample t-test was conducted using these observations. The returned t-value is 5.093, which is higher than the t-value for the specific degree of freedom (df = 6) at the 95% confidence interval (t = 5.093).

Statistical evaluation suggests that there is significant difference in the number of errors between the group who used the Visual Prompts and the group who used textual prompts [$t(6) = 5.093$, $Sig_{(2\text{-tailed})} = 0.002$].

4.2 Completion Time

The data, shown in Table 3, obtained from the experiment to compare the efficiency between visual and textual prompt by measuring and comparing the task completion time by both prompts. These observations were then subjected to SPSS software for statistical analysis. These observations were collected through with-in group arrangement. A single group of children evaluated both types of prompts. Although some safeguard measures were applied to remove the biasness of experiment. Later, a paired-sample t-test were applied on the observations. The readings obtained through this experiment is mapped into a boxplot as shown Fig. 7, in to have a better insight of the outcome.

The returned t-value is 10.093, which is higher than the t value for the specific degree of freedom (df = 9) at the 95% confidence interval (t = 10.993).

A paired-sampled t-test for task completion time suggests that there is a significant difference between the groups who used the Visual Prompts and textual prompts to perform specific task [$t(6) = 10.093$, $Sig_{(2\text{-tailed})} = 0.00$].

Table 3. Time completion time

Participant	Task completion time (textual prompt)	Task completion time (Visual Prompt)
1.00	10.00	3.00
2.00	14.00	2.00
3.00	13.00	2.00
4.00	10.00	4.00
5.00	12.00	3.00
6.00	5.00	1.00
7.00	11.00	2.00
8.00	14.00	2.00
9.00	10.00	3.00
10.00	11.00	1.00

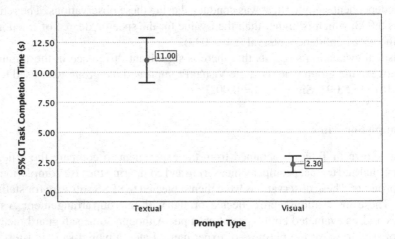

Fig. 7. Task completion time

4.3 Optimum Visual Prompt

In the Table 4, data obtained from experiment to compare different types of Visual Prompts on basis of its efficiency i.e., time completion time to perform a specific task is given. This data is collected through with-in group arrangement. This data is then subjected to SPSS software to perform paired-sample t-test to evaluate the significance.

When different kind of Visual Prompts were evaluated on basis of time completion time. It was found that there is no significant difference in the task completion time for each type of Visual Prompt.

Table 4. Optimum visualization

Participant no	Task completion time (visual type 1)	Task completion time (visual type 2)	Task completion time (visual type 3)
1	2	3	1
2	3	2	1
3	1	2	2
4	2	4	1
5	3	2	2
6	1	1	1
7	1	2	1
8	1	2	1
9	3	1	1
10	2	2	1

5 Discussion

The experiment explored and answered the research question by using statistical analysis on the obtained observations, to analyze the efficacy and efficiency of Visual Prompts and cues. The results deduced from these observations have verified our hypotheses (H-1) and hypotheses-2 (H-2). These results also negate the null hypotheses (N-1) and null hypotheses (N-2).

Hence, we can say our Hypotheses (H-1) "Visual Prompts and Cues will enhance the usability of meetings clients in terms of efficiency" and hypotheses-2 (H-2) "Visual Prompts and cues enhance the accuracy of input by kindergartener" were proved to be true.

In terms of Efficacy, Visual Prompts and cues reduces the number of wrong pickups significantly as compared to textual prompts. When these children were subjected to evaluate textual prompt, their clicks on wrong icons or background were taken as wrong inputs by the facilitator. From the observations number of errors in textual prompt were quite high which means that Visual Prompts are more comprehendible by the young children and there are less chances of errors to be committed by them. The results of Independent Sample t-test on these observations proved that there is a significant between these two types of prompts in terms of Errors prevention and children are more prone to errors in textual prompts as compared to Visual Prompt.

Regarding the efficiency, the task completion time drops significantly when children were using Visual Prompt to complete the task. However, when textual prompts were used their performance dropped significantly. They completed the task in long interval of time. When these observations were projected to Paired Sample t-test to analyze them, it was found that there is a significant difference between task completion time using two different types of prompts. It suggests that Visual Prompts are efficient means, to communicate information to these young children as compared to textual prompts. From the results it was proved that Visual Prompts are a better choice to enhance the usability of a software for kindergarteners.

The answer to research question RQ, whether Visual Prompts and cues enhance the usability in terms of efficacy and efficiency is affirmative from the results. As mentioned earlier, these results were concluded by applying appropriate statistical analysis over the observations obtained from experiment. The type of statistical was chosen according to experiment arrangement. Experiments conducted over same children to analyze both visual and textual were subjected to paired-sample t-test. But the observations obtained from experiments arrangements in which visual and textual cues were tested on different were subjected to independent sample t-test.

These results have proven Visual Prompts significantly efficient and effective. As suggested by Piaget, young children of age less than 3 years are in their developing stage. Their cognitive and fine motor skills are not fully developed yet [18]. So, it might be assumed that younger children of age 2–3 years will not be able to perform well under Visual Prompts. They might have issues dealing with this interface without adult guidance. This must be considered by designers, while developing a software for common use to include children as young as three years old for their targeted users. To include these users, Visual Prompts have proven themselves to be effective and efficient.

Finally, the result for optimum design of Visual Prompts suggested that there is no significant difference between efficacy or efficiency of all types of Visual Prompts. This result obtained through paired-sample t-test suggests that every design has optimized efficacy and efficiency, with some insignificant difference between them.

6 Conclusion

In this work we analyze the interface of the most popular online meeting application Zoom meeting [20] in terms of its usability for kindergarteners. The above-mentioned application used textual prompts and cues to communicate information between host and guest. These technical scaffoldings in the form of textual prompts were found to be ineffective and inefficient, to communicate the information. Therefore, they were not helpful for the targeted user (children aged between 3 to 7).

The findings from the experiment proved that technical scaffolding in the form of Visual Prompts and cues are more helpful to communicate the information regarding the task in an effective manner. This was evident from the experiment results. Both the results showed a very high t value. To evaluate the success rate, $t = 5.093$ and for evaluation of Task completion time it was $t = 10.093$. Which indicates that use of Visual Prompts enhances the learnability of an application for young children because it fits the human mental model, whereas textual prompts lag due to under development language skills.

However, to select the most appropriate and suitable Visual Prompts is a challenging task. In complex operations and complicated task, it is a difficult task to create and evaluate a visual expression for that operation, which not only represent that operation but also fits the human mental model perfectly.

The plan for future work includes, designing a collaborative platform for kindergarteners based on Visual Prompts and cues. The present collaborative platform such as

Microsoft Teams (which is used for document sharing, online meetings, and communications), lacks this flavor of Visual Prompts. In addition, the study also aims in future to measure the cognitive load of textual prompts on human-brain by analyzing the behavior of adults.

References

1. Rajhans, V., Memon, U., Patil, V., Goyal, A.: Impact of COVID-19 on academic activities and way forward in Indian Optometry. J. Optom. (2020). https://doi.org/10.1016/j.optom.2020.06.002

2. Patricia, A.: College students' use and acceptance of emergency online learning due to COVID-19. Int. J. Educ. Res. Open 1, 100011 (2020). https://doi.org/10.1016/j.ijedro.2020.100011

3. Bonneton-Botté, N., Fleury, S., Girard, N., et al.: Can tablet apps support the learning of handwriting? An investigation of learning outcomes in kindergarten classroom. Comput. Educ. 151, 103831 (2020). https://doi.org/10.1016/j.compedu.2020.103831

4. Danby, S., et al.: Talk in activity during young children's use of digital technologies at home. Aust. J. Commun. 40, 83 (2013)

5. Zoom: Zoom Support Center (2020). https://support.zoom.us/hc/en-us

6. van der Meij, H., van der Meij, J.: A comparison of paper-based and video tutorials for software learning. Comput. Educ. 78, 150–159 (2014). https://doi.org/10.1016/j.compedu.2014.06.003

7. Kähkönen, M., Ovaska, S.: Initial observations on children and online instructions. In: Proceedings of the 2006 Conference on Interaction Design and Children, New York, NY, USA, pp. 93–96. Association for Computing Machinery (2006)

8. Markopoulos, P., Bekker, M.M.: How to compare usability testing methods with children participants. In: Bekker, M.M., Markopoulos, P., Kersten-Tsikalkina, M. (eds.) Proceedings of the International Workshop, pp. 153–158 (2002)

9. Neumann, M.M.: Parent scaffolding of young children's use of touch screen tablets. Early Child Dev. Care 188, 1654–1664 (2018). https://doi.org/10.1080/03004430.2016.1278215

10. Wood, E., et al.: Parent scaffolding of young children when engaged with mobile technology. Front. Psychol. 7, 1222 (2016)

11. Neumann, M.M.: Young children and screen time: creating a mindful approach to digital technology. Aust. Educ. Comput. 30, 1–15 (2015)

12. Nacher, V., Garcia-Sanjuan, F., Jaen, J.: Evaluating simultaneous visual instructions with kindergarten children on touchscreen devices. Int. J. Hum. Comput. Interact. 36, 41–54 (2020). https://doi.org/10.1080/10447318.2019.1597576

13. Nacher, V., Jurdi, S., Jaen, J., Garcia-Sanjuan, F.: Exploring visual prompts for communicating directional awareness to kindergarten children. Int. J. Hum. Comput. Stud. 126, 14–25 (2019). https://doi.org/10.1016/j.ijhcs.2019.01.003

14. Triyason, T., Tassanaviboon, A., Kanthamanon, P.: Hybrid classroom: designing for the new normal after COVID-19 pandemic. In: Proceedings of the 11th International Conference on Advances in Information Technology, New York, NY, USA. Association for Computing Machinery (2020)

15. Niemi, H., Ovaska, S.: Designing spoken instructions with preschool children. In: Proceedings of the 6th International Conference on Interaction Design and Children, New York, NY, USA, pp. 133–136. Association for Computing Machinery (2007)

16. Baloian, N., Pino, J.A., Vargas, R.: Tablet gestures as a motivating factor for learning. In: Proceedings of the 2013 Chilean Conference on Human - Computer Interaction, New York, NY, USA, pp. 98–103. Association for Computing Machinery (2013)

17. Hiniker, A., Sobel, K., Hong, S.R., et al.: Touchscreen prompts for preschoolers: designing developmentally appropriate techniques for teaching young children to perform gestures. In: Proceedings of the 14th International Conference on Interaction Design and Children, New York, NY, USA, pp. 109–118. Association for Computing Machinery (2015)

18. Piaget, J.: The Child and Reality: Problems of Genetic Psychology. Trans. by A. Rosin. Grossman, Oxford (1973)

19. Dix, A., Finlay, J., Abowd, G., Beale, R.: Human-Computer Interaction, 3rd edn. Pearson Education Limited, Harlow (2004)

20. Boyarsky, K.: The 10 best video meeting apps, 4 November 2020

Gamification Design Predicaments
for E-learning

Adam Palmquist[1]($\boxtimes$), Robin Munkvold[2], and Ole Goethe[2]

[1] University of Gothenburg, Gothenburg, Sweden
adam.palmquist@ait.gu.se
[2] Nord University, Bodø, Norway
{robin.munkvold,ole.goethe}@nord.no

Abstract. We introduce how gambling techniques slurred as gamification can be abusive and how adapting it for HCI can lay a practical basis for unethical designs, both in the commercial and applied research sectors. Based on the original notion of game theory, we argue that these techniques can be pervasive in our everyday socio-technical ecosystem. The digital technology industry's commercial underpinnings frequently promote irrational user-behavior and using these design techniques in educational technology could foster negative user learning behaviors. Given the complexity of these concepts' legal issues, it is not always easy to ensure that one does not cross the line. This study presents four gamification design predicaments that demand attention when designing gamification in (e)learning. The research has both theory and practical implications.

Keywords: Information technology · Gamification · Gamblification ·
Instructional design · E-learning · Information systems · Design heuristics

1 Introduction

The phenomena of "gaming the system," could be when a learner attempts to succeed in an educational environment by exploiting properties of the system's irregularities rather than by attempting to learn the matter [1, 2] In the last years, there is a particular growing interest in understanding users' motivation to use a system and the Human-Computer Interaction research community has long been interested in the design, development, and evaluation of games and playful systems [3].

Gamification and gamblification is a rapidly emerging form of media convergence between the more chance-based activity of gambling and the more skill-based activity of gaming. The marriage of video gaming and gambling has been theorized as bringing about new forms of gambling-related cognitive processes such as the: "near-miss" effect (erroneous processing of outcome); gambler's fallacy (mistaken ideas that an inevitable result is more or less likely, given a previous series of events); "chasing" effect (increased persistence and risk-taking to recoup what has been lost). These processes affect individuals in which they approach and evaluate gambling situations. As such, a pertinent research problem is whether existing measurement instruments designed to identify

© Springer Nature Switzerland AG 2021
X. Fang (Ed.): HCII 2021, LNCS 12790, pp. 245–255, 2021.
https://doi.org/10.1007/978-3-030-77414-1_18

gambling related cognitions can be employed in this new context and population, and if not, how they can be adapted [4].

Gamblification is yet to become a full-on household term, as it is solely used to denote a specific practice that is rising in popularity among online gambling operators and social platforms alike [5]. Its origins are traced back to gamification, known as the practice of using non-game elements to enhance personalization and achieve proximity to each individual player [6].

While many, if not most games include some element of chance, this is something we argue designers should add to learning games with caution. Of course, we still need randomness in the games [7] like which assignment you get out of a set of possible assignments or a quiz, but any time a random element is included, think very carefully about why you are doing it, what you hope to accomplish by it, and what you think your students will get out of it [8].

In this paper, we are furthering our research on the ethical issue related to gamefulness and addresses that gamification design patterns are nonuniversal and some of the more frequent used design practices in gamification has footing in gambling. Unthoughtful practice of these patterns to influence the users/players can potentially negatively affect the individual.

2 Related Work

Gameful design in non-game products has during the last decade has transformed from being a buzzword to become to be nothing out of the ordinary in Information Technology and Information Systems (IS) and has become more and more accepted by the everyday user [9, 10]. Corresponding a there is a growing discussion concerning influencing systems and persuasive digital technology [11]. In this discussion the use and application areas of gamification is a reoccurring topic [12–14].

Simultaneously online gambling has grown in North America and Europe in the last decade [15]. The normalization of online gambling different media spaces parallel with the public acceptance of gameful design has opened for "gamblification" a convergence of video gaming and gambling co-existing in a software [16, 17]. The amalgamation of gaming and gambling exist in several digital businesses such as software using virtual items, currencies [18] and games with a free-to-play business model [19]. Concerns about the potential harmful effects of gamblified media have resulted in a debate about the moral, ethical, and legal status of gamblified products and services [20, 21]. Scholars have theorized that the combination of skill-based video gaming and chance-based gambling may result in cognitions which differ from those endorsed by non-gaming gamblers. Potential perceptions can be the effect of gaming on perceptions of control over chance-based events [22]; the role of Locus of Control [23]; the desirability of gambling and manner of video game consumption [19].

Also, with the current debate between the World Health Organization and American Psychiatric Association (APA) on the classification of Gaming Addiction [24] and how Problematic Gambling best shall be approached and preserved [25] there it appears that examining, measuring, discussing and understanding when and when not, behavior design patterns become negative.

3 Game Theory: Background

Game theory is a theoretical framework for comprehending social situations among competing agents in a competitive situation. A strategy or optimal decision-making of independent and competing actors in a strategic setting [26]. Game theory analyses the social structures within which the consequences of an agent's action is contingent and in a conscious way for the agent alter the options of actions of other agents in the existing structure [27]. The game theory considers the rational model of the individual decision or limited rationality of the agents and how to direct multilateral relations between them is non-mediatized. The agent situations can be competition and cooperation between several involved parties by using mathematical methods. This is a broad definition, but it is consistent with many applications, including strategic inquiries in conflict situations, understanding economic competition in companies, problems of fair distribution in economics, animals' social behavior in competitive positions, parlour games, political voting systems etcetera [28].

One requirement for the theory is the existence of presupposed agents', and their viewpoints about their probabilities in a situation can match different objective probabilities. In choice situations, agents must rely on their subjective estimations or perceptions of their probabilities [26]. Behavioral and social science game theory is presented as incorporating agents' subjective probabilities and relationships regarding their preferences over the risk [29]. Indicating that individuals in several situations saw themself as agents (players) determine to solve a game have marked the actual maturity of game theory as a tool for application to behavioral and social science and was recognized [30].

4 Gamification Design Predicaments

Like most technologies, the introduction and use of persuasive technology to persuade a transformation of mind and behavior could positively and negative effects the user. Gamification has recently gained in popularity as an enabler of persuasion since it is supposed to increase engagement by using game elements. Gamification could be a catalyst to increase the effects of the designed and intended persuasion. The study of unintended negative consequences of behavioural interventions is becoming an important research area [31–35].

In game design different design patterns have been highlighted as a reusable solution for different problems [36]. A pattern solution frequently captures more solutions rather than one exact solution. However, so-called dark patterns are when the different design elements functions to trick the user into doing things that are not in the user's best interest [37]. Dark patterns are design strategies used to benefit the business rather than the target audience, using unethical applications such as coercion, deception, and fraud. The dark patterns are likely to occur without the consent of the user. The scientific discussion on dark design patterns concluding them as questionable and unethical [11, 37, 38]. The ethical discussion on gamification exists but are still in its infancy [20, 39]. Dark gamification design could be defined as the craft of purposefully designing gamification that does not have the user's well-being in mind.

As gamification has a firm footing in the marketing and service industry [40] transferring a successful gamification pattern from one context to another could have severe outcomes. A design that seems harmless in one context could in another have be contra productive.

In user experience (UX) design, increasing user engagement researchers and specialists aspire to produce a flow experience and immersion in a software product. This not necessarily incentives the desired outcome for the user. Even though improving user engagement using game elements is an exciting idea, contrary to the marketing perspective, the goal of UX is not to make the user loyal to the system, but rather increase the user experience in the system. This, of course, has its own drawback when it comes to do UX for hedonic, utilitarian (pragmatic) [41] or multipurposed [42] information systems. The following paragraph will present four predicaments (or patterns) that may rise when transferring gamification patterns from one software system to another without thorough reflections of the context (see Fig. 1).

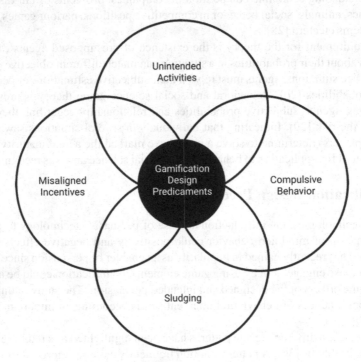

Fig. 1. Gamification design predicaments

Unintended Activities. At present, the process of implementing gamification to accomplish the intended objectives effectively is vague. The literature on gamification design both from researchers [43, 44] and practitioners [45, 46] provide imperfect, limited and context-dependent rules of thumb. Consequentially, both researchers and practitioners are restricted to a tentative, speculative, and costly implementation process [47]. To transfer game design philosophies with often hedonic purposes to the utilitarian learning environment is challenging [3]. Not being intimate with the context being gamified is problematic. As users of game systems in educational settings are usually aware of how the system's designers position them, gamification challenges the existing didactic contract in settings where pre-existing systems have game-like features, like education. How the implemented gamification system is merged with the existing systems (how levels, XP, and missions relate to formal education and grades) can significantly impact user behaviour [48].

Palmquist & Linderoth [48] shows that if the gamification design does not align with the learning systems outcomes intended, the game features can be a distraction. Even if the user likes to use the system, s/he will not learn more. To offer features that provide social cohesion for the users, such as commentator functions, discussions threads or online forum and then force the user to post in these entities may increase time on site and provide stickiness. However, these resources may not directly be related to the intended learning behaviour, sustaining the learners to spend time in the system without focusing on the actual reason for using it in the first place.

Another common gamification pattern is playful customization features (e.g., avatars). These features affect user- retention, time allotted on the system and scroll rate of the users. It is beneficial to promote hedonic values, though utilitarian users are not beneficent. Gamification and its features related to social media must be applied based on the understanding of different systems [41].

Users usually sweep past various posts, and occasionally find information, causing them to pause and read, leaving a like or a comment. A similar mechanism is used in slot machines: users are browsing towards anticipation of reward (a payoff of three cherries, a post you would like to interact with). However, because the reward is dispensed, arousal happens unpredictably, making the dopamine retain a continuous flow, and users remain occupied with the feed for a more extended time. This design feature is also known as "stickiness" and is something every tech agent reveres and aims for as the pinnacle of efficient design [49].

Misaligned Incentives. Skilled game designers are often competent at implementing incentives as motivational triggers for maintaining player interest, stretch commitment and repeat usage [50]. Misaligned incentives usually transpire in the absence of well-designed rule systems that control the rewards or penalties for the player actions. The fundamental idea of this is that unless a set of rules incentivize game participants do specific tasks, they tend to act in their self-interest, which may not always be what the game designer intended. Incentive alignment of the learning goals and gamification goals are imperative in gamification design for learning. Several gamification designs promote competition amongst the users for providing a sense of competence. Still, it can be detrimental to casual users with low representation and low self-efficacy since they can feel forced to compete with their peers, negatively affecting their incentive and reducing their interest and engagement. It can also foster negatively U2U behaviour. In a work environment, playing games is mainly associated with the competition. Individuals tend to turn work duties that they are paid to do into competitions because of the underlying motivational factors that make employees excel at their work [51]. The practice of employee advocacy and company-wide social media sharing with our colleagues and social media networks has a lot to do with competition. While everyone within the team sees what their colleagues are sharing and a leaderboard indicates the top-performing employees, it is in our human nature to strive to be best, especially when there are other incentives in play. In its simplest form, we can be either intrinsically or extrinsically motivated or de-motivated to do something – are we motivated from within, from our work, or are we motivated just by external factors, such as monetary rewards, badges or collector's points? The question also applies to the group that is not equivalent to high representation and high self-efficacy. That group of people would not want to compete and feel pushed or forced to be a part of such a competitive environment. For many users, it is not always about competition but motivation. However, the gamification design in the HCI environment, characterized solely by competition and linked to external rewards, may be negatively associated with such groups' morale, motivation, and engagement levels [52]. Therefore, overall, in general, gamification has the potential to satisfy the needs for competence, autonomy, and social relatedness, on the one hand, but on the other, it can drastically decrease the engagement and motivation level of individuals who feel pushed to compete.

Compulsive Behavior. Researchers identify that some game features and sensations, like flow, producing a distinguished dopamine stream can affect learning negative and even be harmful [53, 54, 55]. Thus, fixation on the flow-state in gamification design could be a potential problem in gamified environments. Unlike the behaviour of alcoholics or gambling addicts, addiction in such environments should not have more significant effects, such as loss of personal property or family disruption. However, concerning the dependency created by the game-like experience in the educational environment, the users can resource to "game the system" to get rewards. They are not using the system for learning but to receive a sense of recognition and assistance of self-esteem, which can be disturbing for the other learners. The user could change the focus from learning the subject due to gamified system aspects. Earning points to get a higher position in a leaderboard or unlock one exclusive or rare content in the system and gain visibility with his peers drives activity. Virtual goods procurement or high ranking in gamified solutions depend on the system's primary goal, but it is not uncommon for users to seek alternative strategies to get their desired results [1].

Also, the user creates a dependence on the game elements and starts to focus on the game system more than acquire knowledge. Thoughtfully designed gamification in a learning system should positively be correlated to the progress and the students learning outcomes, not devising students to initiate social media behaviour. A behaviour that mainly involves only gradual participation and is not inspiring production [56]. Also, gamification overuse may go unnoticed for teachers or instructors identifying the behaviour as positive students' engagement. Therefore, in a gamified learning environment, regular monitoring of the students' peer-to-peer interactions is suggested and familiarizing teachers/instructors of this negative learning behaviour.

Sludging. Another behaviour design theory often compared [57] or combined [58] with gamification is the Thaler and Sunstein Nudge theory [59]. Like gamification, this theory of choice architecture and libertarian paternalism by the design or redesign of an object or situation propose the more optional choice in relevance to benefit the user's health, wealth and happiness. This theory's theoretical grounding comes from behavioural economics and is based on the Kahneman & Tversky studies on their Prospect Theory [60]. The theory proposes two distinct systems for processing information and making decisions:

System 1, the fast and un-logical system, and *System 2*, the slow and logical system. The nudging method uses this theory to help people make improved decisions that will benefit them and society in the long run – like eating healthier, saving money for retirement, or preventing littering. Thaler and Sunstein have emphasized that this knowledge is not novel; entrepreneurs have used these methods for ages [61]. One example is the buy bait rebate – not for the sake of the environment but to increase profit. Thaler demands that when nudging is used to trick individuals, it should be termed *Sludging* [61]. Even if the resemblance concerning nudging and gamification is striking, there is a significant difference: Nudging has a straightforward ethical ethos from the beginning, while gamification has not. Even so, the application context can transform a nudge into a sludge.

For instance, a student who collects digital badges in different courses hypothetically absorbs more knowledge and, therefore, may complete upper secondary education 20% faster than the non-gamified course participants. This would by most be viewed as beneficial for the student as well as society. However, if a blue color operator adopts the same behaviour in a corporate training course and finishes the training 20% faster due to gamification, the company is the clear winner since the operator has used his/her spare time to study to learn novel company policies.

In the gamified education, while the student gained virtual badges for educational accomplishments s/he simultaneously gained beneficial knowledge and more spare time when compulsory education was completed. In the gamified training, while employee gained virtual badges for educational accomplishments, s/he just absorbed how the company's new routines should function, so in contrast with the student, the employees gained limited knowledge of a domain nor more spare time. In fiscal terms, the workers receive nothing for their additional effort; instead, s/he gave away time, while the employer received incremental profit, decreasing the assumed training-time. Even if the design pattern in one context were nudging, in another, it became sludging.

5   Discussion

As this study shows every case of implementing gamification must, therefore, be ethical consider separately, which complicates the principled analysis of gamification. There must exist an understanding of how gamification is linked to the context and how they interact. The gamification predicaments: *Unintended Activities*, *Misaligned Incentives*, *Compulsive Behavior*, and *Sludging* presented in this study could function as design heuristics that need to be considered when designing an ethical gameful experience. There have been voices highlighting the need for innovation in both business and research regarding gamification [62]. The authors of this paper agree, but at the same, we stress that a more established debate on the (un)ethical aspects of gamification, especially regarding transferring gamification design patterns amid different contexts. Dewinter et al. [63] emphasize that there are no clear boundaries in the field of gamification; what is appropriate in one context may be problematic in the other [63]. Correspondingly, as the young field of gamification is deemed multidisciplinary [9, 64] a professional gamification designer, is undoubtedly working in several different fields. Therefore, participatory design methods and approaches, such as design workshops with different stakeholders, is necessary to generate cohesiveness and uphold users' values. Nevertheless, to take the time determining what a meaningful gamification design is and what is not.

6 Conclusion

The authors of this paper endorse that the identified gamification predicaments can be perceived with two lenses:

1) The gamification practitioner lens; providing heuristic implementing designing and implementing ethical gamification.
2) The gamification researcher lens; providing research propositions for further studies in the field of gamification.

The use of creative business models and strategies involving contests, sweepstakes and gambling-like activities in social games and other online media has increased dramatically. These strategies aim to balance capitalizing on users' engagement for the mechanics inherent in gambling while not crossing the line into illegal activity but not necessarily ethics. The persuasiveness of gamblification experience mainly lies in the idea that something of monetary value is in the grasp of the player just by participate. However, in terms of learning, gamblification may not be considered a meaningful mimic of gamification as gamification-led learning experiences are not random, and neither are the rewards nor value they carry for the learners.

References

1. De Angeli, A., Brahnam, S., Wallis, P., Dix, A.: Proceedings of the CHI 2006 Workshop on Misuse and Abuse of Interactive Technologies, Montreal, Canada, pp. 1647–1650 (2006)
2. Baker, R., Walonoski, J., Heffernan, N., Roll, I., Corbett, A., Koedinger, K.: Why users engage in "gaming the system" behavior in interactive learning environments. J. Interact. Learn. Res. 19(2), 185–224 (2008). Association for the Advancement of Computing in Education (AACE), Waynesville, NC. https://www.learntechlib.org/primary/p/24328/. Accessed 11 Dec 2020
3. Deterding, S.: The lens of intrinsic skill atoms: a method for gameful design. Hum. Comput. Interact. 30(3–4), 294–335 (2015)
4. Barata, G., Gama, S., Jorge, J.A., Gonçalves, D.J.: Relating gaming habits with student performance in a gamified learning experience. In: Proceedings of the First ACM SIGCHI Annual Symposium on Computer-Human Interaction in Play - CHI PLAY 2014, pp. 17–25. ACM (2014)
5. Mullin, S.: Gamblification an overview of legal issues with gambling in social games and social media (2020). https://www.mygamecounsel.com/wp-con-tent/uploads/sites/32/2018/03/Gamblification-Article-1015.pdf
6. Hanus, M.D., Fox, J.: Assessing the effects of gamification in the classroom. Comput. Educ. 80, 152–161 (2015)

7. Marczewski, A.: User types. In: Even Ninja Monkeys Like to Play: Gamification, Game Thinking and Motivational Design, 1st edn, pp. 65–80. CreateSpace Independent Publishing Platform (2015)
8. Nicholson, S.: A RECIPE for meaningful gamification. In: Reiners, T., Wood, L.C. (eds.) Gamification in Education and Business, pp. 1–20. Springer, Cham (2015). https://doi.org/10.1007/978-3-319-10208-5_1
9. Koivisto, J., Hamari, J.: The rise of motivational information systems: a review of gamification research. Int. J. Inf. Manage. **45**, 191–210 (2019). https://doi.org/10.1016/j.ijinfomgt.2018.10.013
10. Nacke, L.E., Deterding, S.: The maturing of gamification research [editorial]. Comput. Hum. Behav. **71**, 450–454 (2017). https://doi.org/10.1016/j.chb.2016.11.062
11. Nyström, T., Stibe, A.: When persuasive technology gets dark? In: Themistocleous, M., Papadaki, M., Kamal, M.M. (eds.) EMCIS 2020. LNBIP, vol. 402, pp. 331–345. Springer, Cham (2020). https://doi.org/10.1007/978-3-030-63396-7_22
12. Landers, R.N., Bauer, K.N., Callan, R.C., Armstrong, M.B.: Psychological theory and the gamification of learning. In: Reiners, T., Wood, L.C. (eds.) Gamification in Education and Business, pp. 165–186. Springer, Cham (2015). https://doi.org/10.1007/978-3-319-10208-5_9
13. Toda, A.M., Valle, P.H.D., Isotani, S.: The dark side of gamification: an overview of negative effects of gamification in education. In: Cristea, A.I., Bittencourt, I.I., Lima, F. (eds.) HEFA 2017. CCIS, vol. 832, pp. 143–156. Springer, Cham (2018). https://doi.org/10.1007/978-3-319-97934-2_9
14. Nyström, T.: Exploring the darkness of gamification – you want it darker? In: Intelligent Computing: Proceedings of the 2021 Computing Conference. Presented at the Computing Conference 2021, London, UK, 15–16 July 2021
15. Markham, F., Young, M.: "Big gambling": the rise of the global industry-state gambling complex. Addict. Res. Theory **23**(1), 1–4 (2015). https://doi.org/10.3109/16066359.2014.929118
16. Lopez-Gonzalez, H., Griffiths, M.D.: Understanding the convergence of markets in online sports betting. Int. Rev. Sociol. Sport **53**(7), 807–823 (2018). https://doi.org/10.1177/1012690216680602
17. Macey, J., Hamari, J.: Investigating relationships between video gaming, spectating esports, and gambling. Comput. Hum. Behav. **80**, 344–353 (2018). https://doi.org/10.1016/j.chb.2017.11.027
18. Hamari, J., Keronen, L.: Why do people buy virtual goods: a meta-analysis. Comput. Hum. Behav. **71**, 59–69 (2017). https://doi.org/10.1016/j.chb.2017.01.042
19. Gainsbury, S.M., et al.: Convergence of gambling and gaming in digital media, p. 147. Victorian Responsible Gambling Foundation (2015)
20. Kim, T.W., Werbach, K.: More than just a game: ethical issues in gamification. Ethics Inf. Technol. **18**(2), 157–173 (2016). https://doi.org/10.1007/s10676-016-9401-5
21. King, D., Delfabbro, P., Griffiths, M.: The convergence of gambling and digital media: implications for gambling in young people. J. Gambl. Stud. **26**(2), 175–187 (2010). https://doi.org/10.1007/s10899-009-9153-9
22. King, D.L., Ejova, A., Delfabbro, P.H.: Illusory control, gambling, and video gaming: an investigation of regular gamblers and video game agents. J. Gambl. Stud. **28**(3), 421–435 (2012). https://doi.org/10.1007/s10899-011-9271-z
23. Toprak, P.: The psychology of control and video games. In: Ctrl-Alt-Play: Essays on Control in Video Gaming, pp. 21–33. McFarland (2013)
24. Pontes, H.M., Schivinski, B., Sindermann, C., et al.: Measurement and conceptualization of gaming disorder according to the world health organization framework: the development of the gaming disorder test. Int. J. Mental Health Addict. **19**, 508–528 (2019)

25. Petry, N.M., et al.: Cognitive-behavioral therapy for pathological gamblers. J. Consult. Clin. Psychol. **74**(3), 555–567 (2006)
26. Peters, H.: Game Theory Springer Texts in Business and Economics, 2nd edn. Springer, Heidelberg (2015).978-3-662-46950-7
27. Walliser, B.: The principles of game theory. In: Bourgine, P., Nadal, J.P. (eds.) Cognitive Economics, pp. 55–78. Springer, Heidelberg (2004)
28. Kuhn, H.W., Harsanyi, J.C., Selten, R., Weibul, J.W., van Damme, E.E.C.: The work of John Nash in game theory. J. Econ. Theory. **69**, 153–185 (1996)
29. Savage, L.: The Foundations of Statistics, 2nd edn. Dover Publications, New York (1972)
30. Harsanyi, J.: Games with incomplete information played by "Bayesian" players, I-III Part I the basic model. Manag. Sci. **14**(3), 159–182 (1967)
31. Etkin, J.: The hidden cost of personal quantification. J. Consum. Res. **42**(6), 967–984 (2016)
32. Fishbach, A., Choi, J.: When thinking about goals undermines goal pursuit. Organ. Behav. Hum. Decis. Process. **118**(2), 99–107 (2012)
33. Hutton, R.: The gamification of finance. TOPIA Can. J. Cult. Stud. **30**, 207–218 (2014)
34. Lupton, D.: Self-tracking modes: reflexive self-monitoring and data practices. In: Imminent Citizenships: Personhood and Identity Politics in the Informatic Age - Workshop. SSRN (2014)
35. Stibe, A., Cugelman, B.: Persuasive backfiring: when behavior change interventions trigger unintended negative outcomes. In: Meschtscherjakov, A., De Ruyter, B., Fuchsberger, V., Murer, M., Tscheligi, M. (eds.) PERSUASIVE 2016. LNCS, vol. 9638, pp. 65–77. Springer, Cham (2016). https://doi.org/10.1007/978-3-319-31510-2_6
36. Bjork, S., Holopainen, J.: Patterns in Game Design (Game Development Series). Charles River Media Inc., Rockland (2004)
37. Zagal, J.P., Bjork, S., Lewis, C.: Dark patterns in the design of games. In: Proceedings of the Conference on Foundations of Digital Games 2013 (2013)
38. Linehan, C., Harrer, S., Kirman, B., Lawson, S., Carter, M.: Games against health: a player-centered design philosophy. In: Proceedings of CHI EA 2015, pp. 589–600. ACM, New York (2015)
39. Goethe, O., Palmquist, A.: Broader understanding of gamification by addressing ethics and diversity. In: Stephanidis, C., et al. (eds.) HCII 2020. LNCS, vol. 12425, pp. 688–699. Springer, Cham (2020). https://doi.org/10.1007/978-3-030-60128-7_50
40. Huotari, K., Hamari, J.: Defining gamification - a service marketing perspective. In: Proceedings of the International Academic MindTrek Conference, pp. 17–22 (2012)
41. Heijden, H.: User acceptance of hedonic information system. MIS Q. **28**, 695–704 (2004). https://doi.org/10.2307/25148660
42. Wu, J., Lu, X.: Effects of Extrinsic and Intrinsic Motivators on Using Utilitarian, Hedonic, and Dual-Purposed Information Systems: A Meta-Analysis. J. Assoc. Inf. Syst. **14**, 153–191 (2013). https://doi.org/10.17705/1jais.00325
43. Arnab, S., et al.: Mapping learning and game mechanics. Br. J. Educ. Technol. **46**, 391–411 (2015). https://doi.org/10.1111/bjet.12113
44. Morschheuser, B., Hamari, J., Werder, K., Abe, J.: How to gamify? A method for designing gamification (2017). https://doi.org/10.24251/HICSS.2017.155
45. Argilés, F.T.: Yu-Kai Chou (2016). Actionable gamification: beyond points, badges and leader-boards. Octalysis Media: Fremont. AC. Int. J. Organ. (18), 137–144 (2017). https://doi.org/10.17345/rio18.137-144
46. Zichermann, G., Cunningham, C.: Gamification by Design: Implementing Game Mechanics in Web and Mobile Apps. O'Reilly Media, Sebastopol (2011)
47. Hassan, L., Morschheuser, B., Alexan, N., Hamari, J.: First-hand experience of why gamification projects fail and what to do about it (2018)

48. Palmquist, A., Linderoth, J.: Gamification does not belong at a university. In: Proceedings of the 2020 DiGRA Conference, Tampere (2020, in press)
49. Wixom, B.H., Todd, P.A.: A theoretical integration of user satisfaction and technology acceptance. Inf. Syst. Res. **16**(1), 85–102 (2015)
50. Richter, G., Raban, D.R., Rafaeli, S.: Studying gamification: the effect of rewards and incentives on motivation. In: Reiners, T., Wood, L.C. (eds.) Gamification in Education and Business, pp. 21–46. Springer, Cham (2015). https://doi.org/10.1007/978-3-319-10208-5_2
51. Sepehr, S., Marie, M.: Competition as an element of gamification for learning: an exploratory longitudinal investigation. In: Proceedings of the First International Conference on Gameful Design, Research, and Applications, pp. 2–9 (2017)
52. Vorderer, P., Hartmann, T., Klimmt, C.: Explaining the enjoyment of playing video games: the role of competition. In: Proceedings of the Second International Conference on Entertainment Computing (2003)
53. Sun, Y.Y., Zhao, Y., Jia, S., Zheng, D.: Understanding the antecedents of mobile game addiction: the roles of perceived visibility, perceived enjoyment and flow. In: Proceedings of the Pacific Asia Conference on Information Systems, p. 141 (2015)
54. Chou, T., Ting, C.: The role of flow experience in cyber-game addiction. Cyber Psychol. Behav. **6**(6), 663–675 (2004)
55. Jeong, E.J., Lee, H.R.: Addictive use due to personality: focused on Big Five personality traits and game addiction. Int. J. Soc. Behav. Educ. Econ. Bus. Ind. Eng. **9**, 1995–1999 (2015)
56. Heinonen, K.: Consumer activity in social media: managerial approaches to consumers' social media behavior. J. Consum. Behav. **10**(6), 356–364 (2011)
57. Lieberoth, A., Jensen, N.H., Skovgaard, T., Bredahl, T.V.G.: Differential effects of gamification, nudging and rational information on travel behavior: a field experiment. In: Game Scope (2016)
58. Holler, M.J.: Paternalism, gamification, or art: an introductory note. Homo Oeconomicus **32**(2), 275–283 (2015)
59. Thaler, R.H., Sunstein, C.R.: Nudge: Improving Decisions About Health, Wealth, and Happiness. Yale University Press, New Haven (2008)
60. Kahneman, D., Tversky, A.: Prospect theory: an analysis of decision under risk. Econometrica **47**, 263–291 (1979)
61. Thaler, R.H.: Nudge, not sludge. Science **361**, 431 (2018)
62. Raftopoulos, M.: Has gamification failed, or failed to evolve? Lessons from the frontline in information systems applications. In: CEUR Workshop Proceedings, vol. 2637, pp. 21–30 (2020)
63. Dewinter, J., Kocurek, C., Nichols, R.: Taylorism 2.0: gamification, scientific management and the capitalist appropriation of play. J. Gaming Virtual Worlds **6**(2), 109–127 (2014)
64. O'Donnell, N., Kappen, D., Fitz-Walter, Z., Deterding, S., Nacke, L., Johnson, D.: How multidisciplinary is gamification research? Results from a scoping review (2017)

Game Design, Creativity and e-Learning: The Challenges of Beginner Level Immersive Language Learning Games

Tiago Barros Pontes e Silva[1]([✉]) [iD], Raquel Pereira Pacheco[1] [iD],
Mariana da Silva Lima[1] [iD], Mauricio Miranda Sarmet[2] [iD],
Maria Luísa de Carvalho Cascelli de Azevedo[1] [iD],
Vitor Henrique Malcher Ferreira[2] [iD], and Carla Denise Castanho[1] [iD]

[1] University of Brasília, Brasília, Brazil
tiagobarros@unb.br
[2] Federal Institute of Education, Science and Technology of Paraíba, Paraíba, Brazil

Abstract. Games have been used for a variety of educational purposes. The immersive nature of games, however, becomes a challenge when the goal is to promote language learning for beginners. In this sense, this research investigates the key strategies for using games in the context of a foreign language learning course for beginners. Specifically, this study is being carried out in partnership with the Brazil-Finland Cultural Center (CCBF) and it aims to improve student engagement in learning Portuguese as foreign language in a distance learning modality. The research was organized in two stages: A diagnostic, that aims to understand the experience and the needs with the current edition of the course; and an interventionist, that seeks the student engagement and learning by the introduction of digital mini games as complementary teaching material. Therefore, the challenges identified in the first stage and some possible ways to address them with the second were presented as results. The next steps involve an evaluation of the first generation of games, which must follow iterative cycles until reaching the idealized solution. Although it was not feasible to implement all the raised attributes in these first versions, we understand that those characteristics are central to expanding the agency of teachers and students in the learning process and should guide the evolution of this platform.

Keywords: Game design · e-learning · Learning games · Language acquisition

1 Introduction: Remote Learning for Language Acquisition

There are various reasons for learning a foreign language. As migration has been more and more common, the need of learning a new language goes from being able to communicate in a new country, for work or educational purpose or even as leisure. Migration can also happen for family, work, education and refuge, in which immigrants search for stability and safety (Fritz and Donat 2017).

© Springer Nature Switzerland AG 2021
X. Fang (Ed.): HCII 2021, LNCS 12790, pp. 256–275, 2021.
https://doi.org/10.1007/978-3-030-77414-1_19

Language is one of the key manifestations of a culture (Van Der Veer and Valsiner 2001) Being able to master a certain language broadens possibilities of access to knowledge, job prospects and social integration in professional and personal situations (Bednarz 2017). Not only language aids in content but also in context and meaning making. A new language opens the door to changes in cultural identity and reinforced the idea of global citizenship. In this article we are going to explore the other side of migration: how does a member of the residing country can grasp an immigrant friend's or partner's culture?

Language acquisition in adults is a very different process from language acquisition in children. Adult learning principles must be taken into account, with a more practical and contextualized approach to language learning. Participatory methods are praised for their proximity to concerns and need of individual learners, as well as giving autonomy to understand their own learning outcomes and build their own path. Adults are motivated by learning what is most relevant for them, therefore, mapping topics of interest and practicing authentic speech around them is a great pedagogical strategy. Most contexts aim for a mother-tongue based dual language approach, however, there are a few cases when that is not possible (Nieuwboer and Rood 2017).

A noticeable trend in adult language learning is remote learning. There are synchronous and asynchronous options, some with a very structured curriculum, activities and evaluations, and others with the primary objective of making practice the easiest. Beyond traditional courses offered online, there are games, services for exchanging letters, and informal conversation platforms. Most language online courses offer a predominant individual experience, activities which used to be printed and filled by the learner in a physical classroom become a virtual version of the task, without actually embracing and exploring the full potential of a classroom that can be anywhere and anytime, without borders (Schiepers *et al.* 2017). Even in remote learning, there's still the need of offering social experiences and cultural exchange as a way to contextualize learning.

There are a few studies that discuss what should be the language learning experience for an adult (Schiepers *et al.* 2017):

1. Repetition and practice in challenges connected to learners needs.
2. Diversify authentic input in target language, utilizing written and spoken resources, as well as videos, newspapers and music.
3. Perform meaningful tasks connected to real life application.
4. Learner control in skills, difficulty and complexity of challenges.
5. Immediate and individualized feedback.
6. Access to a social space for interaction.
7. Easy access and accessibility for people of various income, social classes, education and digital literacy.

From these items we can infer that language learning (a) needs to challenge the learner with experiences that can be translated to the real world, as well as (b) creates a space for social interaction and also (c) offers opportunities of authentic language output. In this perspective, we understand that games become a relevant opportunity as complementary teaching material to foster those strategies. Thereat, considering their potential to increase motivation and fascinate students at different ages, games have already been used for a variety of educational purposes. The immersive nature of games, however, becomes also a challenge when the goal is to promote language learning for beginners. Therefore, this research investigates the key strategies for using games in the context of a foreign language learning course for beginners. Specifically, this study is being carried out in partnership with the Brazil-Finland Cultural Center (CCBF) and it aims to improve student engagement in learning Portuguese as foreign language in a distance learning modality.

2 Games as Learning Facilitators

Gamified education has already demonstrated its potential. In this article we adopt the *gamification* approach in broader terms: as implementing game elements in non-game scenarios, like game mechanics or achievement systems; but also, as using games themselves as teaching tools, whether they have been designed or not for this purpose. When applied to educational contexts, both these methods have the potential to promote more learner engagement. When the learning experience is mixed with a gamified experience, a combination of extrinsic and intrinsic motivation through game context can make learning more meaningful. It is possible to go beyond applying knowledge. For that to happen, the gamified experience must aim to provide an ecosystem where the learner can build his or her knowledge focusing on learning tasks in context rather than repeating content (Palomino et al. 2019a, 2019b; Toda *et al.* 2019). Applied to language acquisition, this could immerse the player in the new language by focusing on practical aspects of the language rather than grammar.

Toda *et al.* (2019) cite game elements in their gamification taxonomy in 5 categories:

- **Performance:** elements related to environment response and feedback, such as Points, Progression, Level, Stats and Acknowledgement.
- **Ecological:** elements related to the context and environment of the gamified experience, such as Chance (randomness, luck or probability), Imposed choice, Economy, Rarity and Time Pressure.
- **Social:** elements related to interactions between players, such as Competition, Cooperation, Reputation and Social Pressure.
- **Personal:** elements related to the player, such as Sensation, Objective, Novelty and Renovation (boosts or extra lives).
- **Fictional:** mixed dimension related to the user and environment, which unifies the user experience with the game context. In this dimension there are Narrative and Storytelling.

With these elements in mind, it is necessary to make a brief description of the status of gamified education. Formal Education itself already presents a few of these elements, the most common being the traditional PBL (Point-Badge-Leaderboard) approach. We can observe these elements in apps such as Duolingo (which focused on foreign language learning), Kahoot (which serves as a support for classroom activities) and even in websites such as CodeAcademy (which provides free and paid coding courses) and

Khan Academy (which also provides free and paid courses of various themes and disciplines). Most of the elements present in these examples are related to the categories Performance, Ecological, Social and Personal. The Fictional category, however, hasn't been explored in mainstream gamified apps and learning experiences (Palomino *et al.* 2019a; 2019b).

In language learning the storytelling and narrative dimensions offer a unique perspective for the learners to internalize words and expressions. We define **storytelling** as the sequence of events that happen in a story, and the **narrative** as the way this story is told. Everything in the learning experience can contribute directly to shape this narrative experience and create an immersive experience. The content then can be very contextualized, which in turn makes the learning experience more meaningful, as stated before (Palomino *et al.* 2019a).

Narratives shape the way we construct reality. They are culturally transmitted and mediated by symbols and language alike. They also distribute intelligence in a network pattern. We tell stories to remember, to teach, to dream. For Bruner (1991), narratives have the attribute of establishing dialogues, they are versions of reality that need have their meaning and interpretation negotiated by both parties. It is the way we experience culture and create shared meaning and is also the way we can create meaningful learning (Newman 2005).

Agency, autonomy and authorship are the combination of the Fictional dimension and adult learning principles. More than repetition, it is necessary to provide experiences that the learners can transform and create meaning that goes beyond of what was first proposed. Games can create emergent narratives – narratives that are created by the user choices or actions. These narratives are personalized experiences that can be created in a number of different ways and is what we aim to find as a newfound path for foreign language learning experiences from this research.

3   Case Study: Portuguese as Foreign Language Course

The research opportunity arose from a demand to improve the Portuguese as a foreign language course offered by the Brazil-Finland Cultural Center (CCBF). In recent years, the Center has offered the course in person in Helsinki. The classes were held in the Center's facilities. In 2019, a migration to a virtual edition of the course was organized, aiming to reach a larger audience of students in Finland. In the process, the teachers produced and adapted the official content for the remote modality, making most of the learning experience asynchronous. For this, the online course platform Claned was chosen. It allows the presentation of content in several formats, like texts, pictures and videos, as well as incorporates external plugins to perform more specialized exercises, such as the use of H5P for proposing rich and interactive internet content in HTML5. Also, it highlights some of the students' analytics about their progression through the course (completed content and exercises feedback). With the platform migration, the pedagogic team had specialized trainings, as how to create video contents and how to act in front of cameras. The trainings occurred through a partnership with the Aalto University.

We understand this as a relevant opportunity because it was not a simple adoption of an already consolidated perspective on distance education that separates the roles of content writer, tutor and the responsible teacher for the discipline, with all the associated issues of impersonality (Umekawa and Zerbini 2015). This new edition focused on the careful monitoring of students and the enhancement of interactivity as a learning tool in the same way as they did in the classroom course. Therefore, as the entire team gets involved in all stages of the process – the creation of content, the class monitoring, the assessments, the feedback providing, and the synchronous activities, it became onerous compared to traditional models of online teaching. It now demands the teacher's attention continuously in order to keep the class engaged with the activities and in frequent communication with their colleagues. This presented a scaling challenge for future editions of the online course.

The investigation started at this time, seeking to understand how students interacted with each other during classes and how they engaged with the learning process. In addition, it aims to study whether it would be possible to add asynchronous modules such as digital mini games to the new edition of the course in order to stimulate the students' commitment and learning, considering Hung *et al.* (2018) suggestions on the effects of using games on language acquisition. Only one edition of the remote course had been held up to this point.

3.1 Research Methods

As previously discussed, this study is being carried out in partnership with the Brazil-Finland Cultural Center (CCBF). To investigate the student's engagement in the new distance learning course, the research team consisted of nine members: Three research professors in the areas of Computer Science, Psychology and Design, a Master of Education, a Bachelor of Linguistics and Literature, two Bachelors of Design and two undergraduate students in Computer Engineering.

The research was organized in two stages: Diagnostic and interventionist, inspired by the ergonomic approach (Guérin *et al.* 2001). The former aims to understand the experience with the current edition of the course; and the latter seeks to promote student engagement and learning by the introduction of digital mini games as complementary teaching material. This chapter addresses the first stage, and the second is described by the next chapter.

The research design consisted of a qualitative approach (Flick 2008) inspired by ethnographic methods (Flick, 2008; O'reilly 2012) that aimed to understand the participants motives and contradictions about their roles, especially regarding the changes related to the new edition of the course. Also, the team adopted the ergonomic approach (see Guérin *et al.* 2001; Abrahão *et al.* 2009) grounded in Activity Theory (see Leont'ev 1978; Engeström 1999) to understand the prescribed tasks and the organization of labor from each participant's perspective, as well as to elucidate the elements that constitute their activity in a real context.

With that in mind, the participants' backgrounds, motivations, strategies and struggles with the new modality were acknowledged. For that to happen, it was necessary to adopt several techniques with procedural flexibility (Guérin *et al.* 2001; Abrahão *et al.* 2009) to elucidate the distinctive perspectives of the participants, such as the combination of semi-structured interviews and global observations. Also, the team used shared boards to represent the main raised issues. This allowed the formulation of new interpretations to be validated by the participants in a cyclical process. The boards were created and shared using the Miro online collaboration software.

The procedure started with a negotiation with the CCBF and the Brazilian Ministry of Foreign Affairs with representatives from different hierarchical levels of public management. The team then made a technical visit to Finland in 2019 for the initial observations and interviews with the course organizers. This step meant to explain the context of the course creation, the experience with its presential version, expectations regarding its results and the future expansion of the course to other Cultural Centers.

During the same visit all the environment and support structure used for the previous editions of the course, as well the new remote edition, was observed, following the ergonomic orientation (Guérin *et al.* 2001) for an understanding of the organization of labor and all the involved constraints. Additionally, teachers and students from previous editions were approached at events promoted by the Cultural Center in Finland. This initial exploration sought to contextualize the new course and allow a global view of how the different stakeholders articulated themselves to conduct the course.

The next stage addressed the general coordinator of the Cultural Center (n = 1), the coordinator of the presential and distance courses (n = 1) and the teachers who produced content and guided the online classes (n = 4). This was the main stage of the diagnosis process, dedicated to understanding the proponents' perspective of the course and the controversy around the new tools. The script for the interviews was organized in three parts, with questions about the course, the teachers and the students, respectively. Some matters demanded a deeper investigation and further discussions with the participants. In general, each initial interview session lasted about two hours. Although the script was not strictly followed, being adapted for each profile and modified according to the responses, the main covered topics are described below.

Concerning the course, we asked what were the reasons for the migration from the presential to the remote version; what is their standpoint of the entire process; who were the people involved with the migration; what were the main practices that were transposed to the remote modality; how is the use of the platform; why they made the decision for the use of English instead of Finish as the support language; how is the selection of supplementary technologies; how was the new content production process; what are the expectations about the remote version; what were the main difficulties they faced; and also the positive aspects of the first experience with the new edition.

We asked the teachers for their background (from their academic and professional training to how they got involved with the course); how is their daily life in Finland; their experience with presential and online teaching; how is the communication process with the other teachers and with the course coordinator (technologies and periodicity); what are the teachers' formal assignments; and what really happens in practice in their work routine; how they feel about these processes; how the learning assessment occurs; and what is the level of autonomy of the teachers in performing these tasks.

We also asked about the students' profile from the previous versions of the presential course and the first online edition; who else they intend to reach with this new modality; what are the main interaction opportunities with the students; what are the ignition points of these processes; how is the student engagement; what are the main perceived cultural dissimilarities; how it affects the course dynamics; how the socialization among students and between teacher and students occurs; how is the students' proactivity towards events; what is the attitude of students in the online course and what are the differences for the classroom previous version.

After these initial interviews another discussion round was held with the course coordinator and teacher to analyze the process of creating practical exercises from the original content. The intention was to understand in detail the main strategies and difficulties in imagining possible training solutions for the students that were linked to the official content of the course. We aim to use this moment to understand the way the teachers evoked previous experiences with the face-to-face and remote editions of the course to suggest potential actions, motivations and themes that enabled the training of specific skills. In addition, this step allowed the validation of the reports of experiences with the students, emphasizing how they deal with cultural differences and the approaches that most promoted student engagement.

Moreover, complementary studies were also performed seeking to foster the forthcoming interventions, based on the proposition of online mini games for the students. First, a desk review was made to ensure an understanding of the official content for the first teaching modules of Portuguese as foreign language. Also, the team analyzed the current version of the course and the platform Claned to comprehend the opportunities and constraints for the future actions. After that, a survey of specialized literature in distance learning, educational games and foreign languages acquisition was done.

Concluding the survey phase, a questionnaire was applied to a group of students (n = 35) of the current edition of the online course to assess an appropriate representational language, compatible with the cultural differences between the two countries – the team from Brazil and the students from Finland. Five types of illustration were added to the instrument, which sought the greatest affinity in terms of visual language for the course in the student's opinion. For each figure, a five-point scale was presented, anchored at the extremes as "not suitable at all" and "entirely suitable". An open question at the end allowed the students to share any other observations regarding the visual style of the illustrations for the online environment.

We also highlight that most of the research happened in 2020, the year the coronavirus pandemic started. This had a huge effect on the research procedures. Not only it affected the interviews, conducted remotely from Brazil, but it also affected the team's organization in planning the research, collecting and analyzing the data, which also had to be done at a distance due to the necessary social isolation in Brazil.

3.2 First Results and Discussion: Challenges and Opportunities

From the previously described procedures of the qualitative research, we emphasize some of the most relevant understandings and challenges for beginner level immersive language learning games. One of the most evident findings was the teachers' need for the learning objects to behave as digital responsive tools that focuses on communication and self-expression in contextualized situations. This means that games should seek to represent situations close to real contexts, in which the effectiveness of communication should be the main focus of the students. This does not mean that realistic or figurative representations are more suitable. Rather, it means that students should be challenged to solve relevant communicational problems in order to appropriate the didactic contents and adapt them to the situation (Paz 2006). The focus of the training is on their production. The communication strategies are the ones that should have the potential to be transposed to the students' reality (Santos 2010). Therefore, we understand games embrace this opportunity as cultural products that offer circumscribed human experiences, providing feedback to the culture itself (Salen and Zimmerman 2004), which in turn is shaped by language. As Salen and Zimmerman (2004) suggest, the Huizinga's (1950) magic circle is accessed from the outside in, but it also returns to the external environment the internally produced meanings, as a model of open culture.

Furthermore, training should take place in a structural way when communicating, not only by artificially reproducing translations, but by creating a repertoire that also incorporates syntaxes, expressions and other inseparable cultural elements. Consequently, the main abilities that should be trained are speaking, listening, writing, and reading as means of communicating. In other words, the action of playing the game must relate to the understanding and self-expression in written and spoken language.

This challenge also relates to inherent issues of the game development: optimizing the amount of offered content and the feeling of freedom of choice by the players. This can be unraveled by the narrative structure with convex choices, as suggested by Rabin (2005). But even with simpler games, we believe that the main question remains as how to approach the game design process, relating the learning strategy with its most structural elements: its narrative and action space, as suggested by Ferreira *et al.* (2019). In this approach, the fundamental elements of the game that guide the design process – Aesthetics, Mechanics, Story and Technology (Schell 2008) should be considered in the same level as the Learning Strategy (Winn 2009), added as a fifty element for the serious game design processes. Besides that, it should be placed at the same structural level of the players actions and progressions in the Schell's tetrad: The Mechanics and the Story (Ferreira *et al.* 2019; Schell 2008), that are reinforced by the game *stimuli* (Aesthetics – more visible) and supported by the appropriate Technology (less visible dimension of the game). This perspective is opposed to the superficial approach for serious games and gamification systems that simply create artificial relations between the essence of the game and the learning process, making them become meaningless repetitions. In summary: the learning content must match how you learn to play the game itself (see Fig. 1).

From that perspective, it is also possible to associate the explicit communication strategies to the students' motivations for language acquisition. We believe that making this association visible to students could not only guide the learning process (Vygotsky 2001), but also make the gaming experience more engaging by evoking its internal meaning (Schell 2008). Hence, the choice of narratives to contextualize the language use could also be related to the students' interests and desires, making the process more meaningful to them. Games have high potential to more easily associate educational content with their contexts of use, a relevant quality for language learning processes. In this sense, the articulations between internal elements of the games and the students' reality become an opportunity to promote engagement, as it can act precisely at the students' motivations.

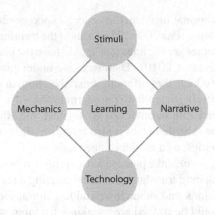

Fig. 1. The fundamental elements of the game that guide the design process (adapted from Schell 2008) combined with the Learning Strategy (adapted from Winn 2009) for the serious game design processes, added as a fifty element in the structural level. Adapted from Ferreira *et al.* (2019).

Another interesting aspect of the ludic approach is the perspective of the game itself: students operate within a universe that allows them to make mistakes with tranquility, making the errors become part of the learning process (Huizinga 1950). For this, it is necessary to create a system that encourages the students to return to the game, increasing its repeatability factor reinforcing the training but changing other elements that could make the experience still meaningful. Palomino *et al.* (2019a) reflects on procedural content generation to allow replayability, and multiple possibilities of narrative creation and interference.

All these requirements were frequently expressed during the interviews when the coordinator and teachers felt a lack of interactivity with the students, as well as between the students and with the pedagogical contents too. The teachers felt the need for more autonomy, as well as when in person, when the teacher can observe the student's behavior in search of feedback and eagerly adapt the narrative to a more interesting topic for the students, adjusting in real time the approach to the content according to the students' attention level. This factor might be increased by the cultural distinctions between the teacher and students and also by the different students' motivations (Pöyhönen and Tarnanen 2015). In this regard, it was discussed that the digital tools could demonstrate some level of personalization, allowing teachers to adjust it according to the class profile or any other situated conversation making the process more relevant to each group of students.

With that, we realized that one of the biggest changes regarding the course modality was the loss of the teachers' autonomy in relation to the didactic strategies for each class. It happens because in the asynchronous version of the course, the contents and exercises need to be prepared in advance and made available to the students. Therefore, the team considered appropriate that the games allow, in addition to a minimum level of configuration, the possibility of personalization for groups or individuals. This would allow games to have more relevance, possibly impacting its longevity and increasing their replayability potential, serving as more useful tools for teachers in a broader range of scenarios. In contrast, this preparation should not be time consuming and should not require any extra knowledge of digital game development tools.

In addition, the need for an initial vocabulary repertoire and the absence of a content mediator requires the use of an adequate graphic language to assist the students. Even with graphic support, direct translation of some of the terms was necessary for beginners, interfering with the game interface. Addressing the issue in more depth, when teaching languages, exercise commands and instructions purposefully written in target expressions can significantly help students to internalize words. However, if the Design team are not used to the fundamentals of teaching, it is easily misleading to write one of those. That happens because words and expressions that seem simple for a native speaker can turn out to be complex for beginner students (level A2 or lower, based on the Common European Framework of Reference for Languages).

It is common practice for the teacher to add a new word to one in every few instructions, to enhance language acquisition. However, if written by an inexperienced professional, the instruction can end up being more difficult than the content being taught or practiced. If the student is faced with complex structures and new vocabulary words, the teacher might invest a long time expatiating on the meaning of that sentence, which can stall the didactic structure of the class. In order to avoid it, tutors usually choose to translate the sentence. This deprives students of the precious time they could have spent acquiring the language if the instruction was either written in their mother tongue or described in an understandable manner for their level. As Halliday (1966) puts it, "given the right conditions one can make positive use of the student's mother tongue; and in such cases to neglect it may be to throw away one of the tools best adapted to the task in hand."

With this in mind, the team considered relevant to both add new words or translate when applicable. *Id est*, based on the experience of English language teachers, we used instructions in Portuguese (the target language) when it was feasible and presented translations to an understandable language (English) when the sentence structure was too advanced for that level. That way, we suggest the stimulation of language acquisition based on meaningful uses while, at the same time, the reduction of anxiety when trying to understand the main objectives of the game.

The use of English as a translation language was not a decision based on didactic grounds, but a requisite from the context. Not all teachers who currently work at CCBF are fluent in their students' native language (Finnish). Since this could lead to some ambiguous or equivocal explanations, they use English when they need to avoid using Portuguese structures that are too complex for the level of the students.

Despite the switching of languages being not an obstacle to game development per se, it might become a struggle as the team is envisioning an online platform that can be reached by thousands of people, requiring only the internet and a digital device. Since the objective of the project is to be scalable for other countries and Cultural Centers, it is relevant to ask oneself what is the influence of using a third language as a mediator between the target and native languages. Taking our case in mind, we can already note significant distancing between them. For instance, using the dichotomous reference (stress-timed and syllable-timed) of the classification of languages based on their rhythm (James 1940; Abercrombie 1967), it is interesting to note that both Portuguese and Finnish are considered to be syllable-timed while English is stress-timed. Taking that into consideration, we cannot know for sure how switching to a stressed-timed language (English) can affect learning when both your native language (Finnish) and target language (Portuguese) are syllable-timed.

It is important to note that a few linguists (Dauer 1983; Bertinetto 1989; Barry *et al.* 2003; and others) consider the rhythm of languages to be an outdated reference for classifications, with some even arguing that Finnish presents characteristics of both groups (Sajavaara and Dufva 2001). However, it does not invalidate the claim that the three aforementioned languages are different. Studies based on genetic comparison of population place Germanic (English), Finnic (Finnish), and Romance (Portuguese) in very distant positions (Harding and Sokal 1988). In addition, classifying languages deriving from the proto-language Indo-European, based on the study of linguistic reconstruction (Fennell, Barbara A.; 2001), theorizes a similar distance. While Portuguese and English derive from the Latin and Germanic families respectively, two very distinctive branches, Finnish is so peculiar in its etymological structure that it is considered by the author as part of a separate branch, not even derived from the proto-language Indo-European tree. Other scholars comment on how uncertain the positioning of Finnish is in the attempts of placing it in a family tree, although it is certain it does not belong to either Latin or Germanic branches (Marcantonio 2002).

With that, we are faced with the foreshadowing of an obstacle. Although in the described project it was not a restrictive point, using a third language as a mediator might lead to language barrier limits. Not knowing the students' mother tongue fluently is a real situation in several countries and it is exponentially more likely to happen if the teaching is placed online. While the Finnish students of CCBF are fluent in English, we cannot guarantee students from future benefited language centers will be. Using only Portuguese, the target language, can lead to previously discussed problems. A possible solution is to require a language localization person or team, based in the area of future centers, in order to provide accurate translations in their mother language and optimize the platform to receive new language inputs without the need of the development team.

The difficulty level of the game was another point of attention for the team. When designing a game, it is important to consider challenges and rewards as tools for the intricate balance of engagement that is called flow. Flow is first defined by researcher Mihaly Csikszentmihalyi (2000) as a state of consciousness of deep focus and emotional involvement, a concept envisioned and widespread to the field of Game Design by Chen (2007).

"[…] when your ability matches really well to a particular challenge you can enter the flow state. If your skill is much greater than the challenge offered by a given activity, you'll be bored. If your skill is far below the level of the challenge provided, you'll be frustrated. Or, as in the case of rock climbing and other dangerous activities, you'll be anxious. […] Video games especially have numerous advantages in creating and maintaining flow, such as providing clear goals; a limited stimulus field; and direct, immediate feedback." (Swink 2009).

However, when designing a serious game for educational or instructional purposes, it is of extreme importance to keep in mind that this formula has to be applied with attention. Beyond the distress already embedded in learning the mechanics of a game, learning how to play a game while also learning a language brings new intrinsic hardships. Namely, the player is not only faced with the struggles and challenges of the game itself, but also with limited comprehension of the text presented. In this sense, game designers have no control over the player's level of proficiency in the target language, but they do have on the game mechanics. Thus, adjusting the game difficulty can help serious game designers achieve an adequate balance of struggles to keep the game interesting and not frustrating.

It was also considered a challenge to provide a complete freedom of expression to the students in view of the boundaries inherent to closed systems, such as games. In this case, the possibility of content production by the students themselves was considered an exciting path to explore, despite not viable at the moment. It could enhance the students' interactions in terms of complexity and emergence, being useful to insert contextualized content to the games. It would be opportune that the act of playing the games is an effort taken advantage of by the system itself to stimulate its own growth. This could be possible with tasks that guide the students to insert language elements recognizable by the system, for example, the inclusion of nouns related to a given theme, with images, descriptions and related translations. These new elements could be used by students in narrative compositions within the game environment, attributing the assessment of its contextual meaning to the exercises.

Finally, the main challenge of the suggested approach is to control the system's scalability, since it needs to be customizable by teachers and students in different classes, courses, or even in different countries. To learn how to improve the system and to understand the students' behavior, the team considered that some indicators are also needed to monitor the performance of the class. This data should be useful for different groups: By the students themselves as a part of the learning process; for the teachers' assessments; and also, to provide further data through analytics to future research and game design processes.

In summary, the main challenges about the use of language learning games identified in this research are: The games must bring the practice closer to the context of language use; and the gameplay should train language skills (speaking, listening, writing and reading). To do that, the students must solve specific communicational situations; meaning that the practice is about to use their own repertoire to develop a way of communicating. Also, the use of games is an opportunity to link practices to students' motivations, in order to make the experience more meaningful to them. Besides, games should encourage interactions between teachers, students and content; always considering the game perspective: making mistakes with ease and making mistakes to learn. The training should not be boring and bureaucratic, encouraging students to return (replayability); and the game difficulty should be balanced accordingly to the role of a serious game: learning the game must not mislead the language learning process. In order to do that, the games must be flexible to promote autonomy for the teacher in the content creation and also when conducing the classes. Optimizations on the content creation by teachers and students are welcome and could be used as a source of unpredictability and emergence in gameplay. The system must be designed as a scalable model in terms of the number of students, parallel courses and staff; developed with responsive techniques that do not have high performance hardware requirements. As the games will be developed from scratch, the research team could also embrace the opportunity to develop analytics mechanisms that allow the performance monitoring of the class and also to carry out further studies.

4 Game Design: Negotiating with Reality

4.1 The Game Design Process

The game design process took place with the full team of researchers. It followed a mixed model inspired by the Double Diamond presented by the Design Council (2005), internally organized according to Simon and Newell's problem-solving approach (1971) and Simon's Design Science (1981), as suggested by Pontes e Silva (2015a,2015b), where the design activity is understood as an incremental heuristic search through a problem space with divergent (analysis) and convergent (synthesis) cycles (see Fig. 2).

In addition, the game conception was guided by the game design fundamentals, as suggested by Ferreira *et al.* (2019), which adopts Schell's elemental tetrad (2008) incorporating the Learning Strategies as a central component, following the suggestion of Winn (2009). Notwithstanding the game's several distinct components, the MDA framework of Hunicke *et al.* (2004) was also adopted, organizing the game creation process from the intended aesthetic experience to the components' specifications, seeking to orchestrate its integrality. They were organized following Winn's (2009) perspective of Design, Play and Experience (see Fig. 3).

That summarizes the different combined approaches to the organization of the game design process. For more information about the development and evaluation cycles of its initial interfaces, see Silva Lima *et al.* (2020). As in the previous stage, the Miro software was used for the remote game design due to the social isolation caused by the pandemic of the new coronavirus. The entire process was repeated for the development of each game.

At this time, two games were concluded from a total of ten planned games for the first two modules of the course. The games were developed using Strapi (Headless CMS), MongoDB for the databank with the MongoDB online service, hosted on Heroku and tested online with CI/CD (Continuous Integration/Continuous Deployment) for the back-end. For the front-end the development team used React.js, hosted on GitHub and tested online via Github Pages.

Regarding the ideation stages of the process, the deliverables were organized as follows. Initially, the official didactic content to be addressed by the game was specified. It was associated with possible topics of interest (becoming the game's high concept), validated by the coordinator and teacher, as described in the previous stage. Then, a sub-team was responsible for detailing the game's progression structure associated with a core loop mechanic cycle that corresponded to the learning strategy defined for that content. This result is documented as a progression/action flow, and eventually with low-fidelity wireframes to detail any specific scene. Jointly, the software architecture was defined to organize its main components into smaller functionalities, verifying their suitability level with use cases.

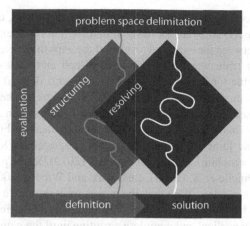

Fig. 2. Design process as an incremental heuristic search through a problem space, where the structuring stages result in a better definition of the problem and the resolving stage search for possible configurations to the specific deliverable as an abductive process. The solution is understood as an integral artifact with all the defined attributes from the structuring stage. Adapted from Pontes e Silva (2015a, b).

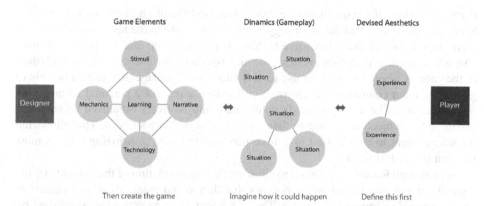

Fig. 3. Organization of the game specification process: first prioritizing the intended experience, then defining the game situations that could foster them; and only after that working on the different components of the game. To this end, a fifth element was added to the fundamental pillars of the serious games: and learning contents and strategies. Adapted from Ferreira *et al.* (2019).

With the structural stage initiated, the other work fronts took place in parallel. The complete asset survey was carried out in a list and then organized by format (illustrations, verbal sentences and interface elements). From this list, the other teams proceeded with the illustrations' drawings and the preparation of the written material. Meanwhile, another sub-team was responsible for specifying what would be the most appropriate feedbacks for students in the learning process, as well as the reports provided to teachers on the use of games. Also, this team defined the most relevant variables for conducting a survey via game analytics to investigate the association between the use of games and the students' engagement. Still, another team specified the high-fidelity wireframes, which were gradually replaced by the produced assets. At certain times, these surfaces were modeled using Adobe XD software for navigation tests. This moment was substantial to ensure consistency between the expected result and the gaps that arise during production.

The development team was organized in front-end and back-end groups. While the first was responsible for implementing all the elements defined in the high-fidelity wireframe, the second programed all the internal functionalities of the system, such as the main methods, database, etc. After the first developed versions, an intrinsic evaluation was carried out on the interfaces in search of the most evident usability and playability problems based on the joint use of the parameters suggested by Kumar *et al.* (2019) usability guidelines for mobile learning; Jahnke *et al.* (2019) Design principles for mobile microlearning; and Pinelle *et al.* (2008), Desurvire and Wiberg (2009), and Jerzak and Rebelo (2014) game heuristics. With that, the games went through a review process and the main hypotheses for the user's test were formulated as an extrinsic evaluation. The process continued in a cyclical and cumulative routine until the games were considered suitable for their inclusion as complementary material in a future edition of the online course. After that, the further research should continue with the analytics approach.

4.2 Beginner Level Immersive Language Learning Games

From the results of the qualitative research stage and the discussions with the Design team, we understand that the main suggestion to contribute to the investigated environment must be an adaptive expansive system. This conception encompasses four main characteristics that reach their greatest potential together. The first one comprehends that, in the context where the students use several educational games, they should be able to gather the main content of the games as collectable assets for a personal record. This documentation, like a diary or study notebook, could be freely organized by students, grouping the subjects according to their own interest or study strategy. This allows the didactic content to be accessed in a more personalized way, prioritizing what is most relevant for each student.

As a second feature, in addition to allowing this appropriation of the contents by the students, it was considered an opportunity that they could create their own objects in an interpretable format by the game. This can occur in some activities established by teachers and serve as a source of expansion and customization of games between different editions of the course. For example, when the class content addresses a specific cultural event, such as the New Year, students with different backgrounds could incorporate their cultural experience into the content. In addition to favoring the specific learning context of the class, these contents already inserted in the platform could be evoked later by teachers in new editions, making the experience broader and more dynamic, also favoring replayability.

Combining the two attributes, these collectibles could be exchanged and disseminated throughout the platform, reducing the effort of teachers when creating new content, generating more significance for the students, who can use their own collection of assets in communication activities with their colleagues. This occurrence can currently be seen in the use of some social media platforms, which incorporate collectible pictures, such as stickers, which are used in different contexts, disseminating some specific representations in different networks.

The third suggested feature is that, instead of designing only games as closed systems, we should design a game creation tool. It could be organized as a direct application of the inventory of collectible objects linked by sets of simple rules. This repertoire of rules could involve sequences of actions, with appropriate triggers, effects and feedbacks, associated with specific mechanics such as: time control, use of randomizers, action shifts, numerical and string checking mechanisms, among other raised possibilities. With that, teachers could design more open activities, with autonomy to include their own content and define the learning strategies for each class, adapting the tools as the course is conducted. We believe that it would be possible to design a tool that produces a series of games in point and click style, using basic mechanics inspired by other games such as: memory, dominoes, broken telephone, crosswords, hangman, or even slightly more complex structures, such as the management resources genre, Pictionary, among other popular, casual or board games. It is true that this approach imposes a limit on the potential of the games created by the tool. The complexity of the tool needs to be coupled with the technical knowledge necessary for teachers to use it.

The last defined attribute was the need for multiplayer games. The interaction between students and with the teacher was considered a defining factor for engagement (Dixson 2010). That could happen with some possible scenarios: the teacher with a pre-defined role; the whole class participating in the same instance of the game; or even students in smaller groups for independent game sessions in synchronous or asynchronous modalities. This would be a significant feature to incorporate socialization and communication through the platform.

Developing a platform with all of these characteristics broadened the scope of this research. Thus, in order to reach this level, it was defined that for the first stage only an initial set of ten games would be produced and tested, organized into five thematic pairs. These preliminary products must be designed according to the broader rules defined for the platform and will be evaluated in real context of use in some editions of the course for improvement. The initial versions must contain data output for further analysis, in order to allow a broader understanding of the factors that may be associated with student engagement. Over time, we hope to be able to more accurately assess the validity of using these low-complexity games and their role in the students' learning process. Thus, it will be possible to launch new versions of the games until we reach the idealized platform with all the four described attributes.

As an example of this first generation of products, the initial pair of games is briefly presented. It was established that the main learning strategy for these contents should be the communication in specific contexts. Thus, the two games address a problem situation in which the interpretation of the dialogues is the main element of the mechanics. For the first game, the goal is to transpose elements of the dialogue to a record on the avatar's phone. To do so, the player needs to understand the characters' context and speeches. In the second game, the goal is to identify a specific person at a work environment. To do this, the player needs to collect tips from other characters in conversations. The assessment of the player's understanding occurs in the choice of the possible responses that must be related to the context of the conversation. When performed two successful cycles of conversation, the character provides a tip about the person sought. After a while, the player should have enough information to identify the right person. Figure 4 presents some of the described situations from both games.

Fig. 4. Scenes from the first two games, which focus on training communication skills in work situations. Representations of internal environments, dialog interfaces and representations of smartphone environments were used to establish the gameplay context.

5   Conclusion

This research aimed to investigate the challenges of using educational games in the context of a course on learning Portuguese as foreign language. To this end, it was organized in two stages, a qualitative investigative approach and another as a propositional interventional Design process. Therefore, the challenges identified in the first stage and some possible ways to address them were presented as results. The next steps involve an evaluation of the first intervention, which must follow iterative cycles until reaching the idealized solution. Although it was not feasible to implement all the raised attributes in these first versions, we understand that these characteristics are central to expanding the agency of teachers and students in the learning process and should guide the evolution of this platform.

Moreover, the research team understands that this utopic proposition of creating a platform that creates games may be the best solution for all the complex challenges this project has been facing. By understanding the new learners' need, we conclude that it is imperative to provide a software that can be shaped by people – be it the teachers or the students – and allow them to create their own experiences. If we aim to offer real world tasks and real-world context, we should also acknowledge that the world changes fast (and is continuing to change). A task that is relevant today might not be in one or two years. So, our software needs to have the ability to change with it.

These accelerated changes require learning that expands the learner's horizon and helps the learner to grasp practical knowledge. This demands that not only our game allows agency for the students but also agency for the teachers and educators alike. When aiming to construct complex learning experiences, we must go beyond content acquisition or classroom participation. Our mid-term goal is to expand knowledge through virtual learning experiences empowering teachers and students as the main agents of the change (Engeström and Sannino 2010).

References

Abercrombie, D.: Elements of general phonetics. Edinburgh University Press, Edinburgh (1967)

Abrahão, J.I., Sznelwar, L., Silvino, A.M.D., Sarmet, M.M., Pinho, D.: Introdução à ergonomia: da prática à teoria. São Paulo: Edgard Blücher LTDA (2009)

Barry, W.J., Andreeva, B., Russo, M., Dimitrova, S., Kostadinova, T.: Do rhythm measures tell us anything about language type? In: Proceedings of the 15th ICPhS, pp. 2693–2696. Barcelona (2003)

Bednarz, F.: Professional and social integration of migrants and language learning: convergences and challenges at the European level. In: The Linguistic Integration of Adult Migrants. Berlin/Boston: Walter de Gruyter GmbH (2017)

Bertinetto, P.M.: Reflections on the dichotomy stress vs. syllable-timing. Revue de phonétique appliquée, vol. 91(93), 99–130 (1989)

Bruner, J.: The Narrative Construction of Reality. Crit. Inq. 18(1), 1–21 (1991)

Chen, J.: Flow in games (and everything else). Commun. ACM 50(4), 31–34 (2007)

Csikszentmihalyi, M.: Beyond boredom and anxiety. Jossey-Bass (2000)

Dauer, R.M.: Stress-timing and syllable-timing reanalyzed. J. Phon. 11(1), 51–62 (1983)

Design council. a study of the design process – The double diamond (2005)

Desurvire, H., Wiberg, C.: Game usability heuristics (PLAY) for evaluating and designing better games: The next iteration. In: Ozok, A.A., Zaphiris, P. (eds.) OCSC 2009. LNCS, vol. 5621, pp. 557–566. Springer, Heidelberg (2009). https://doi.org/10.1007/978-3-642-02774-1_60

Dixson, M.D.: Creating effective student engagement in online courses: what do students find engaging? J. Sch. Teach. Learn. 10(2), 1–13 (2010)

Engeström, Y.: Activity theory and individual and social transformation. Perspect. Act. Theor. 19(38), 19–30 (1999)

Engeström, Y., Sannino, A.: Studies of expansive learning: foundations, findings and future challenges. Educ. Res. Rev. 5(1), 1–24 (2010)

Fennell, B.A.: A History of English: A Sociolinguistic Approach. Blackwell, Oxford (2001)

Ferreira, V.H.M., Pontes e Silva, T.B., Maynardes, A.C.: Design de jogos educacionais para o ensino de LIBRAS. Revista Educação Gráfica, vol. 23(1), 24–42 (2019)

Flick, U.: Introdução à pesquisa qualitativa-3. Artmed editora (2008)

Fritz, T., Donat, D. What migrant learners need. In: The Linguistic Integration of Adult Migrants. Berlin/Boston: Walter de Gruyter GmbH (2017)

Guérin, F., Laville, A., Daniellou, F., Duraffourg, J., Kerguelen, A.: Compreender o trabalho para transformá-lo: a prática da Ergonomia. Tradução de: L. Sznelwar et al. São Paulo: Edgard Blücher LTDA (2001)

Halliday, M.A.K.: General linguistics and its application to language teaching. In: Patterns of Language: Papers in General, Descriptive and Applied Linguistics, pp. 1–41 (1966)

Harding, R.M., Sokal, R.R.: Classification of the European language families by genetic distance. Proc. Natl. Acad. Sci. 85(23), 9370–9372 (1988)

Huizinga, J.: Homo Ludens: A Study of the Play-Element in Culture. The Beacon Press, Boston (1950)

Hung, H.T., Yang, J.C., Hwang, G.J., Chu, H.C., Wang, C.C.: A scoping review of research on digital game-based language learning. Comput. Educ. **126**, 89–104 (2018)

Hunicke, R., LeBlanc, M., Zubek, R.: MDA: a formal approach to game design and game research. In: Proceedings of the AAAI Workshop on Challenges in Game AI, vol. **4**(1) (2004)

Jahnke, I., Lee, Y.-M., Pham, M., He, H., Austin, L.: Unpacking the inherent design principles of mobile microlearning. Technol. Knowl. Learn. **25**(3), 585–619 (2019). https://doi.org/10.1007/s10758-019-09413-w

James, A.L.: Speech signals in telephony. Sir I. Pitman & sons, Limited (1940)

Jerzak, N., Rebelo, F.: Serious games and heuristic evaluation – the cross-comparison of existing heuristic evaluation methods for games. In: Marcus, A. (ed.) DUXU 2014. LNCS, vol. 8517, pp. 453–464. Springer, Cham (2014). https://doi.org/10.1007/978-3-319-07668-3_44

Kumar, B.A., Goundar, M.S., Chand, S.S.: Usability guideline for mobile learning applications: an update. Educ. Inf. Technol. **24**(6), 3537–3553 (2019). https://doi.org/10.1007/s10639-019-09937-9

Leont'ev, A.N.: activity, consciousness, and personality (1978)

Marcantonio, A.: The Uralic language family: facts, myths and statistics. (2002)

Newman, K.: The case for the narrative brain. In: Proceedings of the second Australasian conference on Interactive entertainment (IE 2005). Creativity and Cognition Studios Press, Sydney, AUS, 145–149 (2005)

Nieuwboer, C., Rood, R.: Progress in proficiency and participation: an adult learning approach to support social integration of migrants in Western societies. In: The Linguistic Integration of Adult Migrants. Berlin/Boston: Walter de Gruyter GmbH (2017)

O'reilly, K.: Ethnographic methods. Routledge. Chicago (2012)

Palomino, P.T., Toda, A.M., Oliveira, W., Cristea, A.I., Isotani, S.: Narrative for gamification in education: why should you care?. In: IEEE 19th International Conference on Advanced Learning Technologies (ICALT), Maceió, Brazil, pp. 97–99 (2019a)

Palomino, P.T., Toda, A.M., Oliveira, W., Cristea, A.I., Isotani, S.: Exploring content game elements to support gamification design in educational systems: narrative and storytelling. In: VIII Congresso Brasileiro de Informática na Educação (CBIE 2019) (2019b)

Paz, D.M.D.S.: Formação de conceitos de ensino de leitura em português como segunda língua. In: Doctoral dissertation, Universidade Federal de Santa Maria (2006)

Pinelle, D., Wong, N., Stach, T.: Heuristic evaluation for games: usability principles for video game design. In: Proceedings of the SIGCHI Conference on Human Factors in Computing Systems (2008)

Pontes e Silva, T.B. A.: Cognição no processo de design. InfoDesign - Revista Brasileira de Design da Informação, vol. **12**(3), 318–335 (2015a)

Pontes e Silva, T.B.: Um campo epistemológico para o Design. Revista de Design, Tecnologia e Sociedade, vol. **2**(2), 23–41 (2015b)

Pöyhönen, S., Tarnanen, M.: Integration policies and adult second language learning in Finland. In: Simpson, J., Whiteside, A. (eds.) Adult Language Education and Migration: Challenging agendas in policy and practice, pp. 107–118. Routledge (2015). https://doi.org/10.4324/9781315718361-8

Rabin, S.: Introduction to game development. Charles River Media (2005)

Sajavaara, K., Dufva, H.: Finnish-English phonetics and phonology. Int. J. Engl. Stud. **1**(1), 241–256 (2001)

Salen, K., Zimmerman, E.: Rules of Play: Game Design Fundamentals. MIT Press, Cambridge (2004)

Santos, D.D.: A experiência de um aprendiz de português como segunda língua em ambiente de imersão (2010)

Schell, J.: The Art of Game Design: A Book of Lenses. CRC Press, Boca Raton (2008)

Schiepers, M., et al.: Creating a dynamic and learner-driven online environment for practicing second language skills: guiding principles from second language acquisition and online education. In: The Linguistic Integration of Adult Migrants. Berlin/Boston: Walter de Gruyter GmbH (2017)

Silva, L.M., Pontes e Silva, T.B., Pacheco, R.P., Castanho, C.D.: Design de jogos sérios para aprendizagem de Português como Língua Estrangeira. Revista Educação Gráfica, vol. **24**(3), 245–263 (2020)

Simon, H.A., Newell, A.: Human problem solving: the state of the theory in 1970. Am. Psychol. **26**(2), 145 (1971)

Simon, H.A.: The sciences of the artificial. massachusetts institute of technology (1981)

Swink, S.: Game Feel: a Game Designer's Guide to Virtual Sensation. CRC Press, Boca Raton (2008)

Toda, A.M., Klock, A.C.T., Oliveira, W.: Analysing gamification elements in educational environments using an existing Gamification taxonomy. Smart Learn. Environ. **6**, 16 (2019)

Umekawa, E.E.R., Zerbini, T.: Evasão e persistência em ações educacionais a distância: análise do perfil discente. Rev. Psicologia Organizações e Trabalho **15**(2), 188–200 (2015)

Van Der Veer, R., Valsiner, J.: Vygotsky: Uma Síntese. São Paulo, Loyola (2001)

Vygotsky, L.S.: A Construção do Pensamento e da Linguagem. São Paulo, Martins Fontes (2001)

Winn, B.M.: The design, play, and experience framework. In: Handbook of Research on Effective Electronic Gaming in Education. IGI Global, pp. 1010–1024 (2009)

Design and Application Research of Gamification in University Curriculum——Taking the Course of TV Camera for Example

Yuan Yao[1], Ling He[2], and Junjie Shang[1(✉)]

[1] Lab of Learning Sciences, Graduate School of Education, Peking University, Beijing, China
{yaoyuan2016,jjshang}@pku.edu.cn
[2] School of Education, Jiangxi Science and Technology Normal University, Nanchang, Jiangxi, China

Abstract. It has been generally considered as one of the effective ways of teaching reform to add gamification into college courses. This study mainly discusses the specific methods of improving the learning effect of university courses through gamification, and tries to put forward a set of design framework and apply it to a university course. From the perspective of learning engagement, this paper analyzes the effect of gamification design and application, and investigates the relationship between gamification learning experience, learning motivation, personality traits and learning engagement. The significance of this study lies in, on the one hand, enriching the practical experience of improving learning engagement through gamification, on the other hand, providing reference for constructing the theoretical model of the relationship between gamification and learning engagement.

Keywords: Gamification · Design · Application · Learning engagement · Learning motivation · Personality traits

1 Introduction

In recent years, Gamification has been widely concerned. It is generally believed that gamification is the application of game elements to non-game fields. According to this definition, gamification is a method, means or way of thinking used to improve user experience and participation in non-game environment. Educational games and game-based learning are to learn knowledge and skills through a complete game. Gamification, instead of letting learners play a certain game, only involves some activities including game elements, such as points, levels, badges, rankings, etc. [1]. It is not necessary to use pure games in teaching, but the characteristics of gamification such as challenge, curiosity, competition and control can be applied to the design of learning activities [2].

During the Novel Coronavirus Pneumonia epidemic period, many university teachers spontaneously applied gamification elements such as points, badges and rankings to

X. Fang (Ed.): HCII 2021, LNCS 12790, pp. 276–293, 2021.
https://doi.org/10.1007/978-3-030-77414-1_20

online classroom teaching, or organized students to carry out gamification activities at home, which enhanced the interest of courses and stimulated students' learning motivation. Adding game elements into instructional design has become one of the trends in the development of learning methods. In the post-epidemic era, people will pay more attention to active learning. How to integrate gamification into university curriculum to make learning process more interesting, learning content more useful and learning results more valuable, is a meaningful topic, which deserves the attention of university teachers and researchers.

This study mainly discusses the specific ways to improve the learning effect of university courses through gamification, and tries to put forward a set of design framework, which is applied to the university course of Television Camera. From the perspective of learning engagement, this paper investigates the effect of gamification design and application, and analyzes the relationship between gamification learning experience, learning motivation, personality traits and learning engagement. The significance of this study lies in, on the one hand, enriching the practical experience of improving learning engagement through gamification, on the other hand, providing reference for constructing the theoretical model of the relationship between gamification and learning engagement.

2 Design

2.1 The Design Principles of Gamification

The design of gamification needs to follow some general principles, which is the basic consensus reached by researchers after many practices. Marache-Francisco and others summed up six principles of gamification design, which mentioned that gamification must be beneficial to both the owner and the user; Through tailor-made triggers, different users can experience different gamification designs; The interaction and motivation should be considered [3]. The gamification design principles summarized by Morschheuser et al. mainly include: understanding the user's needs, motives and behaviors, and also understanding the background of gamification application; Identify and clearly define the goal of gamification; Verify the idea of game design as early as possible; Follow the iterative design process; Rich knowledge of game design and human psychology; Participants and organizers must understand and support gamification; Always pay attention to user needs in the process of iteration; Define and use indicators to evaluate and monitor the success of gamification; Continuously optimize the design through management and monitoring; Users are invited to participate in the conception and design stage [4]. Li Chaobo believes that the gamification design of adult training courses should follow four design principles. One is interest orientation, which stimulates adult learners' interest in the course content. This can be achieved through perceptual awakening, stimulating inquiry and multiple stimuli. Second, experience-oriented, considering establishing the relationship between adult learners and learning content. Methods include motivation association, knowledge association and goal association. The third is action-oriented, which includes "small steps" thinking and goal stratification, establishing a clear rule system, designing competition mechanism and confirmation and feedback mechanism; Fourth, development orientation. Always aiming at improving adult learners' knowledge, skills or changing attitudes [5]. Darina Dicheva and others summarized

14 principles of educational gamification design, among which the social participation principles include individual and group competitions, participation in group activities and team projects, and cooperation and interaction with other students [6].

Based on the previous studies, it can be seen that the curriculum design of gamification needs to pay attention to the following key principles (see Fig. 1): First, pay attention to stimulating learners' learning motivation; Second, always focuses on the study of curriculum knowledge and the improvement of skills; The third is to promote links between learners, curriculum objectives and old and new knowledge; The fourth is to achieve competition and cooperation through social participation; Fifthly, evaluate the design effects through iterations, dimensions and indicators.

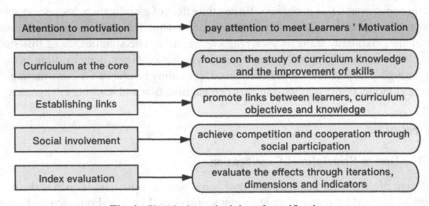

Fig. 1. Key design principles of gamification

2.2 The Design Framework of Gamification

Gamification design of university courses is not a simple combination of games and learning, nor is it to apply games to study a certain knowledge point or as a means of practice. Instead, it should apply the spirit, thinking and motivation of games to the teaching, motivate learners through tasks, challenges, competition, cooperation and rewards, and guide learners to strengthen interaction and learning, increase learning enthusiasm and improve learning engagement. The gamification design of university courses is instructional design, and it should also refer to educational games and game-based learning design.

After the Novel Coronavirus Pneumonia epidemic, one of the major changes in the college curriculum is that various means are widely used to enrich the teaching process, and blended learning has become a trend. Huang Ronghuai and others believe that the curriculum design of blended learning is an inevitable requirement of class-based teaching system. It is also the need of developing students' professional skills. The design framework should roughly include three stages: frontal analysis, activity and resource design and evaluation design. The frontal analysis includes learner characteristics, learning objectives and blended learning environment, while activity and resource design includes blended learning overall design, unit design and resource design and development. The evaluation design is mainly based on the contents determined in the previous two stages [7].

The gamification design framework proposed by Werbach and Hunter includes six steps. One is to define goals, list all possible potential goals and make each goal as accurate as possible, identify the final goal by the importance of goals; The second is to describe the target behavior. Before the behavior is promoted, the definition of the ultimate goal should be specific and clear. In the user analysis stage, it is necessary to understand the scope and characteristics of the user group, subdivide the user group if necessary, and ensure that the gamification system can adapt to each subdivision group; The third is user analysis, which clarifies who the user is, what kind of relationship he has with the designer, what may motivate the user, and decides which incentive factors to adopt; The fourth is to design the activity loop, including participation loop and advanced design; The fifth is to keep fun and keep the system interesting in order to attract users better; The sixth is to configure appropriate tools, which is the stage of system implementation [8].

Based on the above framework of blended learning curriculum design and gamification design, this study attempts to put forward the design framework of gamification (see Fig. 2), that is, the design process, for the reference of designers to improve curriculum design. According to this framework, the design of gamification can be divided into six steps: the analysis of curriculum, the analysis of learning background, the analysis of incentive mechanism, the design of gamification elements, the implementation of gamification and the evaluation of gamification effect. These six steps can be summarized into three modules.

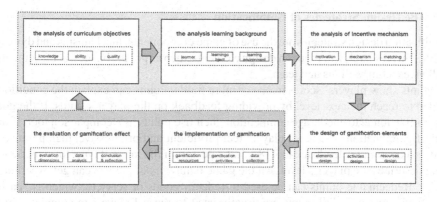

Fig. 2. The design framework of gamification

First, the analysis of curriculum objectives and learning background. Teachers and instructional designers should first have a clear understanding of the learning objectives of the course, that is, to clarify the specific requirements that students need to meet in terms of knowledge, ability and quality. At the same time, they should know the characteristics of learners, such as preparatory knowledge, learning styles and preferences, and classify the knowledge to be learned, such as theoretical knowledge and practical knowledge, and know the learning environment, such as learning resources, learning space, learning tools, teaching methods and strategies, etc.

Secondly, the analysis of incentive mechanism and the design of gamification elements. According to the curriculum objectives, teachers and instructional designers need to make clear which driving forces may stimulate students' learning. In other words, teachers want which learning motivation to be stimulated, so as to choose appropriate gamification elements and design the curriculum activities, resources and presentation methods concretely. In this module, gamification design elements can be embedded into existing curriculum activities and resources, and they can also be completely new.

Third, the implementation of gamification and the evaluation of gamification effect. After the gamification design, teachers and instructional designers should collect learners' learning data in time in the process of implementation, so as to select appropriate evaluation dimensions and indicators, and promote the evaluation and feedback of gamification effect after the course. In this module, we need to answer whether the game design has an impact on the learning effect, which factors work and which factors don't.

Finally, it should be noted that in this design framework, the design of gamification may be carried out after or at the same time as the curriculum design, and it must be closely combined with the curriculum objectives and teaching plans no matter when it starts; Game design is a dynamic and adjustable process, and the six design steps can be adjusted and leapfrogged in sequence according to the actual progress of curriculum; Gamification design is also a cycle and iterative process. The evaluation result of the previous round can be the basis for improvement of the next round of design, and enough design practice can better verify the reliability of gamification effect model.

2.3   The Design Strategies of Gamification

Gamification design strategies are the use of game components, mechanisms and dynamics [8]. This research will focus on design elements such as points, badges, achievements, challenges, competitions and teams.

Points show players' scores in one or more fields. Points can explain the conditions needed to reach the next level by providing feedback on the player's status. If the goal of gamification is to encourage competition, then use points as a comparison tool. If the goal of gamification is to make players feel proficient and progressive, then points are used as a continuous feedback tool [8]. In the design of the integral type, the experience value describes the player's level. All the game behaviors of players can get experience values; Redeemable points can be used to redeem goods or services, which is "cash" in virtual economy; Skill points are usually used to reward players to complete some special and non-core tasks [9].

Badges are used to visualize players' achievements, which can be used in combination with points, grades and achievements, or can be used as a single system. The badge system should have five characteristics. First of all, badges can set goals, stimulate and challenge players to achieve their goals. Secondly, badges can guide players' behaviors, explain what activities can be carried out in the system, and guide the establishment of behavioral norms. Third, badges build a reputation for players, and players can show their professional reputation and ability by displaying medals. Fourth, badges are status symbols. Badges illustrate the achievements of players and represent their social and economic status in the game. Fifthly, badges are the identification of specific people, and players with the same badge combination may have a sense of unity [8]. Collecting badges can become people's motivation, and well-designed badges also attract players.

Challenges are often used with social elements such as competitions and teams. When designing a challenge, designers should pay attention to originality, sufficient time interval and increasing difficulty level by level. The challenge also needs to provide instant and personalized feedback for individuals and teams. When designing the team, the number of people should be kept within a small range, and attention should be paid to the use of seats that are conducive to communication [10].

3 Application

In this study, the above design principles, framework and strategies are applied to a university course. According to the design process, through specific implementation and evaluation, the improvement of learning effect under the gamification is investigated.

3.1 Curriculum Objectives and Background Analysis

Television Camera is the main compulsory course of the major of educational technology, which emphasizes both theory and practice, especially practice. The goal of the course is to enable students to have the following five professional abilities: to be familiar with and reasonably use cameras and related equipment; to master the basic knowledge of television photography; to be able to write scripts of television works; to be familiar with the creative process of television cameramen; to master the technology and skills of television photography, to be able to integrate disciplines and innovate, and to cooperate with others. Among the five goals, the second one is the knowledge requirement, the first and third are the skill requirements, and the fourth and fifth are the professional quality requirements.

The learners of TV Camera are sophomores majoring in educational technology, radio and television journalism and advertising, and have completed the study of photography technology and skills. There are three main types of learning environments. Learning space includes multimedia classrooms, studios, outdoor environment, software of Learning Pass and QQ; Learning tools include digital cameras, tripods, lighting rocker arms and tracks, acquisition systems, multimedia courseware and traditional paper textbooks; Teaching methods mainly include teaching, practical operation, visual demonstration, group discussion, cooperative learning and classroom report, etc.

3.2 The Choice of Gamification Elements

Classifying and transforming the curriculum objectives into the requirements for students' abilities, we find that the acquisition of knowledge, especially skills, can be driven by progress and sense of accomplishment and ownership, and the professionalism of innovation and cooperation can be stimulated by social influence and association (see Table 1). According to Yu-kai Chou's octagonal behavior analysis method [11], we tried to match the incentive factors with the gamification elements. The achievement system design elements including points, badges and grades are selected to promote the learning of knowledge and skills, and the individual competition and team task design elements are selected to promote the acquisition of professional qualities such as innovation and cooperation.

The reason why the achievement system can stimulate is that people are more likely to like the activities they are good at, so the ability needs may play a regulatory role in the development of intrinsic motivation. Under certain conditions, positive feedback is a method that can enhance the sense of ability and produce intrinsic motivation. In gamification, the best example of positive feedback is the achievement system. In the design of gamification courses, the achievement system can be composed of points, badges, grades, feedback, progress reports, etc., so that learners have the feeling of climbing up the ladder and moving step by step [12].

Table 1. Curriculum objectives, incentive factors and elements choice

Curriculum objectives	Competency requirements	Incentive factors	Gamification elements
Master the basic knowledge of TV camera	knowledge	Progress and sense of accomplishment, ownership	Points, badges, grades, achievement systems, convertible points, challenges
Using professional camera equipment, writing scripts	Skills		
Master camera skills, be able to innovate and cooperate	Professionalism	Social influence and connection	Individual competition, team task

3.3 The Design of Gamification Elements

Achievement System Design The purpose of this course is to cultivate quasi-professional cameramans, so we customize a set of cameramans' achievement system, which includes badges, points and grades. The achievement system of is also a system of grade upgrading. It is divided into eight levels, and each level is divided into three sub levels: gold, silver and bronze. Through the promotion of the level, it provides feedback for learners to complete each challenge task, which marks the continuous improvement of camera knowledge and skills.

The design of badges pattern mainly considers the characteristics of learners and learning objects. The patterns should represent the camera skills, and show the differences of camera skills through the different images of each badge. The main picture of the badge takes the camera equipment as the theme, and the main level is distinguished by the icon in the center. According to the order of the complexity of camera equipment from simple to complex and camera skills from weak to strong, the main pictures are as follows: phone camera - intern cameraman, card digital camera - new cameraman, pick-up head - junior cameraman, hand-held digital camera - intermediate cameraman, shoulder digital camera - senior cameraman, tripod - highly qualified cameraman, clip-stick - expert cameraman, finished film - master cameraman. Sub levels are distinguished by color and number of stars, and the design patterns are as follows: bronze - one green star, silver - two gray stars, gold - three yellow stars (see Fig. 3).

Fig. 3. Badges design of TV camera course

The middle position of each badge shows the student's head image and name, which is to make students have a strong sense of achievement and ownership through customization. Badges will be published through QQ group of this course, and achievements will be sent to students through QQ individually in the form of display chart (see Fig. 4), so that students can know their learning progress in time. As can be seen from Fig. 4, students can clearly and intuitively understand their badges, points, competition ranking and other information.

Competition and Challenges Design. Aiming at the curriculum objectives with innovation, cooperation and other professional qualities as the core, this study designed a team competition which was highly consistent with the course content through repeated discussions with the course teacher and teaching assistants. The elements such as treasure hunt, time limit and story were embedded into the competition rules (see Fig. 5). Students were required to look for specific elements under the specified theme and within a limited time, shooting short stories with the main line. This competition design hopes to stimulate learners' awareness of cooperation and competition, so as to promote learning engagement. Besides, in order to master the knowledge of photography, the researchers designed the challenge task of multiple knowledge contests, and the results were used as the basis for awarding badges.

The gamification achievement system embedded into the curriculum system needs to design challenging learning activities and tasks. The course of TV Camera is divided into eight chapters, so the researchers have designed eight corresponding challenge tasks, and the difficulty of the tasks increases with the improvement of students' ability. The

学号/姓名：**20191200** 张大宝

积分情况：20+20+30+20+30+10+90+20+30+30+10

成就情况：金牌大师级摄像师

个人赛表现：第二名

团队赛表现：第三名

Fig. 4. The display chart of achievement for a student

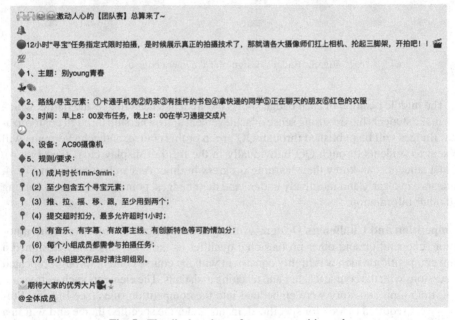

激动人心的【团队赛】总算来了～

12小时"寻宝"任务指定式限时拍摄，是时候展示真正的拍摄技术了，那就请各大摄像师们扛上相机、抢起三脚架，开拍吧！！

◆1、主题：别young青春

◆2、路线/寻宝元素：①卡通手机壳②奶茶③有挂件的书包④拿快递的同学⑤正在聊天的朋友⑥红色的衣服

◆3、时间：早上8：00发布任务，晚上8：00在学习通提交成片

◆4、设备：AC90摄像机

◆5、规则/要求：

(1) 成片时长1min-3min；

(2) 至少包含五个寻宝元素；

(3) 推、拉、摇、移、跟，至少用到两个；

(4) 提交超时扣分，最多允许超时1小时；

(5) 有音乐、有字幕、有故事主线、有创新特色等可酌情加分；

(6) 每个小组成员都需参与拍摄任务；

(7) 各小组提交作品时请注明组别。

期待大家的优秀大片

@全体成员

Fig. 5. The display chart of team competition rules

chapter of knowledge mastery is mainly in the form of online limited time competition, while the chapter of skill mastery is mainly in the form of practical operation, and some of the original assignments of the course are still retained. The gamification design is carried out to improve students' interest in learning. As can be seen from Table 2, in order to give students clear and timely game feedback, there is a corresponding and matching relationship between the course chapters, challenge tasks and gamification achievement system.

In addition to virtual achievement systems, competitions and challenges, learners who have completed all the challenge tasks can also exchange the accumulated points for "real" rewards, which are not in kind but related to the further improvement of students' camera skills. For example, students who have reached a certain point amount can get the opportunity to visit TV stations or participate in feature films. It should be noted that the reward should not exceed the ability of teachers and designers, and should be aimed at improving students' learning enthusiasm and professional ability.

4 Results

4.1 Application Effect Analysis

In this study, the students of the first semester of the 2019–2020 academic year and the students of the first semester of the 2020–2021 academic year as the main data sources, from the perspective of learning engagement, the differences between using and not using gamification instructional design were compared.

Study Design and Data Collection. Regular classroom teaching methods are adopted in the fall of 2019, and gamification design is added to autumn 2020 course. The two semester courses are consistent in terms of teachers, syllabus, teaching contents and teaching arrangements. In this study, through the method of quantitative research, questionnaires are issued to obtain the data of students' learning engagement, and the questionnaire data of students participating in the survey are taken as samples. The learning engagement questionnaire is divided into three parts: emotional engagement, cognitive engagement and behavioral engagement. After the understanding and preliminary analysis of the students' mastery of television camera knowledge in the early stage of the course, the students of two semesters have certain homogeneity. There are 42 valid samples in autumn 2019 and 40 valid samples in autumn 2020. Both questionnaires were completed voluntarily.

Comparison of Learning Engagement. Learning engagement can reflect students' learning effect to a certain extent, including emotional engagement, cognitive engagement and behavioral engagement. The learning engagement data of fall 2019 and fall 2020 can be accepted as normal distribution. SPSSAU software is used to conduct independent sample t test on the data of two semesters. The results are shown in the Table 3. The learning engagement, cognitive engagement and behavioral engagement of the two groups were significant at 0.01 level, and Cohen's D value was greater than 0.8, and the effect was large. In conclusion, there were significant differences in learning engagement, cognitive engagement and behavioral engagement between using and not using gamification instructional design, and the difference was large. This shows that, compared with the autumn course of 2019, the students who have experienced the gamification design in autumn 2020 have a certain improvement in their learning engagement, especially in cognitive and behavioral engagement.

Table 2. The corresponding relationship between the course chapters, challenge tasks and gamification achievement system

Course chapters	Teaching emphasis	Gamification Design				
		Challenge tasks	Titles	Grades	Points	Badges
An overview of television camera	Camera classification, basic and professional camera introduction	Online Time Limit Answers	Intern cameraman	Bronze medal	10	
				Silver medal	20	
				Gold medal	30	
Television footage	The composition of the TV picture, the scene of the TV picture	Online Time Limit Answers	New cameraman	Bronze medal	10	
				Silver medal	20	
				Gold medal	30	
Fixed lens and motion lens	Fixed lens, motion lens and upscale lens	MV of campus scenery	Junior cameraman	Bronze medal	10	
				Silver medal	20	
				Gold medal	30	
Design of split lens	Sub shot script design, long shot	News interview program design (group)	Intermediate cameraman	Bronze medal	10	
				Silver medal	20	
				Gold medal	30	
Shooting AIDS	The use of rocker arm, track and magic leg	Online Time Limit Answers	Senior cameraman	Bronze medal	10	
Television lighting	Introduction, understanding and operation of lighting tools			Silver medal	20	

(*continued*)

Table 2. (*continued*)

Course chapters	Teaching emphasis	Gamification Design				
		Challenge tasks	Titles	Grades	Points	Badges
Use of studio	Studio introduction, studio lighting system, studio background system			Gold medal	30	
		Individual competitions			10-100	Progress presentation
		Short Film for News Interview (Group)	Highly qualified cameraman	Bronze medal	10	
				Silver medal	20	
TV program shooting	TV news shooting, TV feature film shooting, the difference between feature film and TV news, TV advertisement and MV shooting, TV short play			Gold medal	30	
		Theme MV(individual)	Expert cameraman	Bronze medal	10	
				Silver medal	20	
				Gold medal	30	
		Team Competition			20/40/60	Progress presentation
		Offline Time Limit Answers	Master cameraman	Bronze medal	10	
				Silver medal	20	
				Gold medal	30	

4.2 Impact Relationship Analysis

Study Design. In this study, we selected 40 students who participated in the course of TV Camera in autumn 2020 as the research object. They were all sophomores majoring in educational technology. A total of 40 valid questionnaires were collected, including 6 boys (15%) and 34 girls (85%).

In this study, the gamification design of the course of TV Camera is implemented. The process of course experiment mainly includes four parts: early communication with teachers, gamfication design, formal implementation of the course, questionnaire survey and data collection and analysis. The research on the influence relationship mainly

Table 3. Independent sample t test of learning engagement

	Group (mean ± SD)		t	p
	Autumn 2020 (n = 40)	Fall 2019 (n = 42)		
Learning engagement	3.23 ± 0.36	2.93 ± 0.32	4.006	0.000**
Cognitive engagement	3.17 ± 0.49	2.77 ± 0.39	4.057	0.000**
Behavioral engagement	3.43 ± 0.43	3.02 ± 0.48	4.018	0.000**
Emotional engagement	3.13 ± 0.36	2.98 ± 0.38	1.721	0.089

$* p<0.05 ** p<0.01$

adopts the quantitative method, using the quantitative data of questionnaire survey, and analyzing the status of students in the course by SPSSAU.

The main data collection tool of this study is the questionnaire of students' gamification learning experience, learner characteristics, learning motivation and learning engagement. Combined with the existing theories, classic questionnaires and curriculum practice, this study determined the items of the questionnaire, adjusted the content and language expression of the questionnaire on the basis of student interviews. The short version of the Chinese Big Five Personality Questionnaire [13], and the Learning Motivation Scale developed by Amabile et al. [14] have been used. The learning engagement questionnaire of Z wang et al. [15], Skinner et al. [16] and QP Kong et al. [17] was used as the basis of the learning engagement questionnaire. Combining with the actual situation of the course, the learning engagement questionnaire was designed from three dimensions of behavioral engagement, cognitive engagement and emotional engagement. Each item in questionnaires was scored by Likert's scoring system.

Research Hypothesis. The core idea of this study is to explore the relationship between gamification learning experience and learning engagement, and to explore whether learning motivation plays a mediating effect when analyzing the influence of gamification learning experience on learning engagement. In addition, we also pay attention to whether the personality traits play a moderating role in the influence of gamification learning experience on learning engagement (see Fig. 6). Here we try to put forward two kinds of hypotheses:

The first category:

I   Students' gamification learning experience has a significant positive impact on the level of learning engagement of the TV Camera course
II   Students' gamification learning experience has a significant positive impact on learning motivation of the TV Camera course
III Students' learning motivation has a significant positive impact on the level of learning engagement of the TV Camera course
The second category:

IV   The students with a certain higher personality trait showed a higher level of learning engagement in the gamification learning experience of the TV Camera course

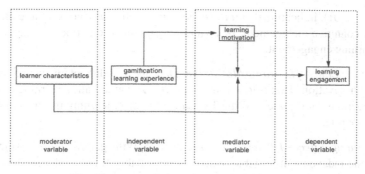

Fig. 6. Impact relationship analysis framework

Research Results. The reliability and validity of the questionnaire were analyzed. The reliability coefficient values were greater than 0.8, and the reliability quality was also high. The validity of the study data was also acceptable. Firstly, Pearson correlation coefficient was used for correlation analysis, and then linear regression was used to analyze the influence relationship. Finally, hierarchical regression was used to analyze the mediating effect and moderating effect.

The Relationship Between Gamification Learning Experience and Learning Engagement. Taking gamification learning experience as independent variable, and cognitive engagement, behavioral engagement, emotional engagement and learning engagement as dependent variables respectively, the regression coefficients of gamification learning experience were 0.483 ($t = 3.220$, $p = 0.003 < 0.01$), 0.601 ($t = 5.321$, $p = 0.000 < 0.01$), 0.405 ($t = 3.830$, $p = 0.000 < 0.01$) and 0.490 ($t = 5.021$, $p = 0.000 < 0.01$). This means that gamification learning experience has a significant positive impact on cognitive engagement, behavioral engagement, emotional engagement and overall learning engagement.

The Relationship Between Gamification Learning Experience and Learning Motivation. The gamification learning experience is used as an independent variable, and the intrinsic learning motivation, extrinsic learning motivation and learning motivation are used as dependent variables respectively for linear regression analysis. It can be found that the regression coefficients of the gamification learning experience are 0.563 ($t = 5.555$, $p = 0.000 < 0.01$), 0.442 ($t = 3.812$, $p = 0.000 < 0.01$) and 0.474 ($t = 5.303$, $p = 0.000 < 0.01$), indicating that the gamification learning experience has a significant positive impact on intrinsic learning motivation, extrinsic learning motivation and overall learning motivation.

The Relationship between Learning Motivation and Learning Engagement. Taking intrinsic learning motivation as an independent variable, and cognitive engagement, behavioral engagement, emotional engagement and learning engagement as dependent variables, we conduct linear regression analysis. It can be found that the regression coefficients of intrinsic learning motivation are 0.595 ($t = 3.363$, $p = 0.002 < 0.01$), 0.624 ($t = 4.272$, $p = 0.000 < 0.01$), 0.365 ($t = 2.686$, $p = 0.011 < 0.05$) and 0.516 ($t = 4.159$, p = 0.000 < 0.01), indicating that intrinsic learning motivation has a significant positive impact on cognitive engagement, behavioral engagement, emotional engagement and overall learning engagement.

The Mediating Effect of Learning Motivation Data analysis did not find significant effect of learning motivation. That is to say, in the process of gamification learning experience affecting learning engagement of the TV Camera course, learning motivation does not play a bridge role.

The Moderating Effect of Learner Characteristics With gamification learning experience as the independent variable, extrovert personality traits as the moderator variable, and cognitive engagement, behavioral engagement and learning engagement as the dependent variables, respectively, the interaction term between gamification learning experience and extrovert personality traits shows significant (t = 3.562, p = 0.001 < 0.05), (t = 2.134, p = 0.040 < 0.05) and (t = 2.692, p = 0.011 < 0.05). This means that when the gamification learning experience affects learning engagement, the extrovert personality traits has a significant difference at different levels.

With gamification learning experience as independent variable, conscientious personality traits as moderator and cognitive engagement as dependent variable, the interaction between gamification learning experience and conscientious personality traits was significant (t = 2.678, p = 0.011 < 0.05). This means that when the gamification learning experience affects cognitive engagement, the conscientious personality traits has a significant difference at different levels.

4.3   Qualitative Analysis

In this study, 12 students who participated in the fall 2020 course were interviewed about the gamification learning experience. Overall, we have received a lot of positive feedback.

In terms of emotional experience of gamification design, students reflected that the course "raised my interest" and "I felt very happy, satisfied and fulfilled to get a medal", "the knowledge I learned in this course is constantly deepening, and my ability is constantly improving." the point system has a greater influence on me, because I would like to get points."

In terms of the design of learning activities, some students think that "the most interesting thing is the challenge of 'Different Youth (team competition)', they string it into a story with various elements, and then shoot a short video, which is very novel."

In terms of the visual effect of gamification element design, the students commented that "the badge design is very exquisite, and the personal photo is designed on the medal, which is very interesting. I really want to get it. The badge is very good-looking."

5   Conclusion and Reflection

5.1   Conclusion

Generally speaking, gamification learning design improves students' learning engagement level in the course of TV Camera. There are significant differences in learning engagement, cognitive engagement and behavioral engagement between using and not using gamification instructional design. After adopting gamification teaching, the students' learning engagement level in the course of TV Camera has been improved to a certain extent.

Students' gamification learning experience has a significant positive impact on learning engagement and learning motivation, and students' intrinsic learning motivation has a significant positive impact on learning engagement. The students with higher extroversion personality traits showed a higher level of overall learning engagement, and the students with higher conscientious personality traits showed a higher level of cognitive engagement in the TV Camera course.

These results confirm the existing research conclusions to some extent. Wad Ghaban and Robert Hendley believe that gamification motivation benefits vary with personality types. Highly extroverts can benefit from gamification design [18]. In an empirical study conducted by Patrick Buckley and Elaine Doyle in 2016, it was found that learners with extraversion personality traits can obtain satisfaction from external motivation and think gamification has positive gains [19]. Another survey conducted by the same two researchers in 2017 shows that gamification design is particularly effective for students with intrinsic motivation [20].

In the process of gamification learning experience affecting learning engagement, learning motivation has no mediating effect, that is to say, in this course, the positive performance of learning engagement is directly caused by gamification learning experience, not by gamification experience to stimulate learning motivation, and then by learning motivation to promote learning engagement. This may be due to the strong direct effect of gamification experience on learning engagement, or it may be related to the small sample size, which needs to be tested in further researches.

5.2 Reflection

Based on the gamification design principles, framework and strategies, this study takes the university course of Television Camera as an example, and verifies the effectiveness of gamification in improving learning engagement through design and implementation. In the process of design and implementation, researchers reflect on the problems existing in the current relevant research.

Moderation is the primary factor in the gamification design of university courses. At present, the gamification design and application in the field of higher education is still not very popular, which may be related to the higher implementation cost. In the university curriculum, it is difficult to reform the curriculum system through educational games. For teachers, excessive game design needs higher time and money cost; for students, complex game design also needs time to master and adapt. Therefore, a moderate gamification design embedded in the teaching process is more operable.

Customization is the core of gamification learning design for university courses. In order to attract students' attention and stimulate learning behavior, gamification design needs to keep cognitive consistency with curriculum objectives and learning process, and can't be divorced from each other. We need to find the combination of the two and tailor-made for the course.

It can be considered to use the ranking table. Although previous studies have shown that rankings may affect students' learning motivation. However, in this interview, many students suggested to increase the ranking list. How to display the ranking list is a key problem for teaching designers. For example, we can show the top 25% or 50% of the competition rankings. The advantage of this is that on the one hand, it can meet the needs of students to understand their own level, on the other hand, if the results are not satisfactory, it will not feel too shameful. Or we can ask students to provide a "care list" to provide students with the performance of their classmates they want to know.

The concept of situational learning can be introduced into the gamification design of practical courses. One of the development directions of future gamification design is to add situational stories, enhance the simulation learning experience, and endow the medal design with professional roles. TV Camera is a professional course with strong practicality. The experience of real situation will also be of great help to students' understanding of professional knowledge. Some scholars have explored this aspect. For example, the educational gamification research team of Peking University has transformed the situation story of MOOC, which has achieved remarkable results. It may be used as a reference for the gamification design of university courses in the next step [21, 22].

Designing and developing a digital tool to help the customizing of the gamification components may also be a more feasible means. Displaying students' achievements and releasing competitions tasks through interactive software are measures taken under the condition of limited manpower and time. If a gamification APP that can be embedded in the learning platform, the efficiency of design can be improved.

About the research limitation, in terms of data analysis, firstly, in the application effect research, although the teachers, curriculum syllabus, course content and students' professional background are the same in the two semesters, the differences in students' homogeneity can not be avoided. Second, restricted by the actual number of students, the sample size is still relatively small, and the reference value of the results is relatively limited. In terms of design and implementation, the design scheme only comes from the researchers' background knowledge, the matching with actual skills needs to be improved. If professionals can be participated earlier in the design work, the effect will be better.

Acknowledgements. This study is funded by The Key Education Research Project in 2020 Sponsored by Yuyue Educational Development Foundation in Center for Research on Pre-K12 Education of Peking University (No: JCJYYJ201902).

References

1. Kapp, K.M.: The gamification of learning and instruction: game-based methods and strategies for training and education. In: The Gamification of Learning and Instruction: Game-Based Methods and Strategies for Training and Education. San Francisco, CA, Pfeiffer (2012)
2. Jiang, Y., Shang, J., Zhuang, S.: Design and application of game-based inquiry learning model. China Educ. vol. 5, 84–91 (2011) [in Chinese]
3. Marache-Francisco, C., Brangier, E.: Process of gamification. from the consideration of gamification to its practical implementation. In: Centric: the Sixth International Conference on Advances in Human Oriented and Personalized Mechanisms (2013)

4. Morschheuser, et al.: How to design gamification? A method for engineering gamified software. Information and Software Technology (2018)
5. Li, C.: Embodied cognition and game learning : return and innovation of adult training. Adult Educ. 6 (2017) [in Chinese]
6. Dicheva, D., et al.: Gamification in education: a systematic mapping study. J. Educ. Technol. Soc. 18(3), 75–88 (2015)
7. Huang, R.H., Ma, D., Zheng, L.Q., Zhang, H.H.: Curriculum design theory based on blended learning. Electr. Educ. Res. (01), 9–14 (2009). [in Chinese]
8. Werbach, K., Hunter, D.: For the Win: How Game Thinking can Revolutionize your Business. Wharton digital press, Newark (2012)
9. Zichermann, G., Christopher, C.: Gamification by design: Implementing game mechanics in web and mobile apps. " O'Reilly Media, Inc.", 9 (2011)
10. Aldemir, T., Berkan, C., Goknur, K.: A qualitative investigation of student perceptions of game elements in a gamified course. Comput. Hum. Behav. 78, 235–254 (2018)
11. Chou, Y.: Actionable gamification - Beyond points, badges, and leaderboards. Packt Publishing Ltd, Birmingham (2019)
12. Chapman, J.R., Peter, J.R.: Does educational gamification improve students motivation? If so, which game elements work best? J. Educ. Bus. 93(7), 315–322 (2018)
13. Mengcheng, W., Dai, X., Yao, S.: The preliminary preparation of the Chinese big five personality questionnaire III : the formulation of the simplified version and the reliability and validity test. Chin. J. Clin. Psychol. 4 (2011) [in Chinese]
14. Chi, L., Xin, Z.: Measurement of college students learning motivation and its relationship with self-efficacy. Psychol. Dev. Educ. vol. 22(2), 64–70 (2006) [in Chinese]
15. Wang, Z., Bergin, C., Bergin, D.A.: Measuring engagement in fourth to twelfth grade classrooms: the classroom engagement inventory. Sch. Psychol. Q. 29(4), 517 (2014)
16. Skinner, E., et al.: Engagement and disaffection in the classroom: part of a larger motivational dynamic? J. Educ. Psychol. 100(4), 765 (2008)
17. Kong, Q.-P., Wong, N.-Y., Lam, C.-C.: Student engagement in mathematics: development of instrument and validation of construct. Math. Educ. Res. J. 15(1), 4–21 (2003)
18. Ghaban, W., Robert, H.: How different personalities benefit from gamification. Interact. Comput. 31(2), 138–153 (2019)
19. Buckley, P., Doyle, E.: Gamification and student motivation. Interactive Learning Environments, 1–14 (2014)
20. Buckley, P., Doyle, E.: Individualising gamification: an investigation of the impact of learning styles and personality traits on the efficacy of gamification using a prediction market. Comput. Educ. 106.MAR., 43–55 (2017)
21. Qu, X., Zeng, J., Shang, J.: Research on MOOC gamification design model from the perspective of situational stories. China Distance Educ. (Integrated Edition) 000.012, 24–33 (2019). [in Chinese]
22. Zhu, Y., Pei, L., Shang, J.: Research on the integration of game and MOOC video - - Taking the MOOC course of Gamification teaching method as an example. J. Distance Educ. 6 (2017). [in Chinese]

Children's Learning Through Touchscreen Games: The Role of Background Music and Touchscreen Experience

Haoxue Yu[1], Hui Li[1($\boxtimes$)], and Kaveri Subrahmanyam[2]

[1] Central China Normal University, Wuhan 430070, Hubei, People's Republic of China
yhxxs@mails.ccnu.edu.cn, huilipsy@mail.ccnu.edu.cn
[2] California State University, Los Angeles, Los Angeles, CA 90032, USA
ksubrah@exchange.calstatela.edu

Abstract. Touchscreen devices have become commonplace in children's lives, and a popular activity among young children is the playing of educational games on touchscreen devices. In these games, background music is used by most game developers as an essential element in increasing player's engagement and interest. The limited research on the effects of background music in educational touchscreen games on young children's learning has yielded mixed results. In addition, past studies have found that touchscreen experience has an impact on children's fine motor skills, which are needed for most touchscreen games. Therefore, the purpose of this study was to explore whether background music and children's touchscreen experience would influence the effect of playing a touchscreen time telling game on children's learning to tell time. Seventy two children aged 5–6 years were randomly assigned to one of four experimental conditions created by crossing two factors - background music while playing the game (Yes or No) and prior touchscreen experience (Yes or No). The results showed that background music promoted learning to tell time among children without touchscreen experience, but had no effect on those who had prior experience. Participants in all conditions were able to transfer the content of touchscreen learning (iPad) to other media (paper clock). The findings have implications for educational game developers, parents, and educators.

Keywords: Background music · Touchscreen experience · Touchscreen games · Learning

1 Introduction

According to a report by Common Sense Media in 2020, video game playing occupies the second place in the proportion of children's daily screen time, with children aged 0–8 spending an average of 23 min a day playing games; this has not significantly changed from trends that were observed nine years ago (25 min per day) [1]. Similar to the U.S., video games are popular among children in China [2]. With the rapid spread of touchscreen devices, touchscreen media have become commonplace in children's lives

© Springer Nature Switzerland AG 2021
X. Fang (Ed.): HCII 2021, LNCS 12790, pp. 294–305, 2021.
https://doi.org/10.1007/978-3-030-77414-1_21

now, with about 97% of American homes with children under 8 owning at least one mobile phone, and 75% of those households owning a tablet computer. As a result, touchscreen games are becoming increasingly dominant in children's lives as early as 2 years [1]. Meanwhile, educational applications based on touchscreen technology and targeted at children are also developing rapidly. By the beginning of 2020, there were more than 180,000 educational apps in the App Store [3]. As of August 2018, the number of children's education app users in China reached 59.13 million, and the total number of children's education apps was more than 40,000, accounting for 7% of the total app market share in China [4].

As educational touchscreen games have become more popular among children, game developers and researchers are beginning to pay attention to the effects of these games on children's development. Li et al. explored the impact of games on children's anthropomorphism, and found that after playing a touchscreen game, six-year-olds' levels of anthropomorphism increased and rated real trains as more human-like [5]. A recent meta-analysis also found that touchscreen games promoted STEM (Science, Technology, Engineering, Mathematics) and vocabulary learning in young children [6]. At present, the scholarship about the science of game learning is still in its infancy, and how to develop educational applications designed to promote meaningful, active, engaged and socially interactive learning in a context that supports learning goals is critical to children's learning through touchscreen games [7]. Therefore, the educational benefit and effects of games need to be better understood. This understanding includes exploring the factors, particularly related to game features, that could affect learning from games [8].

An attractive technique for making games more interesting is the addition of background music, which is one of the elements present in most educational games [9, 10]. It refers to using music as a secondary activity to improve people's auditory environment of current activities [11]. Its effects on games can be understood from two aspects: on the one hand, according to arousal theory [12], music can make players more immersed in a game and more focused because of emotional arousal, so as to promote their learning [13, 14]; on the other hand, it seems plausible that adding music could have a negative effect on learning through games. The theory of limited cognitive resources by Kahneman tells us that new auditory information requires additional processing resources [15], leaving less resources for other cognitive tasks such as processing the game's educational content. In previous empirical studies, no consistent conclusions have been drawn on the impact of background music on educational game learning [9, 16, 17]. Yang et al. explored the effects of in-game background music on video game learning among undergraduates with different cognitive styles such Holism and Serialism. Holists tend to process information in a "whole-to-part" order and Serialists prefer to process information in a "part-to-whole" sequence. The results demonstrated that the learning of Holists was not affected by background music, while the learning of Serialists was negatively affected [16]. Among primary school students, there is evidence that background music in educational adventure games was effective at promoting children's learning motivation, but had no positive or negative impact on learning [9]. In contrast to the negative results of the above studies, some researchers found that the presence of out-of-game background music had a positive effect on college students' learning of historical knowledge and recall accuracy through educational video games [17].

Previous studies on the impact of background music in educational games has mainly focused on elementary school students and undergraduates. Studies examining the role of background music in children's educational game learning, especially with regard touchscreen game learning is limited. Extant research with children has mainly investigated the effects of background music on cognitive processes such as attention, working memory and task transfer when children listen to music while completing a variety of experimental tasks/activities [18–20]. Koolidge and Holmes found that children with an average age of 4.77 years performed better with pure music as general background music than without music when completing jigsaw activities [18]. And one study found that 5- to 6-year–old children can significantly improve their performance on task switching with the presence of background music [19]. In addition, some researchers investigated the effect of background music on children's working memory [19, 20]. Kaniel and Aram used a visual discrimination task that required participants to remember previous stimuli and responses while solving new problems and found that children aged 5–6 performed better in working memory when background music was played in experimental settings than when no background music was played [20]. Overall, studies have mostly provided positive evidence of the effect of background music when completing activities on children's cognition; however findings to the contrary have also been obtained. Dartt found that exposure to background music was detrimental to the concentration of 3- to 5-year-old children while playing [21]. Previous studies have shown a clear link between music played during activities and young children's cognitive performance. Therefore, it is worth exploring whether background music has an impact on children's touchscreen learning.

Based on the widespread use of touchscreen devices by children, researchers have explored the impact of touchscreen experience on children's fine motor skills development [22–25]. On the one hand, it was found that the earlier touchscreen devices were used by children aged 19–36 months, the better their early fine motor level was [22]. On the other hand, some researchers found that compared to participants who received 24 weeks of fine motor activities plan using a touchscreen tablet, children who engaged in a manual play activities program made greater changes in the fine motor precision, fine motor integration and manual dexterity, which meant the extensive use of touchscreen might have negative impact on the fine motor development of preschool children [26]. Webster et al. also found that children aged 3–4 years old who spent more time in contact with screens such as televisions and tablets had poorer performance in hand dexterity [25]. Touchscreen technology provides a variety of touch functions, including clicking, sliding, dragging and so on, which put demands on children's fine motor skills [27]. Whether children without touchscreen experience will be affected by the lack of proficiency in playing games, or whether the prior experience will affect children's learning through touchscreen games still remains to be seen.

The ability to transfer learning from one environment to another is an adaptive skill developed in early childhood and is part of learning [28]. Studies have shown that children between the ages of 4 and 6 can effectively transfer touchscreen learning knowledge.

Some researchers found that children aged 4–6 can learn to solve the Hanoi tower problem through practical operation and touchscreen practice, and transfer their knowledge in both directions [29, 30]. Similarly, preschoolers could successfully transfer skills learned from touchscreen to real life such as measuring and telling time [31, 32]. Furthermore, some researchers have explored the impact of embedded background music on multimedia learning transfer, but the results are mixed [33, 34]. Moreno and Mayer explored the transfer effect of multimedia learning in undergraduates with background music and sound, and found that music and sound had a negative effect on the transfer of knowledge. The researchers explained that background music occupies the participants' limited cognitive resources, which reduces the cognitive resources available for knowledge transfer, and thus may have a negative impact on transferring what they learned [33]. Gong et al. also found that background music had no effect on the transfer of mobile communication knowledge that undergraduates learned through multimedia. They suggested that this may be due to the attention-adaptation effect, which means the cyclic playing of background music makes the subjects quickly ignore the presence of music and focus on knowledge learning [34].

In this study, a time telling game (Moji Clock from the Apple App Store) was used to explore children's learning through touchscreen games. The theme of learning time was chosen because it was one of the themes in Chinese kindergarten curriculum. Meanwhile, two studies have explored the clock learning of Chinese 5- to 6-year-olds through touchscreen games and they considered that children in this age group, who had limited knowledge of reading time, were appropriate participants for this experimental task [32, 35]. Therefore, this study took children aged 5–6 years as participants and selected Moji Clock as a game learning material to discuss the role of background music and touchscreen experience on children's touchscreen learning.

2 Method

2.1 Participants

Seventy-eight children aged 5–6 years were recruited from a large kindergarten affiliated to a university in Central China. All children were ethnically Chinese and from the middle-class. Six children were recruited but not included in the analysis because they were more than 72 months old or they refused to participate in the experiment midway through. In total, data from 72 participants ($M = 67.24$ months, $SD = 3.16$; 36 boys) were included in the study analysis.

2.2 Design

This study used a 2 (background music: with vs. without) × 2 (touchscreen experience: with or without) between-subjects design. Participants were first asked if they had ever played a game on a mobile phone or tablet. Based on their answers, 72 children were randomly assigned to groups with or without background music. There were four experimental conditions in total, including background music-touchscreen experience ($n = 19$, $M = 66.32$ months, $SD = 3.54$; 12 boys), background music-no touchscreen experience ($n = 17$, $M = 67.35$ months, $SD = 3.39$; 8 boys), without background music-touchscreen experience ($n = 19$, $M = 68.21$ months, $SD = 2.70$; 8 boys), without background music-no touchscreen experience ($n = 17$, $M = 67.06$ months, $SD = 2.90$; 8 boys).

2.3 Tools and Materials

In order to consider the suitability of game and avoid the influence of irrelevant sound effects as much as possible, the study adopted the educational app "Moji clock" (see Fig. 1) of Apple App Store as the pre-test and post-test material, which aimed to help children tell time (including on the hour and the half hour) through an interactive touch-screen interface. Children could adjust the clock in this game to match the target time by turning the minute hand according to a voice command (for example, "adjust the time to 2:00"). When children finished the adjustment of the clock and pressed the "OK" button in the lower right corner, the game provided feedback that varied depending on whether the children answered correctly or not. When the answer was correct, the bird on the left would add an ornament. When the answer was wrong, bird droppings would fall from the top left of the game.

Fig. 1. Screenshot from the game "Moji clock"

Because the "Moji clock" lacked background music, Ye's "Happy Time" [36] was selected to be the music that played in the background while the child played the game to simulate a touchscreen game with embedded background music. Eleven research assistants were invited to rate the emotional valence and familiarity of music by using a nine-point Likert scale. In order to control for the influence of volume and rhythm, the background music was played at 60dB equal to the normal speech volume [37]. According to the MixMeister BPM analysis software, the beat of "Happy Time" was 105.60, which was in the medium speed level [38]. Additionally, the researchers adjusted the volume of the game instructions to be approximately 5 dB higher than the background music, so that the background music would not obscure the game's voice commands.

To explore whether children can transfer what they learn from touchscreen to another media, paper clocks (printed in black and white on A4 paper, see Fig. 2) were used as the transfer test material in this study.

Fig. 2. The paper clock

2.4 Procedure

We adopted the research procedure of Wang et al. [32], whose study used a touchscreen game similar to the material used in this study to explore how 5-to 6-year-olds learn clocks through a game. Testing included the pre-test stage, the instruction stage, the learning stage, and the post-test stage (including transfer test).

Pre-test stage: the researcher randomly presented 1–12 number cards to investigate children's number knowledge. Then these children were asked to read out the time (six times, three times on the hour, three times on the half hour) which was randomly demonstrated on the "Moji clock," and scored one point for each correct answer. Children who scored six points were excluded from the follow-up study as they seemed to be proficient at reading a clock and might not benefit from playing the app game.

Instruction stage: the researcher taught children basic clock knowledge (to recognize the hour hand and minute hand, recognized the hour and half hour) and basic operation of the game (get voice instructions by pressing the horn shaped button, submit answers by pressing "OK", and adjust the clock time by turning the minute hand). The instruction lasted approximately 10 min.

Learning stage: children operated the game alone for 10 min. The background music group played "Happy Hour" on a loop in the background while playing the game. The background music did not play for children in the no-background condition.

Post-test stage (also including transfer test): the researcher used the time presented on the "Moji clock" and paper clock (in order to avoid errors caused by the order, the game and paper were randomly arranged in order) to ask the question "What time is it now?" (8 questions for each media, 4 were the times on the hour and 4 were the times on the half hour). If participants answered one question correctly, they would get one point. In order to understand children's subjective feelings towards the whole game operation process, children had to make a subjective assessment (A four-point Likert scale was used, "0" meant "no", and "3" meant "a lot") on their music awareness ("Did you hear the music?"), music affection ("Do you think the music is noisy?"), music interest ("If you play the game again, do you want to have music?") and game interest ("Do you like the music?").

3 Results

All of the 72 children in this study knew numbers 1–12 and successfully played the touchscreen game. An ANOVA confirmed that there were no significant differences in the participants' age as a function of condition, $F(3, 68) = 1.35, p > 0.05$. As for the emotion and familiarity of background music, the analysis of the ratings from the 11 research assistants showed that the music was emotionally positive ($M = 8.09, SD = 1.22$; the higher the score, the more positive the mood), while the familiarity was low ($M = 2.00, SD = 2.05$; the higher the score, the higher the familiarity). This suggests that the music in the study was similar to the background music style of children's educational games in the market, while it also avoided potential threats to validity from the possibility that a few of the participants' would be familiar with the music.

The descriptive data of children's scores on the pre-test, post-test and transfer test are shown in Table 1. One-way ANOVAs revealed no significant differences across four groups (background music-touchscreen experience, background music-without touchscreen experience, no background music-touchscreen experience, no background music-without touchscreen experience) in pre-test scores, $F(3, 68) = 0.62, p > 0.05$.

Table 1. Means and standard deviations of children's post-test in four conditions

	Background music-touchscreen experience	Background music-without touchscreen experience	Without background music-touchscreen experience	Without background music-without touchscreen experience
Pre-test score	1.26 ± 1.91	1.53 ± 2.04	0.74 ± 1.24	1.18 ± 1.88
Post-test score	6.11 ± 2.23	6.53 ± 1.91	6.16 ± 1.98	4.18 ± 2.79
Transfer test score	6.00 ± 2.08	6.35 ± 2.18	6.00 ± 2.19	4.18 ± 3.03

An ANCOVA was conducted with background music and touchscreen experience as the between-subjects variables, the post-test score as the dependent variable, and the pre-test score controlled as the covariate. Results showed that the main effect of pre-test score was significant, $F(1, 67) = 6.68, p < 0.05, \eta2\ p = 0.09$, whereas the main effect of background music, $F(1, 67) = 3.18$, $p > 0.05$, $\eta2\, p = 0.05$, and touchscreen experience, $F(1, 67) = 3.67$, $p > 0.05$, $\eta2\, p = 0.05$, was not significant. In addition, the interaction between background music and touchscreen experience was statistically significant, $F(1, 67) = 5.88$, $p < 0.05$, $\eta2\, p = 0.08$. Further simple effect analysis found that children without touchscreen experience in the background music group performed better on post-test score than those in the no background music groups, $F(1, 70) = 8.82$, $p < 0.01$, $\eta2\, p = 0.12$. However, there was no significant difference in post-test performance among children with touchscreen experience whether or not background music was available during the learning stage, $F(1, 70) = 0.20$, $p > 0.05$. This suggests that background music can promote learning of clock knowledge among children who had no touchscreen experience, but it had no significant effect on learning among children who had prior touchscreen experience.

Then, with background music and touchscreen experience as the between-subjects variables, an ANCOVA was conducted on transfer score with the post-test score as the covariate. The results showed that the main effect of background music, $F(1, 67) = 0.10$, $p > 0.05$, $\eta2\, p = 0.001$, and touchscreen experience, $F(1, 67) = 0.04$, $p > 0.05$, $\eta2\, p = 0.001$, was not significant. The interaction between background music and touchscreen experience did not reach significance, too, $F(1, 67) = 0.03$, $p > 0.05$, $\eta2\, p = 0.001$. In other words, children were able to effectively transfer the learning content of touchscreen to other media (paper), and the transfer was not affected by background music and individual touchscreen experience.

Furthermore, the descriptive values of subjective answers are shown in Table 2. The results of the ANOVA showed that there were no significant differences in the score of music awareness, $F(1, 34) = 1.19$, $p > 0.05$, music liking, $F(1, 34) = 0.15$, $p > 0.05$, music interest, $F(1, 34) = 2.02$, $p > 0.05$, and game liking, $F(3, 68) = 0.53$, $p > 0.05$, among children in the different conditions.

Table 2. Means and standard deviations of children's subjective assessment in four conditions

	Background music-touchscreen experience	Background music-without touchscreen experience	Without background music-touchscreen experience	Without background music-without touchscreen experience
Music awareness	2.47 ± 0.84	2.12 ± 1.11	/	/
Music affection	0.37 ± 0.76	0.47 ± 0.80	/	/
Music interest	1.37 ± 1.26	0.82 ± 1.02	/	/
Game interest	2.53 ± 0.61	2.41 ± 0.94	2.68 ± 0.48	2.65 ± 0.79

4 Discussion

We tested whether background music and touchscreen experience could affect touchscreen learning of preschoolers using a two-factor, between-subject design. The results suggested that music in the background can promote the learning in children without touchscreen experience. This is consistent with previous research showing that background music promotes cognitive activity in young children [18, 20]. Based on arousal theory, music can effectively improve the level of emotion and awareness of children, so that young children can enjoy and focus more on their activities [39–41], and thus have a positive impact on their cognitive performance [39, 42]. However, the study also showed that the accelerating effect of music was only found in children who had no experience with touchscreens, and there was no positive or negative effect on children who had prior experience. In terms of subjective assessment, there were no significant differences in music awareness, music emotional experience, music interest and game learning interest between children with and without touchscreen experience. We infer that children with touchscreen experience have been exposed to more games, and they have become desensitized to the background music in games [43], which means that music may be difficult to arouse their higher interest and promote their touchscreen learning. On the contrary, children without touchscreen experience seemed to be full of curiosity and curious about every detail of the game because they have no prior experience. Therefore, compared with the condition without music in the background, those children's learning effect was better with music.

In addition, the study found that children could successfully transfer the clock knowledge they learned from touchscreen games to paper media, consistent with results of Huber et al. [29], Tarasuik et al. [30], Aladé et al. [31] and Wang et al. [32], which indicated that children over 4 years old can effectively complete the transfer task. Besides, our findings showed that music and touchscreen experience would not affect the transfer of children's clock knowledge. This result is consistent with the findings of Gong et al. [34], but not with those of Moreno and Mayer [33]. The reason may be that the materials selected in this study focused on touchscreen operation and interaction rather than simply watching videos, so background music takes up fewer resources [44]. Furthermore, the transfer test of this study used a verbal measure, and did not need to move the clock's needles, which requires children' fine motor skills. Previous studies have also shown that touchscreen experience may affect children's fine motor development [24, 26], but its effect on children's clock cognition is unclear.

Overall, the results of this study suggest that music in the background had a positive effect on touchscreen learning in children without touchscreen experience, but not a significant effect on children with touchscreen experience. This result deserves the attention of parents, educators and application developers. However, it should be pointed out that this study only focused on the impact of medium-speed, active music (the most common form of music embedded in games) on children's touchscreen learning, whereas other types of music may have different effects on children's touchscreen learning. Note also that to compensate for the limitations of the experimental material (Moji clock has no background music), the music played in the background on the iPad in our study and was not related to game elements, which was different from embedded game music. Therefore, further studies can try to explore whether different music rhythms, different emotions or different music types and relation of game music to game elements may have different impacts on children's touchscreen learning.

Acknowledgments. This research was funded by the Fundamental Research Funds for the Central Universities (CCNU20QN039).

References

1. Rideout, V., Robb, M.B.: The Common Sense census: Media use by kids age zero to eight, 2020. Common Sense Media (2020)
2. Xiao, F.: Study on the status, characteristics and relationship between children's out-of-school life time use and children's development. In: Yuan, L. (eds.) Blue Book of Children: Annual Report on Chinese Children's Development, pp. 49–73. Social Science Academic Press, Beijing (2019)
3. Apps for education. http://www.apple.com./education/products/. Accessed 10 Nov 2020
4. Quest Mobile Online Education Industry Insights Report. https://www.questmobile.com.cn/blog/blog_149.html. Accessed 10 Jan 2021
5. Li, H., Hsueh, Y., Wang, F., Bai, X., Liu, T., Zhou, L.: Do young Chinese children gain anthropomorphism after exposure to personified touch-screen and board games? Front. Psychol. **8**, 55 (2017)
6. Gao, C., Wang, F., Tong, Y., Li, H.: Children in the digital age: touchscreen and child development. Psychol. Dev. Educ. **36**(04), 502–512 (2020)
7. Hirsh-Pasek, K., Zosh, J.M., Golinkoff, R.M., Gray, J.H., Robb, M.B., Kaufman, J.: Putting education in "educational" apps: lessons from the science of learning. Psychol. Sci. Public Interest **16**(1), 3–34 (2015)
8. Fassbender, E., Richards, D., Bilgin, A., Thompson, W.F., Heiden, W.: VirSchool: the effect of background music and immersive display systems on memory for facts learned in an educational virtual environment. Comput. Educ. **58**(1), 490–500 (2012)
9. Linek, S.B., Marte, B., Albert, D.: Background music in educational games: motivational appeal and cognitive impact. In: Patrick, F. (eds.) Developments in Current Game-Based Learning Design and Deployment, pp. 219–230. IGI Global, Hershey (2013)
10. Zhang, J., Gao, X.: Background music matters: why video games lead to increased aggressive behavior? Entertain. Comput. **5**(2), 91–100 (2014)
11. Luo, X.: Effects of different type of background music of online games on aggressive mood, cognition and behavior among college students (Unpublished Master Thesis), Southwest University (2014)
12. Husain, G., Thompson, W.F., Schellenberg, E.G.: Effects of musical tempo and mode on arousal, mood, and spatial abilities. Music Percept. **20**(2), 151–171 (2002)
13. North, A.C., Hargreaves, D.J.: Music and driving game performance. Scand. J. Psychol. **40**(4), 285–292 (1999)
14. Cassidy, G., MacDonald, R.: The effects of music choice on task performance: a study of the impact of self-selected and experimenter-selected music on driving game performance and experience. Music Sci. **13**(2), 357–386 (2009)
15. Kahneman, D.: Attention and Effort. Prentice Hall, Englewood Cliffs (1973)
16. Yang, T., Chen, M., Chen, S.: The effects of background music on game-based learning: a cognitive style approach. Asia Pac. Educ. Res. **28**, 495–508 (2019)
17. Richards, D., Fassbender, E., Bilgin, A., Thompson, W.F.: An investigation of the role of background music in IVWs for learning. ALT-J **16**(3), 231–244 (2008)

18. Koolidge, L., Holmes, R.M.: Piecing it together: the effect of background music on children's puzzle assembly. Percept. Mot. Skills **125**(2), 387–399 (2018)
19. Yang, Q., Xie, Y.: The influence of background music on young children's working memory and task switching in kindergarten. J. Stud. Early Child. Educ. **268**(4), 48–55 (2017)
20. Kaniel, S., Aram, D.: Influence of task difficulty and background music on working memory activity: developmental considerations. Alberta J. Educ. Res. **44**(3), 342 (1998)
21. Dartt, K.M.: Effects of background music on preschoolers' attention (Unpublished doctoral dissertation). University of North Texas (2009)
22. Marsh, J., Plowman, L., Yamada-Rice, D., Bishop, J.C., Lahmar, J., Scott, F., Davenport, A., Davis, S., French, K., Piras, M., Thornhill, S., Robinson, P., Winter, P.: Exploring play and creativity in pre-schoolers' use of apps: final project report. Technology and Play (2015)
23. Cheung, C.H., Bedford, R., Saez De Urabain, I.R., Karmiloff-Smith, A., Smith, T.J.: Daily touchscreen use in infants and toddlers is associated with reduced sleep and delayed sleep onset. Sci. Rep. **7**, 46104 (2017)
24. Bedford, R., Saez de Urabain, I. R., Cheung, C.H., Karmiloff-Smith, A., Smith, T.J.: Toddlers' fine motor milestone achievement is associated with early touchscreen scrolling. Front. Psychol. **7**, 1108 (2016)
25. Webster, E.K., Martin, C.K., Staiano, A.E.: Fundamental motor skills, screen-time, and physical activity in preschoolers. J. Sport Health Sci. **8**(02), 24–31 (2019)
26. Lin, L., Cherng, R., Chen, Y.: Effect of touch screen tablet use on fine motor development of young children. Phys. Occup. Ther. Pediatr. **37**(5), 457–467 (2017)
27. Price, S., Jewitt, C., Crescenzi, L.: The role of iPads in pre-school children's mark making development. Comput. Educ. **87**, 131–141 (2015)
28. Barr, R.: Transfer of learning between 2D and 3D sources during infancy: Informing theory and practice. Dev. Rev. **30**(2), 128–154 (2010)
29. Huber, B., Tarasuik, J., Antoniou, M.N., Garrett, C., Bowe, S.J., Kaufman, J., Team, S.B.: Young children's transfer of learning from a touchscreen device. Comput. Hum. Behav. **56**, 56–64 (2016)
30. Tarasuik, J., Demaria, A., Kaufman, J.: Transfer of problem solving skills from touchscreen to 3D model by 3-to 6-year-olds. Front. Psychol. **8**, 1586 (2017)
31. Aladé, F., Lauricella, A.R., Beaudoin-Ryan, L., Wartella, E.: Measuring with murray: touchscreen technology and preschoolers' STEM learning. Comput. Hum. Behav. **62**, 433–441 (2016)
32. Wang, F., Gao, C., Kaufman, J., Tong, Y., Chen, J.: Watching versus touching: the effectiveness of a touchscreen app to teach children to tell time. Comput. Educ. **160**, 104021 (2020)
33. Moreno, R., Mayer, R.E.: A learner-centered approach to multimedia explanations: Deriving instructional design principles from cognitive theory. Interact. Multimed. Electron. J. Comput. Enhanc. Learn. **2**(2), 12–20 (2000)
34. Gong, D., Liu, D., Zhang, D.: The effect of abstract and background music on cognitive load and multimedia learning. Psychol. Dev. Educ. **1**, 83–87 (2008)
35. Wang, F., Xie, H., Wang, Y., Hao, Y., An, J.: Using touchscreen tablets to help young children learn to tell time. Front. Psychol. **7**, 1800 (2016)
36. Happy time. https://music.163.com/#/song?id=179772&market=baiduqk/. Accessed 21 Oct 2020
37. Dirks, D.D., Morgan, D.E., Dubno, J.R.: A procedure for quantifying the effects of noise on speech recognition. J. Speech Hear. Disord. **47**(2), 114–123 (1982)
38. Dubé, L., Chebat, J., Morin, S.: The effects of background music on consumers' desire to affiliate in buyer-seller interactions. Psychol. Mark. **12**(4), 305–319 (1995)
39. Schellenberg, E.G.: Cognitive performance after music listening: a review of the Mozart effect. In: MacDonald, R.A.R., Kreutz, G., Mitchell, L. (eds.) Music, Health and Wellbeing. Oxford University Press, Oxford (2012)

40. Richter, A., Courage, M.L.: Comparing electronic and paper storybooks for preschoolers: attention, engagement, and recall. J. Appl. Dev. Psychol. **48**, 92–102 (2017)
41. Sarı, B., Başal, H.A., Takacs, Z.K., Bus, A.G.: A randomized controlled trial to test efficacy of digital enhancements of storybooks in support of narrative comprehension and word learning. J. Exp. Child Psychol. **179**, 212–226 (2019)
42. Ilie, G., Thompson, W.F.: Experiential and cognitive changes following seven minutes exposure to music and speech. Music Percept. **28**(3), 247–264 (2011)
43. Zhang, J., Fu, X.: The influence of background music of video games on immersion. J. Psychol. Psychother. **5**(4), 191 (2015)
44. Brünken, R., Plass, J.L., Leutner, D.: Assessment of cognitive load in multimedia learning with dual-task methodology: auditory load and modality effects. Instr. Sci. **32**(1–2), 115–132 (2004)

Gamified Education in K-12

Fan Zhao$^{(\boxtimes)}$, Roger Mendez, Alec Toubin, and Brian Mahan

Florida Gulf Coast University, Fort Myers, FL 33965, USA
fzhao@fgcu.com

Abstract. The lack of engagement throughout a traditional education process is a regular concern among all the educators. Gamification is the application of game-like elements and game principles in non-game contexts. The purpose of this study is to identify key steps to adopt a better gamification method in K-12 educational schools. According to a case study, this research presents a gamification proposition that aims to promote learning engagement in K-12 education with the use of Gamification methods. Six stages compose the method: understand students; find resources; select right resources; students' feedback; cluster students; and customize gamification. To validate the method, we developed an initial experiment in a high school environment. The results is successful.

Keywords: Gamification · Learning · K-12 education

1 Introduction

Gamification is the utilization of components of game playing, such as challenges, competition with others, and leaderboards to any type of activity to encourage engagement in participating in it. Along with increasing engagement, gamification helps users or participants become more motivated in being more involved in the activity. The motivation concept of gamification stems from the rewards that come with it. These rewards come in the form of points, badges, gifts, and any other types of achievements. The purpose of gamification is to create a system where the players can gain a sense of engagement in an activity that allows them to apply problem solving skills to a situation while simultaneously having fun with doing so.

By establishing intrinsic reasons, gamification systems adopt heuristic design patterns and dynamic game elements to enrich user satisfaction [1]. Characteristics of games can better motivate and lead users' interests and concentration, and generate excitement with compelling and addictive experience. [2]. However, the success of a desired gamification system depends on the planning and the in-depth analysis of the proposed aims at the beginning of the gamification system implementation [3]. Even gamification systems were adopted in various areas of training and education, users in different scenarios with different characteristics, such as personality and individual peculiarities, should be treated differently by designing customized gamification systems [4].

The most recognized area where gamification is greatly used is the traditional education, such as K-12. Many teachers struggle to keep their students engaged in class

© Springer Nature Switzerland AG 2021
X. Fang (Ed.): HCII 2021, LNCS 12790, pp. 306–315, 2021.
https://doi.org/10.1007/978-3-030-77414-1_22

and motivated to learn outside of it. Students feel boring and tired while learning some conceptual knowledge, such as Math, Physics, and Chemistry. Gamification is the gateway to increase students' interests and engagement by allowing them to participate in games that pertain to what is being taught in their classes. However, while a method of gamification may seem to work when first implemented, its effect on the students may begin to wear off after a while.

Given this context, we conduct a qualitative study in a K-12 education scenario to explore more hidden patterns of gamified motivation in education. According to the case study, we present a proposal of gamification system design to improve and keep the engagement of students in K-12 education.

2 Literature Review

The quality of teaching is of increasingly significance for the success of educational institutions. It is important for educational institutions to ensure that their students get quality education at all levels. Teachers are expected to fulfill their obligations with the utmost quality so that the students can be well prepared for the classes and jobs. It is crucial that teachers motivate their students in learning. The use of gamification could help provide a solution to the decline in learners' motivation and engagement the education system is facing today [5]. Many schools and teachers face the same problem every day. Traditional schooling, is perceived as ineffective and boring by many students, has become ineffective as students tend to lack motivation and an interest in learning. Plenty of teachers have in turn decided to use gamification techniques and methods to engage their students [6].

Borrowing game elements and incorporating them into a classroom environment can actually facilitate engagement among students. Students tend to be more motivated if they're introduced to game elements comparing to a boring classroom environment. Students increase engagement, motivation and overall performance through instant feedback and collaboration when there are game elements added to the class.

The use of educational games as learning tools can enhance not only student knowledge but also their ability to communicate and cooperate with the classmates in what concerns the understanding of learning content. The use of games in the classroom may help students acquire new study methods, while making them feel more motivated than when they are exposed to more traditional teaching-learning processes [7].

Gamification actually provides the component of fun that helps transform students' attitudes towards learning. Having fun in the classroom can result in more students' willingness going to class, wanting to learn, and staying motivated in class. Video games tend to produce an emotional state for its users with enjoyment [8]. This feeling of fun is created in players through their feeling of achievement, reward for completing a level, or simply winning a game [9]. If this element of play is incorporated into a learning experience, an intrinsic interest in learning can follow. For many learners, the fun part of a gamified environment is the product of solving problems and overcoming challenges as they engage critical thinking skills.

Gamification utilizes the most effective components of video game elements without committing to a specific game resulting in increased levels of motivation and engagement in the learning experience. Gamification in education is an ongoing process that harvests the most engaging game components and applies them to increase motivation and engagement among learners. Gamification creates a long-term effect as it works by adding elements inspired from games to the classroom environment mainly to increase motivation, engagement, and promote desired learning behaviors [10].

The main objective of utilizing gamification in education is to increase student engagement and motivation to participate in the classroom. The point of applying these game-like elements is to teach students that learning can be a fun experience. Whether it is digital or non-digital, children experience feelings of joy and excitement when they are playing a game, along with a feeling of determination to reach a certain goal while doing so.

Gamification in education is a topic that many teachers, professors, and researchers must contemplate on, in terms of its effectiveness. The use of gamification in the education system has the ability to provide solutions to the decline in engagement and motivation of students in schooling systems. The application of gamification "provides some remedy for many students who find themselves alienated by traditional methods of instruction" [5]. Furthermore, game-based learning is a great way for students to take the mindset they have when playing video games and apply it to their learning environment. More schooling systems are starting to see this creative learning technique as an innovative way to bring an incline to student motivation, emotional involvement, and enjoyment of learning various topics [11].

Additionally, it is important that when gamification is used in education and classroom environments, it should be designed to partial level of a challenge for the students to maintain their engagement. If the gamification is of a complicated challenge, it could have a reverse effect on engagement and end up causing a lack of interest. Failure in a game setting can damage the student's self-esteem and cause a lack of interest in re engaging. If students are failing to complete these game-type challenges, they won't stay focused and will be less engaged.

If gamification methods are deemed difficult or frustrating, it will do the opposite of what it intends to do. Instructors use gamification in education to grab student's attention, to keep them engaged and improve their motivation. If an instructor intends to create engagement and a fun learning environment, the challenge should be doable but still enough of a challenge to make the students work and think.

It is critical to understand the importance of using games in an educational context but bearing in mind that it must satisfy students and instructors. The use of games gives teachers a chance to create challenges that are suitable for the students' level of knowledge. Teachers can begin to give more difficult challenges as new information and skills are acquired.

3   Research Method

To properly answer our research question regarding users' education and training, we adopted case study method to find hidden facts behind daily K-12 education. We have used a combination of information from the reviewed literature and interview data in two local high schools in southwest Florida. One of them is a private school with 328 students and the other is a public school with over 1800 students. Semi-structured, in-depth interviews were adopted for data collection in the case study. The interview process aimed to explore the subjective ideas/opinions of teachers working in the high school.

As part of the research process, a pair of interviews with teaching perspectives were held with two teachers and 5 students in their classes from two different high schools. The interviews were an exploratory interview of daily education at school. Information was gathered concerning student learning and learning engagement in class. The teachers in the high schools developed several gamified methods in class to encourage student learning. They also adopted a game software to attract students in learning. Both teachers got over 10 years of teaching experience in the high school.

For each teacher, there are two interviews completed. The first interview is an overall exploratory of the teachers' teaching experience. The second interview is more focused on gamification applications adopted in their classrooms.

4   Case Study

4.1   Reward Systems

There are two gamification methods adopted in the two high schools. Both teachers adopted a gamification method with reward systems. People by nature are most likely to accept and interested in active interactions com-paring to passive interactions [12]. The methods to motivate students in gamification are to establish active interactions in the learning process rather than passive instructions, such as lectures in class. Change & Wei [13] identified categories of educational interactions in gamification:

- Learner-content interaction: includes self-expression, pattern recognition, time pressure, and status;
- Leaner-instructor interaction: includes goal settings, instruction, and rewards;
- Learner-learner interaction: includes reputation points, peer tutoring, competition, altruism, group identification, and peer appraisal.

In Learner-instructor interaction, reward is borrowed from game elements. It is a crucial motivation factor that affects students' perception of the benefits of the gamification application [14–16].

With this methods, three forms of rewards were developed: points, badges, and levels. Points are an incentivization tool that is used to motivate students to participate in class. In most cases, a student receives a point for whenever they accomplish something in class, such as giving the correct answer to a question or doing well on an assignment or test. The way both teachers implemented points was by giving "bonus points" to each student if the majority of the class receives an A on an exam.

Badges are similar to points, in that they are a symbolization of a student's achievement in class. A certain number of badges can lead up to the student receiving a potential reward for their accomplishments. The way both teachers used badges in their classrooms was by giving a badge to a student for every three times they voluntarily participated in class. After earning ten badges, a student would receive a gift card to a restaurant such as Chipotle, Starbucks, or Chili's.

The third reward offered by the two teachers was levels. Levels can be used in a classroom as a series of learning stages in which students increase their levels each time after they reach a certain goal. Students who are provided the reward method of levels tend to receive higher grades than students who do not [17]. In both teachers' classes, students would move up a level for every time they received a one hundred percent on a homework assignment. By the time they reach the fifth level, they receive a "free day," where they can do whatever they please while in class. The teacher in the private school had mentioned that three years ago, there was a teacher-faculty meeting regarding gamification. The two principals of the high school and students felt that the teachers should start using some forms of gamification to increase student engagement. The public school teacher adopted this system a year ago after knowing the success of the system from the private school. Along with points and badges, both teachers felt that levels in particular would really motivate students into having their own free days. As a result, the number of students receiving one-hundred percent scores on their homework increased tremendously.

4.2 Software Game System

Most children of this generation truly enjoy playing video games during their free time. One popular online game that many teachers and professors use to increase student engagement is called 'Kahoot!.' Kahoot! is a game-based learning platform that brings engagement and fun to students from elementary school to college. The concept of Kahoot! is to make multiple choice quizzes for students to compete against their classmates. Whoever answers the correct questions the fastest holds the title of first place.

The private high school teacher used this game in his classes (unfortunately, it is not adopted in the public high school yet). Many of his former students recalled the experience of using Kahoot! in their ninth grade Human Geography class when it first came out. All of them expressed how much they enjoyed the game and wished to continue using it when we interviewed them. To this day, the teacher still uses it in all of his classes as a way to make his students more engaged in his classes. Eventually, he started to add prizes, such as a free pen or a piece of candy, to those who would finish in first place. When asked how exactly he felt the use of gamification techniques have impacted his students, this teacher spoke on the comparison of playing a game with learning. He felt that adding game-like elements to his curriculum would take away the boredom that students feel. He mentioned that the engagement from his students has increased after adding them.

While certain subjects might be boring to a good amount of school students, it is games like Kahoot! that take student engagement to a completely higher level. Kahoot! is an online application that drives competition among students. Increasing competition between a student and his/her classmates can help them become more involved in the sense that he/she becomes more motivated to finish in first place and possibly win a prize at the end. In addition, competition between children and teenagers can actually help them become closer and form relationships with each other, and eventually learn how to cooperate with one another. It has been stated that the activities gamified with the Kahoot application has a more positive impact on students who use it compared to students who do not [18].

5 Discussion

Even both systems are very successful in two different high schools, there are still problems need to be fixed. Both teachers admitted that, even they tried their best to modify the reward systems and games, there are still some students never been motivated by the gamification systems.

Both teachers have stated that they believe that reasons why students don't feel as motivated to apply themselves is because there aren't enough resources that might pertain to their interests. One student told us during the interview "High school students of our generation today are so drawn to their laptops and smartphones, that anytime they need to research a certain topic or play a game, they instantly turn to these devices." This will weaken the attractions of the gamification in learning. Therefore, finding enough, rich, and various gamified resources is necessary to strength the gamification education to the students.

Additionally, the teacher from the private school emphasizes that not all gamification techniques or methods are accepted by students. Certain gamification techniques and methods can cause students to lose interest and then engagement. Certain students may show dissatisfaction in the game design elements that are incorporated into the classroom. Finding a medium is important when using gamification in education. During the interview, this teacher was asked how students felt about his gamification methods used in his classroom. Students still showed a lack of interest in the subject and topic and even went as far as to say that they were disengaged in the topic.

Gamification won't always engage all students. Students express different attitudes towards the gamification techniques that their instructors may implement into a classroom setting. It is up to the teachers to figure out what gamification techniques get the most engagement out of their students. An easy way to figure that out is to try several gamification methods and get feedback from students. Teachers can also take a look at their students' overall performance in the class as a result of gamification techniques used to motivate students.

Kahoot! is one the gamification methods he used which is very popular among students and teachers across the nation. However, not everyone may enjoy the gamification education through this software. Some students may just not feel engaged due to the topic they are being asked to focus on or they may prefer different game elements. Many classes used to have Jeopardy trivia review games right before exams and offer extra bonus points or rewards if a group won. That gamification method is another great way to engage the whole class because it boosts competitive motivation and engagement. If students are offered the opportunity to receive bonus points and they are divided into groups, they will put together their knowledge and collaborate with one another because they are motivated by game elements and rewards. Some students may prefer different gamification methods. Some students may just be entirely disengaged and may not care for any gamification methods.

Therefore, according to the literature review and our interviews with teachers and students, we propose a six-step gamification design guideline to help instructors develop a better gamification education tool in their classes (Fig. 1).

- Step 1: teachers need to understand students' needs and their interests. For example, some students need to strengthen their logical or reasoning ability while some other students may need to memorize more concepts or terms. Additionally, regarding to the style of games, some students enjoy playing action or adventure games while some other students may like animal or nature games.
- Step 2: teachers need to find appropriate resources according to students' needs and interests. For example, a teacher may adopt "Logo Quiz" app to help students who likes nature games and need to memorize all the country trademarks or flags.
- Step 3: teachers want to adopt a few resources in the class for 2–3 weeks. This is the testing period to exam the matching style between students and different resources. For example, a teacher may use three different apps for three different sections and summarize the results of learning among students.
- Step 4: after the testing period, teachers need to collect students' feedback about the resources adopted before.
- Step 5: according to students' feedback, teachers' perspectives, and learning outcomes from the students during the testing period, teachers need to analyze the students' needs and their interests quantitively. Based on this analysis, teachers can identify groups of students who have similar needs and interests.
- Step 6: for each clustered student group, teachers need to identify the best resource and design the best gamification method in class.

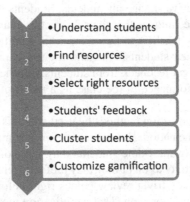

Fig. 1. Proposed gamification methods selection model.

To test this research model, we worked with the private school teacher and completed a simple initial experiment. First, he is well aware how much his students rely on technology to go throughout their day. There are times where he asks them to take out their laptops to complete an assignment. Taking note of this, he has decided he will focus on the change with new technology or software in class.

After thinking about which devices his students use the most, this teacher has decided that it would be good to try and use some learning-based mobile applications, as he always sees his students walking around the halls with their phones in their hands.

Two mobile applications that he has decided to let his students use are called "Geography: Quiz Game" and "Logo Quiz." The Geography: Quiz application is a learning app that helps students in Human Geography learn more about each country and how their human cultures and economies differ from one another. As students are learning they will eventually be quizzed on what they have learned through the app thus far. The Logo Quiz application is a learning app where students must identify specific logos or trademarks that pertain to a certain country. The graphics and the game-like elements of both apps caught the students' attention and increased their engagement and motivation even more.

Since the teacher didn't want to break the pre-defined curriculum, he found a simple method to get students' feedback toward these two new gamification packages. He had a presentation in class about the games and let students play them in class. Every student in each of his classes had expressed how much they all have enjoyed the mobiles and how they felt much more engaged and motivated to learn more about the subject. The teacher then went as far to relate these games with the video games that his students played in their spare time. His logic was that if children can find immense pleasure in games such as 'Fortnite' and 'Mario Kart,' they can find that same pleasure in the learning-based education games.

We didn't have time to cluster all the students in his class. However, after testing the two mobile applications as new resources of gamification, the teacher has come to the conclusion that the use of technology and mobile apps serves as a stronger form of gamification for all of his students. While his original techniques of points, badges, and levels were all good forms of gamification, it was the learning-based mobile applications that really brought student engagement and learning motivation at their peaks. He believes that mobile applications are modern forms of gamification, therefore students are more likely to adopt to them. By taking advantage of this belief, he teaches his students that the learning-based mobile applications can be as fun as playing actual video games.

Overall, the initial testing of our research model is successful! We are excited to continue this experiment in the future, especially to see the results after clustering the students in class.

6 Conclusions

In summary, gamification can promote behavioral change in a classroom. It helps make learning experience more exciting to the students who show little or no interest in learning or engaging in class. If students are being rewarded for learning and engaging in class, it can help learning to be more effective and smoother. Engaging and entertaining students by capturing their attention through game elements can be very beneficial to the teacher and the students. If students are willing to learn and are engaged, it makes a teacher's job much easier to do. Students willingly engaged create a more productive classroom which allows teachers to teach with much ease. Productivity will increase within the classroom and it is a great teaching technique that allows for cognitive and physical development among students depending on the gamification methods used.

The aim of gamification is to support and motivate users to perform a given task by engaging them in the activities and to foster their interest in a certain area that may enhance learning. Gamification has a great potential to motivate students and make the school environment more attractive so as to improve educational activities. Learning shouldn't be a dull experience for students. Learning experiences should be motivating and pleasant. Gamifying education while rewarding effort and success have a great impact on motivation, engagement, and learning experience. According to a case study in two local high schools, we propose a gamification method design guideline to help educators, not only the high school teachers, develop a better educational methods in their classrooms to encourage students learning. We completed an initial test of this design guideline and the results is successful.

Understanding the key steps influencing gamification design is crucial to the success of K-12 education today. This study explores how teachers use gamification methods in their classes to improve student learning outcomes. The proposed research model presented in this study provides helpful guidelines to help educational game designers better understand needs from both students and teachers in education and develop more appropriate games for students. Additionally, the findings and the proposed research model would be beneficial in the theoretical understanding of the adoption behavior of both students and teachers. It may also help in driving the development and execution of new theories in educational gamification research.

References

1. Zichermann, G., Linder, J.: Game-Based Marketing: Inspire Customer Loyalty Through Rewards, Challenges, and Contests. Wiley, Hoboken (2010)
2. Bai, S., Hew, K.F., Huang, B.: Does gamification improve student learning outcome? Evidence from a meta-analysis and synthesis of qualitative data in educational contexts. Educ. Res. Rev. **30**(100322), 1–20 (2020)
3. Alsaleh, N., Alnanih, R.: Gamification-based behavioral change in children with diabetes mellitus. Procedia Comput. Sci. **170**, 442–449 (2020)
4. Nasirzadeh, E., Fathian, M.: Investigating the effect of gamification elements on bank customers to personalize gamified systems. Int. J. Hum Comput Stud. **143**, 1–19 (2020)
5. Alsawaier, R.S.: The effect of gamification on motivation and engagement. Int. J. Inf. Learn. Technol. **35**(1), 56–79 (2018)
6. Van Roy, R., Zaman, B.: Need-supporting gamification in education: an assessment of motivational effects over time. Comput. Educ. **127**, 283–297 (2018)
7. Silva, R.J.R.D., Rodrigues, R.G., Leal, C.T.P.: Gamification in management education: a systematic literature review. BAR-Braz. Adm. Rev. **16**(2), 1–31 (2019)
8. Klimmt, C., Hartmann, T., Frey, A.: Effectance and control as determinants of video game enjoyment. Cyberpsychol. Behav. **10**(6), 845–848 (2007)
9. Gee, J.: Good Video Games + Good Learning. Peter Lang, New York (2013)
10. Huang, B., Hew, K.F.: Implementing a theory-driven gamification model in higher education flipped courses: effects on out-of-class activity completion and quality of artifacts. Comput. Educ. **125**, 254–272 (2018)
11. Hartt, M., Hosseini, H., Mostafapour, M.: Game on: exploring the effectiveness of game-based learning. Plan. Pract. Res. **35**(5), 589–604 (2020)
12. Acar, A.: Testing the effects of incidental advertising exposure in online gaming environments. J. Interact. Advert. **8**, 45–56 (2007)

13. Change, J., Wei, H.: Exploring engaging gamification mechanics in massive online open courses. Educ. Technol. Soc. **19**(2), 177–203 (2016)
14. Drèze, X., Nunes, J.: Feeling superior: the impact of loyalty program structure on consumers' perceptions of status. J. Consum. Res. **35**(6), 890–905 (2008)
15. Eason, C., Bing, M., Smothers, J.: Reward me, charity, or both? The impact of fees and benefits in loyalty programs. J. Retail. Consum. Serv. **25**, 71–80 (2015)
16. Kivetz, R., Simonson, I.: Earning the right to indulge: effort as a determinant of customer preferences toward frequency program rewards. J. Mark. Res. **39**(2), 155–170 (2002)
17. Saran, M., Mohammed, D., Al-magsoosi, A.D.: Gamification in e-learning: the effect on student performance. In: Annual International Conference on Computer Science Education: Innovation & Technology, pp. 25–32 (2018)
18. Orhan Göksün, D., Gürsoy, G.: Comparing success and engagement in gamified learning experiences via Kahoot and Quizizz. Comput. Educ. **135**, 15–29 (2019)

Mixed and Virtual Reality Games

Virtual Reality for Rich Interaction with Cultural Heritage Sites

Nouf AlMuraikhi, Fatima AlMalki, Fadeela AlDahnim, and Osama Halabi(✉) ⓘ

Qatar University, 2713 Doha, Qatar
ohalabi@qu.edu.qa

Abstract. Archaeological sites represent an important dimension of history and civilization. The aim of this work is to is to document the heritage buildings as part of a preservation process of the heritage environment by creating a three-dimensional model of one heritage site in Qatar including all the details of the site using photogrammetry technique. Different techniques for constructing the 3D model of the site has been explored and tested. The model then rendered in a game engine to create interactive virtual reality (VR) experience. Artifacts integrated with the VR environment, moreover, smart avatars that represent people's life and appearance during that period were created in order to bring the place back to life again. Usability, game experience, and simulator sickness evaluation were carried out to test the system.

Keywords: Virtual reality · Photogrammetry · Culture heritage · Serious games

1 Introduction

The new era of digital age and recent advancement in cutting-age immersive technology have opened new opportunities for accessing and presenting cultural heritage in interactive and interesting style. Virtual reality provide a new medium to provide experience and training for different application in education, medical, and industry [1–3]. VR can provides an immersive experience for different cultural heritage sites [4] in contrast to traditional methods of digitizing the heritage using basic storage medial such as video and audio. This could be sufficient documentation and not for preservation. For heritage preservation it is important to convey context and experience of the heritage community [5]. Virtual environment (VE) enable participants to explore, interact, examine, and have the sense of presence in the same atmosphere of old times. This work aims at capturing the heritage sites and convert it to 3D models and create interactive virtual environment of the site with animations, interaction, and avatars that can bring back the site to live.

Creating VR experience for many cultural heritage have been explored actively in the recent years, especially with advancement of VR headsets in the recent years where it becomes affordable and available to consumers and gamers. Fen et al. presented a virtual experience of Han Chang'an City [6]. Häkkilä et al. developed a virtual reality experience to visit the inaccessible Salla World War II graveyard where they created an accurate simulation and atmosphere [4]. There are many applications In the context of

© Springer Nature Switzerland AG 2021
X. Fang (Ed.): HCII 2021, LNCS 12790, pp. 319–328, 2021.
https://doi.org/10.1007/978-3-030-77414-1_23

introducing the concept of serious games to the culture sites such as a serious game for learning Egyptian hieroglyphs where it uses immersive and interactive virtual learning worlds to support transfer of knowledge [7]. A serious game for the ancient Agora of Athens was presented in where it provided virtual tours of the area and a game quiz [8]. Eslam and his colleagues presented a cultural learning environment of heritage artifacts for Young Museum [9].

Creating a realistic 3D models of the site is another challenge, especially if the scale of the site is large. Many research papers had different approaches in order to utilize photogrammetry to create highly immersive virtual reality experience. Vajak and Livada [10] case study focuses on converting images of real time world captured using photogrammetry to a 3D model. Photogrammetry was done by capturing eight hundred images using Samsung Galaxy s6 phone. The photos were processed in different software to get the generated textured 3D model. The generated model was imported to Unity3d to create scripts, write code, add objects and mechanics to accomplish a high-quality VR interface. Grun et al. [11] mentioned a workflow that combines photogrammetry and virtual reality to restore cultural heritage. Photogrammetry and laser scanning were used for the interior structure of the temple. A set of steps and different software were used to construct a virtual reality interface with the help of photogrammetry. Yastikli [12] has done experiments that involved using digital photogrammetry and terrestrial laser scanning and concluded that using any of these methods can restore and document cultural heritage. The experiments include the workflow for each method from acquiring data, building of texture mesh to get the final product needed. Leonov et al. [13] had a different approach as laser scanning methodology was used on Shukhoov Hyperboloid tower in Moscow. It was mentioned that there are different techniques required to restore cultural heritage sites. Their approach was to create a 3D model of the tower and develop a software application for public users. Nevertheless, many approaches in how a three-dimensional model can be created and how it can be turned into an immersive interface using different workflows and techniques.

The presented work combines the previous researches by mixing between historical retrieval and creating an immersive and interactive scene by adding Game components, avatars and scenarios with the usage of a modern interactive head mounted display (HMD). The goal is to bring the historical sites to life by adding these elements together using game engine as well as photogrammetry.

2   System Architecture

Photogrammetry technique was selected mainly because it is a low-cost and affordable solution. The laser scanning has a smaller footprint and higher accuracy but very expensive. Our main target is to provide the workflow for an affordable and cheap solution with high accuracy. The first step is to capture the site using camera or drone, then will create a 3D model from the image using photogrammetry software. The 3D model needs cleaning to make it ready to export to the game engine. AgiSoft MetaShape was used to convert images to 3D model and MeshLab was used to clean the model. Also, Blender was used to remodel and re-sculpt some errors and finalize the final model and make it ready for rendering in the game engine. Some textures were damaged and needed editing, therefore, Paint3D from Microsoft was used to fix textures. Once the model and the textures are ready, it will be imported as a game components. In the game engine navigation as well as scenarios and characters were added that allows the users to interact with in the environment. Support for virtual reality is achieved by converting the system to VR components and implemented interaction with controllers. HTC Vive Cosmos were used as an HMD where it allows freedom of interaction and walking in a room-scale mode. This will make the interaction more intuitive by not restricting the user movement and apply walkaround and natural interaction with ability to move around and grasp objects. Figure 1 shows the overall system architecture.

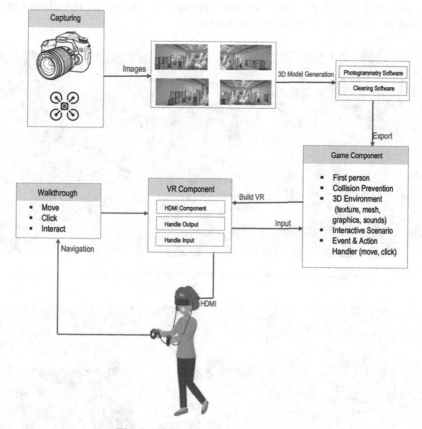

Fig. 1. The overall system architecture.

3   User Interface Design

Our aim is to build a user-friendly interface where user interaction is not done by a mouse and a keyboard, instead the user will use a wand or controller and a headset instead of a monitor to view the scene. The user can navigate and move freely in the scene. The interactivity in the system is what enhances the usability. The user has the ability to roam freely on valid locations and has the option to teleport as shown in Fig. 2, the system will show the teleportation in green as an indicator that it is a valid point. The user can point at the button on the board where it will change color upon hovering to blue and red when pressing. Once pressed the tour guide will walk towards the building and begin to speak as shown in Fig. 3. The user has the ability to interact with the many objects in the scene as they usually do in the real site. The user can interact with the well in the site, once he walks up to the handle, it will be highlighted in yellow as shown in Fig. 4 and he can rotate the handle which will produce a bucket of water. The user can also interact with various artifacts in the scene as shown in Fig. 5 and have a closer inspection of what the object looks like. This is provides a unique experience as it is usually not allowed in the historical and museums to touch such artifacts.

Fig. 2. The user move freely using teleportation technique.

Fig. 3. Screenshots of the smart avatars to provide tour guidance.

Fig. 4. The user can interact with virtual objects as he do in the real site to provide the same experience in real life.

Fig. 5. The user can interact with many artifacts in the scene where usually are not allowed to touch in the real site.

4 Evaluation

The system was evaluated based on different well established gaming questionnaires. Ten subjects were recruited from different background and wide spread ages.

4.1 Game Experience Evaluation

According to IJsselstejin and his colleagues [14], there are three types of categories to ask the users to get the best answers regarding the game experience of the system, so the first section of the survey was divided to three categories, in-game, social presence module, and post-game module.

In-Game Module

The objective of this test is to understand to what extent the users were immersed and their sense of presence in the virtual world. Also, how interesting or boring was their experience. The participants were asked while they are playing inside the virtual environment to get instant answers about what they are feeling at this moment. This is essential for such questions not to be postponed to after finish as they will try to recall how was their feeling which might not be easy to recall. The results shows that over 70% found the simulation impressive, contended, and successful. Between 57% to 62.6% found themselves absorbed and completely immersed in the simulation. Less than 35% felt bored and only 20.4 felt frustrated as shown in Fig. 6.

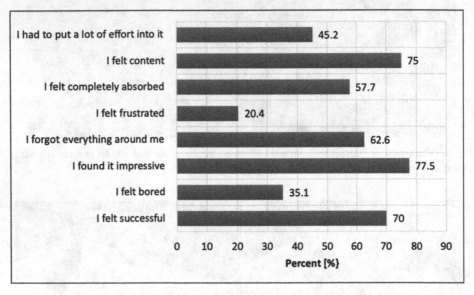

Fig. 6. In-game questions chart.

Social Presence Module
Since the VE include human avatars walking around the scenes and some of them approaching the participants to provide help and guidance, it was necessary to investigate how users reacted to avatars and what was their impression and experience. Therefore, the users were asked while they still testing the system a set of questions to investigates their psychological and behavioral involvement with other social entities. The results shows that 62.5% felt very delighted, 52.5% found the experience enjoyable, 50.1% connected to the avatars, 47.6% paid close attention to others, and less than 25% did not feel that they affected the other's actions (see Fig. 7).

Post-game Module
The objective of this test is to assess how the users felt after finished the whole experiment. Therefore, the users were asked after they had stopped completely and done with the experiment. The results shows that 67.5% felt that they have had a sense that they had returned from a journey which is very important and conclude the purpose of the whole system. 45.4% felt revived and 40.2% felt energized. Meanwhile, less than 20% felt exhausted or felt bad (see Fig. 8).

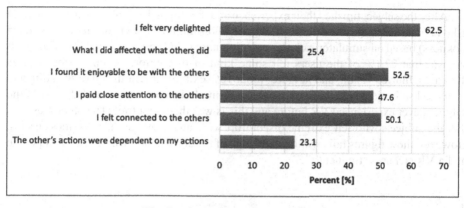

Fig. 7. Social presence module chart

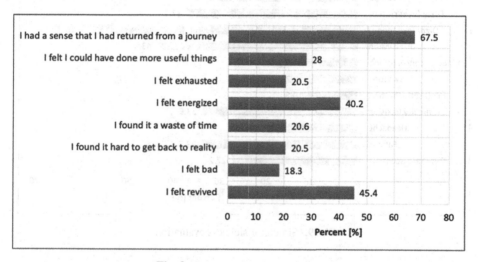

Fig. 8. Post-game module chart. x

4.2 Simulator Sickness Questionnaire

VR headset can cause dizziness and sickness (cybersickness or motion sickness) where some users feel uncomfortable. This was a major issue with the old HMDs since the field of view (FOV) and resolution were very limited, with the advancement of technology the FOV and resolution is drastically improved and this side effect is reduced, however, there are still low percent of people suffer easily experience motion sickness.

In recent study [15], it has been found that more than half the sample (57.8%) have experienced motion sickness whilst 42.2% have never experienced it. For those who experienced motion sickness, 13.7% of people experience VR sickness 'frequently', 19.1% experience it 'sometimes', and 24.9% experience it 'rarely'. These figures explains why we had some low figures in some of our evaluation criteria.

After the subject finished their experience and the stopped completely, the users were asked about their physical state such as general discomfort and vision (motion induced sickness) based on simulator sickness questionnaire (SSQ) presented in [16]. The result showed that 27.1% of the users felt some kind of discomfort which can be seen as dizziness, blurred vision, and fatigue. About 10% extreme discomfort like sweating and increased salivation as shown in Fig. 9. This is might be due to the fact that most of the subject never experienced VR before and this is was there first trail. The other reason is that the subjects who felt extreme discomfort were above 50 and had dizziness issues. However, these figures fails withing the range of the above study where 13.7% of people had a VR sickness 'frequently'.

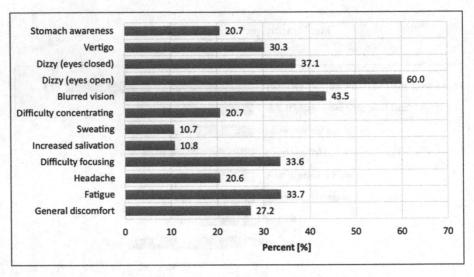

Fig. 9. Simulator sickness evaluation.

4.3 System Usability Scale

Measuring the overall system usability is essential to inspect the users perception of ease of use and consistency. System usability scale (SUS) was used to have a low-cost, reliable and ability to get a global assessment of the system [17]. The overall usability of the simulation is above 82%, however, 27.5% felt that the system was not easy to use and this is reflected on the fact that 37.% thinks that they need the support of a technical person and also 32.8% needed to learn many things before being able to use it. Nevertheless, 55% think that they would like to use the system frequently. This evaluation clarified some issues in the usability of the system that need to be addressed to further increase the overall satisfaction (see Fig. 10).

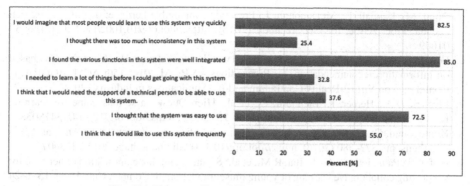

Fig. 10. The overall usability evaluation using SUS.

5 Conclusion

In this work, a workflow on how to create a virtual reality simulation for real world heritage site were explored and successfully were able to create a 3D model using photogrammetry on our targeted site. Many techniques were applied to capture the photos and create the model. Cleaning and mesh editing techniques with different software to make the 3D model ready for game engine rendering were applied. A virtual reality environment based on the site we studied while taking into consideration the realism and implementing immersion. Smart algorithm were implemented to control the avatar motion and make it respondent to the user interaction. The overall result based on many evaluation carried out demonstrated the high potential of such approach to create immersive and enjoyable experience. Most importantly, over 62% felt that they forgot everything around them which indicates that the system successfully achieved immersion. Also, more than 67% felt that they have returned from a journey which demonstrate that the system were able to induce the feeling of visiting and enjoying the virtual tour. With the recent Covid-19 pandemic and restriction to visit many historical sites, this project can provide a solution to have a virtual visit to many locations all around the world and create a unique experience from the comfort of our homes.

References

1. Halabi, O., Balakrishnan, S., Dakua, S.P., Navab, N., Warfa, M.: Virtual and augmented reality in surgery. In: Doorsamy, W., Paul, B.S., Marwala, T. (eds.) The Disruptive Fourth Industrial Revolution. LNEE, vol. 674, pp. 257–285. Springer, Cham (2020). https://doi.org/10.1007/978-3-030-48230-5_11
2. Halabi, O.: Immersive virtual reality to enforce teaching in engineering education. Multimed. Tools Appl. **79**(3–4), 2987–3004 (2019). https://doi.org/10.1007/s11042-019-08214-8
3. Halabi, O., Fawal, S., Almughani, E., Al-Homsi, L.: Driver activity recognition in virtual reality driving simulation. In: 2017 8th International Conference on Information and Communication Systems, ICICS 2017, pp. 111–115 (2017)
4. Häkkilä, J., Hannula, P., Luiro, E., et al.: Visiting a virtual graveyard, pp. 1–4 (2019). https://doi.org/10.1145/3365610.3368425

5. Bonn, M., Kendall, L., McDonough, J.: Preserving intangible heritage: defining a research agenda. Proc. Assoc. Inf. Sci. Technol. (2016). https://doi.org/10.1002/pra2.2016.145053 01009

6. Feng, J., Feng, X., Liu, X., Peng, J.: The virtual wandering system of Han Chang'an City based on information recommendation. In: Proceedings - VRCAI 2016: 15th ACM SIGGRAPH Conference on Virtual-Reality Continuum and Its Applications in Industry (2016)

7. Plecher, D.A., Herber, F., Eichhorn, C., et al.: HieroQuest - a serious game for learning Egyptian hieroglyphs. J. Comput. Cult. Herit. 13 (2020). https://doi.org/10.1145/3418038

8. Kontogianni, G., Georgopoulos, A.: A realistic Gamification attempt for the Ancient Agora of Athens, pp. 377–380 (2016). https://doi.org/10.1109/digitalheritage.2015.7413907

9. Nofal, E., Panagiotidou, G., Reffat, R.M., et al.: Situated tangible gamification of heritage for supporting collaborative learning of young museum visitors. J. Comput. Cult. Herit. 13, 1–24 (2020). https://doi.org/10.1145/3350427

10. Vajak, D., Livada, Č.: Combining photogrammetry, 3D modeling and real time information gathering for highly immersive VR experience. In: 2017 Zooming Innovation in Consumer Electronics International Conference: Galvanize Your Creativity, ZINC 2017 (2017)

11. Grün, A., Remondino, F., Zhang, L.I.: Photogrammetric reconstruction of the great Buddha of Bamiyan, Afghanistan. Photogramm. Rec. 19, 177–199 (2004)

12. Yastikli, N.: Documentation of cultural heritage using digital photogrammetry and laser scanning. J. Cult. Herit. (2007). https://doi.org/10.1016/j.culher.2007.06.003

13. Leonov, A.V., Anikushkin, M.N., Ivanov, A.V., et al.: Laser scanning and 3D modeling of the Shukhov hyperboloid tower in Moscow. J. Cult. Herit. (2015). https://doi.org/10.1016/j.culher.2014.09.014

14. IJsselsteijn, W.A., de Kort, Y.A., Poels, K.: The game experience questionnaire. Prod Exp. (2013)

15. Santiago, A., Nguyen, W.: A survey about VR sickness and gender. In: VR_Marketer. https://venturebeat.com/2020/07/05/a-survey-about-vr-sickness-and-gender/. Accessed 29 Jan 2021

16. Kennedy, R.S., Lane, N.E., Berbaum, K.S., Lilienthal, M.G.: Simulator sickness questionnaire: an enhanced method for quantifying simulator sickness. Int. J. Aviat. Psychol. 3, 203–220 (1993). https://doi.org/10.1207/s15327108ijap0303_3

17. Brooke, J.: SUS: a retrospective. J. Usability Stud. 8, 29–40 (2020)

Towards the Mixed-Reality Platform for the Learning of Children with Autism Spectrum Disorder (ASD): A Case Study in Qatar

Kamran Khowaja[1,2](✉) [ID], Dena Al-Thani[1] [ID], Yasmin Abdelaal[1],
Asma Osman Hassan[1] [ID], Younss Ait Mou[1], and Mohamad Hassan Hijab[1] [ID]

[1] Hamad Bin Khalifa University, Doha, Qatar
{dalthani,yaab34257,ymou,mhhijab}@hbku.edu.qa,
ashassan@mail.hbku.edu.qa
[2] Isra University, Hyderabad, Pakistan

Abstract. This virtual classroom has created a lot of challenges for students with limited access to the technology (computer or smartphone) or the Internet and especially for the parents of children with developmental disabilities, including children with autism spectrum disorder (ASD). ASD is a lifelong disorder and characterized by difficulties in social communication skills and may exhibit a restricted or repetitive set of behaviors. The number of children with ASD is soaring worldwide. There are no platforms that facilitate remote and interactive learning for children with ASD. In this paper, we describe the process of ideation, and design of an interactive educational platform that utilizes the role of mixed-reality (real-time teaching and virtual teaching) to enable remote learning for children with ASD. This work is a product of our continuous collaboration with special education and assistive technology centers based in Qatar in which we have developed an augmented reality (AR) vocabulary learning application for children with ASD in English and Arabic. The application provides the learning of letters and words in an interactive environment. We plan to extend this app to a full-educational platform using mixed-reality. The ideation and design processes were conducted collaboratively with teachers and specialists. In this platform, the child will be learning in a real-time environment when a teacher, child, and parents are all online together at a given time; however, in the absence of a teacher, a robotic talkative avatar would support a child and its parents in a virtual environment. The teachers will also have the capability to communicate with the children and their parents through the platform. It will also allow teachers, specialists, and parents to monitor the child's performance as well.

Keywords: Autism spectrum disorder (ASD) · Mobile augmented reality (AR) · Language comprehension · Vocabulary · Smartphone · Tablet

1 Introduction

The term autistic psychopathology was coined by the Austrian pediatrician Hans Asperger in 1938 in a lecture delivered in German (Asperger 1944). In English, the

© Springer Nature Switzerland AG 2021
X. Fang (Ed.): HCII 2021, LNCS 12790, pp. 329–344, 2021.
https://doi.org/10.1007/978-3-030-77414-1_24

term was first used by Leo Kanner at John Hopkins Hospital in the United States. He introduced the world autism that refers to a condition associated with significant impairment in social, linguistic, and cognitive skills. In his paper, Kanner (1948) described the symptoms that accompany autism. Since then, research has made great progress in better understanding the disorder and in providing suitable interventions. Today, autism is defined as being a spectrum disorder in which a set of different symptoms is apparent during childhood and continues into adulthood. The symptoms of ASD may vary in terms of behaviors and severity. These symptoms range from impaired social behavior to communication and language deficits. Repetitive behavior and difficulty in processing sensory inputs are often apparent (Diagnostic and statistical manual of mental disorders [DSM-5®] 2013). According to the World Health Organization, 1 in 160 children in the world has ASD. However, they stress that this estimate varies substantially across the world (Elsabbagh et al. 2012). The United States reports an ASD prevalence rate of approximately 1 in 59 children (Baio et al. 2018). In Qatar, the Qatar Biomedical Research Institute recently revealed that ASD is prevalent in 1.14% or one in every 87 children (Alshaban et al. 2019). The causes of autism are attributed to both genetic and environmental factors (Landrigan 2010; Lehmann and Murray 2005).

To date, ASD is being clinically diagnosed through behavioral assessment. The treatment regime is tailored to the child's needs, and it usually consists of a set of different educational, behavioral, or medical interventions. The educational and behavioral interventions are the most studied and commonly used approaches with children with ASD. Over the years, a number of approaches were developed and used to address the challenges associated with ASD (Sandbank et al. 2020). These approaches differ in their theoretical background and execution methodology. Applied Behavior Analysis (ABA) has been effective in supporting children with ASD in their daily life (Sulzer-Azaroff and Mayer 1977). Even though it has been used for quite a long time, questions have recently been raised about its effect on inclusive education (Shyman 2016). Other common approaches to support communication and behavioral skills in children with ASD include the Picture Exchange Communication System (PECS) (Rubin et al. 2013) and Social Communication, Emotional Regulation, and Transactional Support (SCERTS) (Rubin et al. 2013). The medical intervention consists of taking specific medication that helps with symptoms.

As a result of the need to support effective learning interventions for children with ASD, the researchers have explored different technological interventions including robotics (Shamsuddin et al. 2015; Tapus et al. 2012), computer-based interventions (Aresti-Bartolome and Garcia-Zapirain 2014; Fletcher-Watson 2014; Khowaja and Salim 2013; Khowaja et al. 2019; Ramdoss et al. 2010; Ramdoss et al. 2012; Ramdoss et al. 2011; Silva et al. 2017), virtual reality (Didehbani et al. 2016; Lahiri et al. 2015; Mesa-Gresa et al. 2018), and Tangible Interfaces (Alessandrini et al. 2016; Cullen and Metatla 2019; Farr et al. 2010; Karanya et al. 2007; McGowan et al. 2017) in order to support the needs of children with ASD. These interventions have been promising and successful in providing effective learning techniques by presenting the educational content in a form that is appealing to children with ASD. These technologies, however, have rarely supported vocabulary learning.

In recent years, augmented reality (AR) gained interest as a number of empirical-based research should its ability to attract ASD children's attention (Mesa-Gresa et al. 2018). Moreover, the research work in the applications of AR with children and adolescents with ASD has been increasing all around the world (Khowaja et al. 2019; Khowaja et al. 2020). However, none have focused on online education and learning for children with ASD. In this research, we build on our previous research work (Khowaja et al. 2020) which focused on designing and developing the initial prototype of a mobile augmented reality vocabulary learning application (MARVoc). The app supported vocabulary learning anytime and anywhere. In this work, we aim to enhance the novelty of MARVoc by incorporating the concept of mixed reality in an attempt to support online teaching and learning. Unlike typical students who can study and excel independently, children with ASD can benefit from the app by connecting with their teachers in real-time regularly and perform a set of tasks within the app environment. To the best of our knowledge, there is no educational platform that caters to the needs of children with ASD. The platform allows parents and teachers to view a child's performance, and teachers can create lesson plans according to the child's needs. The use of the AR app would benefit children with ASD as it would allow them to become independent individuals and live a better life. This paper presents the different stages of requirement, design, and evaluation. The paper focuses on the stages that involved users.

2   Method

The aim of this work is to develop, co-design, and evaluate a mixed reality platform for learning for children with ASD. To achieve this, we adopted human-centered empirical methods in conjunction with participatory design techniques (Muller and Kuhn 1993). We have divided the project into three main stages which involved requirement gathering and evaluation. In all stages, we used semi-structured interviews and focus groups. However, the questions varied in each stage depending on the objective of the stage. Both semi-structured interviews and focus groups facilitated the generation of a multi-disciplinary and variety of viewpoints to be discussed and explored. Our research team consists of two human-computer interaction (HCI) experts, three graduate students, and a software engineering expert. The interviews and focus groups included a group of practitioners that work closely with children with ASD. This group included speech and language therapists, special education teachers, assistive technology experts, and a psychiatrist.

For the analysis of the research of both the semi-structured interviews and focus groups, we adapted thematic analysis. Thematic analysis has been commonly used in the field of HCI (Brown and Stockman 2013) as it is considered as a practical approach when exploring the perspectives of different participants in a particular field and an effective way to address commonalities whilst generating unanticipated insights. We used NVIVO 12 to help us synthesize the interviews and focus groups results. As illustrated in Fig. 1, the project started with the requirements gathering stage which was reported in (Khowaja et al. 2020). This stage shaped the development of MARVoc's first version (MARvoc V1). This stage was followed by an evaluation of the MARVoc V1 with teachers and practitioners. This stage resulted in modifying the first version of MARVoc and we were able to add more features that resulted in developing a mixed reality platform. Lastly, the research team was able to successfully evaluate the platform with the same experts which resulted in the MARVoc V2.1.

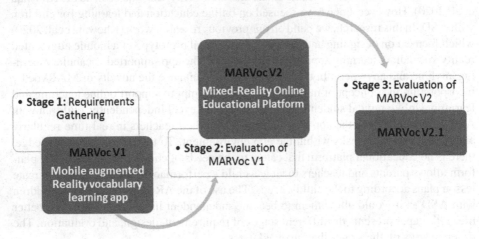

Fig. 1. Stages of the research

2.1 Stage 1: Requirement Gathering for MARVoc V1

Semi-structured Interviews
The semi-structured interviews were conducted with the teaching staff working at two centers located in Doha, Qatar to identify technologies used as a supporting tool for their classroom teaching, instruction methods used, instructional content taught, performance assessment, and the difficulties faced by the children with ASD. The two centers include the Step by Step Center for Special Needs where the English language is used as a mode of instruction, and Shafallah Center for Children with Special Needs where the Arabic language is used as a mode of instruction. Both centers are referred to as CENTER1 and CENTER2 respectively in the manuscript. The interviews conducted at CENTER1 were transcribed in the English language only, while, the interviews conducted at CENTER2 were transcribed in the Arabic language and then translated into the English language. The details of the semi-structured interviews can be read here (Khowaja et al. 2020).

Use Cases Development and Selection
The needs of the teachers working at both centers were analyzed from the transcription of interviews conducted at CENTER1 and translation of interviews conducted at CENTER2. A total of two use cases were created based on the analysis of the needs. These use cases were discussed with the focal person working at both centers to reach a consensus about the selection of one use case. The use case selected after discussion with a focal person at both centers was about the learning of the English alphabet (uppercase

and lowercase), construction of up to four-letter consonant, vowel, consonant (CVC) words, and construction of short phrases/sentences of up to four words. The details of the selected use case can be read here (Khowaja et al. 2020).

Functionalities

The MARVoc provides children with ASD an opportunity to learn and take part in the activities. In the learning, children with ASD can learn mixed-mode letters of the English language, and those three-letter and four-letter CVC words which start with a vowel ('a', 'e', 'i', 'o', 'u') and have visual representation so that children with ASD can see the object and interact with it as well. The activities allow children with ASD to construct words three-letter or four-letter words randomly based on their own choice, or three-letter or four-letter words starting with, ending with, or contains any specific letter, The details of all the mentioned functionalities in the MARVoc V1 from the selected use case can be read here (Khowaja et al. 2020).

2.2 Stage 2: Evaluation of MARVoc V1

Stage 2 included evaluation of MARVoc V1 with teachers and language therapists. During stage 2, one focus group was conducted with 5 participants from CENTER1 in early January 2020 and semi-structured interviews were conducted with 10 special education

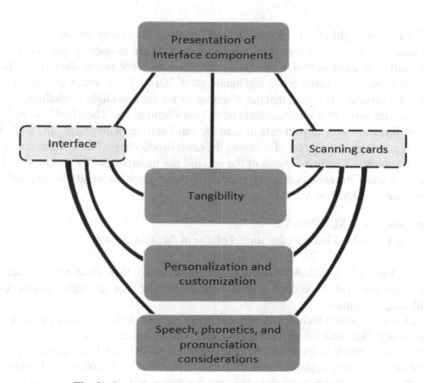

Fig. 2. Stage 2: Evaluation of MARVoc V1 thematic map

teachers and speech and language therapists from CENTER2. The main themes that emerged from the interviews and focus groups can be illustrated in Fig. 2.

The main findings from stage 2 were revolving around the presentation of the app and usability recommendations for the autistic population. Direct quotes and recommendations related to the sub-themes: interface and scanning cards are shown in Table 1.

Table 1. Interface components feedback

Interface related feedback	Scanning cards related feedback
Foreground and background color "The black background is also good as it doesn't cause distraction"	**Foreground and background color** "in general, the background should be simple and clear to avoid distraction"
Icons The icons are pretty small, the letters need to be maximized in size and visible so that the child can see them clearly"	**Texts and letters** "When scanning the letter, a relevant representative figure of the object int the card connected to that letter i.e. (A "ant", p "pot" …etc.)
Text and font "The one we are familiar with, maybe Calibra or Arial. Yes, usually, these are the two interchangeably fonts we use"	**Font face and typeface** The one we are familiar with, maybe Calibra or Arial. Yes, usually, these are the two interchangeably fonts we use
	Shape and size "Its fine, not too big neither too small, its fine"

The experts highlighted the use of card scanning for severe children with ASD is challenging. Research shows that children with ASD are frequently associated with motor malfunctions presented in fine, motor, and gross stability, postural stability deficit, gait, arm movement challenges (MacDonald et al. 2014). In the interviews and focus groups, the participants argued that the scanning part of the app might be challenging for some students given that some students have motor limitations. The MARVoc requires series of fine and motor movements to scan the cards starting with placing the cards for scanning moving to the process of scanning the cards in order to get the AR representation of the vocabulary. The first version of the app did not incorporate any sort of sound or voice-over, which the experts easily pointed out to the research team and was successfully incorporated in MARVoc V2.

Functionalities of MARVoc V2

MARVoc V1 evolved into an educational platform that consisted of:

- Parent View, which includes a performance dashboard of their child(ren) interaction, list of teachers, list of children, access to child view and chat, and videoconferencing with teacher feature.
- Teacher view, which includes an add and remove parent feature, child's performance dashboard, chat, and videoconferencing with parent feature.
- Child view, which includes the functionalities of MARVoc V1. However, different modifications were applied. For example, different levels to support the learning of letters and CVC words were included, and the design of the cards to be scanned was also changed.

We also amended the application in terms of the look and feel of the different application components by applying the changes recommended by the participants. Educational games were added to support the engagement of children with ASD. A robotic-like virtual tutor was added to all screens to guide the child throughout the app.

2.3   Stage 3: Evaluation of MARVoc V2

In this stage, the intention was to evaluate the new enhancements. This stage included three focus group sessions. All of the participants have already participated in the evaluation sessions of stage 2, except for the one assistive technology specialist who was included in this stage. The first session involved one assistive technology specialist from Mada assistive technology Centre in Qatar, whereas the participants in session 2 involved 6 special education teachers, 3 speech and language therapists, and 2 other language therapists. Session 3 included speech and language therapists and one psychiatrist all from Center 2. Due to the COVID-19 pandemic, all the sessions were conducted remotely.

Figure 3 illustrates the thematic map for the findings from the stage 3 evaluation. According to the research in the field of child-computer interaction, the primary goal for new interfaces for children is to be able to start exploring new technology with a minimal range of instruction (Hourcade 2015). The reason being is that as children are less likely to engage in learning activities or receive instructions related to using technologies, the more likely they will learn and know technologies through exploration and play (Hourcade 2015). Another significant finding that we had is related to the AR models used to represent a particular object. The experts highlighted that there should be a clear match between the models used in the interface and the real-life context for generalization purposes. They also highlighted that the technology should provide reasonable feedback in verbal and written form with the use of rewarding and gamification features.

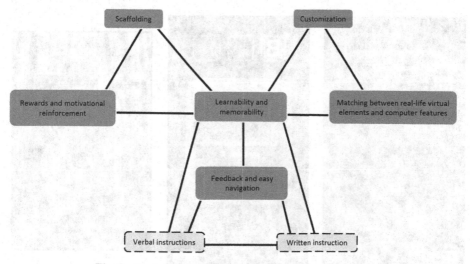

Fig. 3. Stage 3 evaluation of MARVoc V2 thematic map

3   MARVoc Prototypes

3.1   MARVoc V1

The screenshots of MARVoc V1 are shown in Fig. 4 and Fig. 5. The details of each screen can be read here (Khowaja et al. 2020).

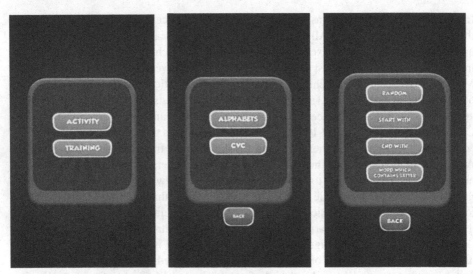

Fig. 4. The first screen allows the user to choose an activity or learning. The second screen allows the user to choose to learn alphabets or CVC words. The third screen allows the user to choose an option to learn or take part in an activity (Khowaja et al. 2020).

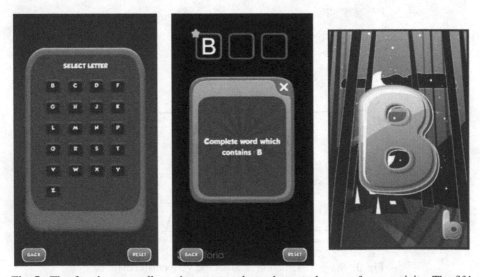

Fig. 5. The fourth screen allows the user to select a letter to learn or for an activity. The fifth screen allows the user to construct a three-letter CVC word as a part of the learning or activity. The sixth screen shows an example of a marker used in the MARVoc (Khowaja et al. 2020)

3.2 MARVoc V2

Drastic changes have been incorporated into the new version of the app in terms of presentation as well as look and feel. As illustrated in Table 1, the new version is kept simple as instructed by the experts. The MARVoc V1 of the app incorporated warm colors which teachers described as "distracting" for a child with ASD as shown in Fig. 4 and Fig. 5. Therefore, ASD-friendly cool colors were used and new features were added to make the experience interactive and joyful for the child with ASD. A robotic avatar was designed to represent the application. As shown in Fig. 6, Marfooq is a new component in MARVoc V2 of the app which refers to and assembles kindness in the Arabic language. Marfooq as illustrated in Fig. 6 will help children with ASD learn vocabulary as it is supported with voice-over features. The robotic character was developed using ASD-friendly colors by a local designer to help the child learn and navigate through the app.

Fig. 6. The robotic character, avatar, and guide for children using the app. The robotic character is called "Marfooq" that will assist the user by providing instructions

Similar to MARVoc V1, the home page components remind the same, but the names were changed to "Learning and Activity" instead of "Activity and Training". The left-side of Fig. 7 shows the home page screens which allows the user to choose learning or activity. The "Activity" allows the child to choose one of three types of activities including creating a word that "Starts with" a certain letter or creating a word that "Ends with" a chosen letter. Lastly, generating a word that "Contains" a letter. All the screens in the app demonstrate the robot, Marfooq which will help children and provide them with verbal instructions.

Figure 8 is an essential upgrade for our application which transformed our application into a mixed-reality platform. An interactive dashboard was added to emphasize inclusivity for parents and teachers of children with ASD during the critical times of the 2020 global pandemic. The dashboard was designed as a communication platform

Fig. 7. The screen on the left allows the user to choose learning or activity. The screen on the right allows the user to choose the different activity types, such as starts with, ends with, and contains a letter. Both screens show the robot, Marfooq

for teachers and parents to monitor the child's progress and to assess the vocabulary learning pattern for their children. There is a live-chatting and scoring log measuring the number of attempts and misses for the child as well as a duration record (in minutes) for how long the child spent in each activity (Fig. 9).

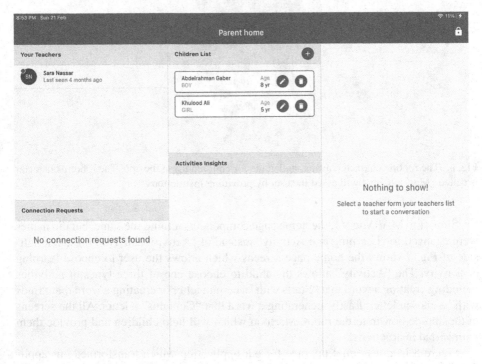

Fig. 8. The screen shows the dashboard of a parent. On the left column, the user can see the list of teachers that can be selected to communicate with. The user can see a list of their children along with activities they have completed in the column shown in the center. On the right column, the user can chat with a teacher by sending text or voice messages

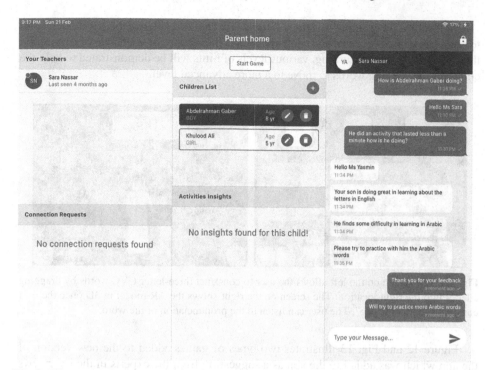

Fig. 9. The screen shows the dashboard of a parent. The format of this figure is same as of format of Fig. 8

The vocabulary learning and the augmented reality screens are shown in Fig. 10. The scanning cards are illustrated on the right side in Fig. 10. The child will need to use the back camera of the iPad to scan the letter to form a three-letter-word; or use the keyboard as shown on the left side of Fig. 10.

Fig. 10. The screen on the left allows the user to select any letter to learn. The screen on the right shows positioning a marker in front of the camera, the letter is then augmented

Figure 11 is an example of a three-letter word. Figure 11 shows the AR models used to represent a three-letter-word and demonstrates the essence of vocabulary learning. As the child progresses in learning, various levels of hints will be demonstrated to help the child master learning words to move to a more advanced level.

Fig. 11. The screen on the left allows the user to construct three-letter CVC words by dragging a letter into the right location. The screen on the right shows the AR model in 3D once the user constructs the word "Big". The user can listen to the pronunciation of the word.

Figure 12 and Fig. 13 illustrates two types of games added to the new version of the app which was added to the app as a suggestion from the experts in the interviews to add entertainment or games to our platform. The first game as shown in Fig. 12 is called "what am I feeling?" which is aimed to engage the child and communicate their feelings using flip cards that assemble one feeling at a time. Whilst Fig. 13 represents another game in the app called "know my colors" which is aimed to engage the child by corresponding and recognizing colors. Both of the games have voice-over or text-to-speech which the child can click on; hear and follow instructions. This approach was not available in version 1 of the app and it was developed based on the recommendations outlined in the thematic map in stage 2 Evaluation of MARVoc V1.

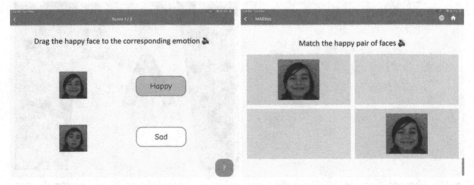

Fig. 12. The screen of the left allows the user to drag the emotion to its name. The screen on the right allows the user to match the correct set of cards representing emotions

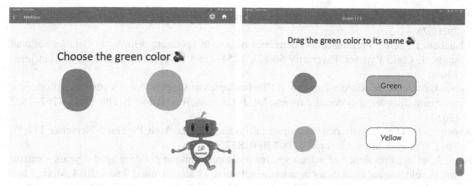

Fig. 13. The screen allows the user to drag the color to its name. The eleventh screen allows the user to select the correct color

4   Conclusion

This paper presents the ideation, design, and evaluation of a mix-reality educational platform for children with ASD. The human-centered approach followed in this research has led to shaping the idea of this research project from merely building an augmented reality app to support vocabulary learning to designing a mixed-reality education platform. The paper presented three stages of design and evaluation. Stage 1 was mainly focused on the requirement gathering and defining the main functionality of the MARVoc application. Stage 2 involved conducting evaluation studies with users in an attempt to enrich the design and functionalities. This phase results in adding major functionalities such as the robotic-like tutor, the different stages of learning, and the specific views for each category of users. The final stage aims to evaluate MARVoc V2 to fine-tune it and prepare it for a longitude user study. The next stage of the project aims to conduct a single-subject design study with the ASD children, and their parents and teachers. A single-subject research design study involves repeated measures for the same participants to understand the individual's normal variability to evaluate the effect of the proposed intervention on children with ASD.

Acknowledgment. We would like to thank the administration of Step by Step Center for Special Needs, Shafallah Center for Children with Special Needs in Qatar, and Mada Assistive Technology Center for allowing their teaching staff, specialists, and super users to take part in the studies related to our ongoing research. We would like to thank Space Crescent and its founder Shk. Abdulrahman Al Thani for the design of the robotic character. This work was made possible by an Rapid Response Call (RRC) award RRC-3-010 from the Qatar National Research Fund (a member of The Qatar Foundation). The statements made herein are solely the responsibility of the author[s].

References

Alessandrini, A., Loux, V., Serra, G.F., Murray, C.: Designing ReduCat: audio-augmented paper drawings tangible interface in educational intervention for high-functioning autistic children. Paper Presented at the Proceedings of the The 15th International Conference on Interaction

Design and Children, Manchester, United Kingdom (2016). https://doi.org/10.1145/2930674. 2930675

Alshaban, F., et al.: Prevalence and correlates of autism spectrum disorder in Qatar: a national study. J. Child Psychol. Psychiatry **60**(12), 1254–1268 (2019). https://doi.org/10.1111/jcpp. 13066

Aresti-Bartolome, N., Garcia-Zapirain, B.: Technologies as support tools for persons with autistic spectrum disorder: a systematic review. Int. J. Environ. Res. Public Health **11**(8), 7767–7802 (2014)

Asperger, H.: Die "Autistischen Psychopathen" im Kindesalter. Arch. Psychiatr. Nervenkr. **117**(1), 76–136 (1944). https://doi.org/10.1007/BF01837709

Baio, J., et al.: Prevalence of autism spectrum disorder among children aged 8 years - autism and developmental disabilities monitoring network, 11 sites, United States, 2014. Morb. Mortal. Wkly. Rep. Surveill. Summ. **67**(6), 1–23 (2018). https://doi.org/10.15585/mmwr.ss6706a1. (Washington, D.C. 2002)

Brown, N., Stockman, T.: Examining the use of thematic analysis as a tool for informing design of new family communication technologies. Paper Presented at the Proceedings of the 27th International BCS Human Computer Interaction Conference, London, UK (2013)

Cullen, C., Metatla, O.: Co-designing inclusive multisensory story mapping with children with mixed visual abilities. Paper Presented at the Proceedings of the 18th ACM International Conference on Interaction Design and Children, Boise, ID, USA (2019). https://doi.org/10.1145/3311927.3323146

Diagnostic and statistical manual of mental disorders [DSM-5®], Washington, DC (2013)

Didehbani, N., Allen, T., Kandalaft, M., Krawczyk, D., Chapman, S.: Virtual reality social cognition training for children with high functioning autism. Comput. Hum. Behav. **62**, 703–711 (2016). https://doi.org/10.1016/j.chb.2016.04.033

Elsabbagh, M., et al.: Global prevalence of autism and other pervasive developmental disorders. Autism Res. **5**(3), 160–179 (2012). https://doi.org/10.1002/aur.239

Farr, W., Yuill, N., Harris, E., Hinske, S.: In my own words: configuration of tangibles, object interaction and children with autism. Paper Presented at the Proceedings of the 9th International Conference on Interaction Design and Children, Barcelona, Spain (2010). https://doi.org/10. 1145/1810543.1810548

Fletcher-Watson, S.: A targeted review of computer-assisted learning for people with autism spectrum disorder: towards a consistent methodology. Rev. J. Autism Dev. Disord. **1**(2), 87–100 (2014)

Hourcade, J.P.: Child-Computer Interaction. Self, Iowa City, Iowa (2015). 201 p.

Kanner, L.: Child Psychiatry, 2nd edn. Charles C. Thomas, Oxford (1948)

Karanya, S., Ajchara, D., Nopporn, C., Patcharaporn, O.: Comparative study of WIMP and tangible user interfaces in training shape matching skill for autistic children. Paper Presented at the TENCON 2007 - 2007 IEEE Region 10 Conference, 30 October–2 November 2007 (2007)

Khowaja, K., Al-Thani, D., Banire, B., Salim, S.S., Shah, A.: Use of augmented reality for social communication skills in children and adolescents with autism spectrum disorder (ASD): a systematic review. Paper Presented at the 2019 IEEE 6th International Conference on Engineering Technologies and Applied Sciences (ICETAS), Kuala Lumpur, Malaysia, 20–21 December 2019 (2019)

Khowaja, K., Al-Thani, D., Hassan, A.O., Shah, A., Salim, S.S.: Mobile augmented reality app for children with autism spectrum disorder (ASD) to learn vocabulary (MARVoc): from the requirement gathering to its initial evaluation. Paper Presented at the HCI in Games, Cham (2020)

Khowaja, K., et al.: Augmented reality for learning of children and adolescents with autism spectrum disorder (ASD): a systematic review. IEEE Access **8**(1), 78779–78807 (2020). https://doi.org/10.1109/ACCESS.2020.2986608

Khowaja, K., Salim, S.S.: A systematic review of strategies and computer-based intervention (CBI) for reading comprehension of children with autism. Res. Autism Spectr. Disord. **7**(9), 1111–1121 (2013)

Khowaja, K., Salim, S.S., Asemi, A., Ghulamani, S., Shah, A.: A systematic review of modalities in computer-based interventions (CBIs) for language comprehension and decoding skills of children with autism spectrum disorder (ASD). Univ. Access Inf. Soc. **19**(2), 213–243 (2019). https://doi.org/10.1007/s10209-019-00646-1

Lahiri, U., Bekele, E., Dohrmann, E., Warren, Z., Sarkar, N.: A physiologically informed virtual reality based social communication system for individuals with autism. J. Autism Dev. Disord. **45**(4), 919–931 (2014). https://doi.org/10.1007/s10803-014-2240-5

Landrigan, P.J.: What causes autism? Exploring the environmental contribution. Curr. Opin. Pediatr. **22**(2), 219–225 (2010). https://doi.org/10.1097/MOP.0b013e328336eb9a

Lehmann, S., Murray, M.M.: The role of multisensory memories in unisensory object discrimination. Cogn. Brain Res. **24**(2), 326–334 (2005). https://doi.org/10.1016/j.cogbrainres.2005.02.005

MacDonald, M., Lord, C., Ulrich, D.A.: Motor skills and calibrated autism severity in young children with autism spectrum disorder. Adapt. Phys. Activ. Q. **31**(2), 95 (2014). https://doi.org/10.1123/apaq.2013-0068

McGowan, J., Leplâtre, G., McGregor, I.: CymaSense: A Novel Audio-Visual Therapeutic Tool for People on the Autism Spectrum. Association for Computing Machinery, Baltimore (2017)

Mesa-Gresa, P., Gil-Gómez, H., Lozano-Quilis, J.-A., Gil-Gómez, J.-A.: Effectiveness of virtual reality for children and adolescents with autism spectrum disorder: an evidence-based systematic review. Sensors **18**(8), 2486 (2018)

Muller, M.J., Kuhn, S.: Participatory design. Commun. ACM **36**(6), 24–28 (1993). https://doi.org/10.1145/153571.255960

Ramdoss, S., et al.: Use of computer-based interventions to teach communication skills to children with autism spectrum disorders: a systematic review. J. Behav. Educ. **20**(1), 55–76 (2010). https://doi.org/10.1007/s10864-010-9112-7

Ramdoss, S., Machalicek, W., Rispoli, M., Mulloy, A., Lang, R., O'Reilly, M.: Computer-based interventions to improve social and emotional skills in individuals with autism spectrum disorders: a systematic review. Dev. Neurorehabil. **15**(2), 119–135 (2012). https://doi.org/10.3109/17518423.2011.651655

Ramdoss, S., et al.: Use of computer-based interventions to improve literacy skills in students with autism spectrum disorders: a systematic review. Res. Autism Spectr. Disord. **5**(4), 1306–1318 (2011)

Rubin, E., Prizant, B., Laurent, A., Wetherby, A.: Social communication, emotional regulation, and transactional support (SCERTS). In: Goldstein, S., Naglieri, J. (eds.) Interventions for Autism Spectrum Disorders: Translating Science into Practice, pp. 107–127. Springer, New York (2013). https://doi.org/10.1007/978-1-4614-5301-7_6

Sandbank, M., et al.: Project AIM: autism intervention meta-analysis for studies of young children. Psychol. Bull. **146**(1), 1–29 (2020). https://doi.org/10.1037/bul0000215

Shamsuddin, S., Yussof, H., Mohamed, S., Hanapiah, F.A., Ainudin, H.A.: Telerehabilitation service with a robot for autism intervention. Proc. Comput. Sci. **76**, 349–354 (2015). https://doi.org/10.1016/j.procs.2015.12.306

Shyman, E.: The reinforcement of ableism: normality, the medical model of disability, and humanism in applied behavior analysis and ASD. Intellect. Dev. Disabil. **54**(5), 366–376 (2016). https://doi.org/10.1352/1934-9556-54.5.366

Silva, C., Da Fonseca, D., Esteves, F., Deruelle, C.: Seeing the funny side of things: humour processing in Autism Spectrum Disorders. Res. Autism Spectr. Disord. **43–44**, 8–17 (2017). https://doi.org/10.1016/j.rasd.2017.09.001

Sulzer-Azaroff, B., Mayer, G.R.: Applying Behavior-Analysis Procedures with Children and Youth, vol. 23. Houghton Mifflin Harcourt School, New York (1977)

Tapus, A., et al.: Children with autism social engagement in interaction with Nao, an imitative robot: a series of single case experiments. Interact. Stud. **13**(3), 315–347 (2012). https://doi.org/10.1075/is.13.3.01tap

Perrugia: A First-Person Strategy Game Studying Movement Patterns in Museums

Christian Y. Limsui[✉]

Ateneo de Manila University, Quezon City, Metro Manila 1108, Philippines

Abstract. This paper shows the creation of a game focused on studying museum visitor path movements. Using existing museumgoer path data collected and floor plans from the Ateneo Art Gallery (AAG), the Philippines' first museum of modern art, a game was created to best observe the way visitors interpret exhibition space based on the concepts of spatial syntax analysis. The steps involved cleaning the existing data to study points of interest in which visitors acted accordingly as well as representing popular and deviated pathways in the game. Design choices also included providing the player with maps and tools to track other NPCs as they explored the museum spaces but only to the point where it provided enough information for them to piece together the rest of the information. In terms of gameplay, the player is expected to look at the artworks and NPCs in order to progress in-game. The study presents a method of employing technology for museums to better understand their visitors, different from the current implementations used for exhibit interaction. The game allows museum professionals to discover the best configuration of artworks and exhibition space without needing to use the physical resources. It also presents a possible tool in learning spatial and social factors affecting the visitor's experience when entering their spaces, providing valuable insights for those in the field.

Keywords: Game and flow · Game immersion · Museum visitorship · Spatial syntax analysis

1 Introduction

Helping visitors understand the museum experience relies on other factors aside from providing textual context. One's understanding of the spatial environment they are in plays an important role in weaving the story in their minds as they undergo the process of meaning-making and narrative hermeneutics [1]. As visitors move through the exhibits' spaces, the experience takes shape depending on the context and sequencing of exhibition pieces [2]. This flow finds basis on the accessibility and visibility of one work towards another, where its interconnectedness is permitted through the physical layout of the exhibition [3]. This takes into consideration a spatial dimension of story-telling, different from the curation and given explanation of the artworks themselves. Another factor which impacts the viewer experience are choices made by both visitors and curators which is explored through an informational dimension of artwork arrangements. This curatorial

© Springer Nature Switzerland AG 2021
X. Fang (Ed.): HCII 2021, LNCS 12790, pp. 345–354, 2021.
https://doi.org/10.1007/978-3-030-77414-1_25

intent, as well as architectural layouts of museums, are the independent factors that help determine visitor movement [4].

Tracking the circulation of museum visitors has been in practice since the early 20th century with focus on questionnaires and manual tracking to gleam information on time spent on exhibits, where people stop, and popularity of exhibitions [5]. Recent advancements in technology have allowed various methods of collecting data on movement patterns such as Bluetooth, WLAN, RFID, video cameras, etc. [6]. While there is a wealth of data that can be gathered from using these methods, there are still limitations in observing visitor interactions. However, incorporating the findings from these studies into another format may allow us to study more qualitative components such as human interaction with the factors mentioned above.

In this paper, we present how a game was designed to better understand path decision and engagement of visitors. By incorporating obtained visitor data from the Ateneo Art Gallery (AAG), the game looks into how building design, exhibit layouts and navigational cues are used to examine possible variations in movement patterns. This allows for a more holistic understanding of decisions that influence visitor behavior. As such, integrating existing visitor traffic data and museum floor plans serve as controlled variables. From there, the study observes what behaviors and strategies translate in-game relation to the phenomena which influences one's museum visitorship.

2 Review of Related Literature

2.1 Spatial Syntax Analysis

The analysis of human interaction with the spatial dimension in museums is better known as "space syntax analysis" [3] which relates spaces in the context of the larger system as compared to the more common study of metric distance between museum objects. Space syntax can be further broken down into two types of links: connectivity, which relates to an object to its physical neighbors, and integration, which relates an object to the exhibition as a whole. The more links are apparent in a path, the more likely the path themselves are to be used by people. In connection to this, visitor paths are more likely to be varied if a space is highly accessible [2, 4].

Wineman et al. [4] utilized two science exhibitions created by the Carnegie Science Center, each evaluated in the Great Lakes Science Center in Cleveland. The site was a moderately-sized open plan area which allowed for randomized sequences of movement and an unobstructed view of the exhibition for the visitors. The exhibitions used for the tests were "ZAP Surgery", which examined technology for medical operations, and "Robotics", focusing on the principles of robot design and function. Spatial context was examined through spatial grouping and visual coordination (e.g. gamma rays, laser beams, cryosurgery). It was noted that these groupings were documented and presented to visitors of the space as well. The study got 100 participants involved to observe their movement patterns within the space, classifying their actions as "contact", being in proximity to an exhibition piece and aware of its existence but nothing further, and "engagement", actively giving said exhibition piece attention.

Tsortzi [2] explored the museum layouts of the Sainsbury Wing, the extension to the National Gallery, London, and the Castelvecchio Museum as one group study on when exhibit pieces were more of permanent fixtures in museums, thus containing spatial designs specific to each area. Tsortzi then examined museums with common spatial themes such as the Pompidou Centre, Paris, and two Tate galleries (Tate Modern and Tate Britain). The framework constructed found that not only did the arrangement of objects provided an "informational" dimension which helped interconnect them to one another, but another factor of a social dimension among visitors is introduced as well should the building layout promote it. Variations in the influence of these two dimensions could exploit the spatial qualities to enhance objects and vice versa. While curators tend to favor the spatial dimension of object distribution and categorization, insights of the interaction provide valuable ideas in understanding underlying principles and how design flow affects overall experience. In light of this study, new ways of handling spatial and display considerations are encouraged.

A visitor's activity can be processed as either moving through an exhibition or being static in a single space (e.g. viewing an artwork) [2]. It should also be noted that a visitor may choose not to view an object, although their path may pass by these said objects. Studies have shown that spatial grouping of themes through integration have had a more powerful draw to visitors over general connectivity, which shows that their behaviors register and prioritize thematic labels.

This understanding of space formed the underlying principle of the game design in this study. The game stage design and how NPCs interact with it in the game were based on these phenomena. While it serves as a good foundation, the study of spatial analysis syntax has mostly stayed in the realm of physical observations. This then serves as an opportunity to study the phenomena in virtual space and pinpoint the similarities of linking themes from real life to computer screen.

2.2 Navigation and Circulation

Navigation within museum spaces may also be broken down into physical determinants which, if following proper guidelines, lead to effective circulation and wayfinding systems [7]. One's navigation process can be broken down into two categories: 1.) patterns of pedestrian movement and 2.) orientation (including conceptual). Unlike most activities, museum spaces require users to move around and engage with exhibitions. Various points of entry coerce visitors to rely on previous patterns of movement they are used to and make pathway choices. This becomes a critical aspect when these movement patterns determine what visitors see or do, as well as help them choose which exhibits to engage.

The study [7] showed how certain layouts could affect certain movement, such as being on the right side of a pathway would give strong tendencies to turn right or go straight unless certain conditions are provided to turn left. Crowd organization also dictated the direction visitors would take, such as in self-organizing to stay on the right in crowded conditions.

Patterns of search-approach-stop also form an important aspect of visitor movement. Visitors are constantly looking for artworks that are of high interest or provocative in their eyes. When a visitor finds an artwork that fits this criterion, they will stop to approach and engage with the subject. An example in a museum space would be to place an attractive art piece at the center of the exhibition to increase the crowd and engagement.

Other factors that determine navigation are patrol strategies to navigate through areas. In most cases, a counter-clockwise movement is employed unless exhibits are present on either side, which a zig-zag method may be utilized instead. The speed of the visitor has an inverse correlation to their thoughtfulness when engaging in exhibits. Engagement, or how long one stops at an artwork, is part of the navigation process as well albeit stopping in front of an artwork does not necessarily mean one is engaging in it.

This study took these factors into consideration when reconstructing the patterns of visitor movement within the AAG. Some aspects such as visitor movement speed can also be adjusted to see how players respond in navigating the space. A limitation of the study is that there is no way to determine as of the moment which of these are to be effective in translation. The layout of the AAG and the gameplay itself may present results that move outside those presented in the study. Players would be encouraged to explore the space within the game freely which may remove inhibitions of following proper circulation.

2.3 Virtual Museum Interaction

The development of technology has not only allowed for the preservation of preserving artifacts but has also expanded exhibit interaction to include the virtual space. Since the first adoptions of the idea through static presentations of text and images [2, 3], the avenues of immersing the visitor through technology has improved through methods such as Augmented Reality (AR), Virtual Reality (VR), and web protocols (HTTP) in addition to devices such as personal computers (PC), CD-ROMs, and personal digital assistants (PDA) [9]. In application, museums have used this for recreating historical events, increase visitor engagement, and for additional educational opportunities about exhibits [10].

Klopfer et al. studied the effectiveness of guided tours and handhelds within the museum space [6]. Aware of the benefits of mobile devices for learning experiences at schools and other centers of learning, a game was designed for the Boston Museum of Science with the goals of visitors to engage with the exhibits more deeply and across one another, as well as engage with one another. The game Mystery at the Museum was designed with past experience in mobile game design and on learning games of the team in mind. Players were deeply engaged in museum exhibits, requiring to get clues from different exhibits within the museum and examine each one closely to piece information together. This combination of depth and breadth of engagement was effective in encouraging participants in thinking about each exhibit in relation to the game's story. Collaboration among players and parent-child interactions received positive feedback from the study as well.

However, games created in this space remain mostly as tools to increase visitor engagement or as marketing tools by the museums [11]. The focus on these tools usually falls under technical aspects of the technology and points for improvement or studying if the visitor's experience with the artworks were heightened through the technology's employment [12]. This current work aims to study utilizing games through a different approach of it being a tool to study the visitors and spatial engagement as a priority aside from the exhibition itself.

3   Game Development

3.1   Bluetooth Beacon Incorporation

Bluetooth Low-Energy (BLE) beacon data gathered in the Ateneo Art Gallery (AAG), the Philippines' first modern art museum, by Casano et al. [13] was used as a controlled variable in-game. The data was collected through the use of phones with a Unity application allowing the conversion of radio signals from BLE beacons into Received Signal Strength Indicator values (RSSI). This provided data on where they stopped by, paths they took, and time spent navigating the exhibit. Testing was conducted with sixty-six (66) participants, many of whom were first-time visitors of the AAG [3]. The study was able to determine the most popular path starting from the first floor to the third floor, increased engagement in interactive exhibits, and the tendency to only explore certain sections only. As they mentioned, it serves as a proof of concept on the utilization and possible limitations of BLE technology [3].

In the game development phase, AAG visitor data was processed to visualize the pathways and points of interest per guest. To ensure playability, the game utilized data from seventeen (17) visitors only who have complete data from the 1st to 3rd floors. To provide a closer estimate to which artworks visitors engaged in, the pathways generated focused on beacons detecting their immediate proximity (1–2 m away from an artwork). Figure 1 shows a generated pathway based on the data from one of the guests.

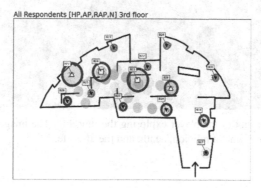

Fig. 1. Orthogonal view of the floor map with a visitor's pathway visualized. Light blue dots indicate the path they took in which they were 1–2 m away from a beacon. The rings around the beacons indicate the engagement of the visitor with how long they stayed in the beacon's radius.

The visualizations were crosschecked with their time logs to verify artwork interest or locate any path deviations. These were then translated into navigation paths in Unity3D. The level design was constructed emulating the AAG's exhibition layout. NPCs were each assigned a path to follow, with configurations for dialogue and to stop at artworks they "enjoyed".

3.2 Recreating the Space

With the inclusion of visitor data from a previous study and the need to be faithful to it, the level design and artworks were made to be accommodating to the data. This meant adjusting artwork placement to align with beacons and, so players would emulate movements by NPCs, refraining from placing artwork in areas that did not correspond with the beacons. The level design was also designed in replicating the wall placements of the floor maps from the visitor pathways. Due to legal constraints of accessing artworks from the Ateneo Art Gallery for the game, there was a need to make custom exhibits and artworks which were arranged into themes and NPC insights adjusted to relate to them. In the game, the story was adapted to a museum-wide curation for the recently deceased artist Gaspar Sousa, whose work mainly focused on religious themes. To correspond to the three floors, the exhibitions were divided into themes of 1.) the timeline of his work, 2.) differences among religions, and 3.) thoughts of religion on death. The figure below showcases the recreated level design, with artworks placed where the beacons were located (Fig. 2).

Fig. 2. In-game screenshot of the player exploring the museum. The image provided is that of the third floor, with the theme of religion, death, and the afterlife.

3.3 Game Design

The game itself focuses on the study of visitor movement patterns and in order to encourage this form of study, the in-game tools should equip players to rationalize the patterns but not spoon-feed them. The game provides the player with tangible and abstract clues for them to piece together information and deduce the best course of action to progress.

As a foundation to better engage with participants, there must be a narrative which encourages exploration. The story is that the Peruggia, a criminal syndicate specializing in museum heists, has been planning to steal from the exhibit. The player, a detective, must find a double agent, the artwork, and the thief in order to successfully catch them. In order to identify these three, the player is given hints based on the interests and movement patterns of NPCs. Aside from hints, players are also provided with a museum map which has descriptions for each exhibition to tie the themes of the artworks in those spaces. A figure showing an in-game screenshot of the map is shown below (Fig. 3).

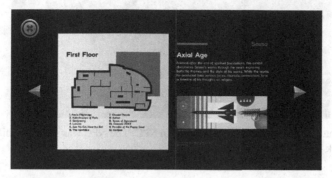

Fig. 3. In-game screenshot of a map as part of the player's tools. The map showcases the layout and brief explanation of the first floor's exhibit.

The player as a detective also has a notebook containing images of each of the NPCs roaming the museum. The player may select any of these images for an arrow to pop up which points to the location of the selected NPC as the building layout spans three floors. An outline also appears over the NPC when they are in the player's field of view. Another figure is provided below showing this feature (Fig. 4).

Fig. 4. In-game screenshot of tracking a selected NPC. Selected NPCs are outlined when seen and an arrow is shown pointing at whatever direction the NPC is. This arrow disappears when interacting with NPCs and artworks.

The player can interact with both artworks, which have fixed descriptions on what the artwork represents, and NPCs, whose dialogues change depending on their location and which artworks they are interested in. Knowing what each NPC is interested in requires the player to have seen the NPC's action and/or have spoken to the NPC to connect their actions to the hints provided. The first-person player also has a constrained field of view to encourage the NPC movement and layout to have influence on the player's actions and to better examine their movements based on what they are looking at. The figure below is a screenshot of the player interacting with an NPC (Fig. 5).

Fig. 5. In-game screenshot of a interacting with an NPC. The NPC was stopped while interacting with an artwork talking about religious tourism.

The player is given 30 min to examine their clues and explore the space and its NPCs. As it is a psychological detective game which studies how the player interacts with the space, the tools provided are designed to encourage players to come up with their own interpretations (which influence their movement) in addition to easing certain tasks, such as tracking visitors, to focus on the game's goals.

4 Discussion

The usage of a game to study visitor behavior in terms of movement patterns shows promise. As a game, it provides another layer of engagement with players through the introduction of actively observing other character's actions as means of gameplay. In turn, there forms an introspection for players and those in arts-related fields to understand psychological influences in the museum experience.

According to Lanir et al., observing the patterns of museum visitors have been an increasingly popular area of study. Museums today are shifting towards a consumer-oriented experience, recognizing each visitor as an active interpreter of the space. Studies conducted in this area help museums allocate their resources more effectively, thus overall improving their exhibits [3]. Architects and museum curators can formulate structural and placement layouts which best serve the narratives they aim to tell in these spaces. This then leads to better audience engagement from the community in their respective museums. In addition, the game itself can be adjusted to study other ways of manipulating visitor engagements in spatial context as compared to a curatorial perspective. As most implements of interactive technology for museums focus on immersion to exhibition pieces, it falls short in focusing on exhibition flow and social interaction [10]. If museums incorporate their own artwork catalogs and floor plans, the game gives museums the opportunity to study the usage of the space with their curatorial intent and look into visitor behavior while cutting the need for physical space and other resources.

There are limitations to the extent of the study as of the creation of this paper, mainly in terms of NPC behavior which could be fleshed out further and expanding the artwork curation process which was had been adjusted in this case. Possible areas of future study through changing the in-game elements to include other factors of visitor interactions (e.g., hypercongestion in museum spaces and established groups that visit can influence one to avoid moving to certain spaces) [14, 15] and the incorporation of spatial dimensions in the digital museum experience.

5 Conclusion

This study presents a different way for museums to learn more about their visitors through means of gameplay. Given that museums have already been tracking visitor patterns in the past and the advance of technology, there are newer, various methods in which they can study how best understand museumgoers to eventually curate their spaces for the most engagement. The method provided through this game is qualitative in nature, presented through the visitor's eyes with the ability to see what they see and interact with. Through the game design, the choices made to have conditions conducive of studying movement patterns were in including paths and points of interest generated by previous visitors in the form of NPCs, recreating exhibition spaces and grouping of exhibit artworks, the addition maps and artwork descriptions supplementing the visitor's understanding, and other tracking tools to have some ease in gameplay. Other than these elements, the game was designed for the player to explore the space for themselves. Further refinements and of in-game elements will help increase the depth of information gathered by museums if done so in future iterations of the game.

6 Future Work

Game testing and deployment will be conducted through functional testing and will be followed with interviews about the experience. The goals of testing are to see if the integration of visitor data and introducing movement patterns as a focus of the game were successful. Participants from the architectural field, arts-related professions, and unaffiliated groups will be invited to collect various insights on the gameplay. Recruitment of testers will be done through online means of communication with screening surveys that asks them about demographics, their professions, and if they have the equipment necessary for testing. Each participant will have a personal session with the researcher who will brief them about the study and what the session will cover. After briefing and if given consent to continue, they will play the game while the researcher observes player input. Once completed, participants will be interviewed about thoughts on the game and certain actions they may have done in-game. Debriefing forms will be given out focusing on additional thoughts on the game and inquiring other points for improvement.

Acknowledgements. We would like to thank Casano et al. for providing the Ateneo Art Gallery data they have collected under the grant entitled "Ateneo Art Gallery Visitor Tracking Study Using Bluetooth Low-Energy Beacons" provided by the Ateneo de Manila University Loyola Schools. We also wish to express our thanks to Ms. Jenilyn Agapito and Mr. Walfrido Diy from the Ateneo Department of Information Systems and Computer Science for reviewing the game creation process and the paper.

References

1. Schorch, P.: The experience of a museum space. Museum Management and Curatorship. 28 (2013)
2. Tzortzi, K.: Museum building design and exhibition layout: patterns of interaction. In: Proceedings of the 6th International Space Syntax Symposium, pp. 072:01–072:16. Turkey, Istanbul (2007)
3. Huang, H.: The spatialization of knowledge and social relationships. In: Proceedings, 3rd International Space Syntax Symposium, p. 43.1– 43.14. Atlanta (2001)
4. Dalton, R.C., Peponis, J., Wineman, J.: Exploring, engaging, understanding in museums. space syntax and spatial cognition. In: The Proceedings of the Workshop held in Bremen (2006)
5. Yalowitz, S.S., Bronnenkant, K.: Timing and tracking: unlocking visitor behavior. Visitor Stud. 12(1), 47–64 (2009)
6. Lanir, J., Tsvi, K., Sheidin, J., Yavin, N., Leiderman, K., Segal, M.: Visualizing museum visitors' behavior: where do they go and what do they do there? Pers. Ubiquit. Comput. 21, 313–326 (2017)
7. Bitgood, S.: The dimensions of visitor movement in museums. Interp News 5, 32–37 (2016)
8. Klopfer, E., Perry, J., Squire, K., Jan, M., Steinkuehler, C.: Mystery at the museum – a collaborative game for museum education. In: Koschmann, T., Suthers, D.D., Chan, T. (eds.) Proceedings of the International Conference on Computer Supported Collaborative Learning 2005, pp. 316–320. Taipei, Taiwan: International Society of the Learning Sciences (2005)
9. Sylaiou, S., Liarokapis, F., Kotsakis, K., Patias, P.: Virtual museums, a survey and some issues for consideration. J. Cult. Herit. 10, 520–528 (2009)
10. Shehade, M., Stylianou, T.: Virtual reality in museums: exploring the experiences of museum professionals. Appl. Sci. 10(11), 4031 (2020)
11. Bergamasco, M., Frisoli, A., Barbagli, F.: Haptics technologies and cultural heritage applications. In: Kawada, S. (ed.) IEEE Proceedings of the CA Conference 2002, Geneva, Switzerland, June 2002, pp. 25–32 [28]. IEEE Computer Society Press (2002)
12. Worden, S.: Thinking critically about virtual museums. In: Bearman, D., Trant, J. (eds.) Proceedings of the Conference Museums and the Web, Pittsburgh, pp. 93–109 (1997)
13. Casano, J.D.L., Agapito, J.L., Moreno, A., Rodrigo, M.M.T.: Quantifying museum visitor attention using Bluetooth proximity beacons. In: Stephanidis, C., Antona, M. (eds.) HCII 2020. CCIS, vol. 1226, pp. 270–277. Springer, Cham (2020). https://doi.org/10.1007/978-3-030-50732-9_36
14. Yoshimura, Y., et al.: An analysis of visitors' behavior in The Louvre Museum: a study using Bluetooth data. Environ. Plann. B: Plann. Des. 41 (2014)
15. Falk, J.H., Dierking, L.D.: The Museum Experience Revisited. Left Coast Press, Inc., Walnut Creek, Calif (2013)

Research on the Interaction Method that Can Alleviate Cybersickness in Virtual Reality Games

Zhenyu Lu[✉] and Ruozhou Mao[✉]

NetEase, Inc., NetEase Building, No. 599 Wangshang Road, Binjiang District, Hangzhou 310052, People's Republic of China
{luzhenyu,maoruozhou}@corp.netease.com

Abstract. Cybersickness is a symptom that is common among game players. Although each player has a different level of symptom, this feeling will occur during the long-term experience of video games. Studies have shown that cybersickness is caused by many factors, including display hardware, screen content, and human factors.

With the development of VR game platforms over the years, cybersickness has become a high-priority in the virtual reality industry, and cybersickness has also been called VR sickness. There have been many different studies on how to alleviate VR sickness, such as adding a virtual nose model to the content, providing Dynamic Gaussian Blur, using Dynamic FOV, etc. These studies are focused on reducing VR sickness by improving the displayed content.

Not like previous studies, in this paper, we looked forward to discussing the VR sickness that was caused by different interaction. In this study, the researchers designed several VR interactions based on different hardware. Then they organized user tests that asked testers to complete several goals in the same VR environment. After comparing multiple sets of test data, the researchers discussed the possibility of an interaction method that will reduce VR sickness and how it looked like. Through this work, we tried to give an insight into the current research findings of alleviating VR sickness and discussing the possibility of long-term VR interaction. In this context, this study aimed to explore a virtual reality interaction method that allows players to alleviate VR sickness during gaming.

Keywords: VR sickness · VR interaction · Self-motion simulation

1 Introduction

In recent years, the VR market has gradually expanded and developed. On March 23, 2020, Valve released "Half-Life: Alyx" with high-quality content to let players once again feel the charm of VR games. The experience of current VR devices has been significantly improved due to the increase in display quality and frame rate.

Although the experience problems caused by hardware has been gradually improved, the inconsistency of the player's body and eyes' view is the main cause of VR sickness.

© Springer Nature Switzerland AG 2021
X. Fang (Ed.): HCII 2021, LNCS 12790, pp. 355–371, 2021.
https://doi.org/10.1007/978-3-030-77414-1_26

Can we improve this problem through game interaction design? There are similar solutions we found, such as "teleportation", "jogging". However, these solutions all have the problem of not being able to fully restore the freedom of movement control.

The purpose of this research is to reduce cybersickness by interaction design. We try to design an approach that can map all movement commands and allow players to generate self-motion. Through user experiment tests, we will discuss the performance of this interaction method compared with the existing method.

2 Related Work

2.1 Causes of VR Sickness

Many previous studies suggest that VR sickness causes players to develop symptoms similar to motion sickness (Kolasinski 1995). In such studies, the specific biological causes of VR sickness cannot be fully determined at this time. The relatively common theoretical frameworks and hypotheses in this field are Sensory Conflict (Sensory mismatch) theory and postural instability theory. Sensory Conflict theory (SCM) provides a very important interpretive framework. The scholars argue that the user's self-motion perception is based on the visual system, the vestibular system and non-vestibular proprioceptors. If these inputs and these receptors are not coordinated, symptoms of motion sickness are likely to occur. Conversely, VR sickness is unlikely to arise when the user's self-motion and perceptual inputs match each other.

Hardware
Hardware plays a very important role in demonstrating virtual content. At present, the VR content created by developers is basically displayed to users through virtual reality headsets and other hardware devices, so the hardware will largely affect the quality of VR content. For example, VR sickness often occurs when the screen refresh rate is not high enough, when the speed of the screen refresh is slower than the brain's expected processing, so the brain's expected screen and the actual presentation of the screen inconsistency will arise. In other words, when the computer-generated picture does not match the speed of movement in the user's brain, motion sickness symptoms will occur. (Rebentisch 2015) (Norman 2017). Another trigger for VR sickness is the mismatch between visual and motor signals obtained from vestibular stimuli. (Groen and Bos 2008). When the eye receives a stimulus and the stimulus transmitted to the vestibule through the inner ear do not match. Therefore, the hardware needs to make the information transmitted from the visual and auditory organs into the brain as consistent as possible.

Since screen display is the most important information transmission channel in the VR system, many current studies have tried to verify the relationship between display-related factors and VR Sickness. A number of studies have shown that the display type and mode are related to the severity of VR sickness symptoms (Benzeroual and Allison 2013; Häkkinen et al. 2002; Sharples et al. 2008). For example, HMD, desktop devices, and real-life theaters have different impacts on VR sickness. (Sharples 2008). Vlad et al. found through experiments that compared with 3D TV, 3D glasses are more likely to cause symptoms of VR sickness to users. Different display modes used by different devices can induce VR diseases to different degrees (Dennison et al. 2016). From this series of studies, users who use HMD show higher scores in VR sickness tests. At the same time, users who watch stereoscopic content are also more likely to have symptoms of VR disease than users who watch monoscopic content (Dennison et al. 2016; Naqvi 2015). Another factor that affects visual presentation is FOV (Field of Vision), which is what the player can perceive visually. Various experimental studies have concluded that reducing the FOV range is one of the effective ways to alleviate VR sickness (Harvey and Howarth 2007).

Content
While most studies have focused on the impact of device-related factors on VR illness, there are still some studies focusing on other factors. Various factors related to VR content, for example, (Fernandes and Feiner 2016), these studies have come to the relatively clear conclusion that narrowing the content FOV can effectively reduce users' VR illness symptoms, which can be verified from both objective and subjective indicators (Fernandes and Feiner 2016; Kobayashi et al. 2015). Therefore, the solution of reducing content FOV while ensuring user immersion is feasible to reduce user motion sickness symptoms and enhance user experience. Human motion sickness symptoms are caused by the mismatch of apparent motion signals, which occurs when the stimulus signals received by the eyes and inner ear are not aligned. Optical flow plays a very important role in this process, so many studies have focused on which characteristics of optical flow can cause VR symptoms in users, including the degree of the speed and the number of moving signals in VR content. Some findings find that the speed of the scene in VR content is positively correlated with the severity of VR symptoms (Chardonnet et al. 2015; Liu and Uang 2012; Lo and So 2001), and the symptoms of VR disorder are exacerbated when there is more rotational motion in the scene (Bonato et al. 2009; Keshavarz and Hecht 2011; Lo and So 2001). Nevertheless, there are previous studies that attempt to investigate the relationship between VR picture quality and VR sickness (Golding et al. 2012; Carnegie and Rhee 2015; Davis et al. 2015) to verify that a high quality, high realistic VR experience and immersion will reduce users' VR sickness symptoms. However, the results showed that the increase in VR quality does not alleviate the symptoms of VR sickness among users.

Human Factors
Many experiments find that different people in the same experiment will have different manifestations of VR sickness, so it is suggested that individual factors such as gender, BMI, and susceptibility to motion sickness can affect the onset and severity of VR sickness in users (Stanney 2003). In general, women are thought to be more likely to experience motion sickness symptoms than men (Freitag et al. 2016), but some scholars argue that there is insufficient evidence for this conclusion (Lawson 2014). Second, the findings on how age affects VR sickness are unclear. Some studies show that older age appears to be associated with a higher susceptibility to VR sickness. However, in a recent study by Saredakis et al. (2020), individuals under 35 years of age show more apparent motion sickness symptoms than older age groups. Since users who receive VR sickness tend to develop motion sickness symptoms, the user's previous motion sickness susceptibility can also help us to predict whether the user will have an uncomfortable experience during the VR experience. The Motion Sickness Susceptibility Questionnaire

(MSSQ) can quantify the motion sickness susceptibility of experimental participants. From the results of some experiments, it can be seen that people with higher motion sickness susceptibility tend to have higher SSQ scores when experiencing VR (Stanney 2003).

2.2 Solutions for VR Sickness

In a broad sense, VR sickness actually includes a variety of uncomfortable symptoms caused by the VR experience, such as Physical Fatigue, Eye strain, Motion sickness and so on. This study focuses on Motion sickness, because it is a crucial factor that prevents many players from using VR for a long time. We have discussed the causes of Motion sickness, and below we will explore some of the solutions that currently exist.

Hardware
The visual performance of VR display has a great impact on the dizziness. Refresh rate, field of view size, and afterglow, etc. Can all become effective factors (Chang et al. 2013). Latency in VR is one of the biggest contributing factors to motion sickness. There are now headsets available that offer faster displays, such as the Valve Index that allows users to adjust between 80 Hz, 90 Hz, 120 Hz and 144 Hz. As the industry develops, the speed of latency will likely decrease, which will significantly help with the problem of motion sickness.

In addition to improving the monitor frame rate and display, some other physical devices can also be used to reduce dizziness and improve the comfort of experience.

Amores and his team designed a necklace to relieve VR sickness by releasing odors. The subjective perception of relaxation increased by 26.1% when using a VR HMD with the olfactory necklace, compared to not being exposed to any stimulus (Amores et al. 2018) (Fig. 1).

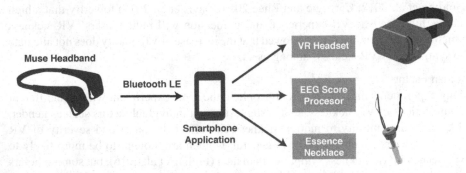

Fig. 1. The prototype of essence necklace made by Amores.

Reliefband is a wearable device that relieves the symptoms by generating electrical signals to stimulate nerves (David Lachowicz 2017). The signals have a rebalancing effect, normalizing nerve messages from the brain to the stomach and reducing symptoms of nausea, retching and vomiting. The Reliefband has also been used in medical research and has been shown to have an effect on symptoms such as vomiting (Habib et al. 2006).

Similar to this solution, Taro Maeda has experimentally demonstrated that the use of Galvanic vestibular stimulation can directly produce the sensation of vection and thus dizziness can be relieved (Maeda et al. 2005).

To sum up, there are two main ways to mitigate dizziness by hardware, which is improving the display effect and soothing nerves. Improving the display does have a significant effect on relieving dizziness, which can be verified in the development of VR headsets in the past few years. However, this method of releasing odor or weak current to relieve dizziness has not been widely used, and it is still a direction worthy of research and improvement.

Display Contents

In fact, to eliminate motion sickness is to help the brain understand that the body is not really moving. Through the processing of the display contents and some auxiliary display system, we can create the illusion that the player is not in motion.

Wienrich, Carolin, et al. attempted to simulate real-life visual perception using the addition of a virtual nose, which is based on the principle of creating a visual reference point that allows the human brain to perceive its own movement (Wienrich et al. 2018). Their study could replicate the results in a very dynamic jump'n'run game and added evidence regarding the effects of a virtual nose on game experience. This approach has also been practiced by other people and has worked to some extent (Fig. 2).

Fig. 2. Left: The model of virtual nose; Right: Nguyen-Vo's frame cave

Thinh Nguyen-Vo and his team tried to reduce player's motion sickness when turning their view by adding a virtual frame cube to the field of view (Nguyen-Vo et al. 2018). This cube follows, and rotates along with the user to simulate a cave automatic virtual environment. EH Chang's research has also shown that rest frames can help reduce motion sickness and increase the sense of presence in VR.

To sum up, most of the approaches to reduce dizziness through screen content are to enhance the player's perception of movement by adding visual references, because the contradictory feeling of no body movement can be alleviated to a certain extent, if players are provided with a relatively static frame of reference visually.

Control Approach

When moving in a real environment, we naturally perceive and believe the fact that we are actually moving. In a virtual environment, however, it is difficult to create this sense of real movement. To connect the virtual with the real and counteract this illusion, we can make it more real through interaction and feedback.

Simulate real movement

This type of solution mainly relies on walking simulators or VR shoes to capture the player's leg movements, thus mapping the player's real physical movement to the virtual character. Such devices are generally large in size, such as virtuix omni's treadmill, and the fully rollable VR motion platform – Eight 360 Nova – developed by Terry Miller and his team ('Omni by Virtuix – The leading and most popular VR motion platform' 2021; Loz Blain 2020) (Fig. 3).

Fig. 3. First: The picture of Omni; Second: The Eight 360 Nova; Third: Cybershoes

In order to improve the portability and reduce the cost of the device, solutions that use wireless wearable shoes to capture leg movements have emerged in recent years. Micheal Bieglmayer and his team have been developing a VR wearable device called Cybershoes since 2015 (Cybershoes 2021). This set of equipment is a pair of shoes with roller soles, through which the player slides back and forth to complete the forward and backward movement orders. When using this device, players need to sit on a rotating seat, through the rotation of the seat to control the direction of the virtual character.

In addition to controlling virtual character movement through assisted hardware, there are also studies that attempt to use the up and down vibration of a person walking as a control signal through an algorithm (Huge Robot 2021). In these studies, the player manipulates the character by running in place. The frequency and amplitude of the up and down shaking generated by running in place is used to control the speed of the virtual character's movement (Slater et al. 1995). However, this scheme also has some drawbacks, for example, it does not achieve backward movement well and requires the use of a controller pointing to control the direction of movement.

To summarize, the core principle of this type of solution is to make the body move so as to eliminate the incongruity between visual and physical senses. The way to control the movement of the character through the motion device is more expensive to implement, while the player is easily fatigued by prolonged movement. Running in place still has problems in the control. The cybershoes sitting solution, on the other hand, is optimized in both aspects, thus far it is a better solution.

Reduce the player's sense of movement

In addition to enhancing the player's body's perception of movement, the opposite app-roach is to reduce the player's visual perception of movement, so that the visual per-ception is consistent with the body's feeling of stillness. Teleportation is the current mainstream game practice, where the player is projected to the target location through the ray emitted from the controller, and then the perspective is switched directly to the target location. This avoids the process of moving in between, so there is no dizziness.

There are also some other practices, such as switching by blinking when turning the view instead of smooth continuous screen rotation. This solution reduces the dizziness, but it can also bring the feeling of unreality. The second approach is to create a relatively static environment, such as placing the player in the cockpit (VR Interactions 2017). In addition, the third-person view can also effectively alleviate the symptoms of VR sickness (Kim et al. 2018), because the movement of objects in the third-person view will be smaller.

By designing the way players interact in virtual reality, it is possible to enhance immersion while mitigating dizziness. However, the current research solutions all still have their own limitations, which makes it the more worthwhile to study and think about.

3 Design Considerations

Through literature review, we can basically understand the causes of VR sickness, which mainly comes from the unsynchronized visual movement perception and body percep-tion. We also did a lot of investigation on current VR technologies and product forms, as this will determine how we should choose the appropriate hardware and algorithms to complete the solution design. Finally, by researching and comparing the current solutions that have a mitigating effect on VR sickness, we clarified our design direction, trying to mitigate the perception of asynchrony between player reality and virtual through interaction design.

In the process of design, we try to solve two problems:

1. How to correspond the way of moving in reality to the control of the virtual character one by one, so as to achieve the same degree of freedom as in real movement.
2. How to make players' bodies feel like moving through interactive movements, and at the same time reduce the fatigue of the player in the process of interaction.

3.1 How People Move in Reality

Franck Multon, in his 1999 study of virtual human walking, summarized that the human body has a total of 30 degrees of freedom (Multon et al. 1999). Based on his research and the observation of people walking in life, it is easy to find that the three main degrees of freedom in movement are:

1. The head controls the viewpoint.
2. The waist controls the orientation of the body.
3. The legs control the direction of human movement (Fig. 4).

Fig. 4. First: Degrees of freedom that human body has; Second: Body facing and the direction of forward is the same; Third: The three main degrees of freedom in movement control.

By studying the movement control of first person/third person games on the current market, it can also be found that the main character movement control is the move direction and body facing, while the direction of perspective and body facing is to maintain the same. Therefore, we can often see the character's head always facing the body directly in front in the match game.

In the VR game, we want to restore the perception of real movement as much as possible. Therefore, we need to design three degrees of freedom control for head movement, body orientation, and character movement, respectively.

Among them, with the use of 6DOF head-mounted display, the problem of vision control can already be well solved. While the body orientation control, and movement control requires more attempts and research.

3.2 How to Generate Motor Perception

It is well established that the visual, vestibular, and somatosensory modalities provide position and rate (e.g., velocity, acceleration) information for estimation of body dynamics (Jeka et al. 2004). When the body perceives imbalance or shaking, the sensation of motion is created. By simulating this sensation, the player's physical senses can be synchronized with visual perception, thus reducing the symptoms of dizziness (Maeda et al. 2005). Keirl J M, in his study of the Motion seat, found that human motor perception comes not only from vestibular judgments, but also from the pressure on skin, and changes in body forces (Keirl et al. 1995). When the body perceives a greater pressure on one side of the skin, the acceleration is felt in the opposite direction. Similarly, when the force on the human body changes, the corresponding sense of movement will be generated. This is how a 6DOF motion seat simulates the driving feeling.

Therefore, to mitigate the player's motion sickness response, it is necessary to allow the player to move visually while the physical forces produce corresponding changes. Bernhard E. Riecke, in his study of Self-Motion Simulation applications in virtual reality, found that providing consistent cues about self-motion to multiple sensory modalities can enhance vection, even if physical motion cues are absent (Riecke et al. 2005; Riecke and Feuereissen 2012).

The design principle of motion seat is to change both the angle of the player's body and gravity, thus producing a corresponding force and skin pressure in the direction of visual movement. This is a solution worth trying and exploring. It tries to change the player's center of gravity in the interactive operation of the motion control, so as to produce a corresponding sense of force.

4 Design

After several attempts and experiments, we designed a relatively feasible interaction scheme. This movement control system is based on the existing VR hardware, so that it will be more universal. The solution adopts a VIVE head-mounted display, two 6DOF controllers, and a Vive Tracker. In order to make the Vive Tracker work properly, two base stations and a signal receiver are required, all of which can be viewed in the official Vive Tracker description (VIVE™ | VIVE Tracker 2021).

4.1 Hardware Setup and Control Rules

First, players need to follow the official guide to set up the VIVE environment, then wear the Vive Tracker on their waist and calibrate it to the front (Fig. 5).

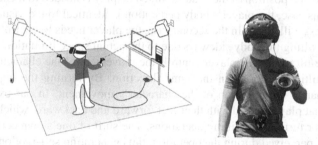

Fig. 5. Left: The schematic diagram of Vive settings; Right: How to wear the devices.

In this system, we implement three independent control: head tracking, orientation recognition, and movement control:

1. The 6DOF system on the head-mounted display is used to capture player's visual changes.
2. The pointing of the Vive Tracker is utilized to determine the player's body orientation.
3. By calculating the position of the head-mounted display and Vive Tracker, we can obtain the state of the player's body tilt, then through the player's body tilt amplitude and direction, to control the direction and speed of the virtual character movement.

The benefits of this implementation are as follows:

1. It can achieve complete movement control without the need for players to wear additional complex equipment.
2. The player is able to control the visual movement, character's orientation and movement independently, without the limitations found in traditional schemes.

3. The player's hand operation is not affected when controlling movement, and the player is able to move once and perform other operational tasks.
4. While controlling the movement, the player will produce self-motion due to the change of body center of gravity caused by the lateral tilt of the body. Through our previous theoretical analysis, this can reduce the inconsistency between the player's visual movement and body perception, thus reducing VR sickness.
5. There is no need for the player to perform walking actions, so the fatigue will be greatly reduced, which can allow the player to control the character movement for a long time.

4.2 Interaction Design

We designed a solution that allows players to control virtual character movement, like walking, running, jumping and other operations, which can basically meet the needs of character movement control in most games today.

Movement

Movement is divided into two cases. In the first case, the player moves by walking freely, and only the position of the head-mounted display is needed to locate the player's position. In this case, the player's body perception is identical to the visual perception, and no dizziness will occur. In the second case, the player needs to control the character movement by tilting the body sideways due to the actual space limitation.

In the side-tilt mode, the player controls the movement of the character in a certain direction by tilting the body in the same direction. By turning the upper body, the player can change the direction of the character's movement. In our experience, we recommend that players stand with their feet forward and backward, which can be more comfortable for turning and tilting operations. The shift of one's own center of gravity can be clearly perceived during the operation, thus generating self-motion (Warren and Wertheim 2014).

The player switches between the two movement control modes by clicking the buttons on the controller. This allows for both closer to realistic movement in a small area and more freedom and comfort when the character needs to be controlled to move over long distances (Fig. 6).

Walking and Running switch

The speed of character is proportional to the player's side tilt, and when the side tilt exceeds a certain angle, the speed no longer increases. We found that the front and back side tilt will be greater than the left and right-side tilt, therefore the angle corresponding to the maximum speed needs to be changed according to the side tilt direction.

Jumping and Squatting

We observed how people jump in the real world: before jumping, people need to lower their center of gravity and then jump upside. When designing this interaction, we adopted the action of crouching with the legs and then standing up to trigger it. This can simulate the real-world body perception, and will not conflict with the directional control.

The crouch operation is triggered by the player's legs crouching down and then staying at that height. When the player stands up, the character becomes upright.

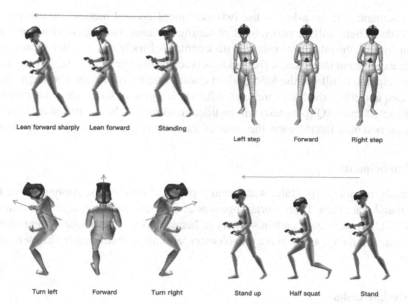

Fig. 6. Upper right: Lean to control move speed; Upper left: Side shift movement; Lower right: Turning movement; Lower left: Jumping gesture.

Summary
Using gesture interaction in VR can improve the player's immersion, but gesture operation is more likely to cause fatigue than joystick and keyboard. Therefore, using self-motion simulation can bring physical sensation to the player while reducing the fatigue caused by gestures. In the design of player movement operation, it is not necessary for players to perform jogging or walking action but by tilting the body to produce the feeling of movement.

5   Evaluation

In order to verify whether different operation methods will affect the player's vertigo, we create a demo containing two different operation methods using Unity. The first method is somatosensory control designed by us, which controls the movement by tilting the body. The second method directly uses the joystick on the controller to control the movement.

5.1   Methodology

The experimental equipment and tools used are as follows:

1.   Hardware: HTC VIVE, A PC with SteamVR.
2.   Demo build by using Unity.
3.   SSQ (Kennedy et al. 1993) and questionnaires.

Participants will be asked to use two movement control methods to complete the same tasks. There will be two rounds of testing for each participant (one time using motion control, the other time using joystick control). Firstly, we inform the participants that the experiment may cause cybersickness (such as dizziness, nausea), and then assist the participants to fill out the MSSQ-short questionnaire, record their susceptibility to dizziness, and fill in the SSQ (pre-test). After each round of test, a short interview will be conducted and SSQ (post-test) will be filled in to record their experience. In order to eliminate potential interference, the order of the tests is random for each participant.

5.2 Participants

This study recruited 10 adults with healthy physical conditions. Among them, 6 are women and 4 are men. Their average age was 26.2 years old (mean age: 26.2 years-old, SD = 2.7). All participants had no history of headaches and vestibular system disorder. Participants in the experiment are all voluntary, and all of them sign the consent before testing.

5.3 Design Tasks

This evaluation experiment is a within subject test, which means that each participant will test both control systems. The purpose of the experiment is to compare the effects of different interaction modes on VR sickness, and whether the interaction mode with self-motion simulation can reduce the player's dizziness. The reason for choosing a within test is that it can automatically control individual variability, which reduces the deviation caused by user differences. In this experiment, the participant's vertigo sensitivity needs to be controlled. Therefore, intra-group testing is appropriate in this experiment.

In this study, there are three tasks:

1. Learn how to move, and complete the basic movements of forward, turn, and back.
2. To move around a large object.
3. Avoid obstacles (Fig. 7).

The first task is an easy one that allows players to adapt the VR experience and learn how to control movement. The second task is to test the player's dizziness when doing circular motion. The third task is more difficult, requiring the player to move forward while avoiding obstacles. The lateral movement will be more intense in the third task. In addition, we provide two operating postures, standing and sitting, which participants can experience during the test.

During the test, more details including body movements, language, interaction, etc. can be recorded for later analysis.

5.4 Results

Interaction & Cybersickness

We subtract SSQ (pre-test) from SSQ (post-test) to get the difference in SSQ score. The table is as follows (Table 1):

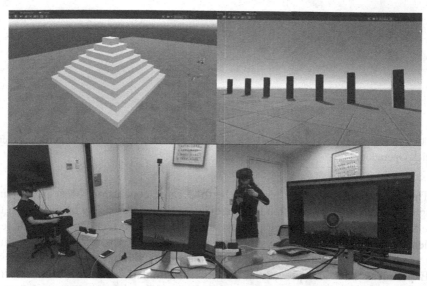

Fig. 7. Upper right: Large object; Upper left: Linear obstacles; Lower right: Sitting operation; Lower left: Standing operation.

Table 1. The SSQ difference of each participant.

Participants	The SSQ difference of somatosensory operation	The SSQ difference of joystick operation
No. 1	12	18
No. 2	14	21
No. 3	2	7
No. 4	1	4
No. 5	5	7
No. 6	9	5
No. 7	− 1	0
No. 8	1	4
No. 9	− 1	24
No. 10	4	11

Then, we use boxplot function in R to visualize the data, and the result is as follows (Fig. 8):

Finally, we use ANOVA to find whether there is a significant difference in the SSQ between two experiments. We get $F = 3.1831$, num df = 1, denom df = 18, p-value = 0.09127. According to p-value < 0.1, it can be shown that the interactive mode has an impact on cybersickness, and it is not surprising for us to see this in the boxplots.

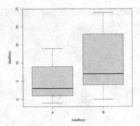

Fig. 8. The Boxplots of SSQ Difference (A represents Somatosensory Operation, B represents Joystick Operation)

Through the interview, we have reached the same conclusion. Most participants thought that the joystick operation is more dizzy than somatosensory operation. At the same time, we also found that participants are more likely to feel dizzy when there is sudden speed change and sideways movements. In addition, when participants collide with an object, or move around closely to an object, they will have a heavy dizziness.

Experiments have also proved that self-motion simulation can reduce the conflict between vision and somatosensory, thereby alleviating cybersickness. But we also found that the relationship between the movement speed and the body slope is the key to make the simulation more real (Table 2 and Fig. 9).

Experience Evaluation

Table 2. Scoring questions

Number	Question	Score
No. 1	It feels real when I was moving	1–5
No. 2	I think the operation is easy to learn	1–5
No. 3	I find it easy to operate	1–5
No. 4	I think the operation is in line with my intuition	1–5
No. 5	I like this operation method	1–5

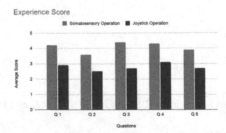

Fig. 9. Average experience score of each question

From the subjective evaluation of participants, the somatosensory interactive experience is better, which can give players a stronger sense of immersion. Participants said that this control method can produce the feeling of moving due to my body actions (self-motion simulation). Secondly, most of the participants also said that sitting operations would be much easier. Some descriptions of the participants are summarized below:

"My body feels more comfortable, and the way of operation and movement is more matched."

"I can imagine myself surfing during somatosensory operation, so I won't be so dizzy."

"The joystick is not very comfortable to control the speed."

"Standing operation is difficult to balance, sitting operation will be much easier and more secure."

There are also a few participants who prefer joystick control. These participants are not sensitive to the dizziness of both scenarios, and they have more FPS gaming experience. After being familiar with the joystick control, this part of the participants can be very accustomed to the control method, and will not feel obvious dizziness. But they also think that the joystick operation is not immersion.

For participants who are very susceptible to vertigo, they said that neither method is comfortable and they had a strong sense of nausea during the test. Especially at the beginning and end of movement, there will be obvious discomfort.

6   Conclusion and Future Work

Through this research, we believe that the control method of VR has an impact on cybersickness. Secondly, the control method with self-motion simulation can reduce the feeling of dizziness during movement, and create a more realistic experience. In our research, we also found that players are extremely sensitive to speed in VR. Many players desire to control the movement speed, and believed that if they could control the speed in a better way, the vertigo would be much weaker. We have also obtained similar conclusions as other studies, that the player feels less dizzy when moving forward, but is stronger when moving sideways. Last but not least, reducing the fatigue of the player can make them feel more comfortable, especially during long periods of movement.

Cybersickness is one of the main factors that hinder us from moving in the VR world. Many engineers and designers are trying to solve this problem. With the development of hardware, the VR experience is getting better and better. But cybersickness also comes from software experience and interaction. Future research can pay more attention to the influence of players' movement speed on cybersickness, and how to let players control their speed easily.

References

VR Interactions: Directed by Anonymous [YouTube]. ACMSIGGRAPH (2017)

Cybershoes. https://www.cybershoes.io/. Accessed 9 Jan 2021

Huge Robot. https://hugerobotvr.com. Accessed 9 Jan 2021

Omni by Virtuix - The leading and most popular VR motion platform. https://www.virtuix.com/. Accessed 9 Jan 2021

VIVE I VIVE Tracker. https://www.vive.com/us/accessory/vive-tracker/. Accessed 18 Jan 2021

Amores, J., Richer, R., Zhao, N., Maes, P., Eskofier, B.M.: Promoting relaxation using virtual reality, olfactory interfaces and wearable EEG, p. 98. IEEE (2018)

Benzeroual, K., Allison, R.S.: Cyber (Motion) sickness in active stereoscopic 3D gaming (2013)

Cargegie, K., Rhee, T.: Reducing visual discomfort with HMDs using dynamic depth of field. **35**(5), 34–41 (2015)

Chang, E., Hwang, I., Jeon, H., Chun, Y., Kim, H.T., Park, C.: Effects of rest frames on cybersickness and oscillatory brain activity, p. 62. IEEE (2013)

Chardonnet, J.-R., Mirzaei, M.A., Merienne, F.: Visually induced motion sickness estimation and prediction in virtual reality using frequency components analysis of postural sway signal. In: Eurographics Association, p. 1 (2015)

Chen, W., Chen, J.Z.: Visually induced motion sickness: effects of translational visual motion along different axes, pp. 281–287 (2011). https://doi.org/10.1201/b11337-47

Davis, S., Nesbitt, K., Nalivaiko, E.: Comparing the onset of cybersickness using the Oculus Rift and two virtual roller coasters, January 2015, p. 3. Australian Computer Society (ACS) (2015)

Dennison, M.S., Wisti, A.Z., D'Zmura, M.: Use of physiological signals to predict cybersickness. Displays **44**, 42–52 (2016). https://doi.org/10.1016/j.displa.2016.07.002

Fernandes, A.S., Feiner, S.K.: Combating VR sickness through subtle dynamic field-of-view modification (2016)

Freitag, S., Weyers, B., Kuhlen, T.W.: Examining rotation gain in CAVE-like virtual environments. IEEE Trans. Vis. Comput. Graph. **22**(4), 1462–1471 (2016). https://doi.org/10.1109/TVCG.2016.2518298

Golding, J.F., Doolan, K., Acharya, A., Tribak, M., Gresty, M.A.: Cognitive cues and visually induced motion sickness. Aviation Space Environ. Med. **83**(5), 477–482 (2012). https://doi.org/10.3357/ASEM.3095.2012

Habib, A.S., Itchon-Ramos, N., Phillips-Bute, B.G., Gan, T.J.: Transcutaneous acupoint electrical stimulation with the ReliefBand® for the prevention of nausea and vomiting during and after cesarean delivery under spinal anesthesia. Anesth. Analg. **102**(2), 581–584 (2006)

Harvey, C., Howarth, P.A.: The Effect of Display Size on Visually-Induced Motion Sickness (VIMS) and Skin Temperature, December 2007, p. 96 (2007)

Jeka, J., Kiemel, T., Creath, R., Horak, F., Peterka, R.: Controlling human upright posture: velocity information is more accurate than position or acceleration. J. Neurophysiol. **92**(4), 2368–2379 (2004)

Keirl, J.M., Cook, R.J., White, A.D.: Dynamic seats - a replacement for platform motion? Flight simulation technology, capabilities and benefits, p. 10 (1995)

Keshavarz, B., Hecht, H.: Axis rotation and visually induced motion sickness: the role of combined roll, pitch, and yaw motion. Aviation Space Environ. Med. **82**(11), 1023–1029 (2011). https://doi.org/10.3357/ASEM.3078.2011

Kim, M., Lee, J., Kim, C., Kim, J.: TPVR: user interaction of third person virtual reality for new presence and experience. Symmetry **10**(4), 109 (2018)

Kobayashi, N., Iinuma, R., Suzuki, Y., Shimada, T., Ishikawa, M.: Using bio-signals to evaluate multi discomfort in image viewing-balancing visually induced motion sickness and field of view, August 2015, p. 6198. IEEE (2015)

Lawson, B.D.: Motion Sickness Symptomatology and Origins' Handbook of Virtual Environments: Design, Implementation, and Applications, pp. 531–600. CRC Press (2014)

Liu, C.-L., Uang, S.-T.: A study of sickness induced within a 3D virtual store and combated with fuzzy control in the elderly, July 2012, p. 334. IEEE (2012)

Lo, W.T., So, R.H.Y.: Cybersickness in the presence of scene rotational movements along different axes. Appl. Ergon. **32**(1), 1–14 (2001). https://doi.org/10.1016/S0003-6870(00)00059-4

Loz Blain: Eight360 Nova: a crazy, untethered, fully rollable VR motion platform (2020). https://newatlas.com/vr/eight360-nova-vr-simulator-ball/. Accessed 9 Jan 2021

Maeda, T., Ando, H., Sugimoto, M.: Virtual acceleration with galvanic vestibular stimulation in a virtual reality environment, p. 289. IEEE (2005)

Multon, F., France, L., Cani-Gascuel, M.P., Debunne, G.: Computer animation of human walking: a survey. J. Vis. Comput. Animation **10**(1), 39–54 (1999)

Nguyen-Vo, T., Riecke, B.E., Stuerzlinger, W.: Simulated reference frame: a cost-effective solution to improve spatial orientation in VR, p. 415. IEEE (2018)

Norman, K.L.: Cyberpsychology: An Introduction to Human-Computer Interaction, 2nd edn. Cambridge University Press, Cambridge (2017)

Rebentisch, L.R.: Cybersickness Prioritization and Modeling. Michigan State University, Michigan (2015)

Riecke, B.E., Feuereissen, D.: To move or not to move: can active control and user-driven motion cueing enhance self-motion perception ("vection") in virtual reality?, p. 17 (2012)

Riecke, B.E., Schulte-Pelkum, J., Caniard, F., Bulthoff, H.H.: Towards lean and elegant self-motion simulation in virtual reality, p. 131. IEEE (2005)

Saredakis, D., Szpak, A., Birckhead, B., Keage, H.A.D., Rizzo, A., Loetscher, T.: Factors associated with virtual reality sickness in head-mounted displays: a systematic review and meta-analysis. Front. Hum. Neurosci. **14**(96), 1–17 (2020). https://doi.org/10.3389/fnhum.2020.00096

Slater, M., Usoh, M., Steed, A.: Taking steps: the influence of a walking technique on presence in virtual reality. ACM Trans. Comput.-Hum. Interact. (TOCHI) **2**(3), 201–219 (1995)

Stanney, K., et al.: Identifying causes of and solutions for cybersickness in immersive technology: reformulation of a research and development agenda. Int. J. Hum.–Comput. Interact. **36**(19), 1783–1803 (2020). https://doi.org/10.1080/10447318.2020.1828535

Stanney, K.M., Hale, K.S., Nahmens, I., Kennedy, R.S.: What to expect from immersive virtual environment exposure: influences of gender, body mass index, and past experience. Hum. Factors J. Hum. Factors Ergon. Soc. **45**(3), 504–520 (2003). https://doi.org/10.1518/hfes.45.3.504.27254

Terzi, K., Hansard, M.: Methods for reducing visual discomfort in stereoscopic 3D: a review. Signal Process. Image Commun. **47**, 402–416 (2016)

Warren, R., Wertheim, A.H.: Perception and Control of Self-motion. Psychology Press, London (2014)

Wienrich, C., Weidner, C.K., Schatto, C., Obremski, D., Israel, J.H.: A virtual nose as a rest-frame-the impact on simulator sickness and game experience, p. 1. IEEE (2018)

Exploring Coordination Patterns in VR-Based Rehabilitation for Stroke Using the Kinect Sensor

Maria F. Montoya[1], Julian F. Villada[1(✉)], John Muñoz[2], and Oscar A. Henao[1]

[1] HCI Group, Universidad Tecnológica de Pereira, Pereira, Colombia
{mf.mv,jfvillada,oscarhe}@utp.edu.co
[2] Systems Design Engineering Department, University of Waterloo, Waterloo, Canada
john.munoz.hci@uwaterloo.co

Abstract. According to the World Health Organization (WHO), acute cerebrovascular diseases represent the third cause of death in the Western world. Access to rehabilitation therapies is very limited and often not very personalized due to its high cost. In recent decades, the use of information and communication technologies (ICT) has become popular as a solution to extend the use of complementary therapies in people with stroke. Particularly, the use of systems that use exercise videogames (Exergames) with motion capture sensors (e.g., Kinect) and virtual reality (VR) headsets has proven to be a feasible and efficient option to promote greater interactivity with the participants and progress quantification. Although the cost of this type of motion capture sensors is low, the type of analysis carried out is often limited to isolated joints and determined by time-series analysis. This paper explores the use of non-linear analysis techniques to investigate the patterns of motor coordination recorded during the interaction with Exergames. A methodology to create phase plane and relative phase diagrams from data captured with the Kinect sensor using both off-the-shelf and VR Exergames is presented. We expose two different rehabilitation scenarios where the coordination analysis could be potentially useful, detailing the multi-joint analysis carried out as well as showing the diagrams and their interpretation. We conclude by reinforcing the need for a more comprehensive and extended analysis of human-body coordination as an important mechanism to validate the use of interactive and virtual technologies in rehabilitation.

Keywords: Phase plane diagram · Relative phase · Coordination · Dynamic system theory · Virtual reality · Exergames

1 Introduction

According to the World Health Organization (WHO), acute cerebrovascular diseases represent the third cause of death in the Western world [1]. Despite efforts to expand the coverage of physical rehabilitation services, access is still very limited [2]. The creation of novel interactive technologies based on gaming systems has been proposed as a feasible and highly motivating method to encourage physical activity and to aid

© Springer Nature Switzerland AG 2021
X. Fang (Ed.): HCII 2021, LNCS 12790, pp. 372–387, 2021.
https://doi.org/10.1007/978-3-030-77414-1_27

the achievement of multiple repetitions of specific movements needed in the rehabilitation process [3]. Research has shown the appropriateness of using exercise videogames (Exergames) as a way to engage older adults in physical activity [4], combat childhood obesity [5], improve mental and social well-being in older adults [6] and affect the cognitive functioning positively in clinical and non-clinical populations [7]. Despite positive aspects, the quantification of the effectiveness of using Exergames as physical therapy still faces many challenges in terms of valid and understandable outcome measurements [8]. Although it has been shown that the understanding of motor patterns associated with the performed movements during Exergaming sessions is a key element to facilitate technology adoption [9], little has been done to further explore this issue. Previous work from Bernstein and colleagues has highlighted underlying biomechanical mechanisms for phase synchronization as key concepts to study the dynamics of human movement [10]. Joint coordination has been explored as one of the biomechanical mechanisms that reveal the quality of the movement; that is why clinicians and researchers put a lot of effort to assess it. The main clinical techniques to measure interlimb coordination are indirect and subjective measurements based on the effects of coordination impairments on patients' function. To this end, most clinical assessments evaluate activities of daily living, and convey a degree of the patients' (in)dependence and the quality of their movement performance [11]. On the other hand, neuroscientist and rehabilitation engineers have focused on the evaluation of motor control witch evidence interlimb coordination through motor patterns. They have proposed measurements motion capture and robotic devices, to extract variables that reflect motor coordination, for instance, an angular representation called relative phase or a time variable called relative reaction time [11].

Therefore, the main goal of this paper is to explore coordination patterns that can be analyzed by plotting angular representations of different coordinative structures after performing specific movements. We design a proof of concept which covers two different scenarios of interactive virtual rehabilitation using Exergames [12]. We use an immersive VR system and off-the-shelf exergames [13] as illustrative examples. We hypothesize that the angular diagrams could reflect the joint coordination changes that participants exhibit while playing Exergames in virtual environments. We provide a comprehensive methodology that uses accessible technology and easy-to-replicate methods to illustrate how these sophisticated biomechanical techniques can be integrated into novel gaming-based rehabilitation therapies.

1.1 Measuring Coordination Patterns with Dynamic Systems Theory

The relationship between human movement and the coordination phase is modeled using coupling angles or sinusoidal identity Euler (Euler angle) in the complex number world. This mathematical concept establishes the relationship of cycles or frequencies of human rhythmic movement in each limb with a particular movement or as a coordinate exercising such as walking, dancing, swimming, etc., [14]. In order to study motor coordination in the human body, accurate capture of data from movements is necessary. One of the best disciplines to study human movement coordination is human biomechanics, not only to describe changes in movement but also to understand why those changes happen [15]. In biomechanical terms, motor coordination is generally defined as the spatiotemporal relationships that exist between different body segments [16]. The phase plane (PPD) and relative phase (RPD) diagrams are two useful techniques for the analysis of coordination patterns since they are qualitative representations of the relationship between displacement and angular velocity, considering one or more segments of the body during the entire movement [17]. These techniques generate diagrams whose trajectories indicate how the different segments are coordinated (e.g., in phase-equal direction or counter-phase-alternating direction) during the movement. These diagrams are the most commonly used concept for simultaneous and congruent interlimb activities [18], widely used by rehabilitation engineers and neuroscientists. Moreover, PPD and RPD has been used to describe stroke patients' coordination during gait, and represent an objective assessment of the motor coordination, alternative to those measurements often developed by clinicians [11].

Phase Plane Diagrams (PPD)
Following the idea of human joints as coordinative structures, the coordination between joints can be described as functional relationships between important anatomical parts of the human body while performing an activity [15]. An initial approach for looking at how human movement is coordinated, is to search for inter-relationships between joints. Phase diagrams have been proposed based on the concept that a system can be graphed as a diagram of two variables called angular position and angular velocity [19]. The phase diagram description is made in a counterclock-wise sense since flexion is a decrement of angle and extension an increment of angle [15, 17].

Figure 1 shows the over-imposed phase diagrams of one running stride that consider the hip and knee for the analysis. On the contrary of angle-angle diagrams, PPD are representations of just one joint; nevertheless, the superimposition of multiple joints is typically carried out to evaluate the coordination between the joints. A phase angle is mathematically defined as the arctan [angular position / angular velocity] for time series respectively [15] which can be seen in Fig. 1 as the angle (seen anticlockwise) of the vector formed from the center of the diagram [0,0] and a point formed by the instantaneous angular position (AP); and the angular velocity (AV). As shown in Fig. 1, the phase angle of the knee "pak" is formed by the vector "vk", and the phase angle of the hip "pah" is formed by the vector "vh". Furthermore, using those two phase angles the relative phase (RP) is defined as the subtraction of the phase angles from both joints at the same instant ($RP = PAh - PAk$) [15, 16]. Thus, the RP can be seen as the angle of the dot product between the vectors "vh" and "vk". The RP as a time series is known as a coordination pattern called "continuous relative phase" (CRP).

Continuous Relative Phase (CRP) and Interpretation
The CRP is a representation of the temporal relationship of two systems; particularly in the body movement analysis, this technique is used to analyze the phase relationship between two body segments [11, 20]. As mentioned in the previous section, the CRP is defined as the difference between the phase angle of the distal segment and the phase angle of the proximal segment at each moment:

$$RP = [PA]_d - [PA]_p \qquad (1)$$

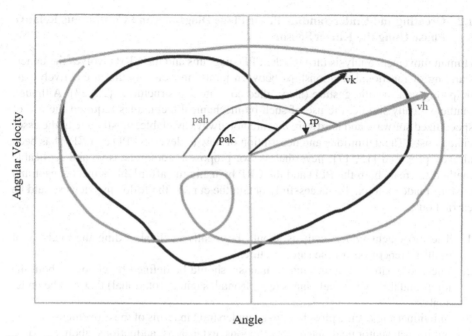

Fig. 1. Superimpose PPD of hip and knee made from non-real data of a gait movement. Gray line: hip phase plane. Black line: Knee phase plane.

Where *RP* is the relative phase, *PAd* is the phase angle of the distal segment and *PAp* is the phase angle of the proximal segment.

The values of the RP allow determining the type of coordination. We define coordination in-phase (0°) if the two segments or joints are moving synchronously. On the contrary, the coordination is counter-phase (180°) if the segments or articulations move on opposite directions [20]. In addition, we can find multiple intermediate coordination modes, called out of phase, between in-phase or counter-phase coordination. On the other hand, the positive or negative sign in the values of the RP, express that a specific segment precedes the other in the coordination of movement. If the values are positive, the distal segment performs the movement before the proximal and if the values are negative, the proximal segment precedes the distal segment.

The CRP, as a movement analysis technique, allows summarizing the coordination, having a strong potential to be a good descriptor of the movement efficiency carried out by the performer [16]. Variability in the CRP reflects the stability of the system as a whole. Motor learning implies that the individual modifies the coordination of the involved segments to adapt to the objective of the task and perform it more efficiently and effectively. Therefore, changes in the values of the CRP between attempts reflect different coordination and are an indicator of the reorganization of the system that normally occurs in the motor learning process [21]. A very structured and well-learned movement shows consistent and very similar CRP curves among attempts, reflecting the neuromuscular control developed to using that specific movement [21].

1.2 Creating and Understanding Phase Plane Diagrams and Continuous Relative Phase Using the Kinect Sensor

Human movement analysis through the PPD diagrams and the CRP involves the understanding of functional relationships between joints' movements that are actively participating in a specific gesture (also called coordinative structures) [22, 23]. Although mathematically simple, the use of such biomechanical techniques required the use of specialized software and hardware that are not always available, mostly due to the associated costs. The definitions and description of how to develop PPD and CRP has been already proposed [15, 17]; nevertheless, we propose a comprehensive and replicable method to create both the PPD and the CRP by using the affordable Kinect sensor and custom-made toolbox. To successfully obtain the curves, the following steps should be carried out:

1. The movement under analysis should be ideally cyclical, aiding the analysis of multiple repetitions of the same gesture.
2. The coordinative structure under analysis should be defined by choosing both the joints and the anatomical planes (e.g., frontal, sagittal, rotational) that will be under analysis.
3. Individual angle-time plots have to be understood in terms of the movements carried out in each anatomical plane (e.g., flexions, extensions, adductions, abductions).
4. Normalization and filtering the time-series might end up being useful in reducing the shakiness of the motion capture data from the Kinect sensor. We develop a normalization to zero mean, and we have used 30-order median filters to remove signal noise from motion capture data of the Kinect sensor [24].
5. Segment the motion capture data, guaranteeing that every segment has a complete repetition of the movement.
6. In the case of PPD: Extract the angular position of each joint and select the plane of interest. A derivative should be applied to the angular position to find the angular velocity information. For each articulation, plot the angular position as an independent variable with the angular velocity as the dependent variable.
7. In the case of the CRP: Once the angular position and angular velocity information of both joints are extracted, a matrix for each joint should be created. The matrix is compound by two rows: i) the angular position and ii) the angular velocity. Finally, it should be extracted the angle of the dot product between these matrices, which should be transformed from radians to degrees, representing the continuous relative phase angle.

2 Methodology

To study coordination patterns with both the PPD and CRP, we decided to use the Kinect sensor. The sensor was used due to its portability and feasibility of being easily integrated into clinical environments as well as the accuracy to capture movement from both upper and lower limbs [25]. Two different scenarios and setups were used considering the current technological advancement of interactive rehabilitation systems: immersive VR and an off-the-shelf Exergaming console.

2.1 Subjects

Five healthy subjects (ages 24.2 ± 5.63), students of Engineering at the local university, were recruited for testing both scenarios in a controlled laboratory environment. The subjects were informed of the experimental protocol using a consent form. The testing procedure was developed in one session; subjects first performed 10 min warm out of joint movements and then played in both scenarios.

2.2 Upper Limb Rehabilitation Using Immersive VR

The HTC Vive VR system was used to immerse the subject in a single-player snowball fight game[1] in a winter wonderland. The subject creates and throws snowballs with the goal to hit targets and score in the game while being under attack from a moving enemy snowman. During the gameplay, several motion recordings were carried out while the subject was learning how to perform the movements that required flexion-extensions of the right arm while throwing the snowball. Although the movement involved several joints, recordings were analyzed using the coordinative structure defined by the elbow and shoulder of the arm associated with the throwing (right arm in this case).

An external Kinect sensor was used to record the motion capture data by using the Brekel Kinect software[2]. Finally, we carried out the steps described in Sect. 1.2 for getting both the PPD and CRP for the flexion-extension of the right shoulder and right elbow. To extract the angular position of the shoulder and the elbow we used a custom-made software tool [20]. Figure 2 shows images of the setup and the VR game used.

2.3 Gait Rehabilitation Using Off-the-Shelf Exergames

In this second scenario, we used one of the most widely explored Exergaming consoles for exercise therapy: the XBOX 360 with Kinect. The Kinect Sports Exergame was used to record users marching in place, a frequently used activity for gait rehabilitation [24]. The Athletics minigame proposes the player a simulation of a competitive race against non-player characters. Repetitions of pronounced and gradually accelerated march in a steady-state were recorded in which the subject performed movements with flexion-extension of the legs while marching rapidly. The right hip-knee coordinative structure was analyzed considering the involvement of these joints in the gait analysis [15].

The recording and processing of motion data were identically carried out as in the first immersive VR scenario. Figure 3 shows images of the setup and the Exergame used in this scenario.

---

[1] https://store.steampowered.com/app/579080/Snow_Games_VR/.

[2] https://brekel.com/kinect-3d-scanner/.

Fig. 2. Upper limb rehabilitation set up. Left: Snow games, the VR game use to the mocap. Right: Kinect position to carry out the mocap, and user position configuration to play the VR game.

Fig. 3. Gait rehabilitation set up. Left: "Athletics Kinect sports" Xbox 360 videogame. Right: Kinect configuration to develop the MoCap, and user position to play the videogame.

3   Results and Discussion

For both scenarios, we carried out the biomechanical analysis considering the PPD and CRP. Although in the previous section the PPD showed the combination of two joints to explain the relative phase measurement, next section shows joints being analyzed separately to avoid the superimposition of excessive information, and also aid graph interpretation. The PPDs were obtained from all sessions, however, we show the best repetitions based on visual inspections from biomechanical researchers. Moreover, continuous relative phases were also computed and plotted. Results and interpretations are presented as follows:

3.1 Upper Limb Rehabilitation Set Analysis

A repetition of the movements performed by subject number 1 was chosen to be represented in the PPD. The phase diagram of the right shoulder in the upper-limb VR scenario is shown in Fig. 4. The graph should be interpreted following a clockwise direction, meaning that extensions are increases of the angle values, and the flexions are decreases of the same.

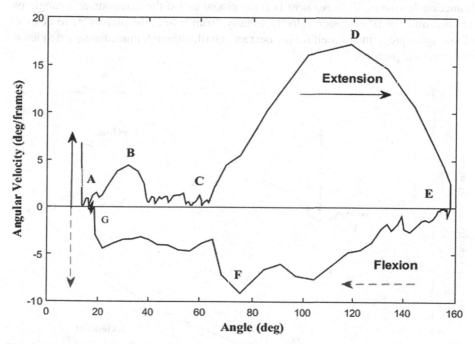

Fig. 4. PPD of the right shoulder for the upper limb rehabilitation scenario using immersive VR. The diagram is divided into letters that represent the segments of the movement. The Extension arrow shows an increase in the angle value while the Flexion arrow shows a decrease.

The complete movement can be described in sub-segments from points A to G. The movement started at point A with an angle of 13° and it had an increase of extension velocity to B until reaching 32°. The segment B-C presented a decrease in the extension's velocity and little oscillations until reaching 60°. From point C to D there was an increase of the angular velocity of 17°/frames in the extension until reaching a peak of 119°, followed by a velocity decrease, to finally get almost a complete shoulder extension of 158° in the D-E segment. The second half of the movement is the shoulder flexion starting at point E, reaching a velocity of flexion of 9°/frames at 75°. Finally, in the segment F-G, a decrease of the shoulder flexion is presented until reaching again a 13° angle.

The PPD of the right elbow is shown in Fig. 5 for the same VR scenario. In this case, the diagram is interpreted anticlockwise direction indicating that flexion movements manifest increases of angle whereas the extensions are decreasing. The movement of throwing the snowballs will be described from point A to F. The elbow in point A started with a flexion degree of 29°. From A to B it can be seen an increase and a posterior decrease of flexion angular velocity with a continuous increase of flexion angle until 51°. Then, from B to C a similar behavior was found, and the angle reaches the maximum flexion at 79°. The elbow extension started in the segment C-D with the player's elbow extension to throw the snowball, that is why in the phase plane can be seen a peek in the extension angular velocity that reaches the 17°/frames at an angle of 41° and it is immediately stabilized. In segment D-E the elbow ended the extension at an angle of 15° reaching the 0° extension velocity. Finally, from E to F, the players try to flex the elbow again preparing himself for the next snowball, although immediately extended it to correct the position.

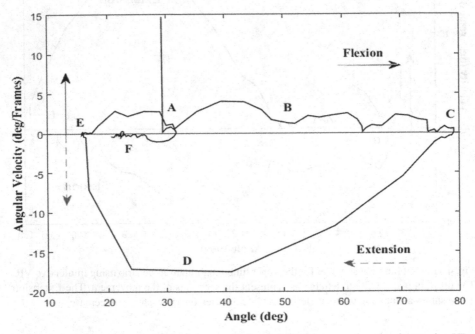

Fig. 5. PPD of the right elbow for the upper limb rehabilitation scenario using immersive VR. The diagram is divided into letters that represent the segments of the movement. The Extension arrow shows a decrease in the angle value while the Flexion arrow shows an increase.

Furthermore, the CRP diagram of each subject that considers both the right shoulder and the right elbow is depicted in Fig. 6. The four different repetitions are superimposed to aid the visualization of motor learning among repetitions. Following the recommendations posed by Barlett and colleagues [15, 17], the CRP was computed by subtracting the phase angle of the distal joint (elbow) from the proximal joint (shoulder). In continuous relative phases, abrupt changes of direction represent poor motor control. While performing multiple repetitions, users naturally learn how to carry out more refined and controlled movements to score in the game.

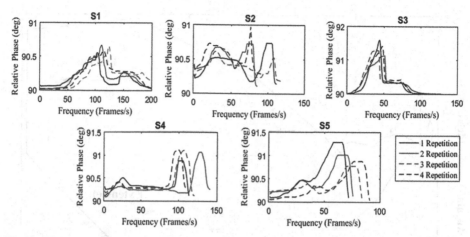

Fig. 6. The CRP diagram of four different repetitions of each subject (S1: subject 1. S2: subject 2. S3: subject 3. S4 subject 4. S5: subject 5) recorded from the upper limb rehabilitation scenario using immersive VR. The continuous black line represents the first repetition, the continuous grey line represents the second repetition, the dashed grey line represents the third repetition, and the dashed black line represents the fourth and last repetition.

For instance, in Fig. 6, the continuous black line represents the relative phase of the first repetition, while the black dashed line represents the relative phase of the last repetition. When compared, the curves show differences that reflect better motor control represented by a smother behavior throughout the task, specifically in subjects 1, 4 and 5 (S1, S4 and S5). Particularly, the throwing movement visualized in CRPs is characterized by two peaks, one more pronounced than the other. Moreover, in the CRP diagram of subject 3 (S3) the first peak is higher than the second one, while in the CRP diagram of subject 4 (S4) the second peak is higher than the first one. In general, changes in the angle values are less pronounced in the last repetition once compared with the first one; thus, indicating a smooth and fine control in the movement.

3.2 Gait Rehabilitation Using Set Analysis

The diagrams of the phase planes in Fig. 7 and Fig. 8 were extracted from the movement performed by subject 1. This diagram should be interpreted clockwise. As shown in the graph, the flexion is an angular increase while the extension is a decrease. The movement started at point A at an angle of 2° and it has an increase in the speed of extension to B until it reaches 3°. The segment B-C shows a decrease in the flexion angular velocity to almost zero, and then in section C-D the angular velocity reaches a peek 6°/frames with a stabilization until reaching the 16° of flexion. From point D to point E, there is a decrease in the flexion angular velocity when the hip flexion reaches the maximum angle of 21°. The second half of the movement started with the hip extension at point E reaching an extension angular velocity of 5°/frames at a maximum angle of 15°. Finally, in the segment F-G, the last part of the movement completes the cycle with a significant decrease of angle extension until 3°.

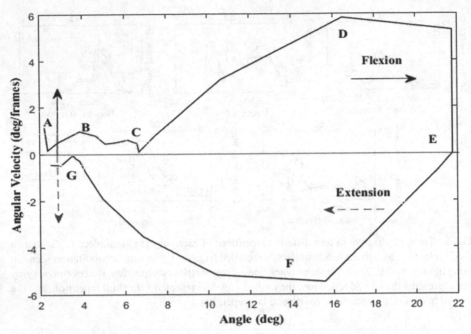

Fig. 7. Phase plane diagram of the left hip for the gait rehabilitation scenario using the "Kinect sports" videogame of Xbox-360. The diagram is divided into letters that represent the segments of the movement.

The PPD in Fig. 8 is interpreted clockwise since the flexion represents an increase in angle and extensions are decreases in angle. The movement began at point A at an angle of 7° and had an increase in the flexion angular velocity to B until it reaches 16°. The segment B-C shows a decrease in the flexion angular velocity to almost 2°/frames finding an angle of 21°. In segment C-D there is a significant increase in the angular velocity until reaching its peak at 38° flexion. From point D to point E, the movement reaches the maximum knee flexion at 38°. The extension of the knee started in the segment E-F reaching an extension angular velocity of 7°/frames at an angle of 30°. Finally, the last part of the movement to close the cycle is given from point F to point G, where there is a significant decrease in the extension to reach 11°.

The CRP between the hip and the knee was calculated from four repetitions of each subject and they are represented in Fig. 9. Following the recommendations in [15] the relative phase was calculated by subtracting the phase angle of the distal joint (knee) from the proximal joint (hip). This continuous relative shows how coordination is improved through repetitions notoriously in subjects 1, 2 and 4 (S1, S2 and S4). The decrease of sudden changes while the movement is repeated, evidences better performance. As can be seen in Fig. 9, specifically for subjects 1, 2 and 4 (S1, S2 and S4), the discontinuous black line (last repetition) is smoother than the continuous black line one (first repetition), and the changes of angles in the discontinuous black line are not as pronounced as in the continuous black line. This behavior exposes a smooth movement in the last repetition. In general, the same shape pattern for the CRP was accomplished for all the subjects.

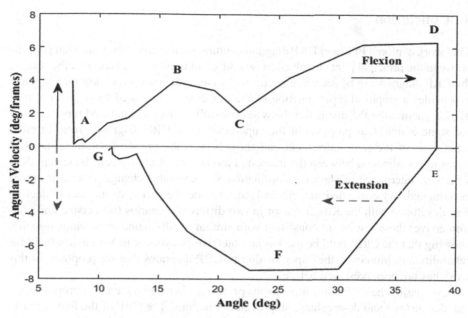

Fig. 8. PPD of the left knee for the gait rehabilitation scenario using the "Kinect sports" videogame from Xbox-360. The diagram is divided into letters that represent the segments of the movement

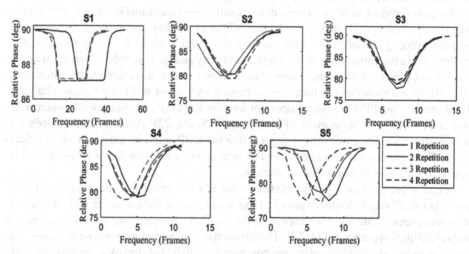

Fig. 9. The CRP of four different repetitions of each subject (S1: subject 1. S2: subject 2. S3: subject 3. S4 subject 4. S5: subject 5) recorded from the gait rehabilitation scenario with the Exergames. The continuous black line represents the first repetition, the continuous grey line represents the second repetition, the dashed grey line represents the third repetition, and the dashed black line represents the fourth and last repetition.

4   Conclusion

This work explored PPD and DRP diagrams aiming to investigate coordination patterns between the principal joints involved in two different movements. Based on the results, the CRP diagram can be seen as a useful tool to analyze intra-joint coordination since it provides a graphical representation of the movement performed by two joints at-a-glance, facilitating the distinction between controlled or non-controlled repetitions of the same action. Our proposal of the superposition of CRP diagrams from different repetitions of the same movement can show how is the progress within sessions in terms of coordination between the interested joints. Therefore, sudden changes in their values are interpreted as a lack of coordination, while smother changes represent a more coordinated and controlled movement [16]. Despite the fact that our data collection was developed with the Kinect sensor in two different scenarios (immersive and non-immersive) these results are consistent with similar results found in previous research showing that the CRP could be used as an objective assessment in VR environment for rehabilitation. Moreover, the superposition of CRP diagrams that we proposed in this work has not been presented before.

Comparing the CRP of the movements performed in the two scenarios proposed, we can deconstruct and de-escalate complex motor actions. The CRP of the first scenario reveals that the throwing movement involving the shoulder and the elbow can have several variations between subjects. On the other hand, a simple movement as the gait showed the same pattern for all the subjects. Furthermore, PPD is also a powerful tool to understand the movement, as proven in the results, these diagrams showed where are the key stages of each joint movement. As the PPD is a compound of the angle position and angular velocity values, it provides valuable information about the acceleration stages of the joint in the entire movement. Angular velocity changes provide information about movement control; for instance, slower movements can be associated with restrictions to perform the movement, which can be caused by pain or muscular fatigue [20, 26]. Furthermore, the PPD provides important angular information often used to determine the correct range of movement of each joint [15, 20, 22]. Although the sample for this study was limited, our results suggest that the CRP could be a useful tool to reflect player's coordination changes present while interacting in a VR environment as a possible scenario for physical rehabilitation therapy.

Finally, we want to highlight the use of the Kinect sensor and specialized software as tools for affordable biomechanical analysis, optimizing the recording and analysis of user's movement and allowing capturing data within a reliable range of measurements for rehabilitation purposes [24, 27]. Therefore, the system that we propose is a low-cost solution to assess joints' coordination compared to others previously proposed [28, 29]. On the other hand, we showed how sophisticated biomechanical analysis techniques of coordination analysis could be used in Exergaming scenarios, reinforcing the idea that measurable and quantifiable benefits can be key in revealing the real benefits of interactive games for health. Future work includes the development of novel kinematic adaptive techniques able to use coordination patterns (e.g., PPD and CRP) to create real-time adaptations of gameplay in real-time [30].

4.1 Limitations

This proof of concept paper has multiple limitations. First, the sample size is small, and it does not allow to reach generalizable conclusions. However, we have provided and comprehensive methodological protocol that shows the feasibility of using the Kinect sensor to explore coordination patterns. The measurement protocol and the described steps for getting the PPD and CRP curves can be easily replicated and extended to other application scenarios.

Second, although the proposed solution can be considered as low-cost, the use of the Kinect as an external sensor especially in clinical settings, can be problematic because in order to capture the movement, an extra computer with specialized and custom-made software to process the data is required. Finally, both the PPD and CRP diagrams require a preliminary and certainly time-consuming analysis and understanding of the angular curves extracted from each joint to ensure they are physiologically correct in their magnitudes.

Acknowledgments. The authors gratefully acknowledge the support of all the members of the Human-Computer Interaction group of the *Universidad Tecnológica de Pereira*. In addition, the CIDT of the *Universidad Tecnológica de Pereira* to provide their facilities for experimentation and content creation. Finally, the authors also thank the clinician Dr. José Fernando López from the Clínica de Dolor del Eje Cafetero, for the constant advisory and his valuable contributions.

References

1. Mathers, C.D., Boerma, T., Ma Fat, D.: Global and regional causes of death. Br. Med. Bull. **92**(1), 7–32 (2009). https://doi.org/10.1093/bmb/ldp028
2. Hanson, K., Ranson, M.K., Oliveira-Cruz, V., Mills, A.: Expanding access to priority health interventions: a framework for understanding the constraints to scaling-up. J. Int. Dev.: J. Dev. Stud. Assoc. **15**(1), 1–14 (2003)
3. Ofli, F., Kurillo, G., Obdržálek, Š, Bajcsy, R., Jimison, H.B., Pavel, M.: Design and evaluation of an interactive exercise coaching system for older adults: lessons learned. IEEE J. Biomed. Health Inform. **20**(1), 201–212 (2015)
4. Kappen, D.L., Mirza-Babaei, P., Nacke, L.E.: Older adults' physical activity and exergames: a systematic review. Int. J. Human-Comput. Interact. **35**(2), 140–167 (2019)
5. Lu, A.S., Kharrazi, H., Gharghabi, F., Thompson, D.: A systematic review of health videogames on childhood obesity prevention and intervention. Games Health: Res. Dev. Clin. Appl. **2**(3), 131–141 (2013)
6. Loos, E., Kaufman, D.: Positive impact of exergaming on older adults' mental and social well-being: in search of evidence. In: Zhou, J., Salvendy, G. (eds.) ITAP 2018. LNCS, vol. 10927, pp. 101–112. Springer, Cham (2018). https://doi.org/10.1007/978-3-319-92037-5_9
7. Stanmore, E., Stubbs, B., Vancampfort, D., de Bruin, E.D., Firth, J.: The effect of active video games on cognitive functioning in clinical and non-clinical populations: a meta-analysis of randomized controlled trials. Neurosci. Biobehav. Rev. **78**, 34–43 (2017)
8. Peng, W., Lin, J.-H., Crouse, J.: Is playing exergames really exercising? A meta-analysis of energy expenditure in active video games. Cyberpsychol. Behav. Soc. Netw. **14**(11), 681–688 (2011)

9. van Diest, M., Stegenga, J., Wörtche, H.J., Roerdink, J.B.T.M., Verkerke, G.J., Lamoth, C.J.C.: Quantifying postural control during exergaming using multivariate whole-body movement data: a self-organizing maps approach. PLOS ONE **10**(7), e0134350 (2015)
10. Whiting, H.T.A.: Human Motor Actions: Bernstein Reassessed, vol. 17. Elsevier, Amsterdam (1983)
11. Shirota, C., et al.: On the assessment of coordination between upper extremities: towards a common language between rehabilitation engineers, clinicians and neuroscientists. J. Neuroeng. Rehabil. **13**(1), 80 (2016)
12. Anguera, J.A., et al.: Video game training enhances cognitive control in older adults. Nature **501**(7465), 97–101 (2013)
13. Levac, D., Glegg, S., Colquhoun, H., Miller, P., Noubary, F.: Virtual reality and active videogame-based practice, learning needs, and preferences: a cross-Canada survey of physical therapists and occupational therapists. Games Health J. **6**(4), 217–228 (2017)
14. Kelso, J.A.S.: Elementary coordination dynamics. In: Interlimb Coordination, pp. 301–318. Elsevier (1994)
15. Barlett, R.: Introduction to Sports Biomechanics: Analysing Human Movement Patterns. Routledge, Abingdon (2007)
16. Burgess-Limerick, R., Abernethy, B., Neal, R.J.: Relative phase quantifies interjoint coordination. J. Biomech. **26**(1), 91–94 (1993)
17. Lamb, P.F., Bartlett, R.M.: Assessing movement coordination. In: Biomechanical Evaluation of Movement in Sport and Exercise: The British Association of Sport and Exercise Sciences Guide (2017)
18. Latash, M.L., Zatsiorsky, V.: Biomechanics and Motor Control: Defining Central Concepts. Academic Press, Cambridge (2015)
19. Parker, H.: Children's motor rhythm and timing: a dynamical approach. In: Advances in Psychology, vol. 84, pp. 163–194. Elsevier (1992)
20. Angulo-Barroso, R., Faciabén, A.B., Mauerberg-Decastro, E.: El ángulo de fase y la fase relativa continua para la investigación de la coordinación motora. Apunts Educación Física y Deportes **103**, 38–47 (2011)
21. Winfree, A.T.: The Geometry of Biological Time, vol. 12. Springer, Heidelberg (2001). https://doi.org/10.1007/978-1-4757-3484-3
22. Spinelli, B.A., Wattananon, P., Silfies, S., Talaty, M., Ebaugh, D.: Using kinematics and a dynamical systems approach to enhance understanding of clinically observed aberrant movement patterns. Man. Ther. **20**(1), 221–226 (2015)
23. Torrents Martín, C.: Teoría de los sistemas dinámicos y el entrenamiento deportivo, La. Universitat de Barcelona (2005)
24. Muñoz, J.E., Villada, J.F., Casanova, S., Montoya, M.F., Henao, O.A.: Dynamic systems theory in human movement exploring coordination patterns by angle-angle diagrams using Kinect. In: 2018 10th International Conference on Virtual Worlds and Games for Serious Applications (VS-Games), pp. 1–4 (2018)
25. Fern'ndez-Baena, A., Susín, A., Lligadas, X.: Biomechanical validation of upper-body and lower-body joint movements of kinect motion capture data for rehabilitation treatments. In: 2012 Fourth International Conference on Intelligent Networking and Collaborative Systems, pp. 656–661 (2012)
26. Angulo-Barroso, R., Faciabén, A.B., MAuERBERg-dEcASTRO, E.: El retrato de fase como una herramienta de análisis del comportamiento motor. Apunts Educación Física y Deportes, **102**, 49–61 (2010)
27. Choppin, S., Wheat, J.: The potential of the Microsoft Kinect in sports analysis and biomechanics. Sports Technol. **6**(2), 78–85 (2013)

28. Scott, S., Dukelow, S.: Potential of robots as next-generation technology for clinical assessment of neurological disorders and upper-limb therapy. J. Rehabil. Res. Dev. **48**(4), 335 (2011)
29. Nordin, N., Xie, S.Q., Wünsche, B.: Assessment of movement quality in robot-assisted upper limb rehabilitation after stroke: a review. J. Neuroeng. Rehabil. **11**(1), 137 (2014)
30. Muñoz, J.E., Cao, S., Boger, J.: Kinematically adaptive exergames: personalizing exercise therapy through closed-loop systems. In: AIVR 2019, pp. 118–125 (2019)

The Woods: A Mixed-Reality Multiplayer Cooperative Game

Kyoung Swearingen[✉] and Scott Swearingen[✉]

The Ohio State University, Columbus, OH 43210, USA
{swearingen.75,swearingen.16}@osu.edu

Abstract. While loneliness in our real lives is increasingly recognized as having dire physical, mental and emotional consequences, cooperative games have also been shown to build empathy and provide positive social impact. In this paper, we present 'The Woods', a local cooperative mixed reality game that provides players with face-to-face interactions in pursuit of a shared goal using augmented reality and 4-channel audio spatialization panning. This paper discusses the technical aspects of the game, the design rationale and development process, and the resulting player experience. The goal of this research is to develop a narrative driven AR game that provides social benefits by prompting players to problem-solve collaboratively, and to leverage the physical and digital experience as fully as possible.

Keywords: Collaborative gaming · Mixed reality · Sonic experience

1 Introduction

'*The Woods*' is a mixed-reality multiplayer cooperative game that addresses the perils of social isolation by promoting connections between people and actively engaging them through play. Using Augmented Reality (AR) and 4-channel audio spatialization panning, players choreograph their movement in <u>real-world</u> space, while interacting with birds, clouds and other objects in <u>virtual</u> space. In pursuit of a shared goal, players experience an immersive sonic narrative of rumbling storm clouds and disconnected voices that culminate in stories of hope and reconciliation. '*The Woods*' provides positive social impact by illuminating our connections to one another and inspiring us to respond through collaboration [1, 2].

Since the 1980's the percentage of American adults who say they're lonely has doubled from 20% to 40%. Research has also indicated that an increase in mobile phone use and online networking (in contrast to face-to-face interactions) in general has had a negative impact on children's health, citing screen time, "phone addiction" and lack of physical activities as potential health-related challenges. These same challenges can be detrimental to a young person's mental and social wellbeing, lead to isolation and depression, cyberbullying, and even contribute to increased suicide rates. While loneliness in our real lives is increasingly recognized as having dire physical, mental and emotional consequences, our goal is to examine through creative inquiry how the same

© Springer Nature Switzerland AG 2021
X. Fang (Ed.): HCII 2021, LNCS 12790, pp. 388–397, 2021.
https://doi.org/10.1007/978-3-030-77414-1_28

technology can be reimagined to strengthen connections between isolated populations through play and collaboration, and to create a dialog at the intersection of the arts, humanities, and human-centered technology [3–5].

'The Woods' was designed to inspire a discourse of contemporary life and explore how technology can cultivate presence and promote positive societal change within it. It is expressive, playful, collaborative and physical. It is designed for people and illuminates our connections to one another. It communicates the importance of fostering mental health through face-to-face engagement, the power of the human voice, and purposefully "combines the strengths of different people from different perspectives" as it examines how technology that is often criticized for inducing isolation can be reimagined to mitigate it (Fig. 1).

Fig. 1. Playing 'The Woods' at Urban Arts Space Gallery, Columbus, OH., USA

2   Narrative

The narrative of 'The Woods' is built upon broken relationships and the hope for their reconciliation. The first narrative follows two adult brothers who have been separated and out of contact with each other for several years. One of the brothers, desperate to reach out and reconcile with the other, is heard leaving a voicemail in an attempt to reconnect. In the beginning, players hear only fragments and distorted chunks of the message, unable to decipher meaning or intent. As the game progresses through player collaboration, the message becomes clearer. Ultimately, players hear the message in its entirety, revealing that although the two brothers haven't spoken in years, there is a palpable yearning to mend their severed ties.

The second narrative follows an aging mother reaching out to her child whom she has not connected with for some time. Similar to the brothers, she also left a voicemail describing her own struggles grappling with an aging parent who had become cognitively disabled. Like the first narrative, this too unfolds as players make progress in the game, concluding with a plea for connection.

These two narratives of reconciliation between these estranged brothers and a mother and a child echoes loudly through the mechanics of the game itself, as the players coordinate their efforts with one another in pursuit of a common goal. The game is designed in a way that it is not enough for one player to do all the work, but rather success can only be achieved through the work of all the players. As players engage one another and contribute to the goal together, the game rewards them with the unfolding narrative of the brothers reconnecting with one another. Furthermore, even if players fail to find success during the game, the mechanics reinforce that they are still connected.

3 Mechanics

What makes 'The Woods' unique is how it enables players to physically collaborate with their whole bodies. Using AR markers and the Master-Client architecture of the Photon Unity Network (PUN), we track the positions of players through their smartphones as they move about the 12x12-foot game space. By tracking the positions of the phones, we connect the players to one another by placing a virtual branch at their mid-point. As players move themselves and their phones through physical space, the branch moves in virtual space. As such, players must choreograph their movement (and the branch by extension) to provide the virtual birds a perch to land on. To accomplish this, the game checks for collisions between the branch and two other virtual objects. If a collision occurs between the branch and a bird, the bird will land on it and a fragment of the aforementioned voicemail will play. By contrast, if a collision occurs between the branch and a storm cloud, a crash of thunder erupts and any birds that were caught scatter and fly away. The mechanics are designed to echo the narrative of the isolated brothers navigating their own obstacles to reconnect with one another.

Players begin by launching the game on their iPhones (assuming a server has already been established on a server located on the same network). Both players/clients must select 'START' to begin the game. See Fig. 2. After doing so, a short cut scene plays that provides the players with an 'in-game' tutorial in the form of an animation. The beginning of the animation shows four birds perching upon a branch. Through secondary movement, we see gusts of wind causing the birds to rebalance themselves so as not to fall off the branch. Dark clouds soon follow as the birds quickly scatter away from the approaching path of the impending storm. At this point, the animation stops, and the game begins.

Fig. 2. Three frames from the intro animation

The animation (in-game tutorial) is important in that it reveals a few key points about the game. First, it shows the goal, or the object of the game: to get the birds in flight back onto the branch. Second, this also reveals the total number of birds that the players must catch: four. Third, we learn that storm clouds are objects meant to be avoided. If not, any birds that happen to be perched will scatter again and the players will have to start once more from the beginning.

Once both players have entered the game, they find their phones attached to either end of an (AR) branch, connected to it by a tether. As players move their phones throughout the gaming environment, the branch responds in turn. In a way, you can think of each player manipulating one of the end points of the branch. This actually provides the players with a high degree of freedom in how they interact with the branch and one another in real-time.

A virtual (AR) bird is then spawned into the game and begins flying to random waypoints that it picks throughout the environment. We designed the experience to have only one bird at a time to let the players fully experience each voicemail message that plays after the bird perches on the branch. As the players choreograph their movement to manipulate the branch which serves as a perch for the spawned bird, the game also introduces a virtual (AR) cloud, a threat that randomly moves across the game space. The cloud serves as an obstacle that the players must avoid as they pursue their shared goal – collect all four birds. If the branch with birds on it intersects this virtual cloud, the phones will vibrate, and the birds will scatter and fly away. If there are no birds on the branch, the phone will simply vibrate. See Fig. 3.

Fig. 3. In-game screenshots from both players' perspectives

4   Audio

While research has shown both physiological and emotional connections drawn through the power of the human voice, 'The Woods' employs it as a mechanism for expressing motivation and intention in its narrative. The immersive real-time audio of 'The Woods' is arrived at with 4-channel audio, using point-source spatialization and amplitude panning. We accomplish this with an embeddable version of the open-source graphical programming environment, Pure Data (PD), that we interface with Unity3D (our game engine). PD is installed on the computer where the server is located and is connected to speakers through an audio interface. We are using the MOTU M4. See Fig. 4 below.

Figure 4, shows main.pd, an array of sound controls created in Pure Data, that was designed to correspond to the mechanics to reflect and magnify the experience of the overall gameplay through sound. In main.pd, 'Tension' blocks indicate there are three levels of intensity to the sound and illustrates that as more birds are collected, the intensity increases. To the left there are levels for 'Birds', 'Ambience', 'Rain' and 'Background'. Their current low levels correspond to the low tension above. As a second and third bird land on the branch, Unity sends messages of these state changes to Pure Data which responds by increasing the tension. Increases in tension are reflected in the 'Birds', 'Ambience', 'Rain' and 'Background' as their volume and intensity are programmed to increase in response. As birds on the branch are lost during gameplay, the tension and the levels of the corresponding sounds also drop. 'Flapping' is played whenever the branch (with birds or without) penetrates a cloud and represents the birds taking flight. 'CLOUD' is also played whenever the branch penetrates a cloud but emits a clap of thunder instead. 'Melody' and 'Notes' play during the intro and ending animations that bookend the entire experience.

At the bottom of Fig. 4, there are controls for 'All speakers and master level' which enables anyone sitting at the server to set the levels for all of the speakers independently,

Fig. 4. Sound design using PD interface

in addition to a subwoofer (if connected). Using Pure Data in this way, in addition to all the individual controls above, allows our audio designer to have significantly more control over the experience, and the ability to fine-tune it in real-time on a per-user basis.

Our audio setup is designed to expand virtual space beyond the phone screen, making the storm clouds perceptible as sonic experiences as they drift by the players. As a metaphor, the storm clouds symbolize obstacles that make connecting with others difficult. In contrast to the global sounds of the storm, the voicemails (delivered by the birds after they have perched on the branch) is played only through the phones' speakers to provide a more intimate and private experience for the players.

While 'The Woods' speaks to concepts of isolation and loneliness in our own lives, the distinction made between global and local audio (i.e., the 4-speaker setup and the phones) motivated the creation of a juxtaposed sonic narrative for the players. The phone speakers provide a more intimate exchange simply by being a localized sonic experience compared to the 4-speaker surround sound setup. But it also takes the same device that the players are using to play the game and uses it as a multimodal device. In addition to expanding virtual space beyond the screen through the use of sound, our goal is also to encourage players to consider how the same technology that is so often criticized for isolating individuals can be reimagined to bring us closer together.

5   Benefits of Collaborative Play

The strength of cooperative games is that they promote social interaction and improve personal relationships by encouraging players to work together to achieve a common goal [9]. And while loneliness in our real lives is increasingly recognized as having dire physical, mental and emotional consequences, cooperative games have also been shown to build empathy and provide positive social impact [10].

Shared activities with peers provide players of all ages with opportunities to learn, practice, and develop their communicative, interactive, and social skills. Because working with a peer can motivate players to attempt difficult and intimidating problems and provide new knowledge about problems and problem-solving strategies by observing one another and imitating their actions. Additionally, cooperative problem solving allows players to discuss their perspectives on a problem, which often leads to conflict, negotiation, and co-construction [3–5].

Computer gaming has often been considered a social affair, and in recent years many video game titles have been accompanied by multiplayer modes to extend their lifecycles in the hands of the consumer. However, multiplayer modes on PC and console games are typically confined to onscreen interactions and lack any real physical collaboration. By contrast, the collaboration that exists in tabletop gaming promotes deep social interactions that stem from verbal communication, and face-to-face problem solving that amplify social connections between the players. 'The Woods' was designed to provide players with a similar sense of community building and promote social connections with their partners as they accomplish a variety of tasks throughout the game as they collaborate with one another.

6 Benefits of Merging Digital and Physical Play

While the social aspects of traditional tabletop games render them interesting enough in their own right, the static nature of their physical media limits the scope of realizable games. Complimentarily, many claim that the drawback to traditional computer games is the lack of social interaction in a face-to-face setting, which tabletop games provide. Therefore, it is only a natural evolution to combine the benefits of computer and tabletop games to provide new and engaging gaming experiences [6].

Physical play offers many opportunities to enhance and stimulate face-to-face interactions and promote active lifestyles that can benefit everyone's quality of life. The innovative mechanics of pervasive games (games that mix the real and virtual worlds) can further motivate its players, both young and old, to increase their levels of social interaction and physical activity. While there are several definitions of pervasive games, in general, their mechanics (or rules) blur aspects of the real world with the 'world of the game'. As an example, since the Global Positioning System (GPS) became available for public use in 2000, many pervasive games have incorporated physical location into their mechanics. 'Pokémon Go!' being one of the most popular [7, 8]. For 'The Woods', it is the physical, collaborative and inclusive affordances of analog games existing in the real world that has inspired it in so many ways.

7   Comparison to Other Cooperative AR Games

The benefits of pervasive games (and especially cooperative ones) are far-reaching as they anchor themselves to physicality, mobility and social interaction. Despite all of its successes, 'Pokémon Go!'s greatest critique was how it suffered from its lack of social interaction, forcing its developer, Niantic, to release a multiplayer version which unfortunately did little to stimulate social interaction between players in the real world – it's most valuable asset! 'The Woods', on the other hand, cannot be played without a real-life partner to choreograph your moves with in-person, and most definitely cannot be won without collaborating with them.

What makes 'The Woods' unique as a cooperative AR game is that it promotes face-to-face interactions over screen-based interactions. While games like 'Codename Neon' and the more recent 'Secret Oops!' have helped to redefine AR games as physical experiences, interactions with other players are still primarily on-screen.

Other games like 'Swift Shot' and 'Real Tag' do support team dynamics, but at the same time lack any narrative component that would otherwise expand Huizinga's 'magic circle' and create space for more meaningful social interactions [11]. By contrast, 'The Woods' was designed as an examination of human connectivity through the lens of contemporary technology. It doesn't come with a non-AR mode, and cannot be played alone. It requires a real, physical coordinated effort between its players which echoes loudly throughout its narrative of reconciliation.

8   Conclusion

The strength of cooperative games is that they promote social interaction, build empathy and improve personal relationships by encouraging players to work together to achieve a common goal. 'The Woods' further expands upon this by promoting real-world physical interactions over screen-based interactions that are made possible through our unique design of AR and audio spatialization. Much of what inspired the digital/analog play that we see in 'The Woods' were observations made of more traditional tabletop and physical games in general. In addition to the affordances of their physical characteristics and the benefits of having real face-to-face interactions with others, there is also an inclusive quality to analog games that is defined by the 'table' that they are played around, and its timeless ability of binding those seated around it in a shared, group activity. By highlighting the importance of physical interaction told through a digital narrative, our goal is to provide positive social impact by illuminating our connections to one another and provoking us to respond through collaboration (Fig. 5 and 6).

Fig. 5. Players collaborating with one another in-game

Fig. 6. POV of a player in-game

References

1. Velez, J.: Extending the theory of bounded generalized reciprocity: an explanation of the social benefits of cooperative video game play. Comput. Hum. Behav. **48**, 481–491 (2015). https://doi.org/10.1016/j.chb.2015.02.015
2. Khuller, D.: How Social Isolation Is Killing Us. The New York Times (2016). https://www.nytimes.com/2016/12/22/upshot/how-social-isolation-is-killing-us.html
3. Jin, B., Park, N.: Mobile voice communication and loneliness: cell phone use and the social skills deficit hypothesis. New Media Soc. **15**(7), 1094–1111 (2013). https://doi.org/10.1177/1461444812466715

4. https://www.floridatechonline.com/blog/psychology/how-smartphones-arecontributing-to-the-loneliness-epidemic/
5. Bekker, T., Sturm, J., Barakova, E.: 2nd workshop on design for social interaction through physical play. In: Gross, T., et al. (eds.) INTERACT 2009, vol. 5727, pp. 952–953. Springer, Heidelberg (2004). https://doi.org/10.1007/978-3-642-03658-3_127
6. Lemle, E., Bomkamp, K., Williams, M., Cutbirth, E.: At the intersection of digital and physical play: the lifecycle of a two bit circus game. In: Lemle, E., Bomkamp, K., Williams, M., Cutbirth, E. (eds.) Two Bit Circus and the Future of Entertainment. SCS, pp. 9–16. Springer, Cham (2015). https://doi.org/10.1007/978-3-319-25793-8_2
7. Piper, A.M., O'Brien, E., Morris, M.R., Winograd, T.: SIDES: a cooperative tabletop computer game for social skills development. In: Proceedings of CSCW 2006, pp. 1–10 (2006)
8. http://teilab-static.arch.tamu.edu/quek/Classes/Aware+EmbodiedInteraction/EmbodiedInteractionPAPERS/MagCMNl05.pdf
9. https://www.researchgate.net/publication/305800486_Pervasive_Games
10. https://www.vs.inf.ethz.ch/publ/papers/hinske-pg07-pervasivegames.pdf
11. Huizinga, J.: Homo Ludens: A Study of the Play Element in Culture. Beacon Press, Boston (1955)

Author Index

Printed in the United States
by Baker & Taylor Publisher Services